People always ask me which character is my favorite. The truth is, I love them all. They're like my children! How could I choose a favorite child? Now, if you were to ask me which character was my favorite from a design perspective, I'd say either Eve or Tearju. Not surprisingly, Train is the most difficult character to draw. (It's his hair that does it!)

—Kentaro Yabuki, 2003

Kentaro Yabuki made his manga debut with *Yamato Gensoki*, a short series about a young empress destined to unite the warring states of ancient Japan and the boy sworn to protect her. His next series, *Black Cat*, commenced serialization in the pages of *Weekly Shonen Jump* in 2000 and quickly developed a loyal fan following. *Black Cat* has also become an animated TV series, first hitting Japan's airwaves in the fall of 2005.

BLACK CAT VOL. 12
The SHONEN JUMP Manga Edition

STORY AND ART BY
KENTARO YABUKI

English Adaptation/Kelly Sue DeConnick
Translation/JN Productions
Touch-up Art & Lettering/Gia Cam Luc
Design/Courtney Utt
Editor/Jonathan Tarbox

Editor in Chief, Books/Alvin Lu
Editor in Chief, Magazines/Marc Weidenbaum
VP of Publishing Licensing/Rika Inouye
VP of Sales/Gonzalo Ferreyra
Sr. VP of Marketing/Liza Coppola
Publisher/Hyoe Narita

Printed in the U.S.A.

Published by VIZ Media, LLC
P.O. Box 77010
San Francisco, CA 94107

SHONEN JUMP Manga Edition
10 9 8 7 6 5 4 3 2 1
First printing, January 2008

THE WORLD'S
MOST POPULAR MANGA

www.viz.com

www.shonenjump.com

BLACK CAT

ブラック・キャット

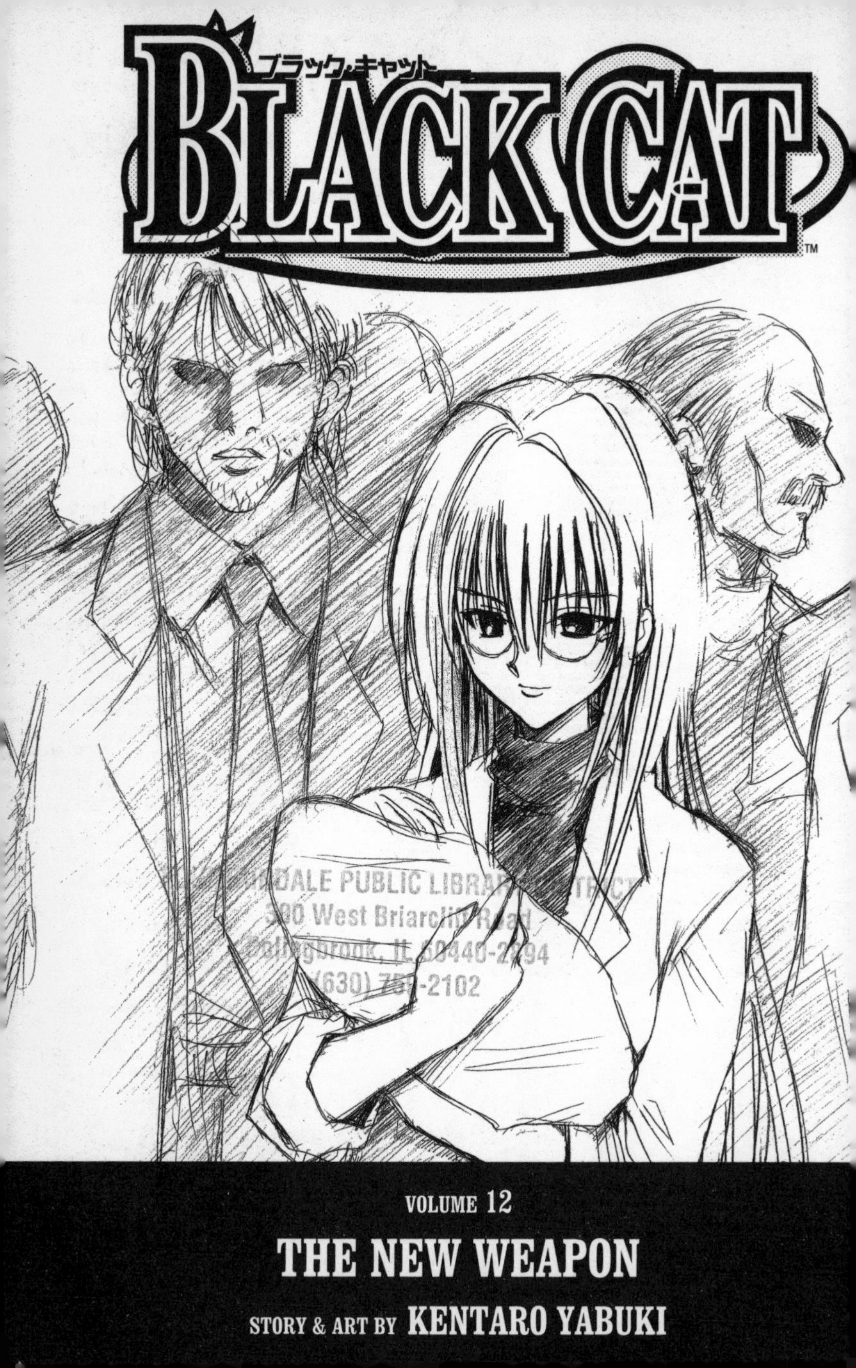

VOLUME 12

THE NEW WEAPON

STORY & ART BY KENTARO YABUKI

characters

BLACK CAT™

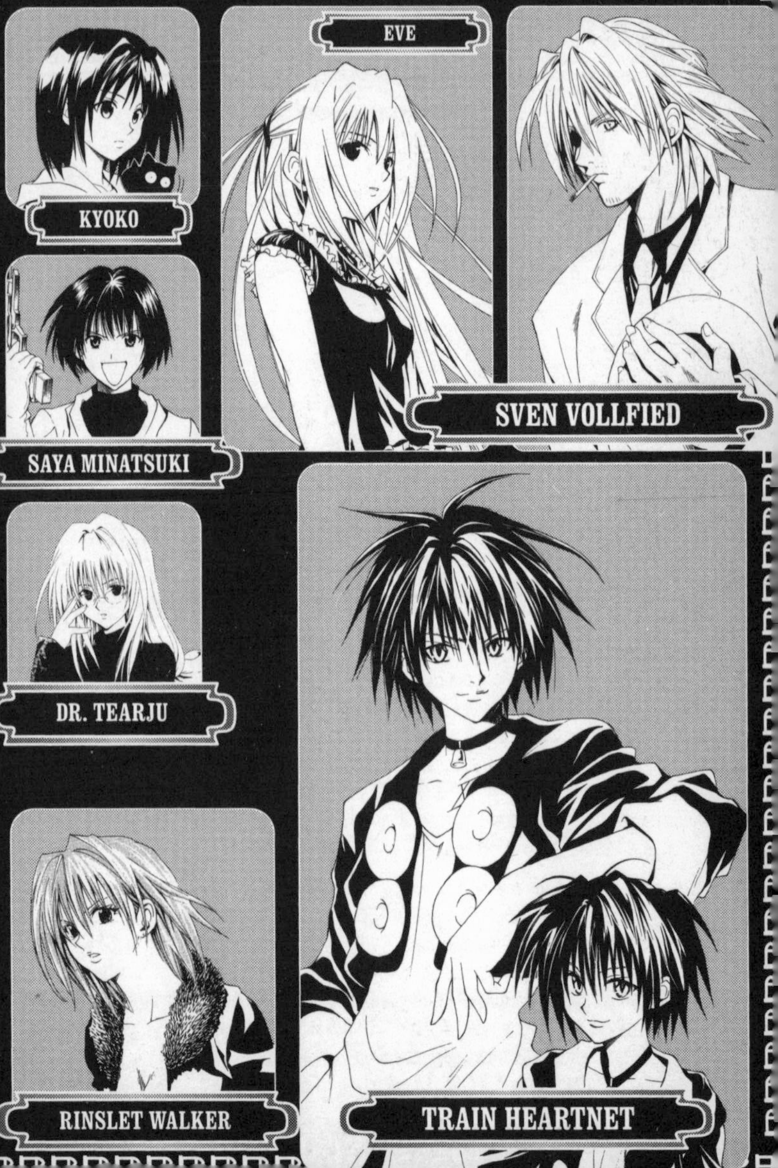

EVE
SVEN VOLLFIED
KYOKO
SAYA MINATSUKI
DR. TEARJU
RINSLET WALKER
TRAIN HEARTNET

APOSTLES of the STARS
CREED DISKENTH
THE DOCTOR
ECHIDNA
No. I SEPHIRIA
No. II BELZE
CHRONO NUMBERS
No. VII JENOS

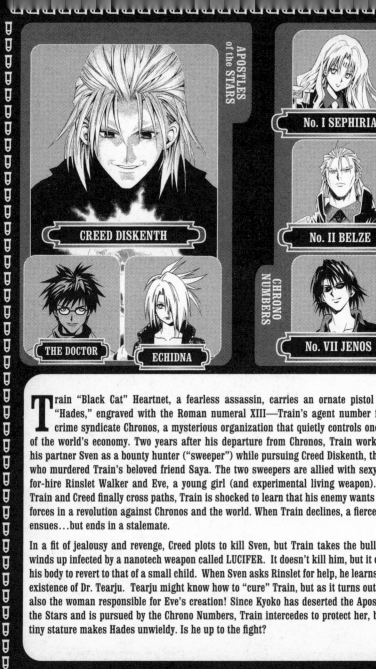

Train "Black Cat" Heartnet, a fearless assassin, carries an ornate pistol called "Hades," engraved with the Roman numeral XIII—Train's agent number for the crime syndicate Chronos, a mysterious organization that quietly controls one-third of the world's economy. Two years after his departure from Chronos, Train works with his partner Sven as a bounty hunter ("sweeper") while pursuing Creed Diskenth, the man who murdered Train's beloved friend Saya. The two sweepers are allied with sexy thief-for-hire Rinslet Walker and Eve, a young girl (and experimental living weapon). When Train and Creed finally cross paths, Train is shocked to learn that his enemy wants to join forces in a revolution against Chronos and the world. When Train declines, a fierce battle ensues…but ends in a stalemate.

In a fit of jealousy and revenge, Creed plots to kill Sven, but Train takes the bullet and winds up infected by a nanotech weapon called LUCIFER. It doesn't kill him, but it causes his body to revert to that of a small child. When Sven asks Rinslet for help, he learns of the existence of Dr. Tearju. Tearju might know how to "cure" Train, but as it turns out, she's also the woman responsible for Eve's creation! Since Kyoko has deserted the Apostles of the Stars and is pursued by the Chrono Numbers, Train intercedes to protect her, but his tiny stature makes Hades unwieldy. Is he up to the fight?

BLACK CAT

VOLUME 12 **THE NEW WEAPON**

CONTENTS

Chapter 104: Train and Sven Disagree

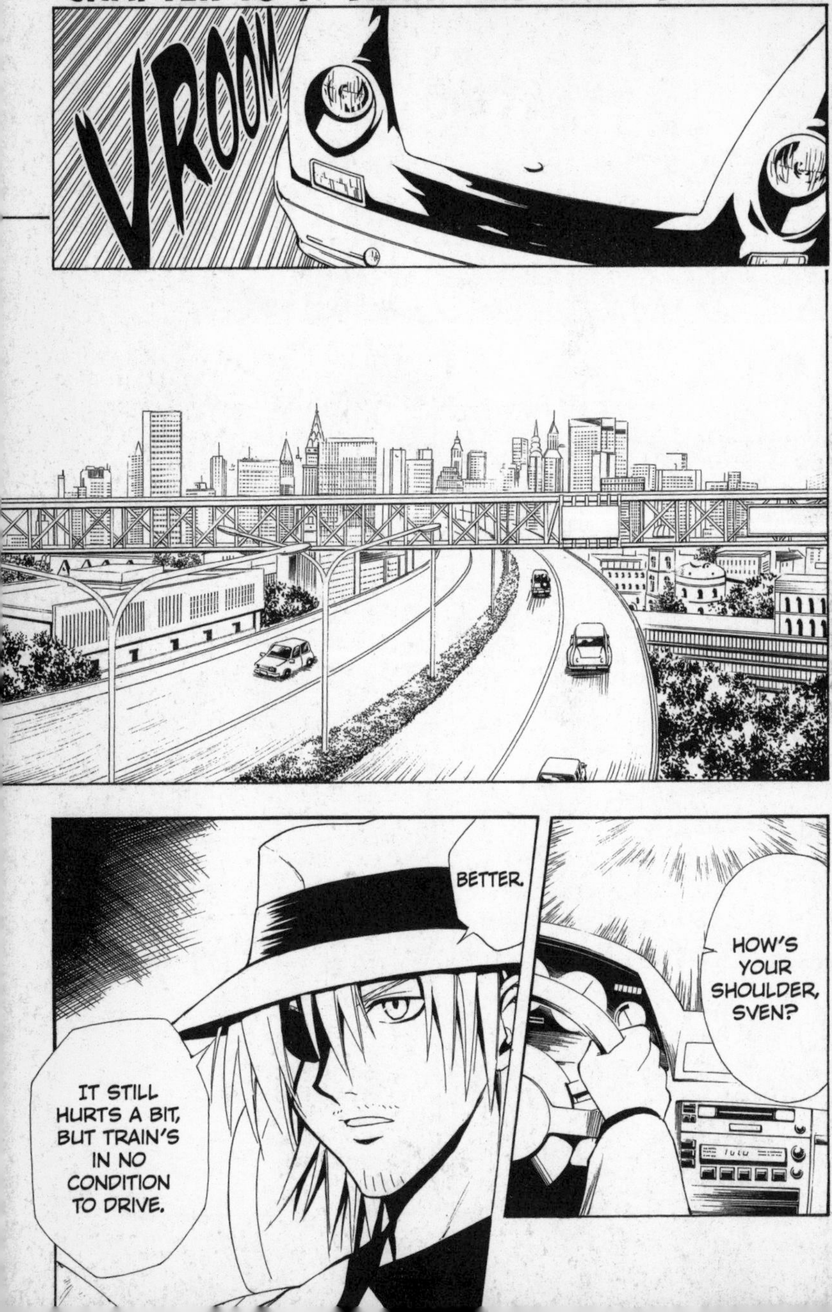
VROOM
HOW'S YOUR SHOULDER, SVEN?
BETTER.
IT STILL HURTS A BIT, BUT TRAIN'S IN NO CONDITION TO DRIVE.

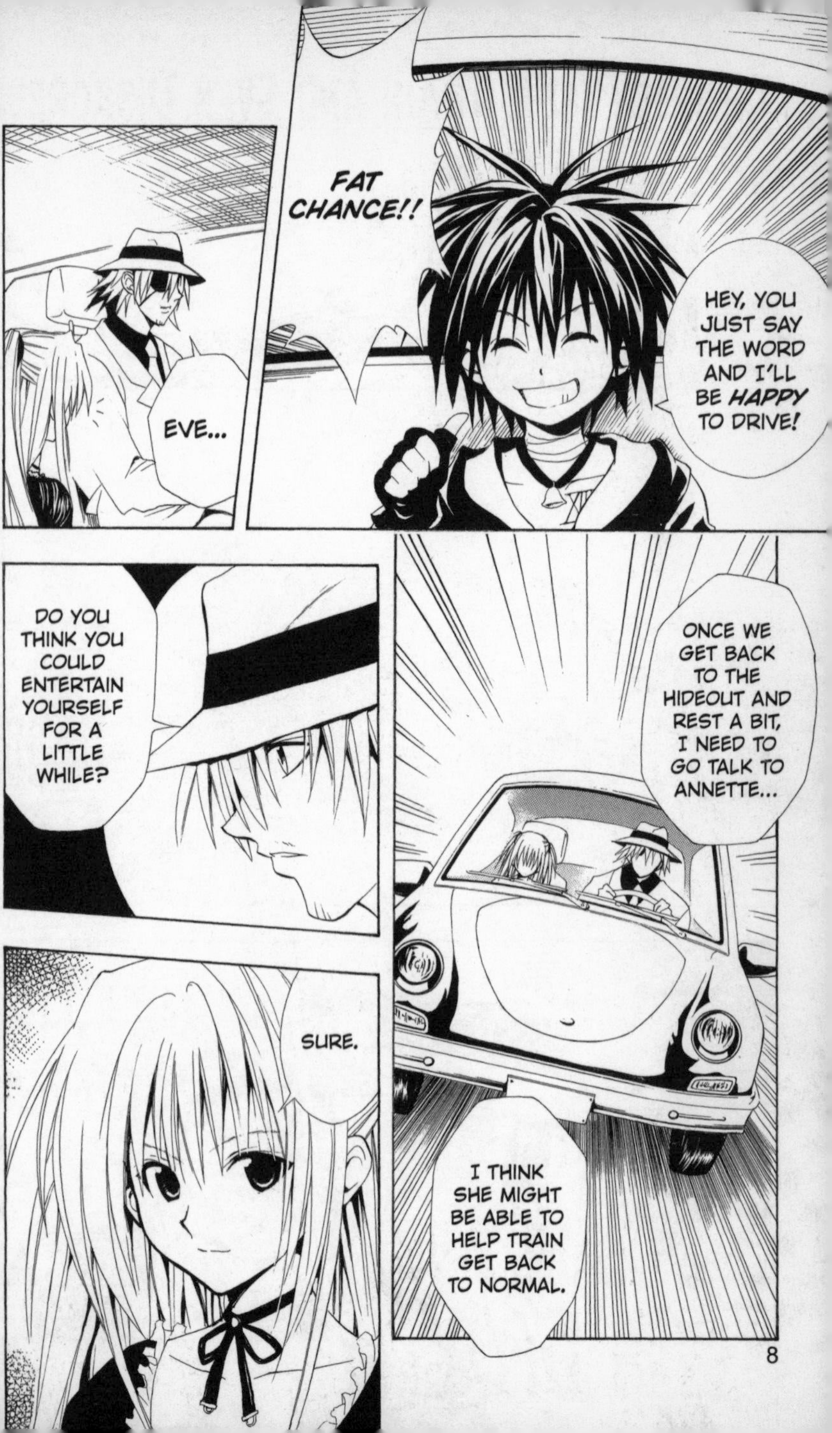
HEY, YOU JUST SAY THE WORD AND I'LL BE *HAPPY* TO DRIVE!
FAT CHANCE!!
EVE...
ONCE WE GET BACK TO THE HIDEOUT AND REST A BIT, I NEED TO GO TALK TO ANNETTE...
I THINK SHE MIGHT BE ABLE TO HELP TRAIN GET BACK TO NORMAL.
DO YOU THINK YOU COULD ENTERTAIN YOURSELF FOR A LITTLE WHILE?
SURE.

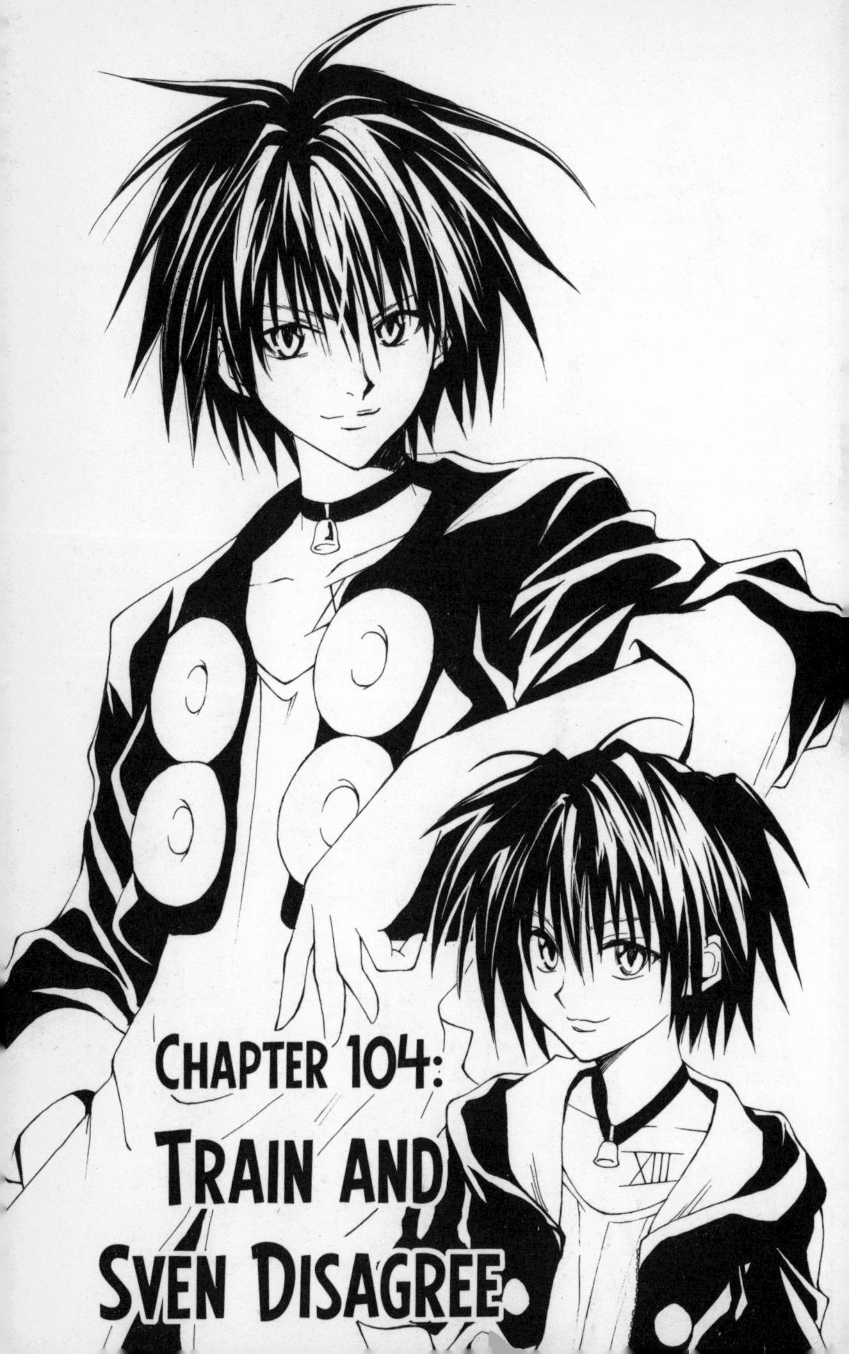
CHAPTER 104:
TRAIN AND SVEN DISAGREE
XIII

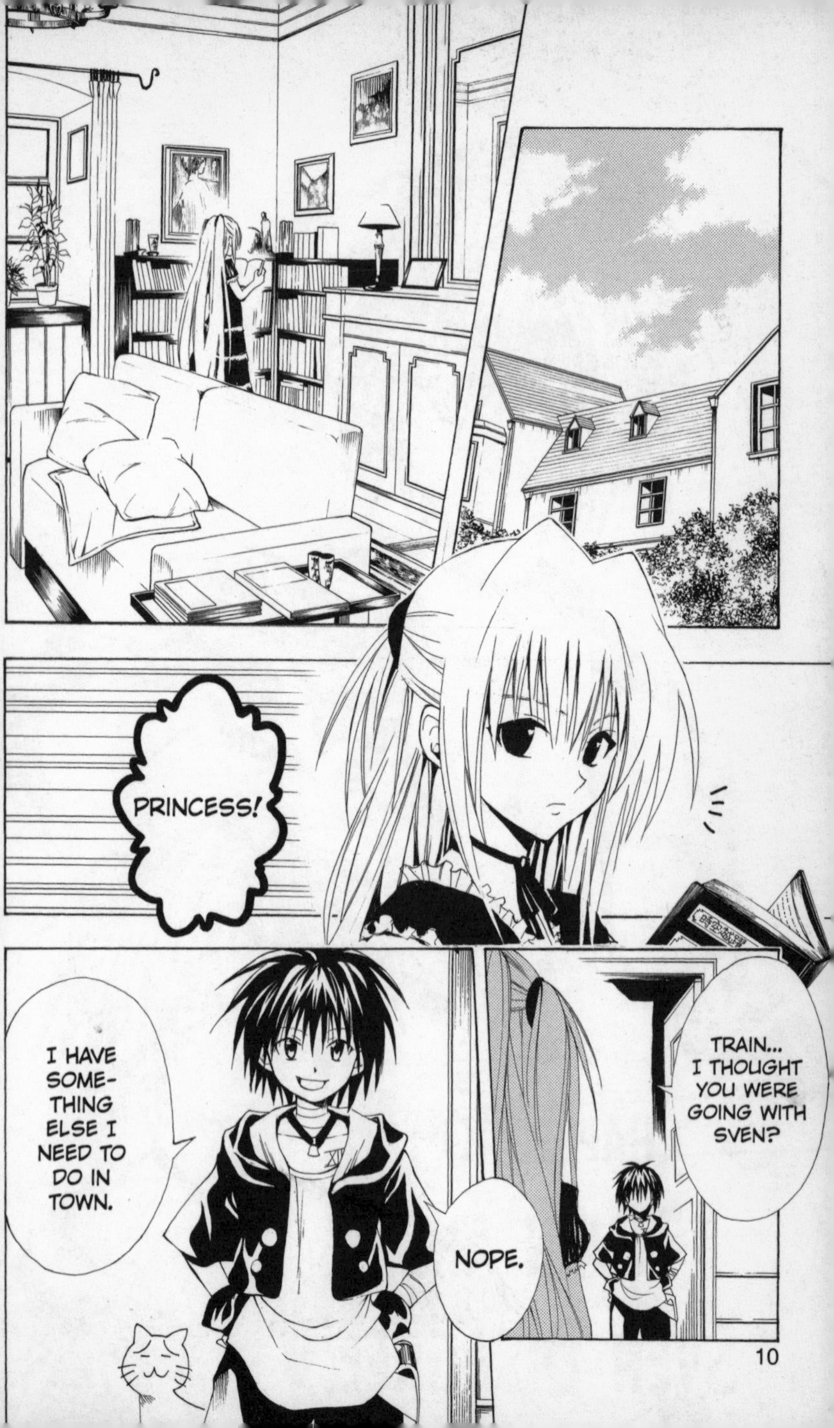
PRINCESS!
TRAIN... I THOUGHT YOU WERE GOING WITH SVEN?
NOPE.
I HAVE SOME-THING ELSE I NEED TO DO IN TOWN.

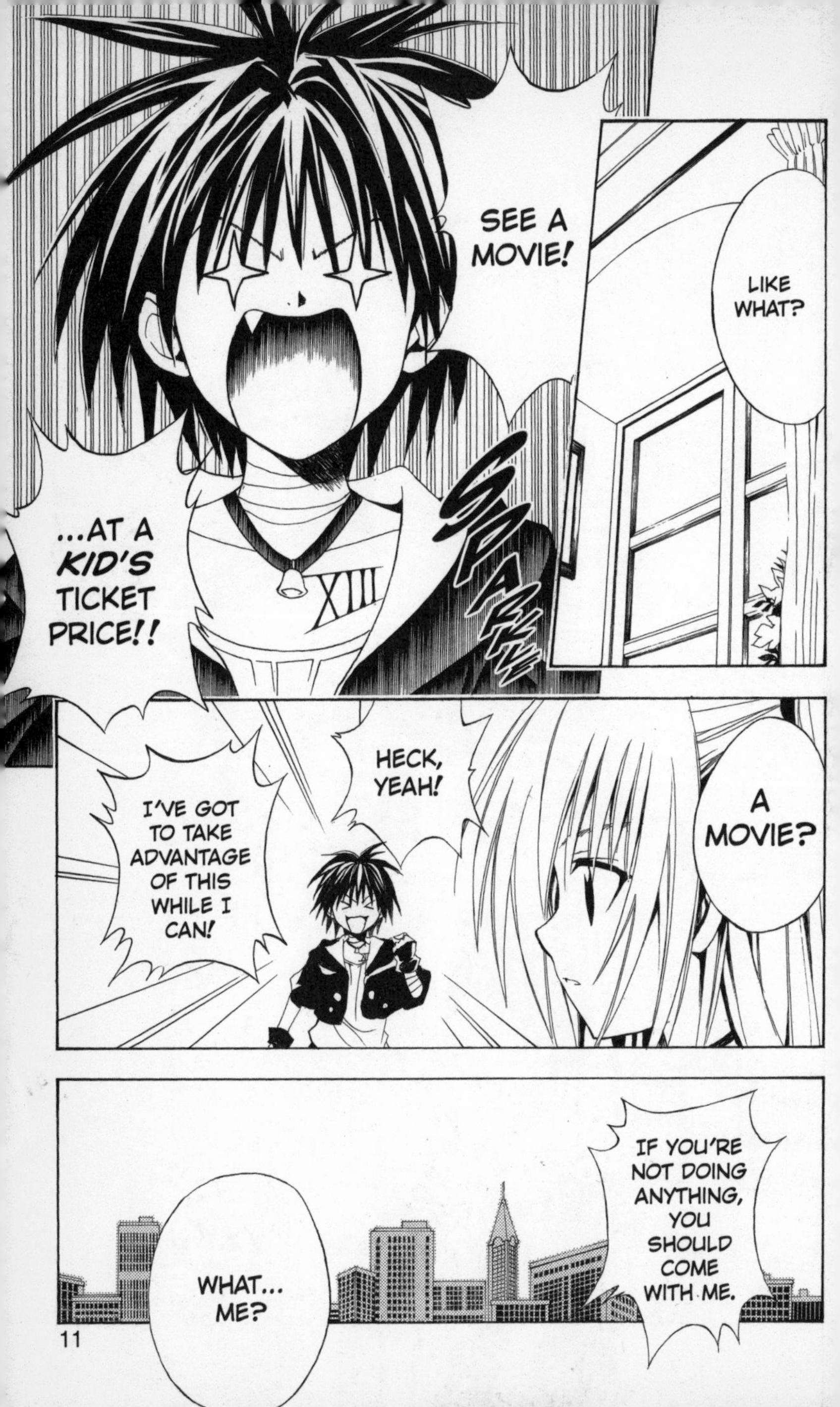
LIKE WHAT?
SEE A MOVIE!
SPARKLE
...AT A *KID'S* TICKET PRICE!!
A MOVIE?
HECK, YEAH!
I'VE GOT TO TAKE ADVANTAGE OF THIS WHILE I CAN!
IF YOU'RE NOT DOING ANYTHING, YOU SHOULD COME WITH ME.
WHAT... ME?

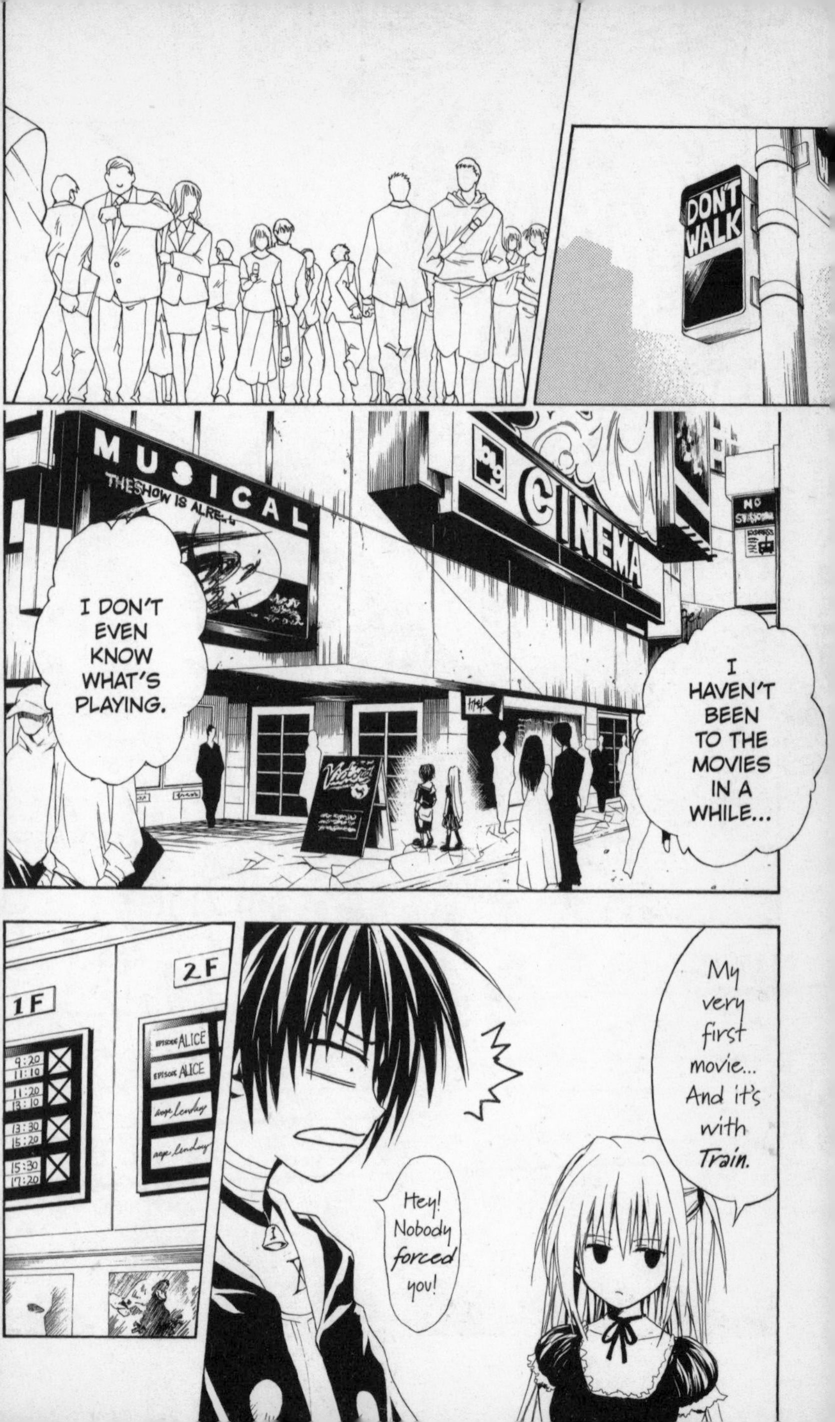
DON'T WALK
CINEMA
MUSICAL
I HAVEN'T BEEN TO THE MOVIES IN A WHILE...
I DON'T EVEN KNOW WHAT'S PLAYING.
My very first movie... And it's with *Train*.
Hey! Nobody *forced* you!
2F
EPISODE ALICE
EPISODE ALICE
1F
9:20 11:10
11:20 13:10
13:30 15:20
15:30 17:20

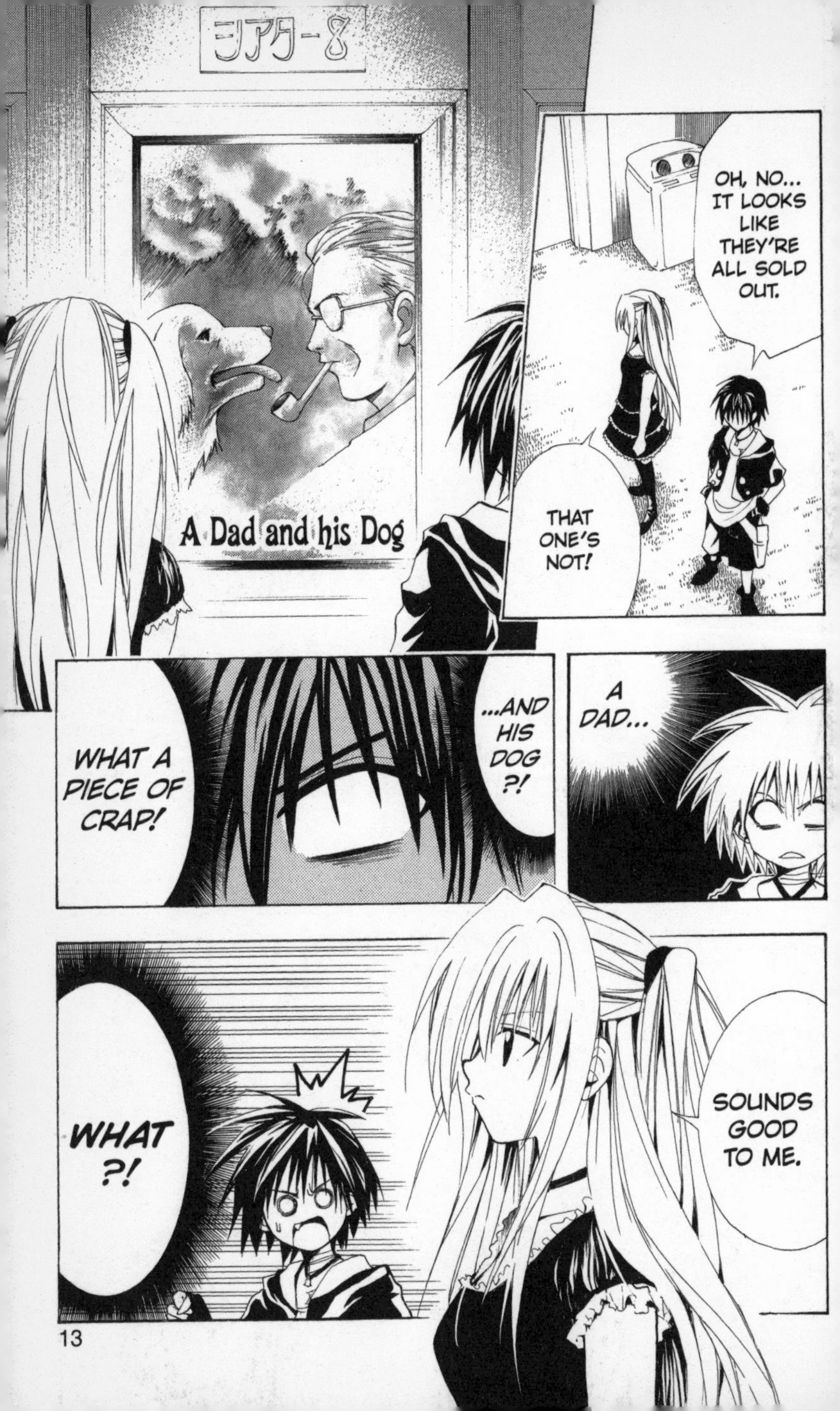

OH, NO... IT LOOKS LIKE THEY'RE ALL SOLD OUT.
THAT ONE'S NOT!
シアター8
A Dad and his Dog
A DAD...
...AND HIS DOG ?!
WHAT A PIECE OF CRAP!
SOUNDS GOOD TO ME.
WHAT ?!

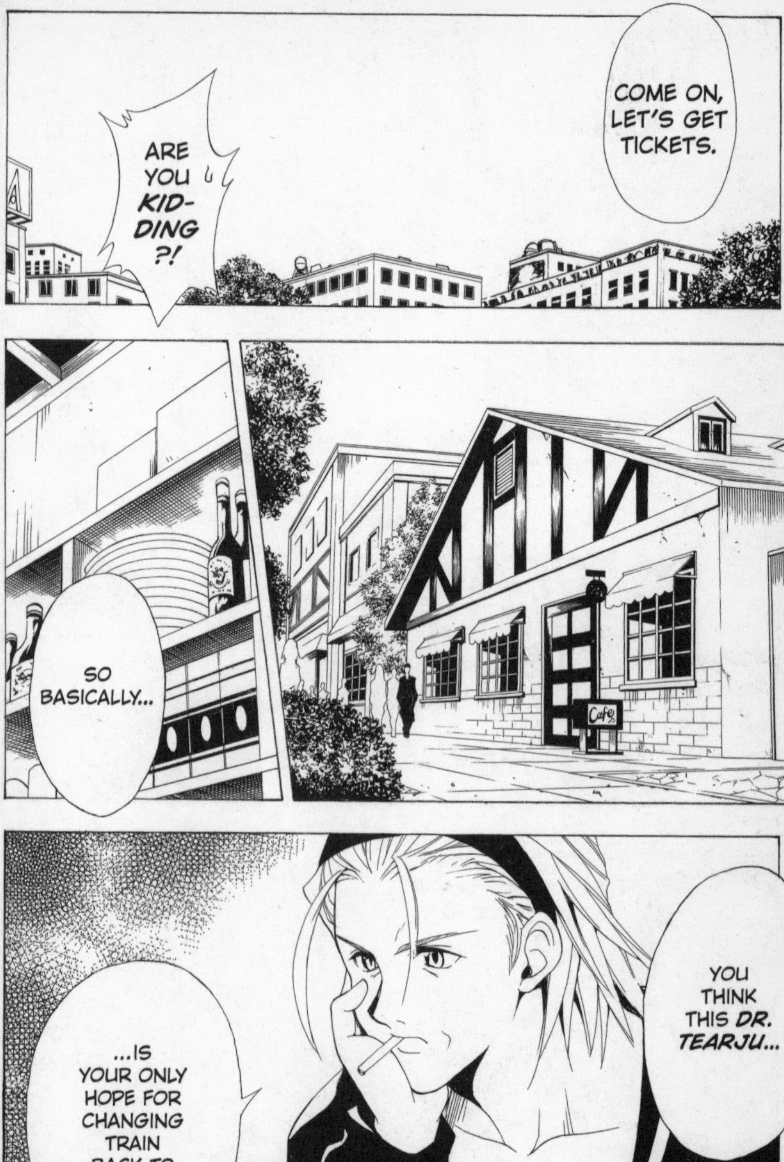
COME ON, LET'S GET TICKETS.
ARE YOU *KIDDING*?!
Cafe
SO BASICALLY...
YOU THINK THIS *DR. TEARJU*...
...IS YOUR ONLY HOPE FOR CHANGING TRAIN BACK TO NORMAL?

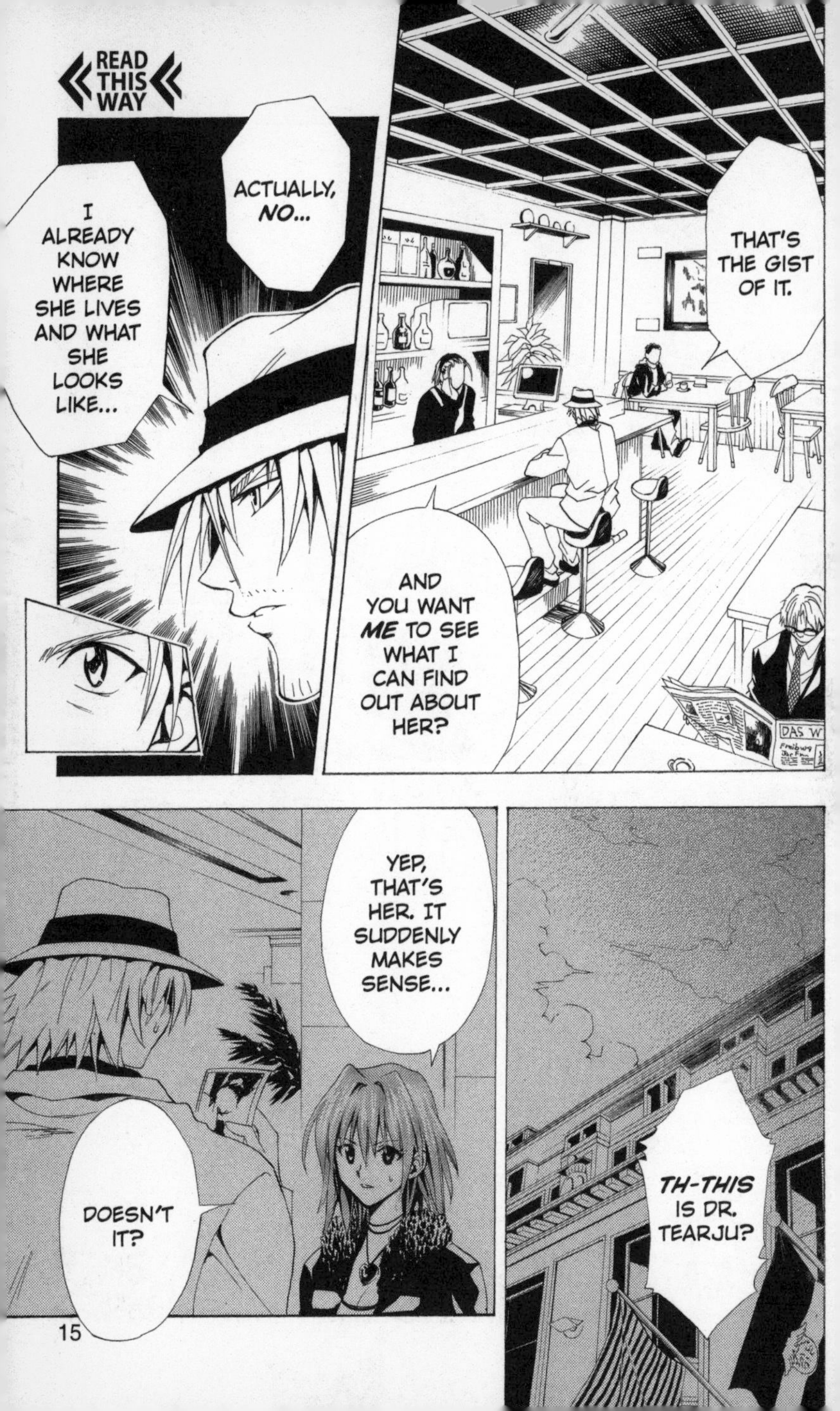
READ THIS WAY
THAT'S THE GIST OF IT.
AND YOU WANT *ME* TO SEE WHAT I CAN FIND OUT ABOUT HER?
ACTUALLY, *NO*...
I ALREADY KNOW WHERE SHE LIVES AND WHAT SHE LOOKS LIKE...
TH-THIS IS DR. TEARJU?
YEP, THAT'S HER. IT SUDDENLY MAKES SENSE...
DOESN'T IT?

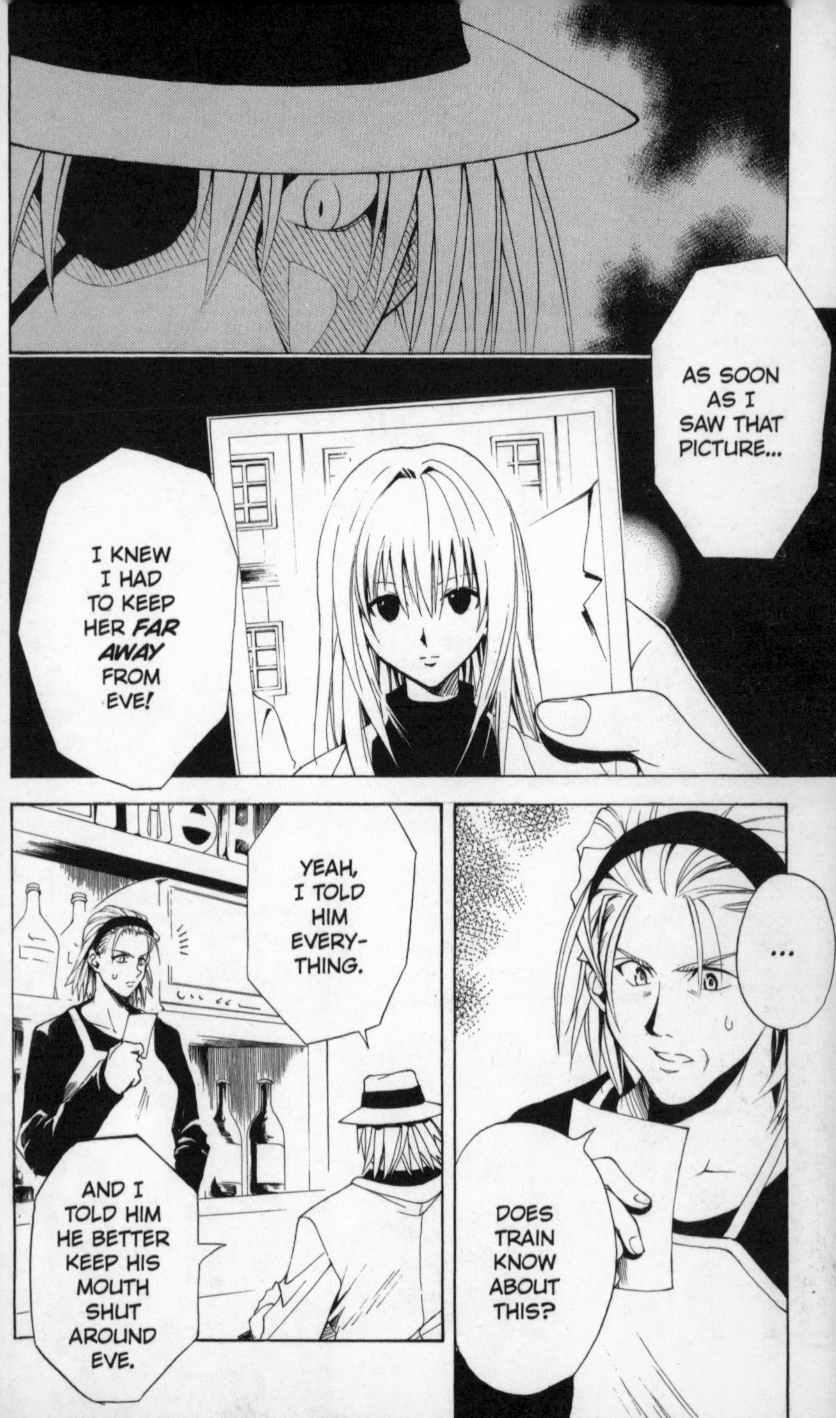
AS SOON AS I SAW THAT PICTURE...
I KNEW I HAD TO KEEP HER *FAR AWAY* FROM EVE!
...
DOES TRAIN KNOW ABOUT THIS?
YEAH, I TOLD HIM EVERY-THING.
AND I TOLD HIM HE BETTER KEEP HIS MOUTH SHUT AROUND EVE.

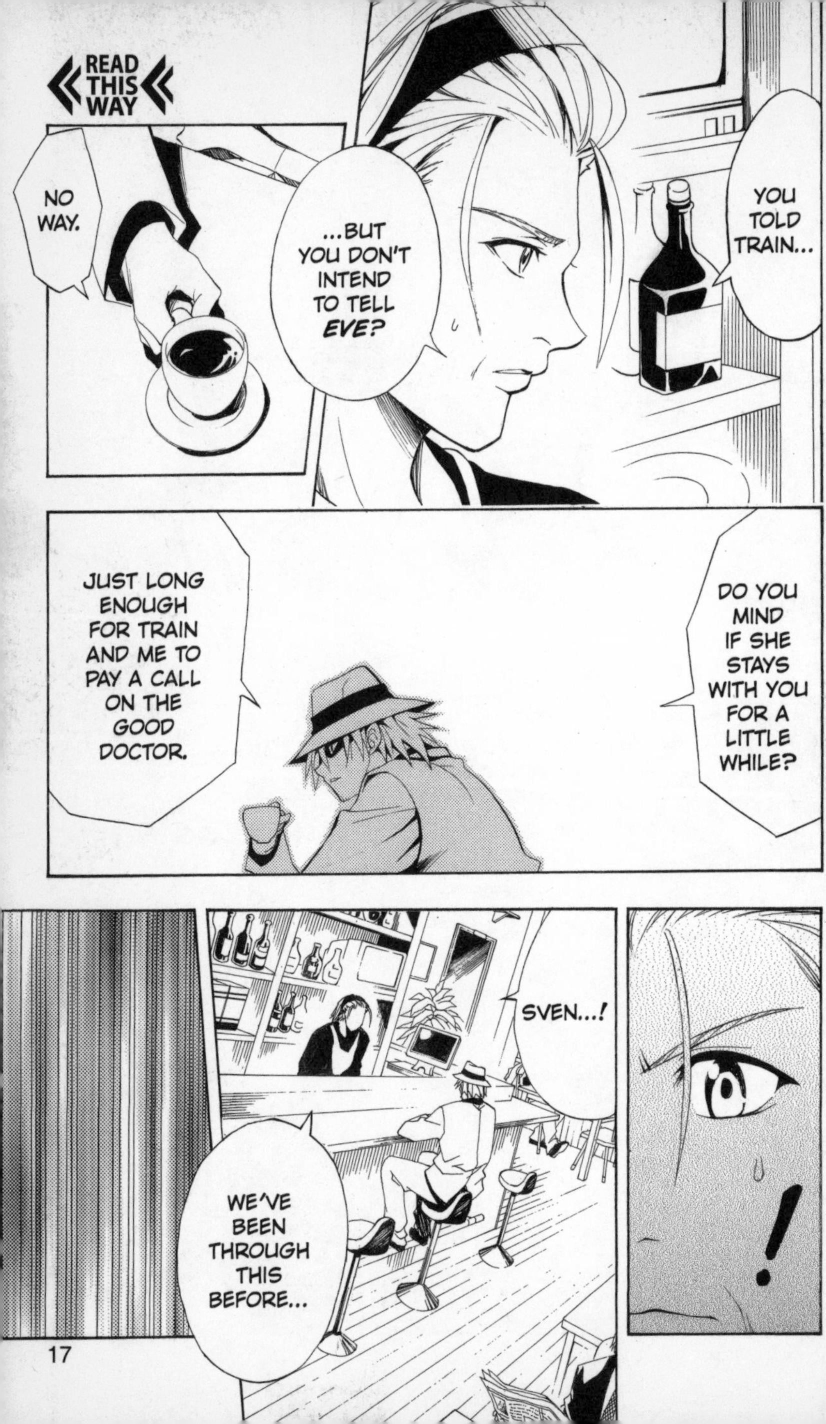
READ THIS WAY
YOU TOLD TRAIN...
...BUT YOU DON'T INTEND TO TELL *EVE*?
NO WAY.
DO YOU MIND IF SHE STAYS WITH YOU FOR A LITTLE WHILE?
JUST LONG ENOUGH FOR TRAIN AND ME TO PAY A CALL ON THE GOOD DOCTOR.
!
SVEN...!
WE'VE BEEN THROUGH THIS BEFORE...

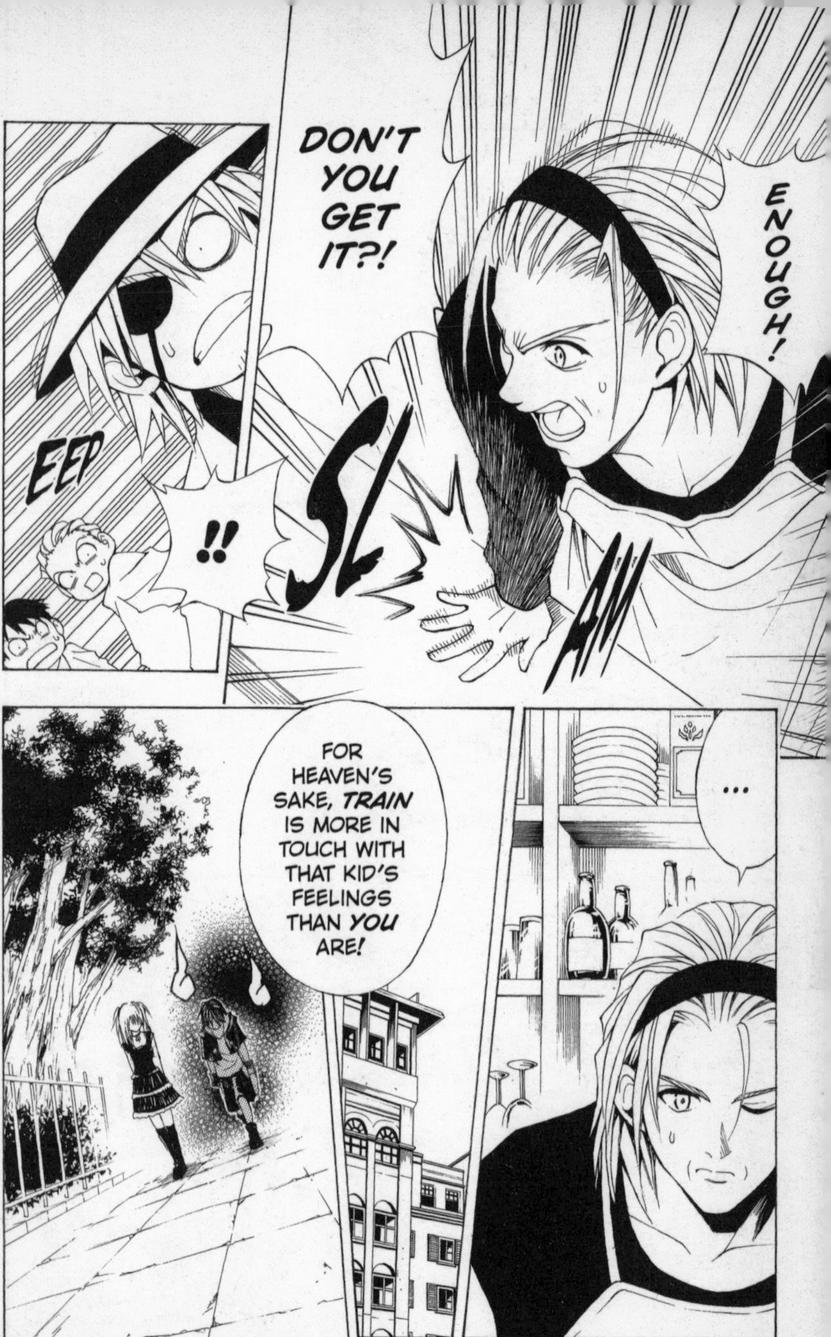
ENOUGH!
DON'T YOU GET IT?!
SLAM
EEP
!!
...
FOR HEAVEN'S SAKE, *TRAIN* IS MORE IN TOUCH WITH THAT KID'S FEELINGS THAN *YOU* ARE!

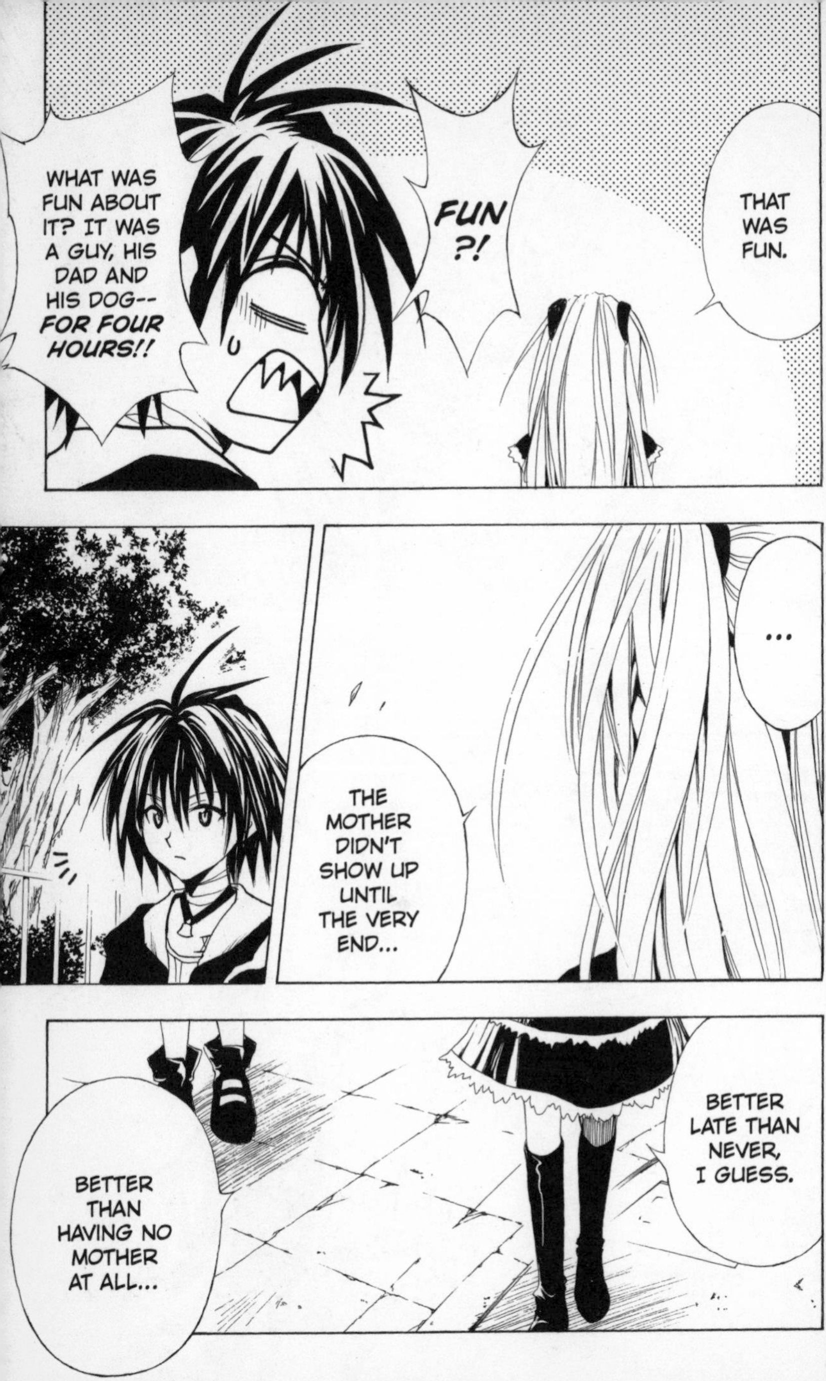
THAT WAS FUN.
FUN?!
WHAT WAS FUN ABOUT IT? IT WAS A GUY, HIS DAD AND HIS DOG-- FOR FOUR HOURS!!
...
THE MOTHER DIDN'T SHOW UP UNTIL THE VERY END...
BETTER LATE THAN NEVER, I GUESS.
BETTER THAN HAVING NO MOTHER AT ALL...

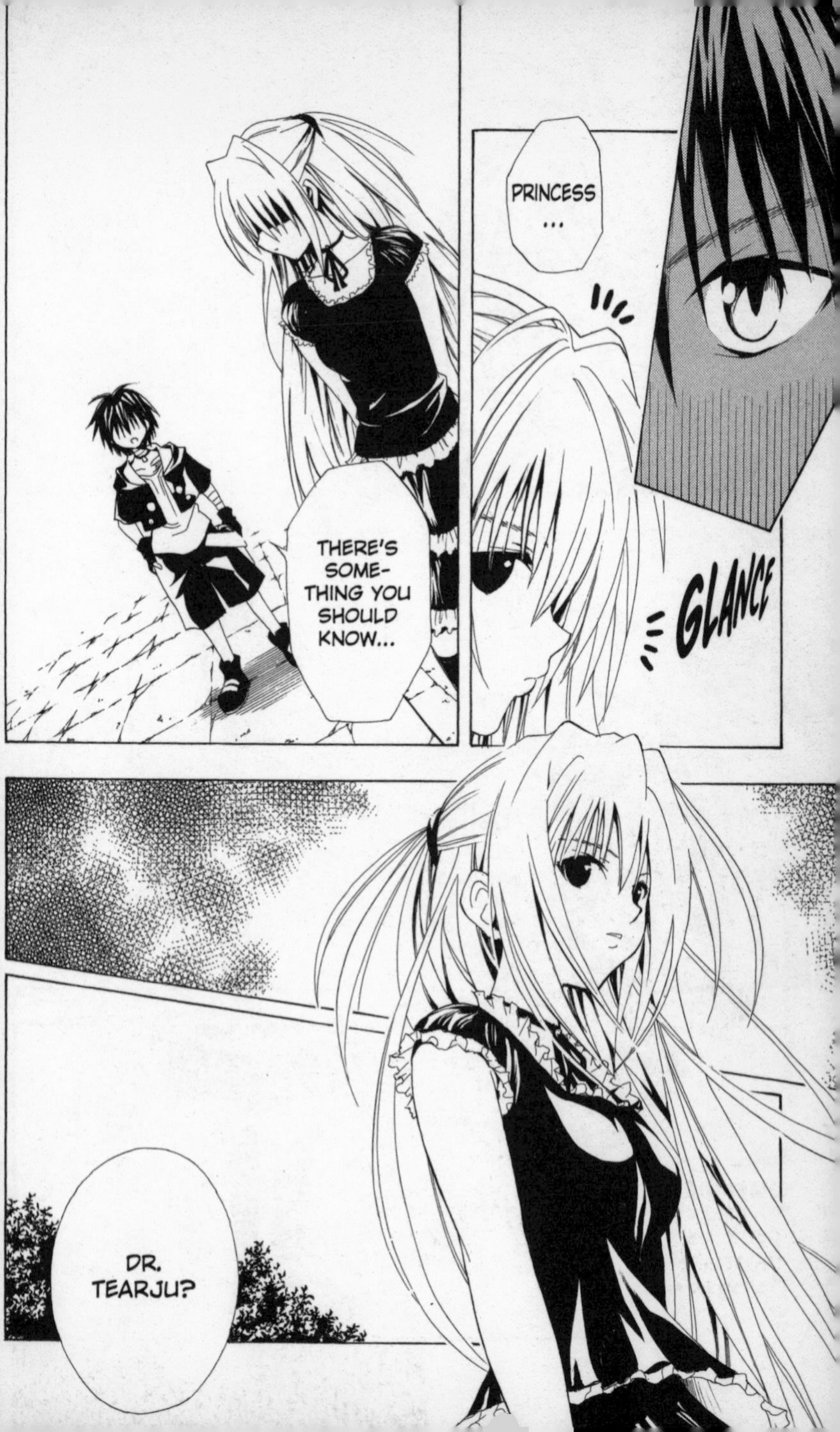
PRINCESS ...
GLANCE
THERE'S SOME-THING YOU SHOULD KNOW...
DR. TEARJU?

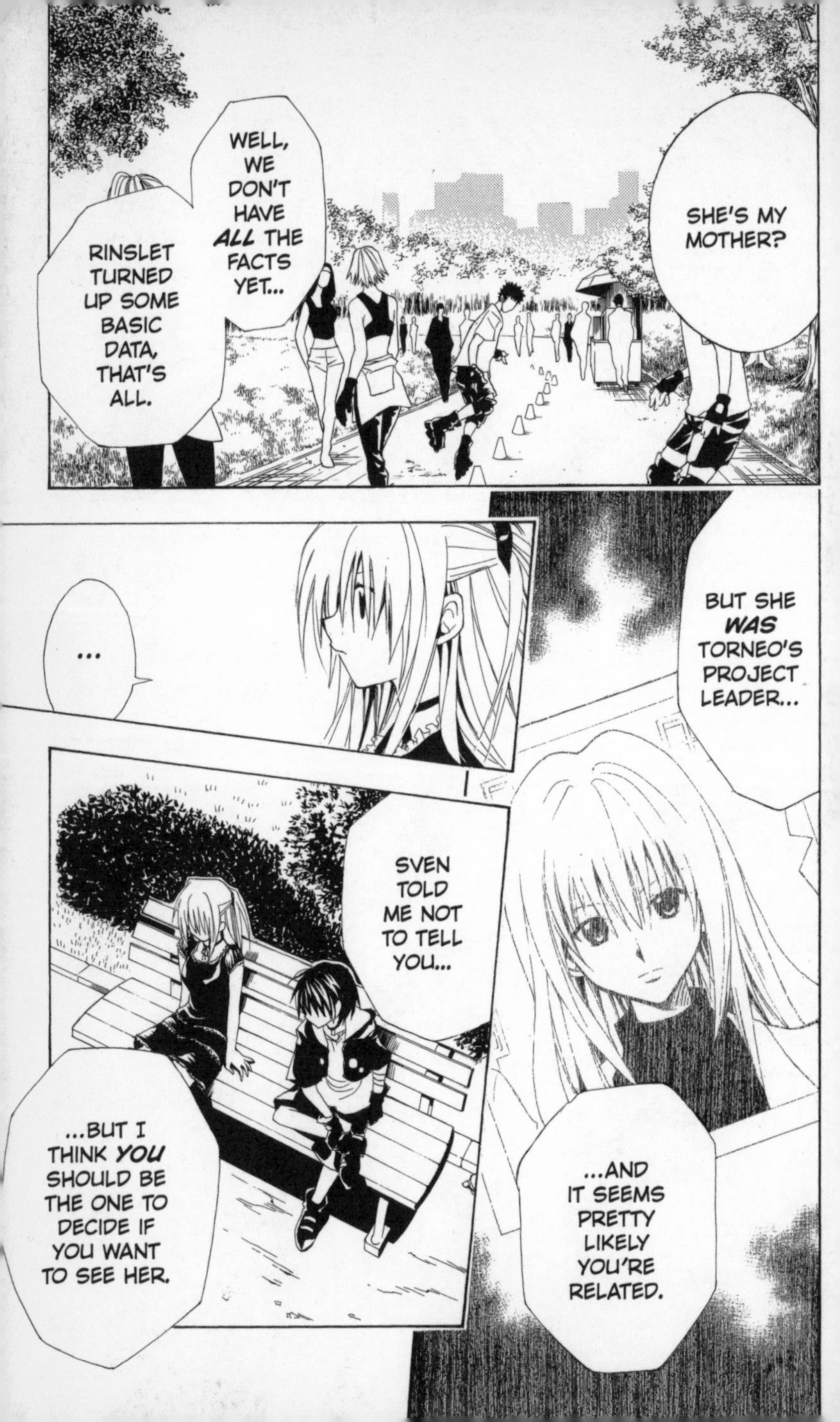
SHE'S MY MOTHER?
WELL, WE DON'T HAVE *ALL* THE FACTS YET...
RINSLET TURNED UP SOME BASIC DATA, THAT'S ALL.
BUT SHE *WAS* TORNEO'S PROJECT LEADER...
...AND IT SEEMS PRETTY LIKELY YOU'RE RELATED.
...
SVEN TOLD ME NOT TO TELL YOU...
...BUT I THINK *YOU* SHOULD BE THE ONE TO DECIDE IF YOU WANT TO SEE HER.

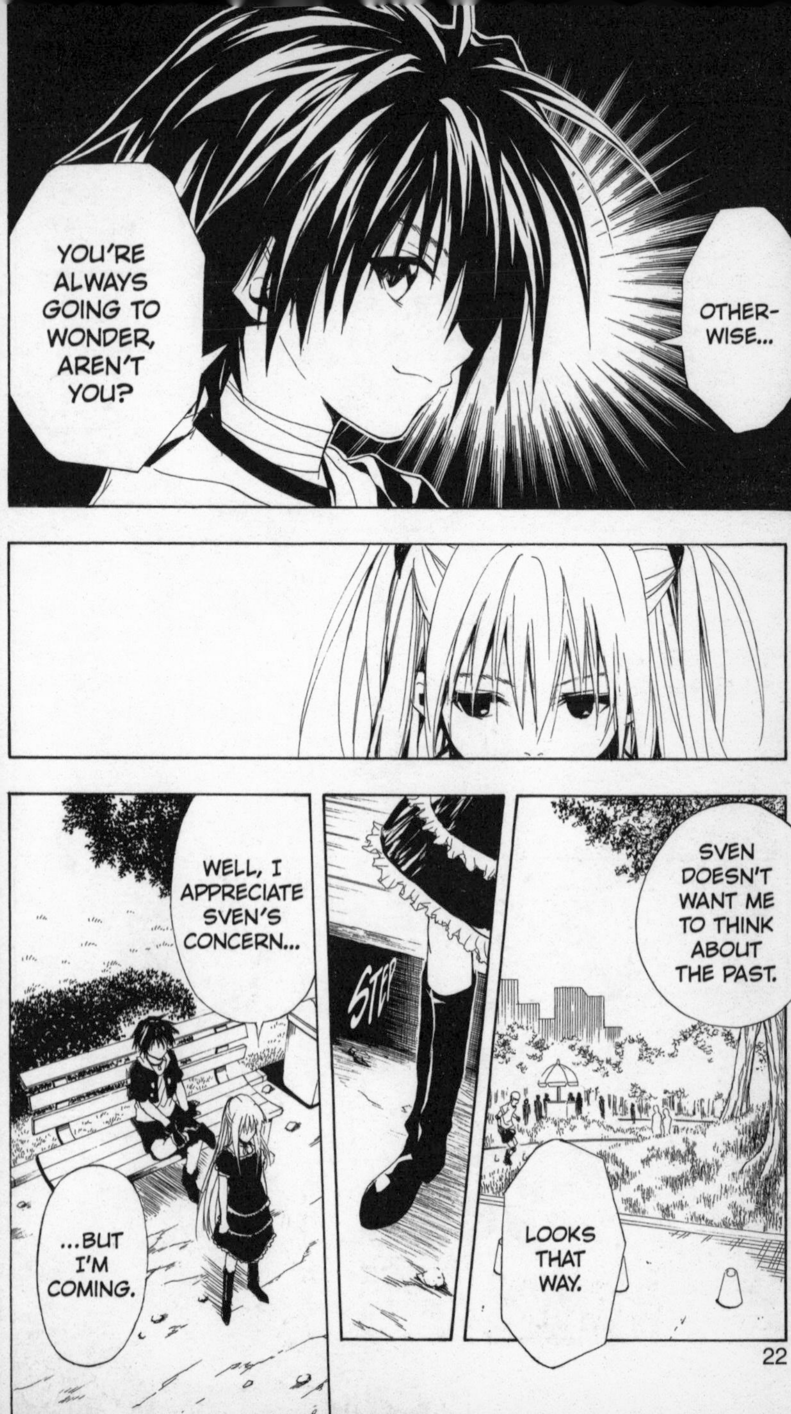
OTHER-WISE...
YOU'RE ALWAYS GOING TO WONDER, AREN'T YOU?
SVEN DOESN'T WANT ME TO THINK ABOUT THE PAST.
LOOKS THAT WAY.
STEP
WELL, I APPRECIATE SVEN'S CONCERN...
...BUT I'M COMING.

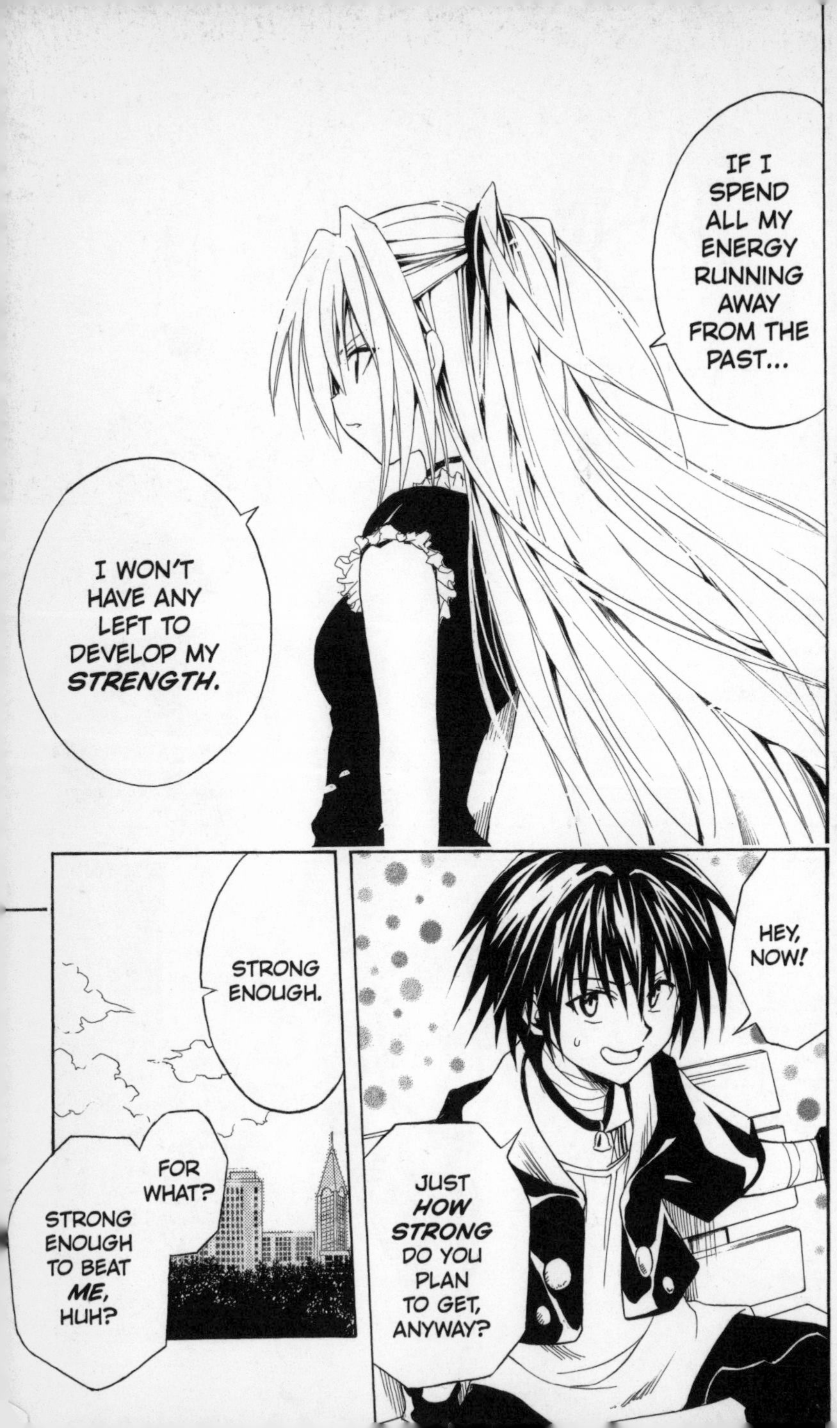
IF I SPEND ALL MY ENERGY RUNNING AWAY FROM THE PAST...
I WON'T HAVE ANY LEFT TO DEVELOP MY *STRENGTH*.
HEY, NOW!
JUST *HOW STRONG* DO YOU PLAN TO GET, ANYWAY?
STRONG ENOUGH.
FOR WHAT?
STRONG ENOUGH TO BEAT *ME*, HUH?

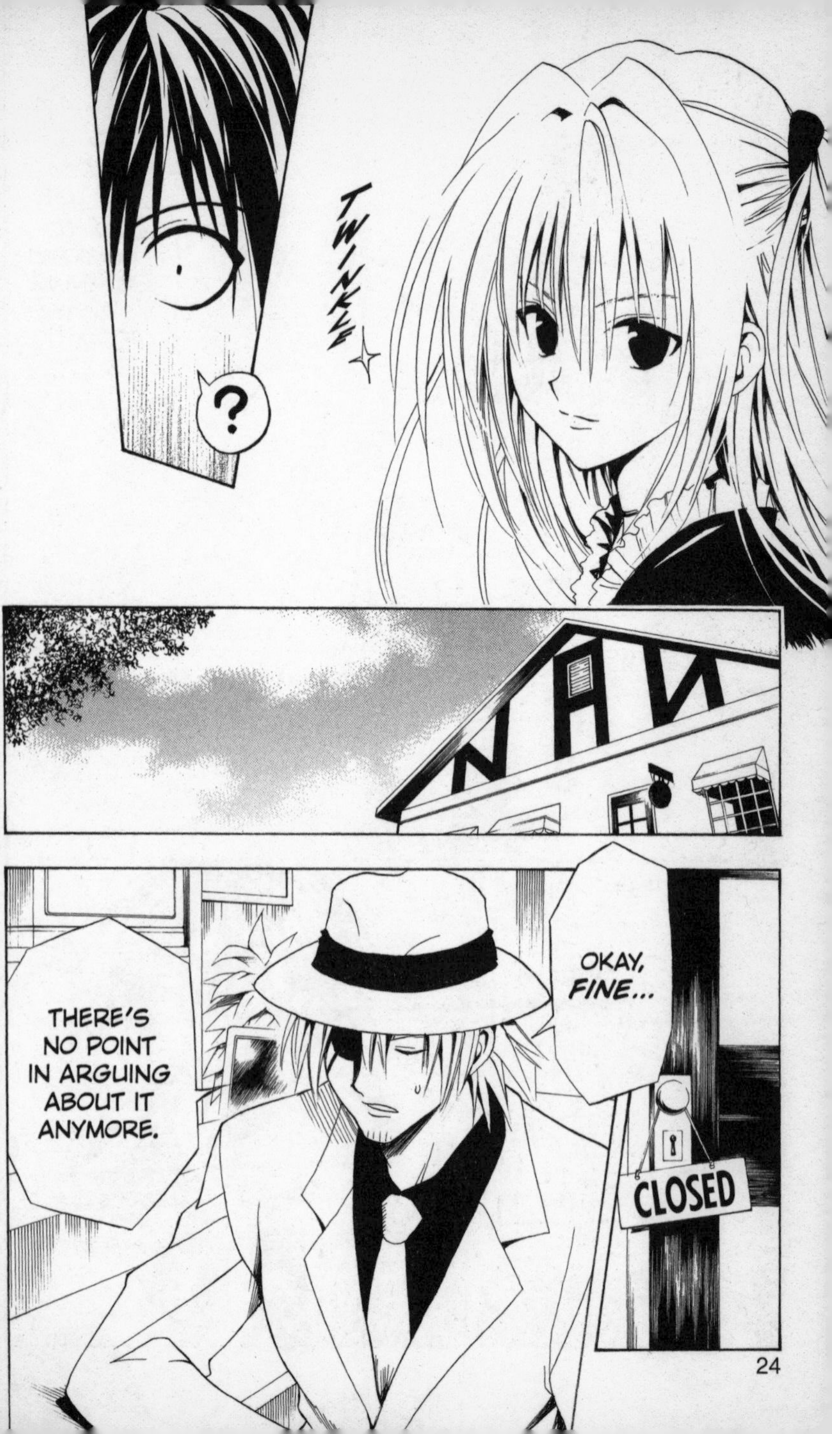
TWINKLE
?
OKAY, FINE...
THERE'S NO POINT IN ARGUING ABOUT IT ANYMORE.
CLOSED

READ THIS WAY

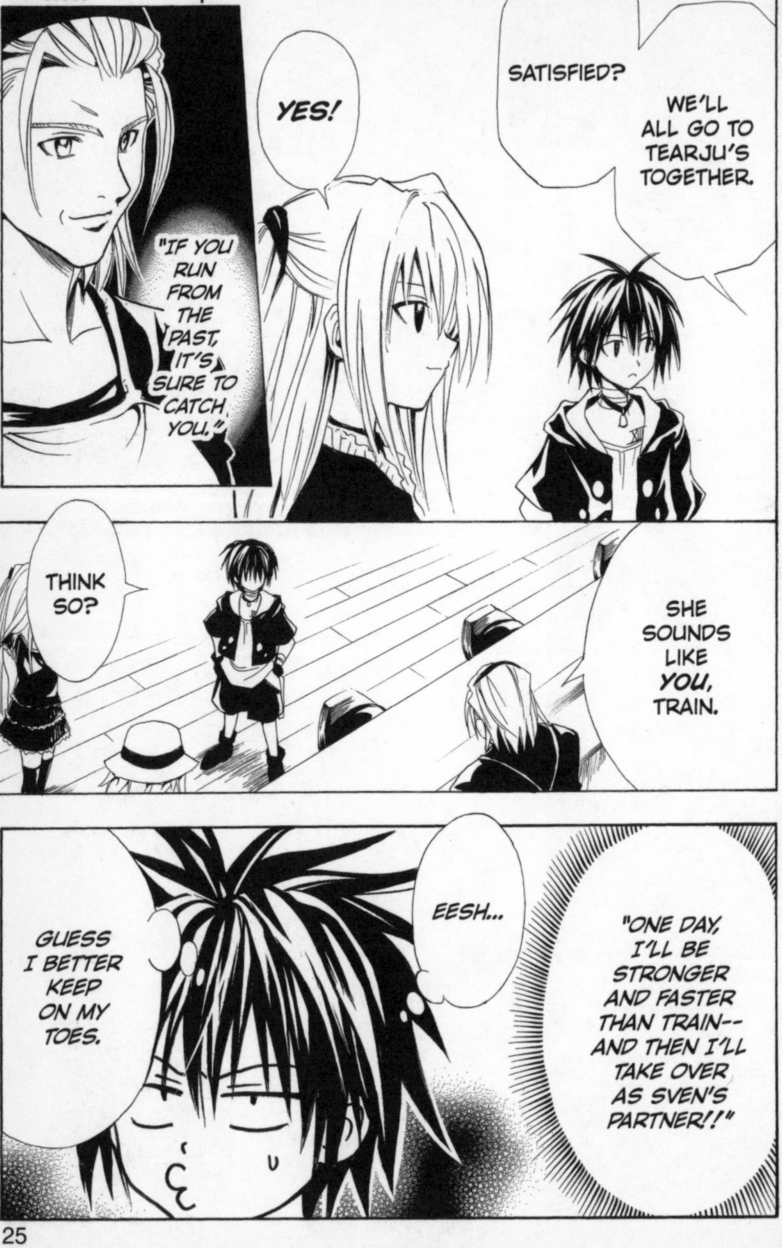
SATISFIED?
WE'LL ALL GO TO TEARJU'S TOGETHER.
YES!
"IF YOU RUN FROM THE PAST, IT'S SURE TO CATCH YOU."
SHE SOUNDS LIKE YOU, TRAIN.
THINK SO?
"ONE DAY, I'LL BE STRONGER AND FASTER THAN TRAIN--AND THEN I'LL TAKE OVER AS SVEN'S PARTNER!!"
EESH...
GUESS I BETTER KEEP ON MY TOES.

BLACK CAT

Chapter 105: Sephiria's Call

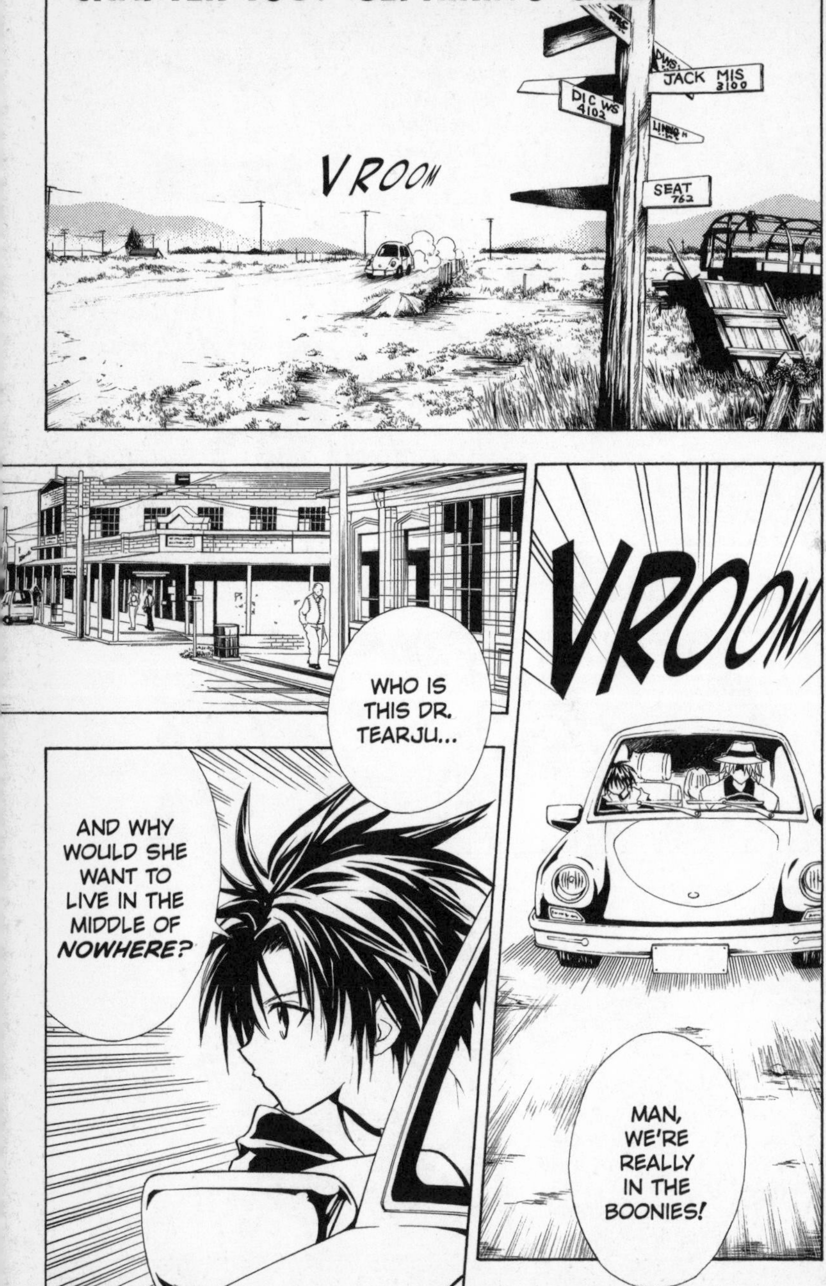
SATZ 583
JACK MIS 3100
DIC WS 4102
SEAT 762
VROOM
VROOM
MAN, WE'RE REALLY IN THE BOONIES!
WHO IS THIS DR. TEARJU...
AND WHY WOULD SHE WANT TO LIVE IN THE MIDDLE OF *NOWHERE?*

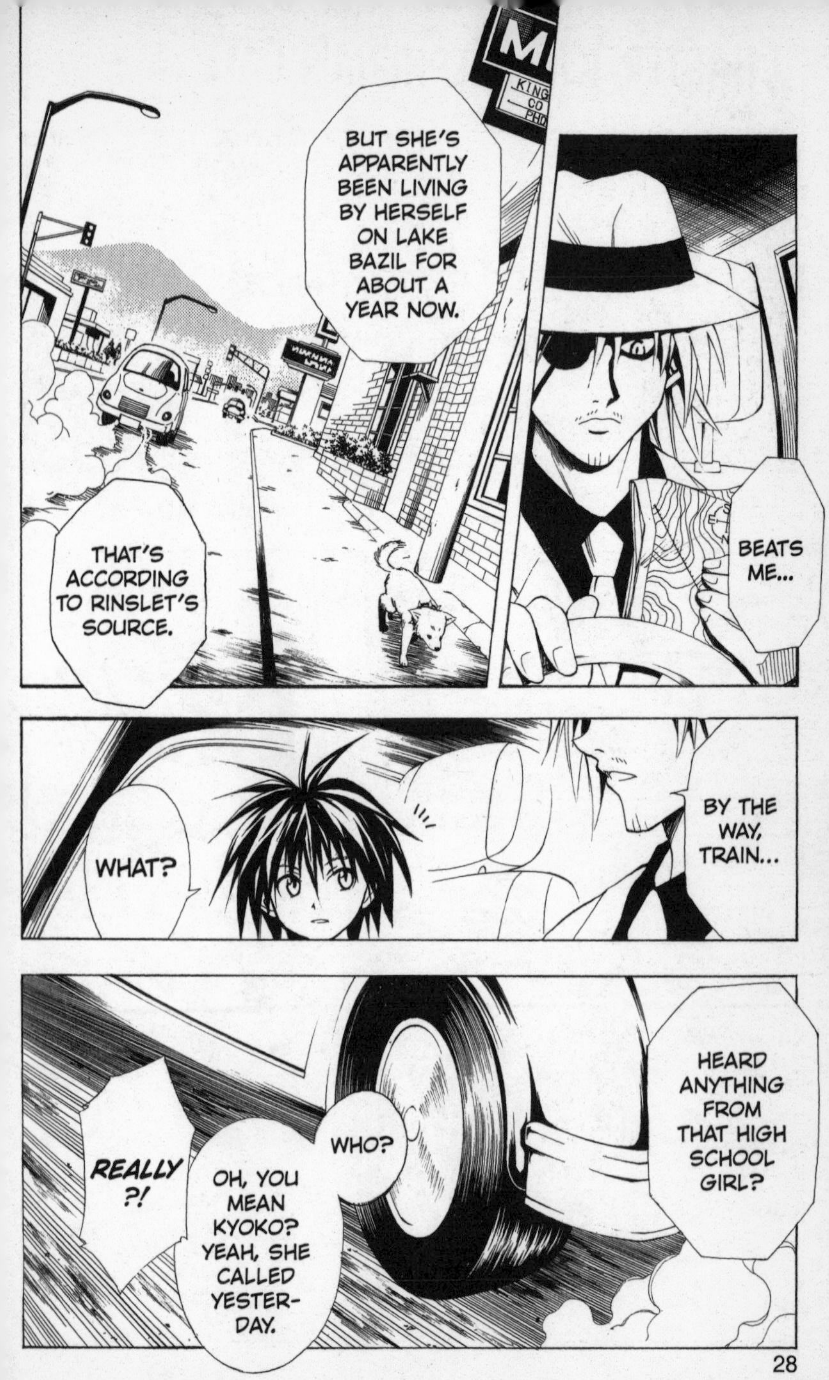
BEATS ME...
BUT SHE'S APPARENTLY BEEN LIVING BY HERSELF ON LAKE BAZIL FOR ABOUT A YEAR NOW.
THAT'S ACCORDING TO RINSLET'S SOURCE.
BY THE WAY, TRAIN...
WHAT?
HEARD ANYTHING FROM THAT HIGH SCHOOL GIRL?
WHO?
OH, YOU MEAN KYOKO? YEAH, SHE CALLED YESTER-DAY.
REALLY ?!

READ THIS WAY

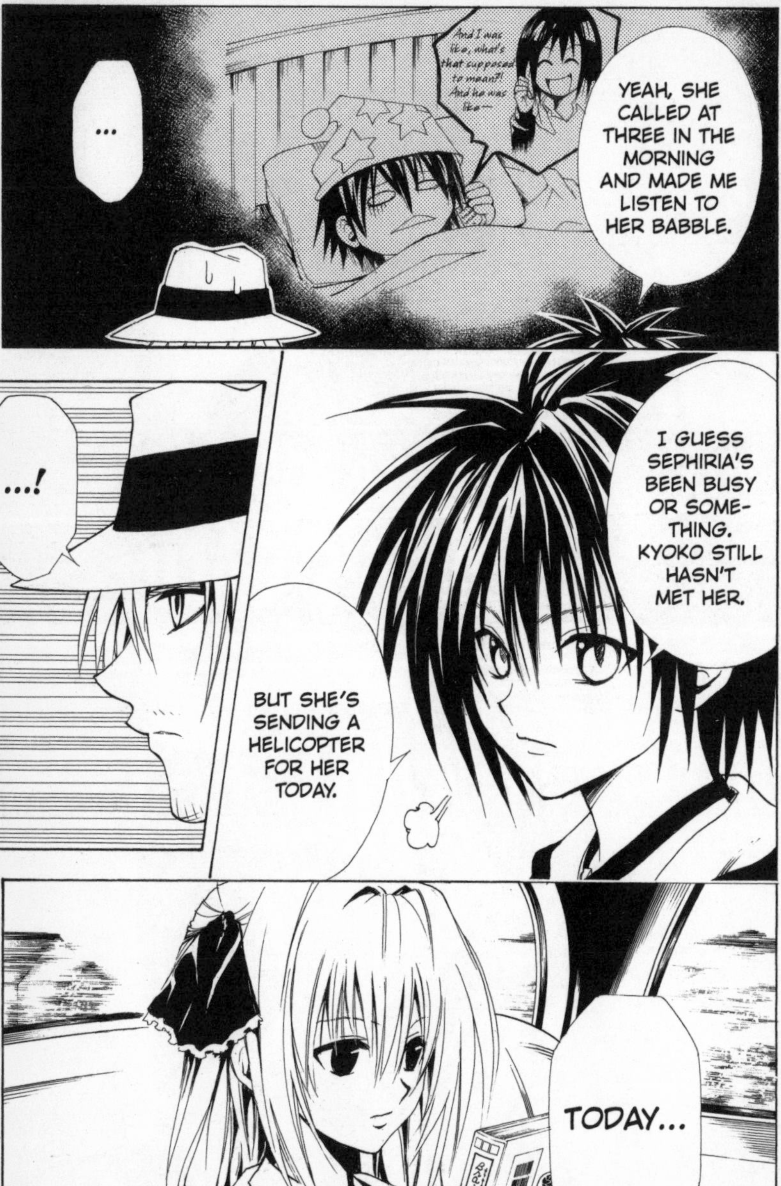
YEAH, SHE CALLED AT THREE IN THE MORNING AND MADE ME LISTEN TO HER BABBLE.
And I was like, what's that supposed to mean?! And he was like—
...
I GUESS SEPHIRIA'S BEEN BUSY OR SOME-THING. KYOKO STILL HASN'T MET HER.
BUT SHE'S SENDING A HELICOPTER FOR HER TODAY.
...!
TODAY...

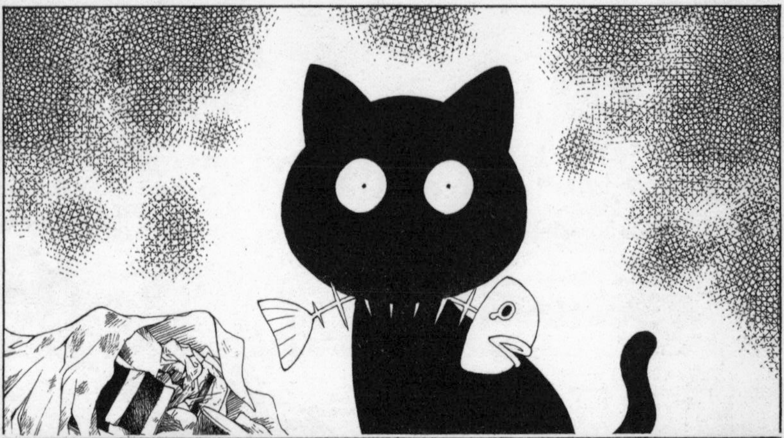

Chapter 105:
Sephiria's Call

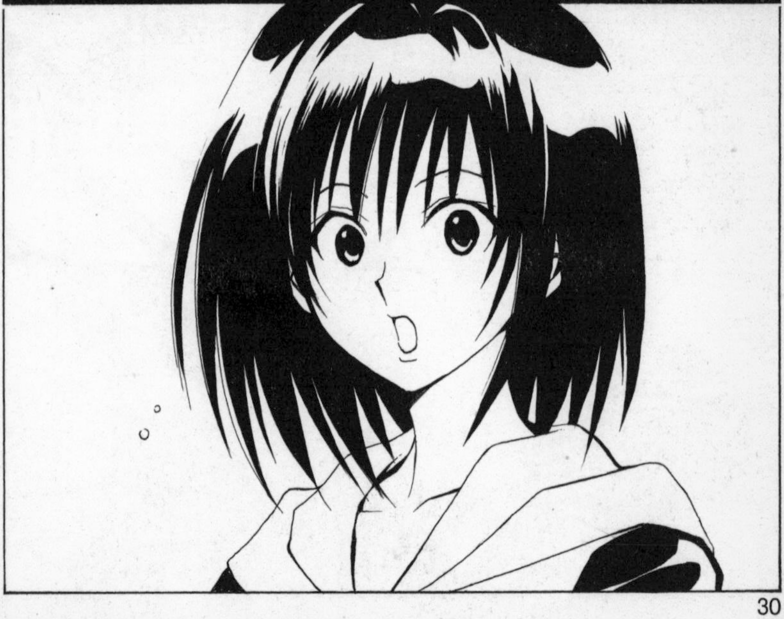

READ THIS WAY

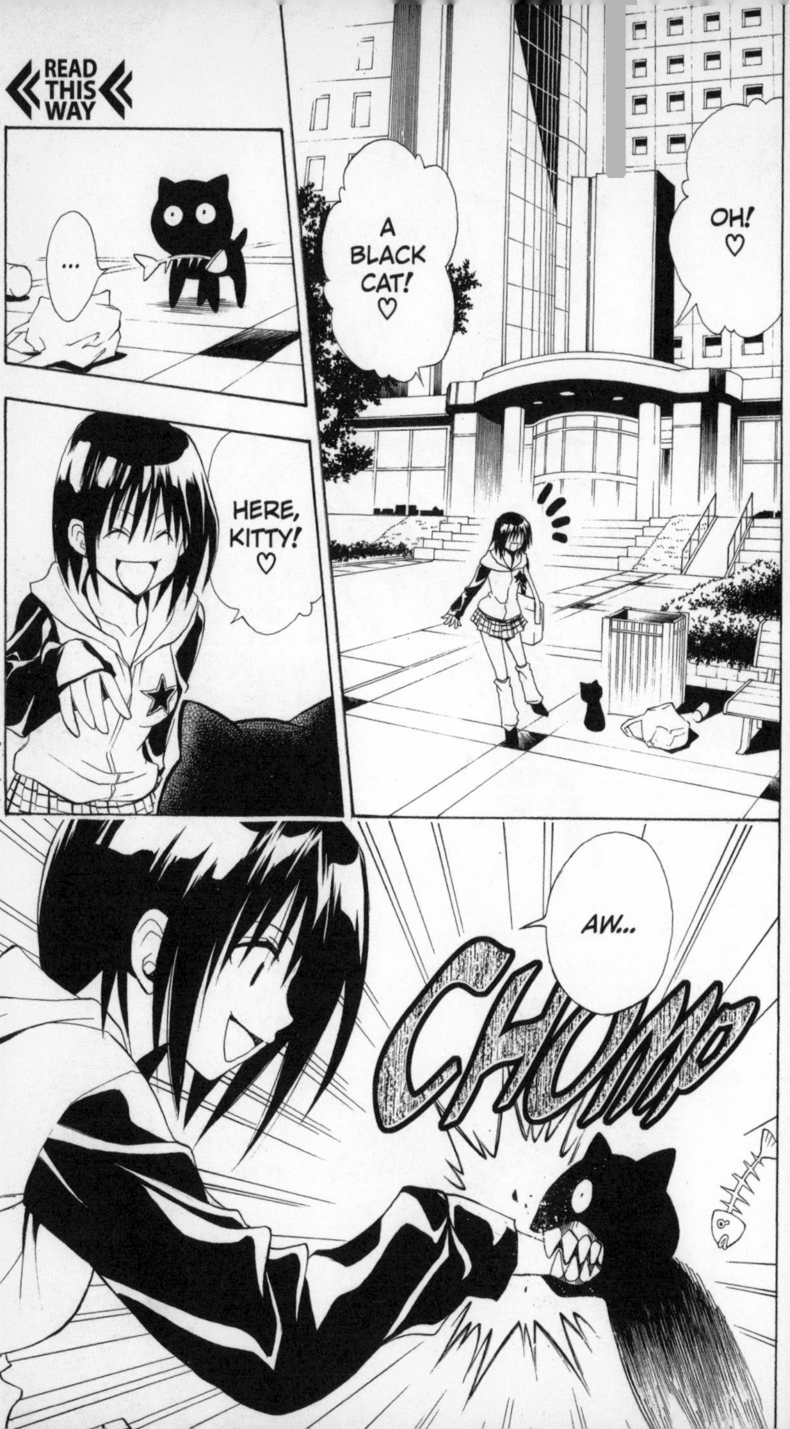
OH! ♡
A BLACK CAT! ♡
...
HERE, KITTY! ♡
AW...
CHOMP

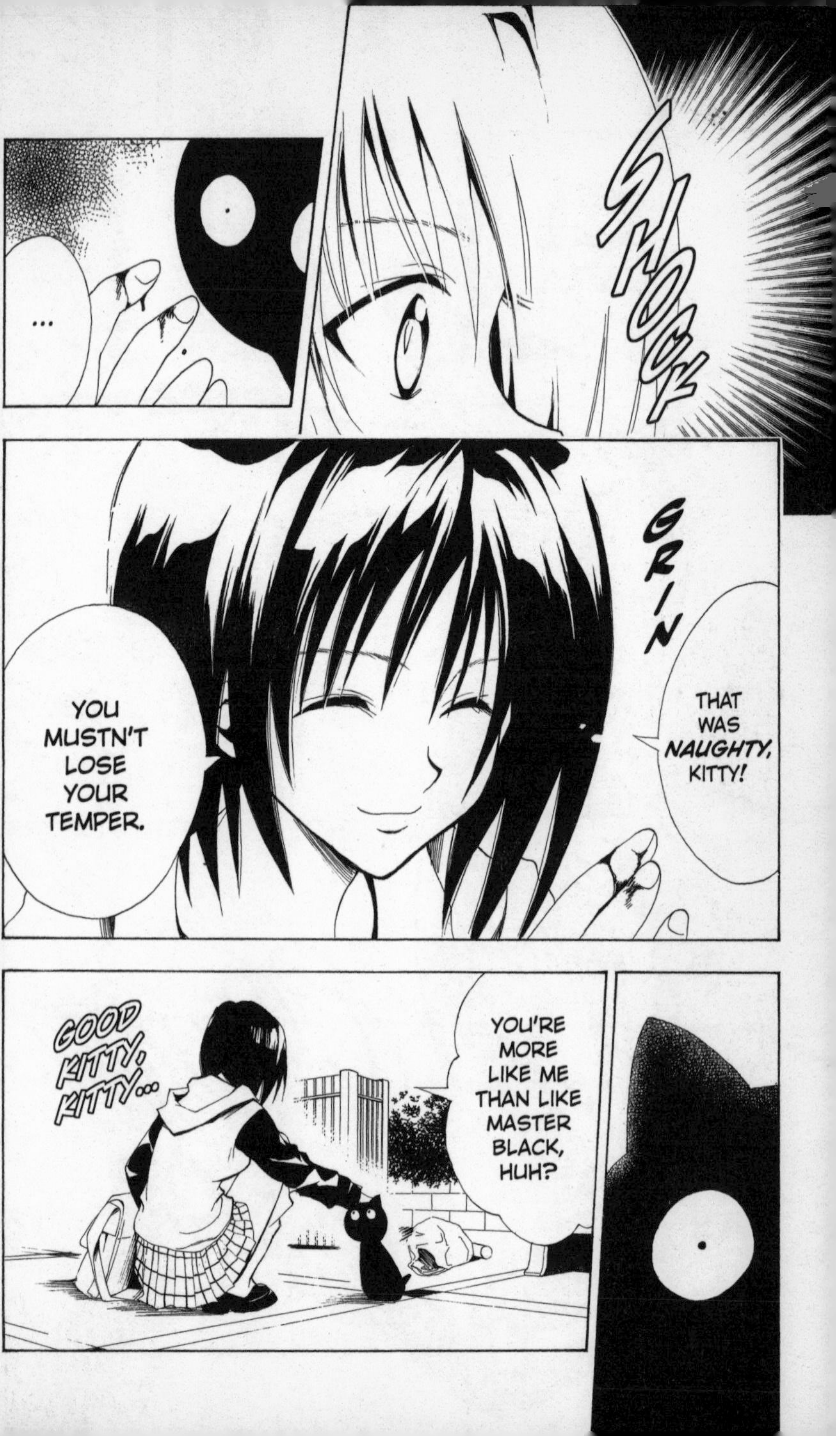
SHOCK
...
GRIN
THAT WAS *NAUGHTY,* KITTY!
YOU MUSTN'T LOSE YOUR TEMPER.
YOU'RE MORE LIKE ME THAN LIKE MASTER BLACK, HUH?
GOOD KITTY, KITTY...

READ THIS WAY

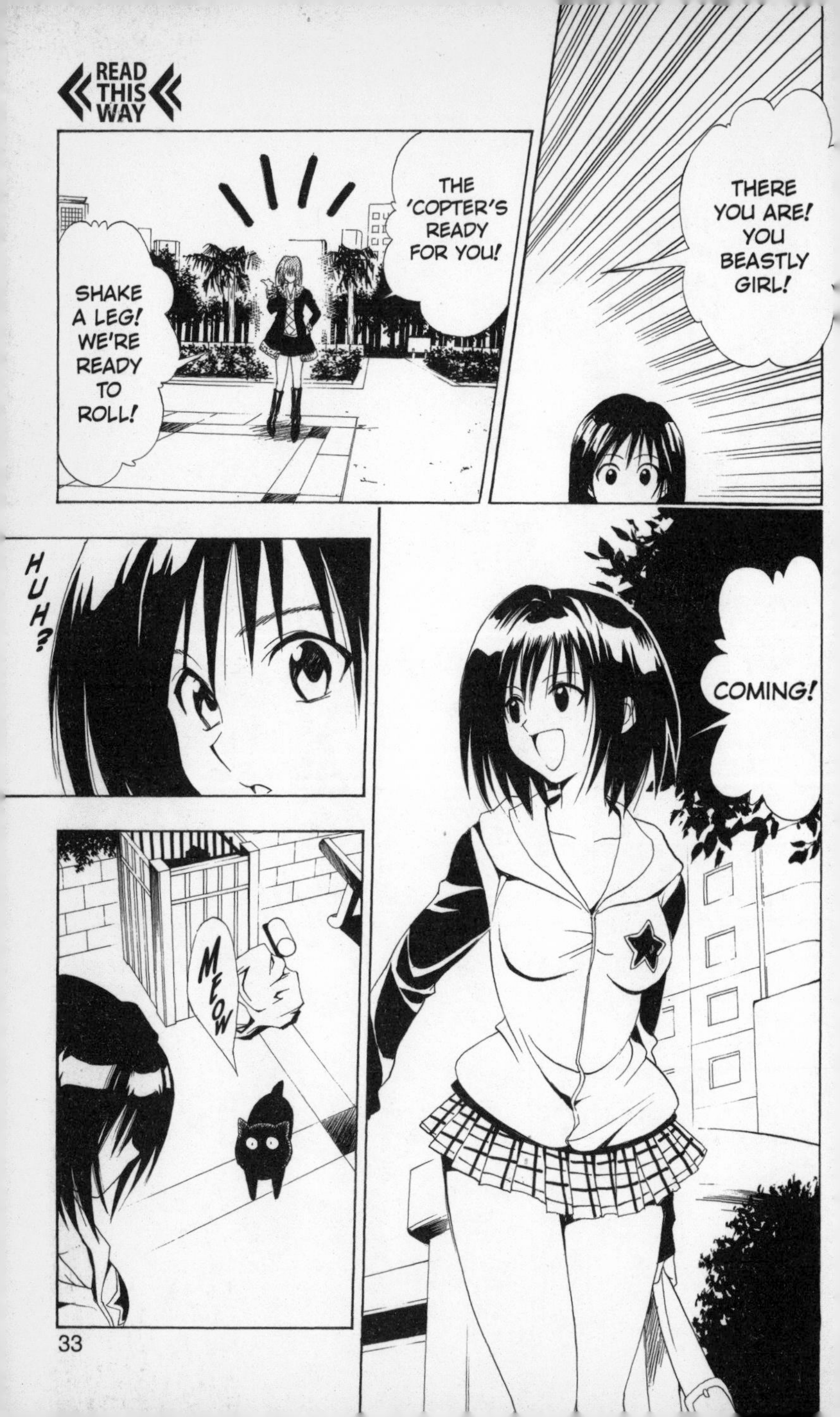

THERE YOU ARE! YOU BEASTLY GIRL!
THE 'COPTER'S READY FOR YOU!
SHAKE A LEG! WE'RE READY TO ROLL!
COMING!
HUH?
MEOW

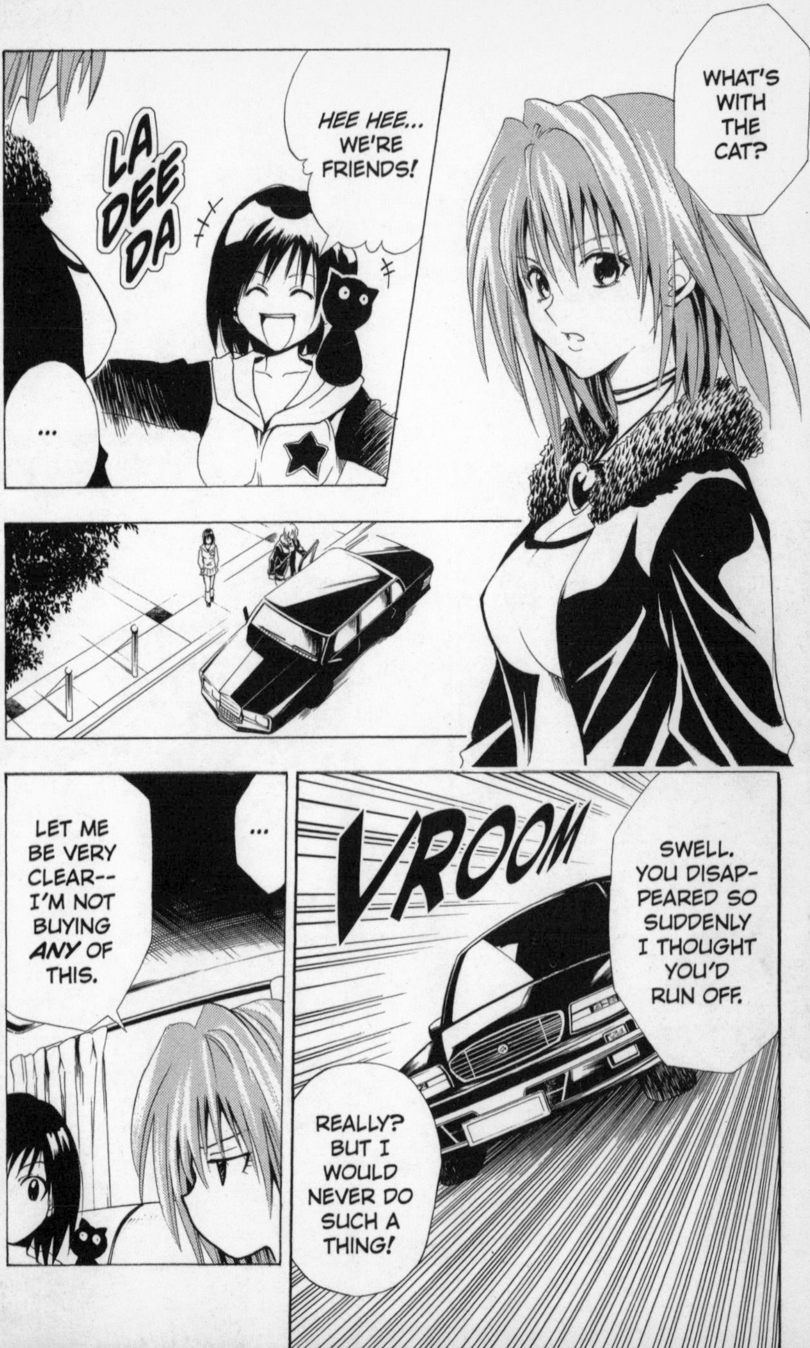
WHAT'S WITH THE CAT?
HEE HEE... WE'RE FRIENDS!
LA DEE DA
...
VROOM
SWELL. YOU DISAP-PEARED SO SUDDENLY I THOUGHT YOU'D RUN OFF.
REALLY? BUT I WOULD NEVER DO SUCH A THING!
...
LET ME BE VERY CLEAR-- I'M NOT BUYING *ANY* OF THIS.

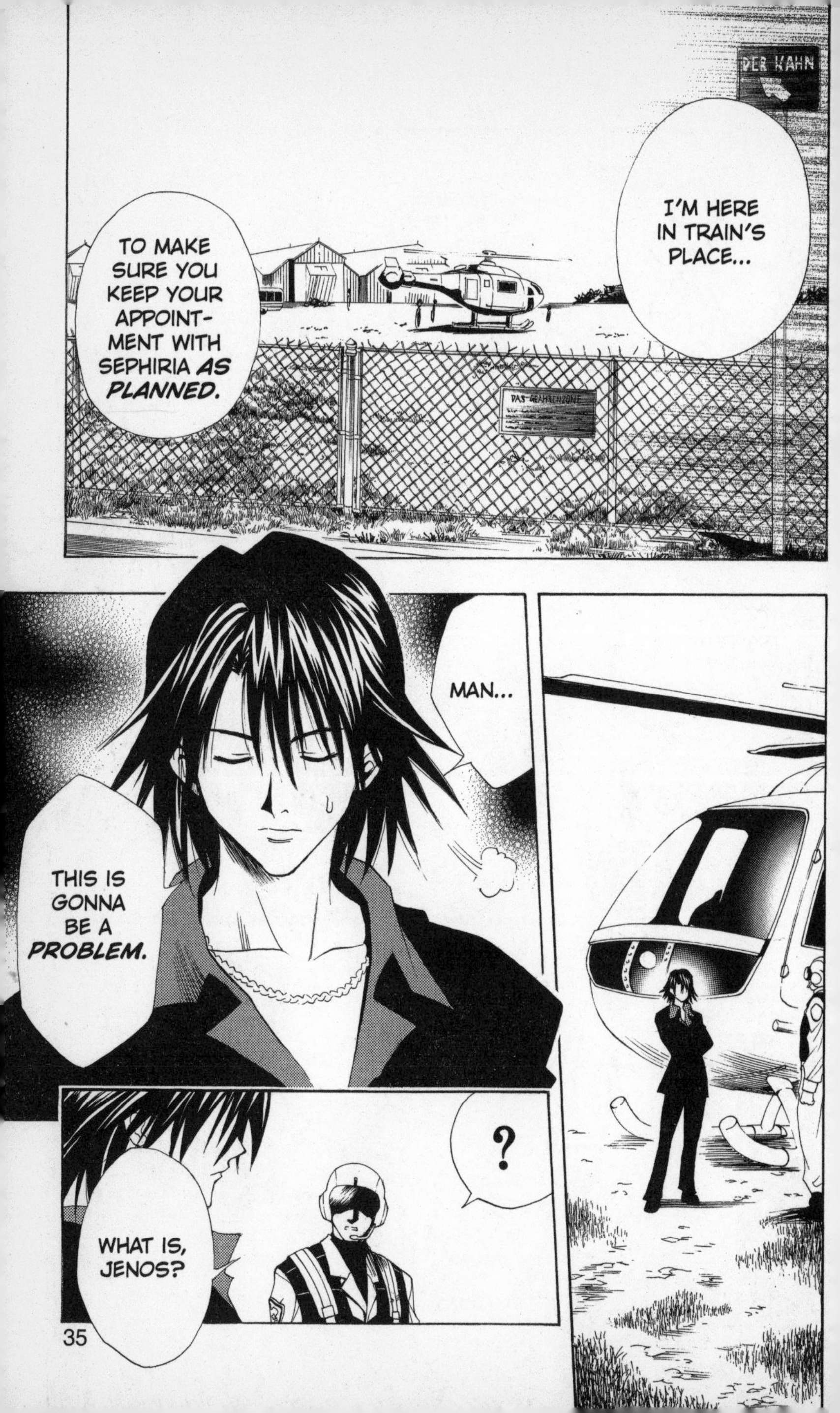
DER KAHN
I'M HERE IN TRAIN'S PLACE...
TO MAKE SURE YOU KEEP YOUR APPOINTMENT WITH SEPHIRIA *AS PLANNED.*
MAN...
THIS IS GONNA BE A *PROBLEM.*
?
WHAT IS, JENOS?

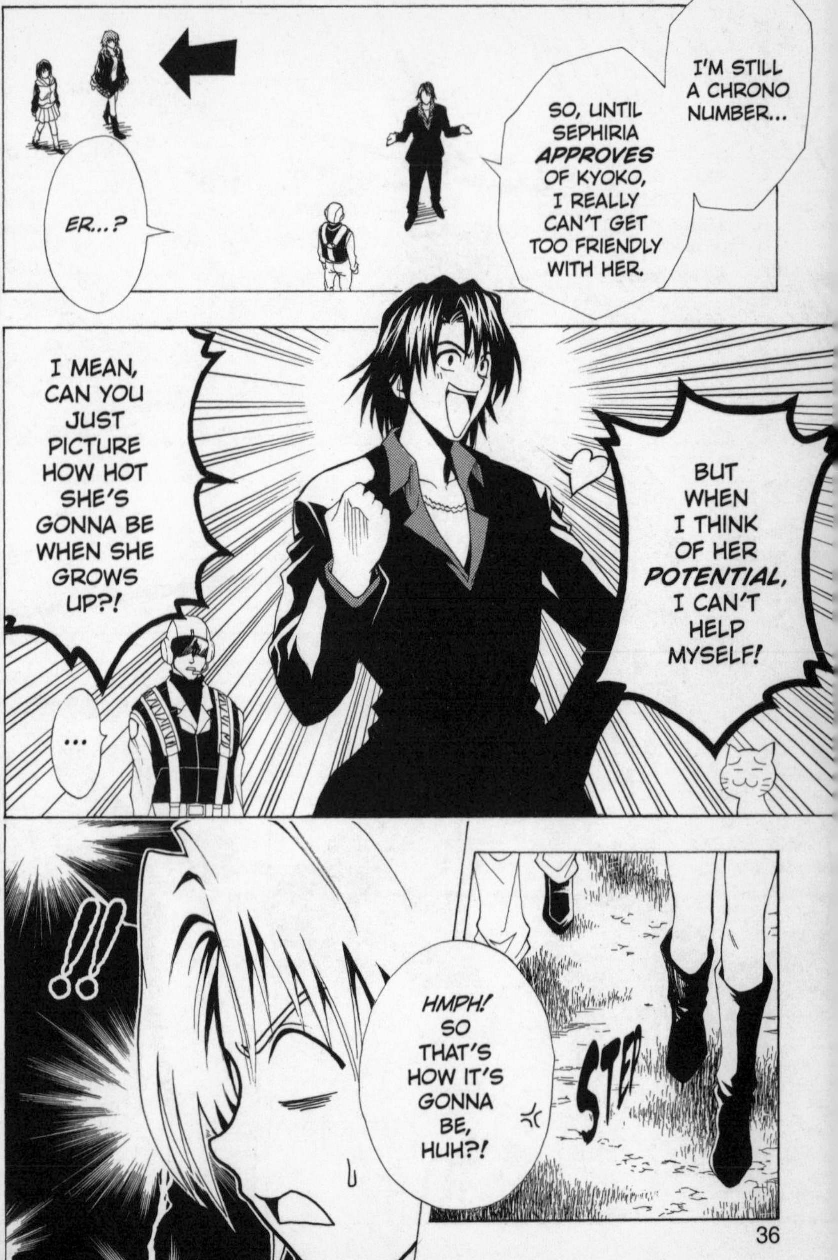
I'M STILL A CHRONO NUMBER...
SO, UNTIL SEPHIRIA *APPROVES* OF KYOKO, I REALLY CAN'T GET TOO FRIENDLY WITH HER.
ER...?
BUT WHEN I THINK OF HER *POTENTIAL*, I CAN'T HELP MYSELF!
I MEAN, CAN YOU JUST PICTURE HOW HOT SHE'S GONNA BE WHEN SHE GROWS UP?!
...
STEP
!!
HMPH! SO THAT'S HOW IT'S GONNA BE, HUH?!

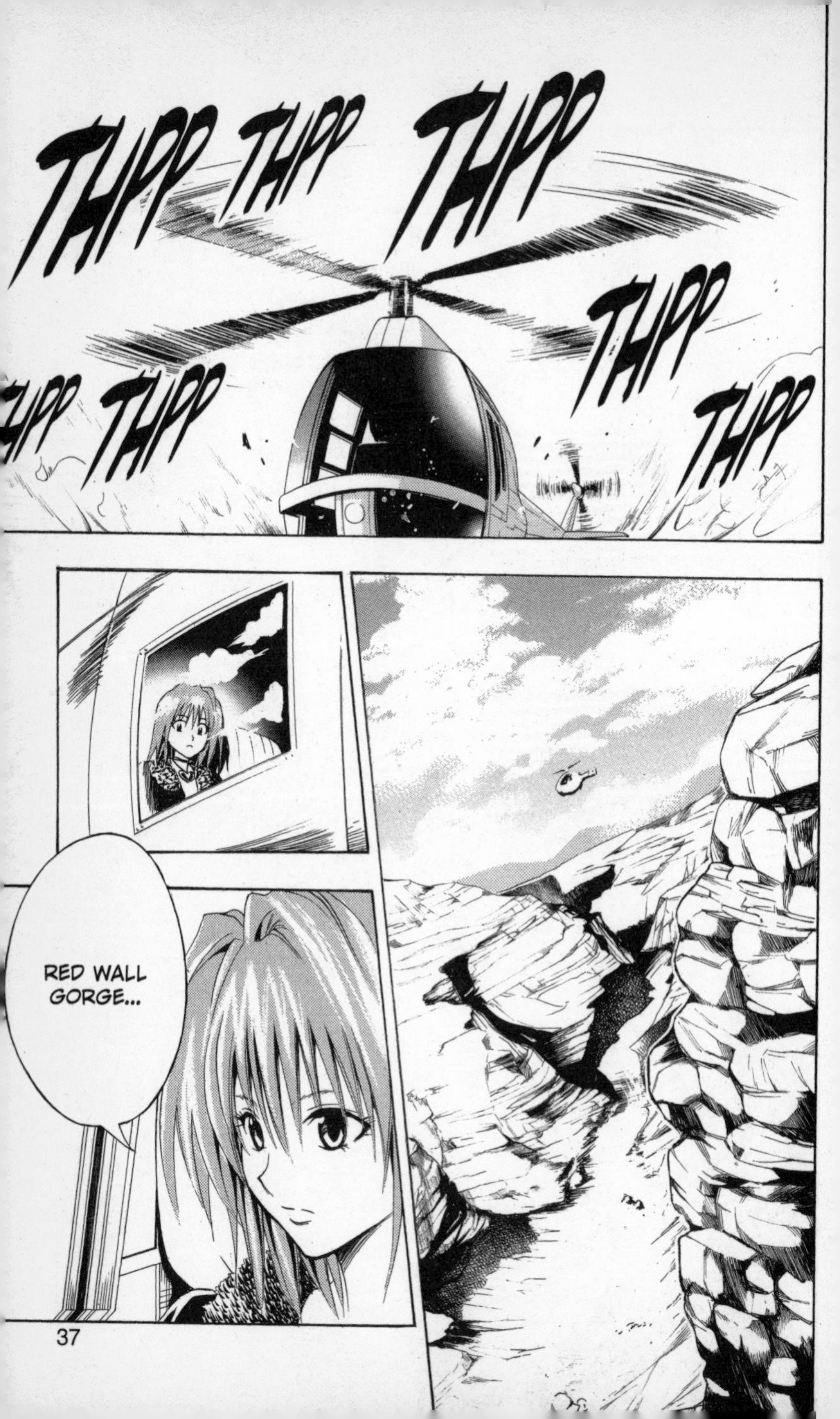
THPP THPP THPP
THPP THPP
THPP THPP
RED WALL GORGE...

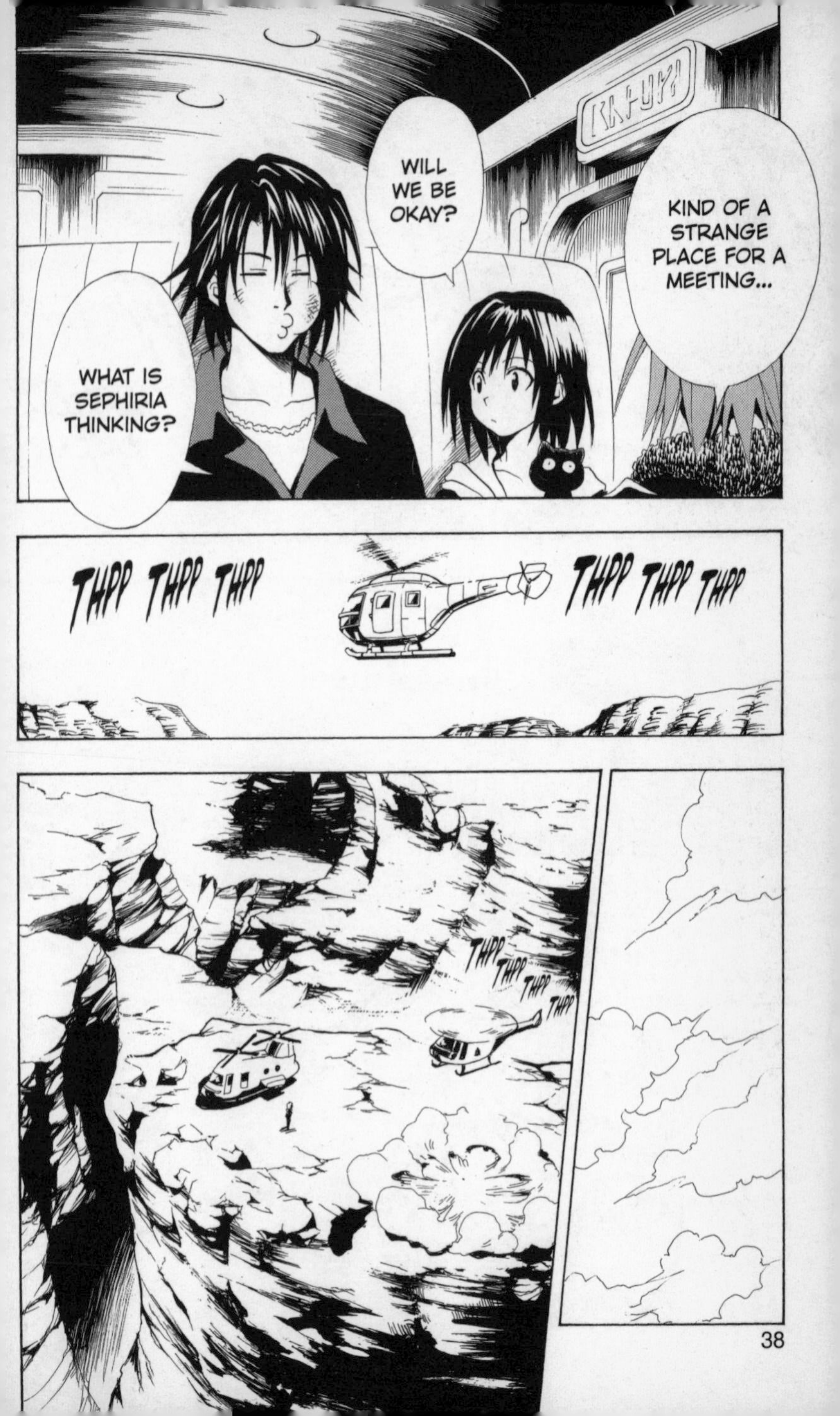
KIND OF A STRANGE PLACE FOR A MEETING...
WILL WE BE OKAY?
WHAT IS SEPHIRIA THINKING?
THPP THPP THPP
THPP THPP THPP
THPP THPP THPP THPP

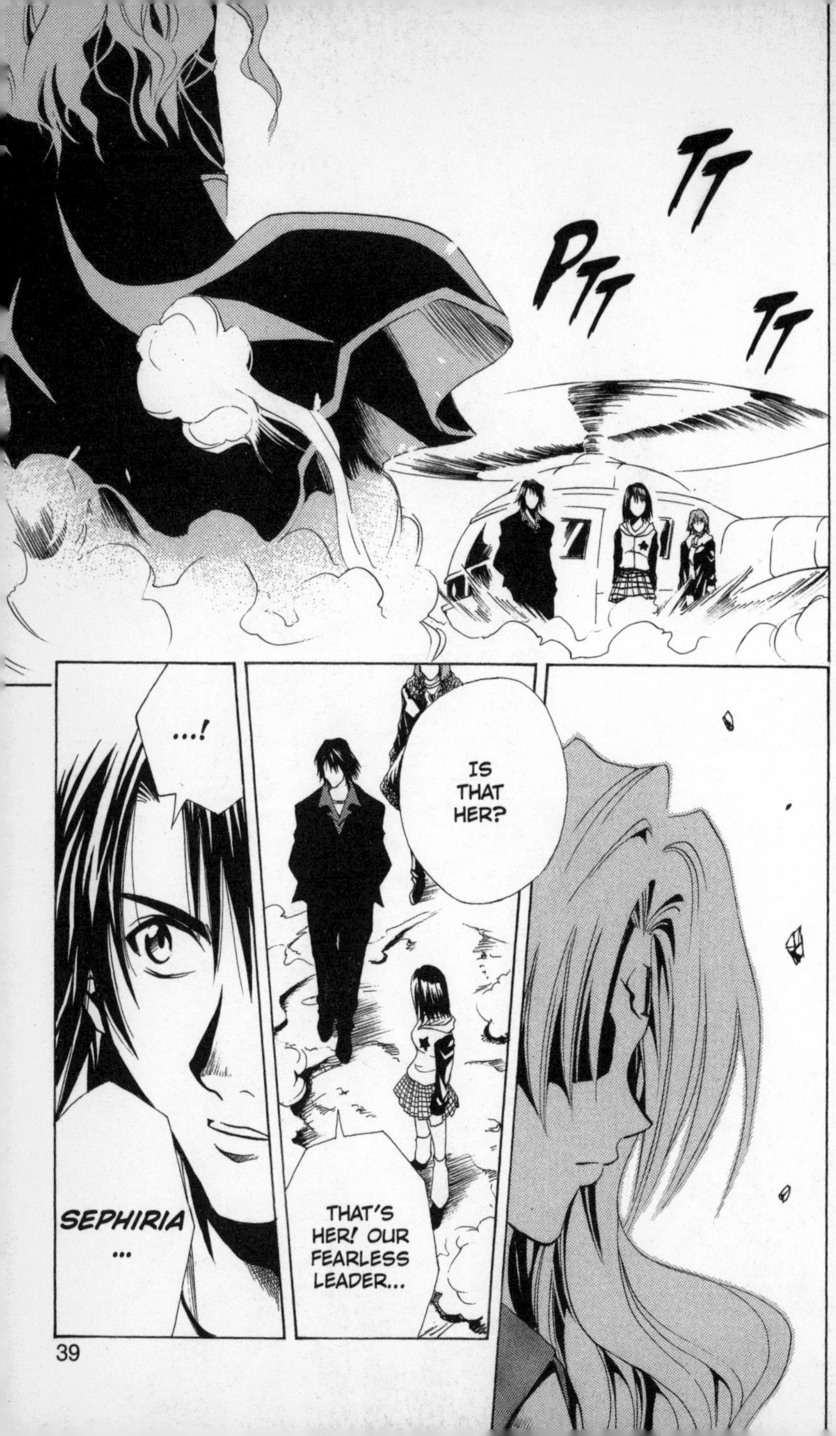
TT
PTT
TT
IS THAT HER?
THAT'S HER! OUR FEARLESS LEADER...
...!
SEPHIRIA ...

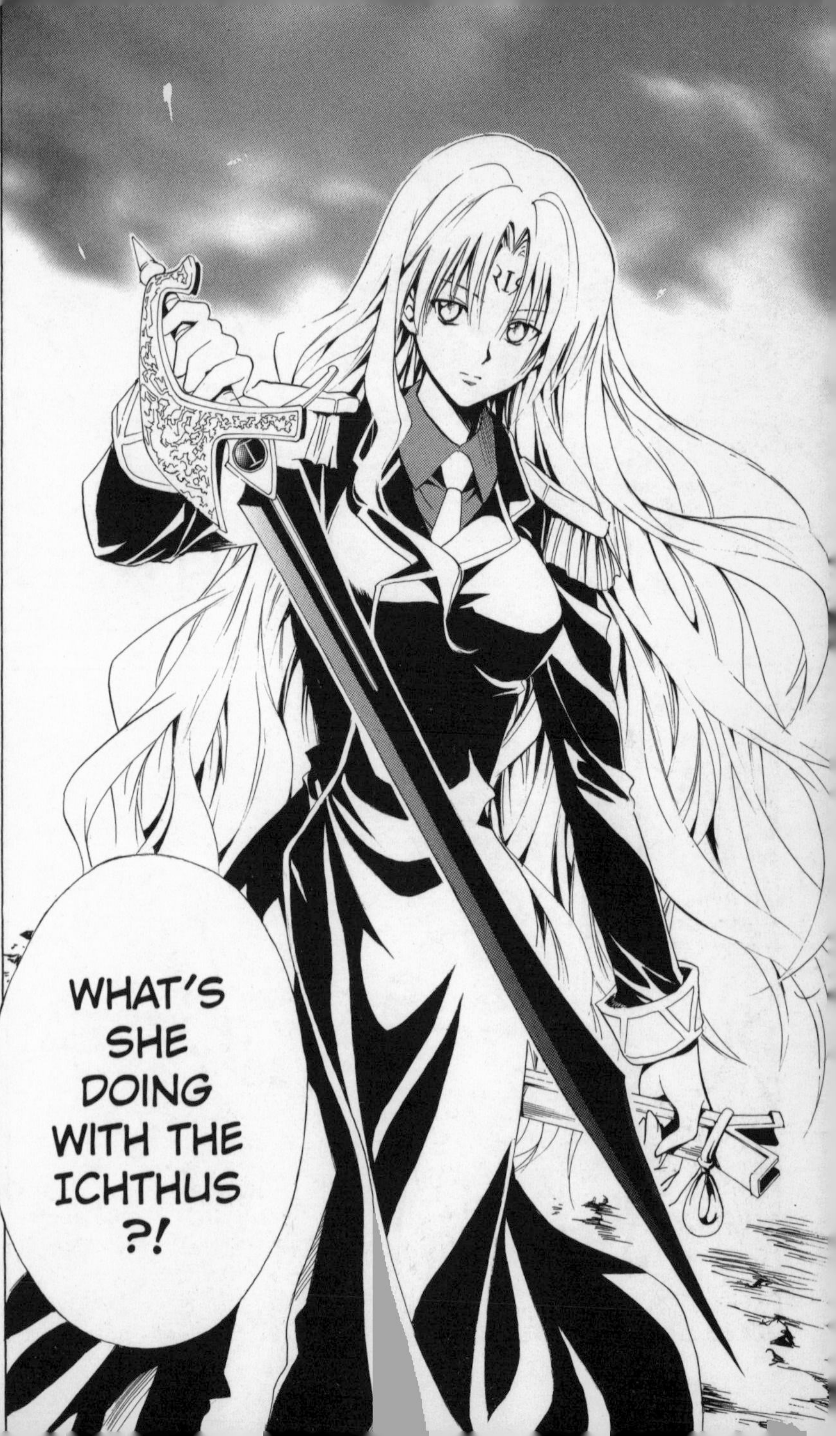
WHAT'S SHE DOING WITH THE ICHTHUS ?!

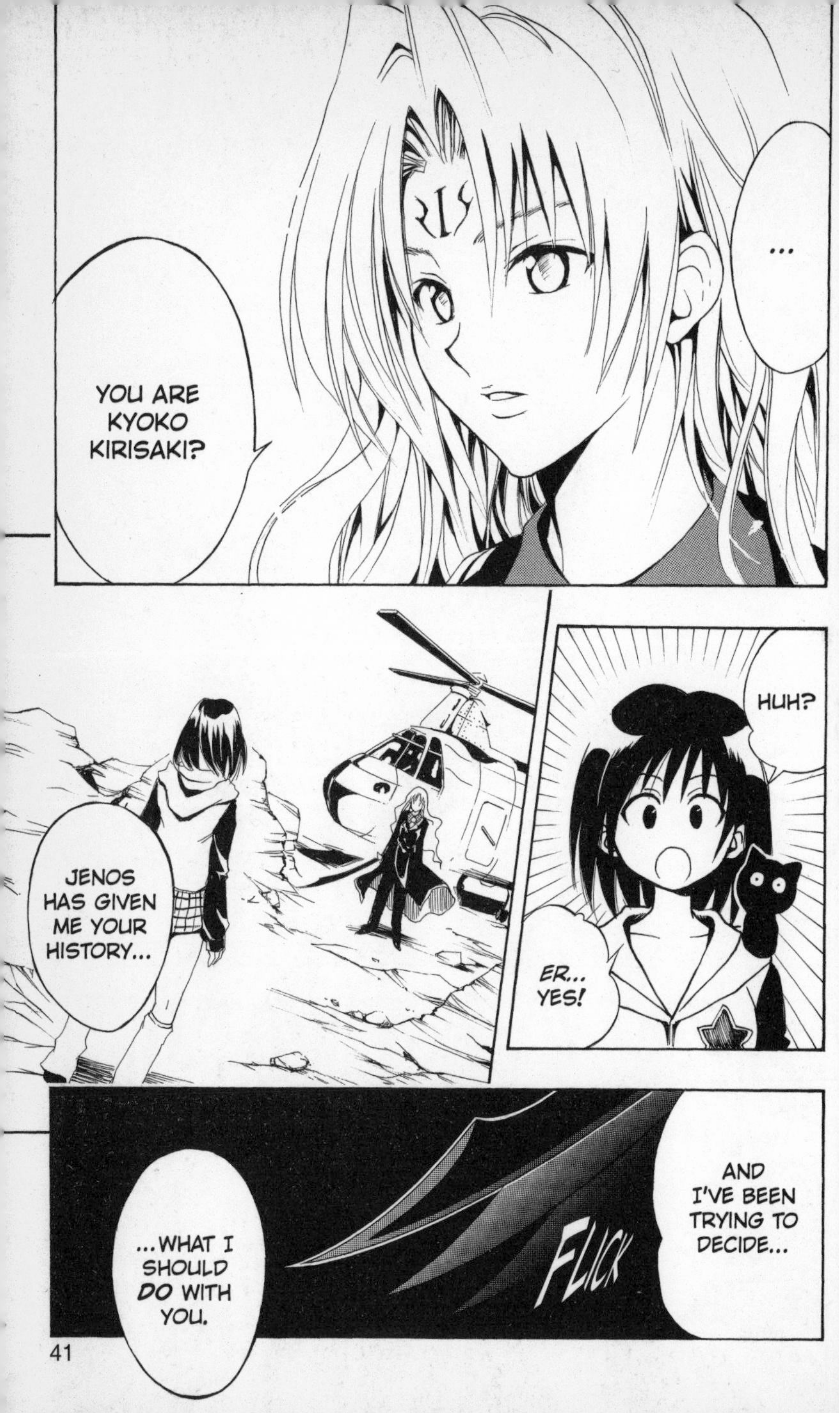
...
YOU ARE KYOKO KIRISAKI?
HUH?
ER... YES!
JENOS HAS GIVEN ME YOUR HISTORY...
AND I'VE BEEN TRYING TO DECIDE...
FLICK
...WHAT I SHOULD *DO* WITH YOU.

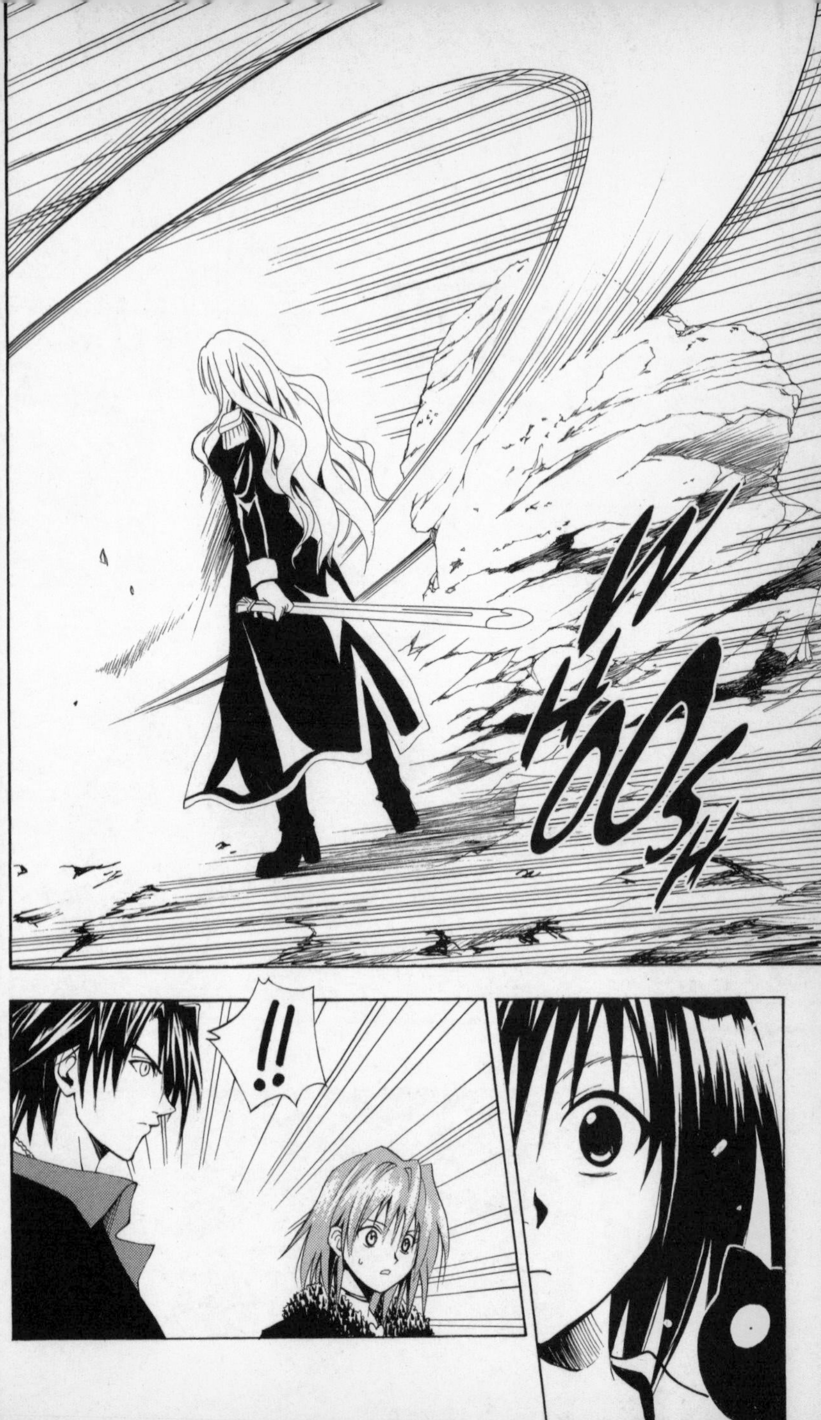
WHOOSH
!!

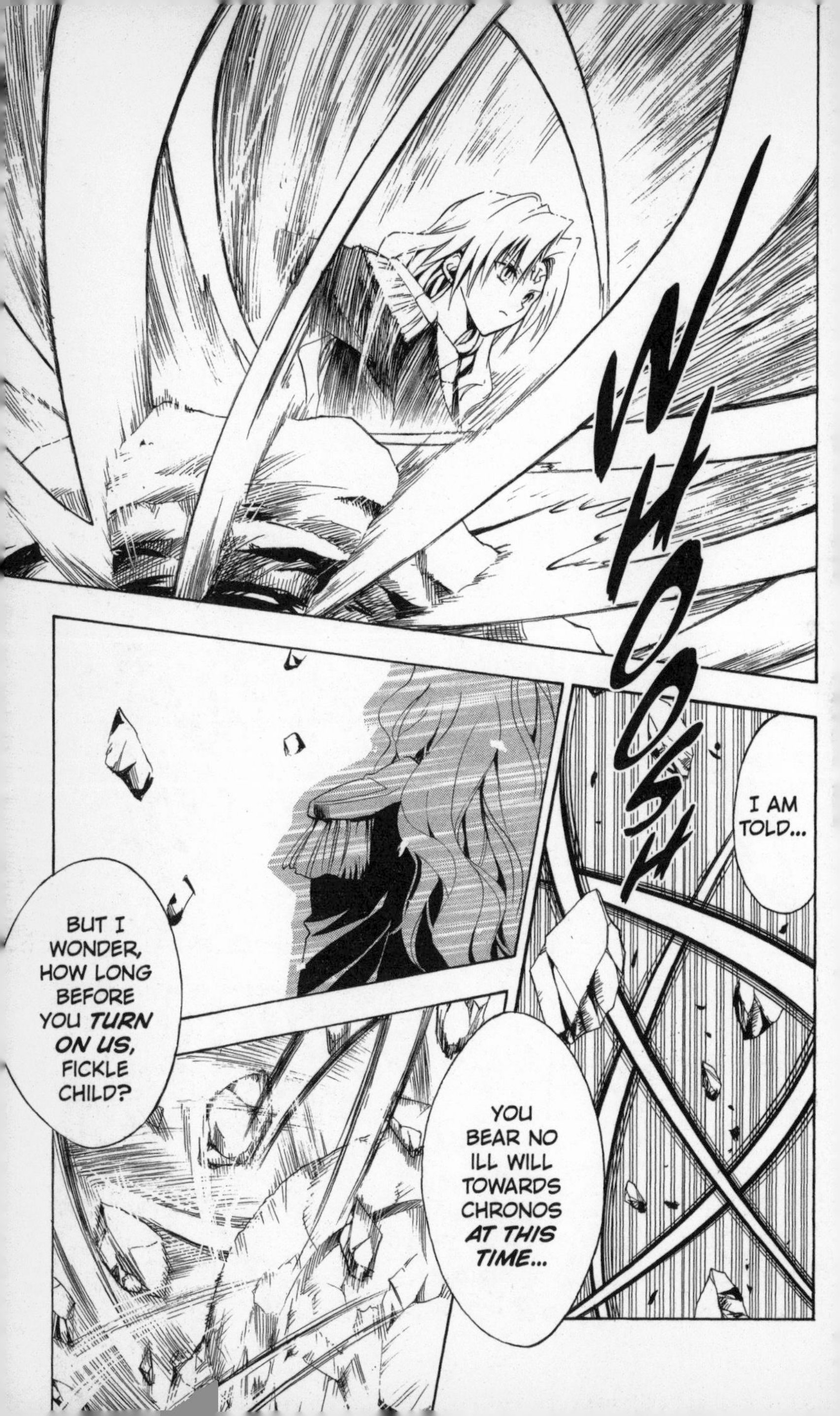
WHOOSH
I AM TOLD...
YOU BEAR NO ILL WILL TOWARDS CHRONOS *AT THIS TIME*...
BUT I WONDER, HOW LONG BEFORE YOU *TURN ON US*, FICKLE CHILD?

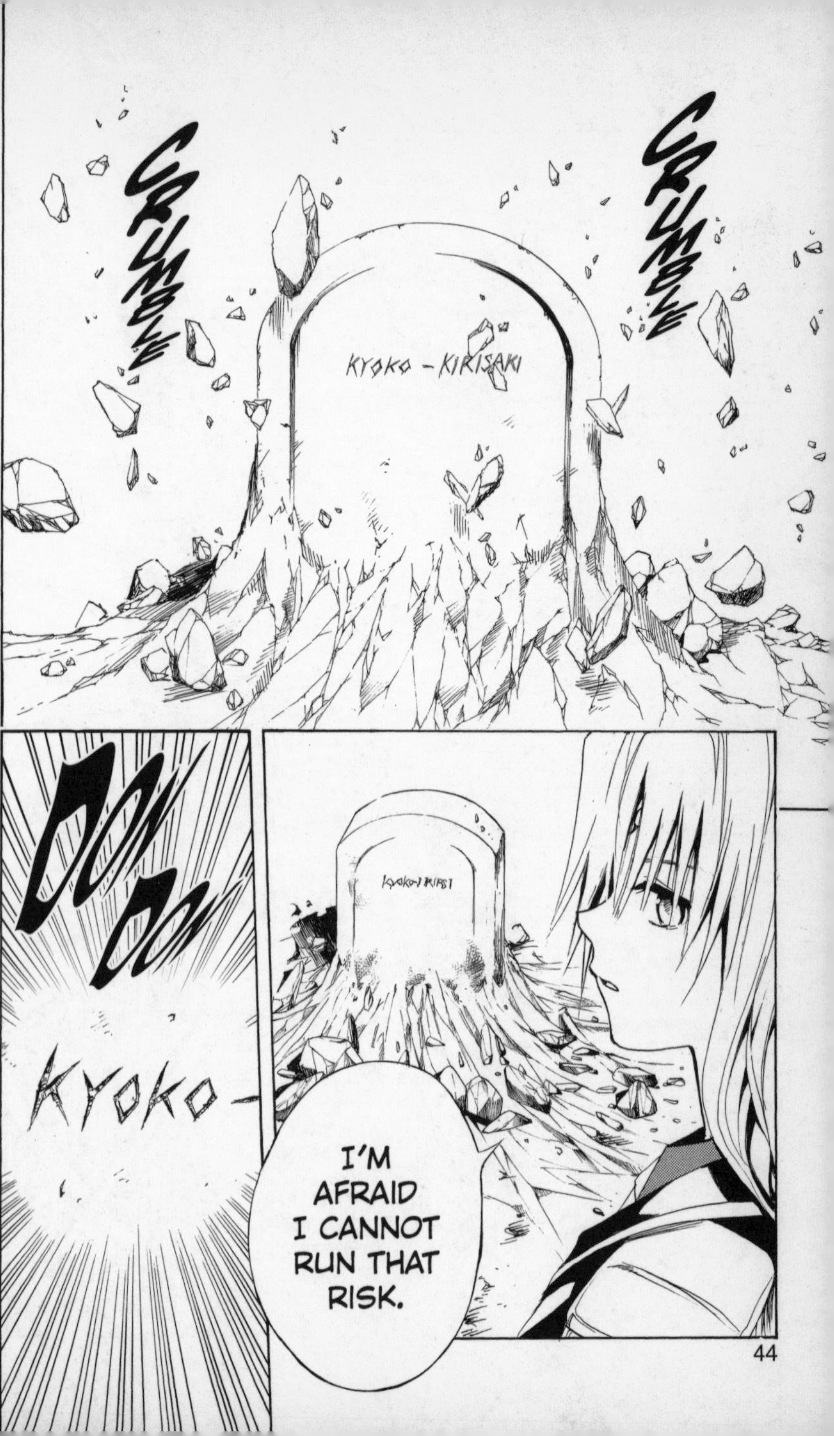

CRUMBLE
CRUMBLE
KYOKO - KIRISAKI
I'M AFRAID I CANNOT RUN THAT RISK.
KYOKO-

READ THIS WAY

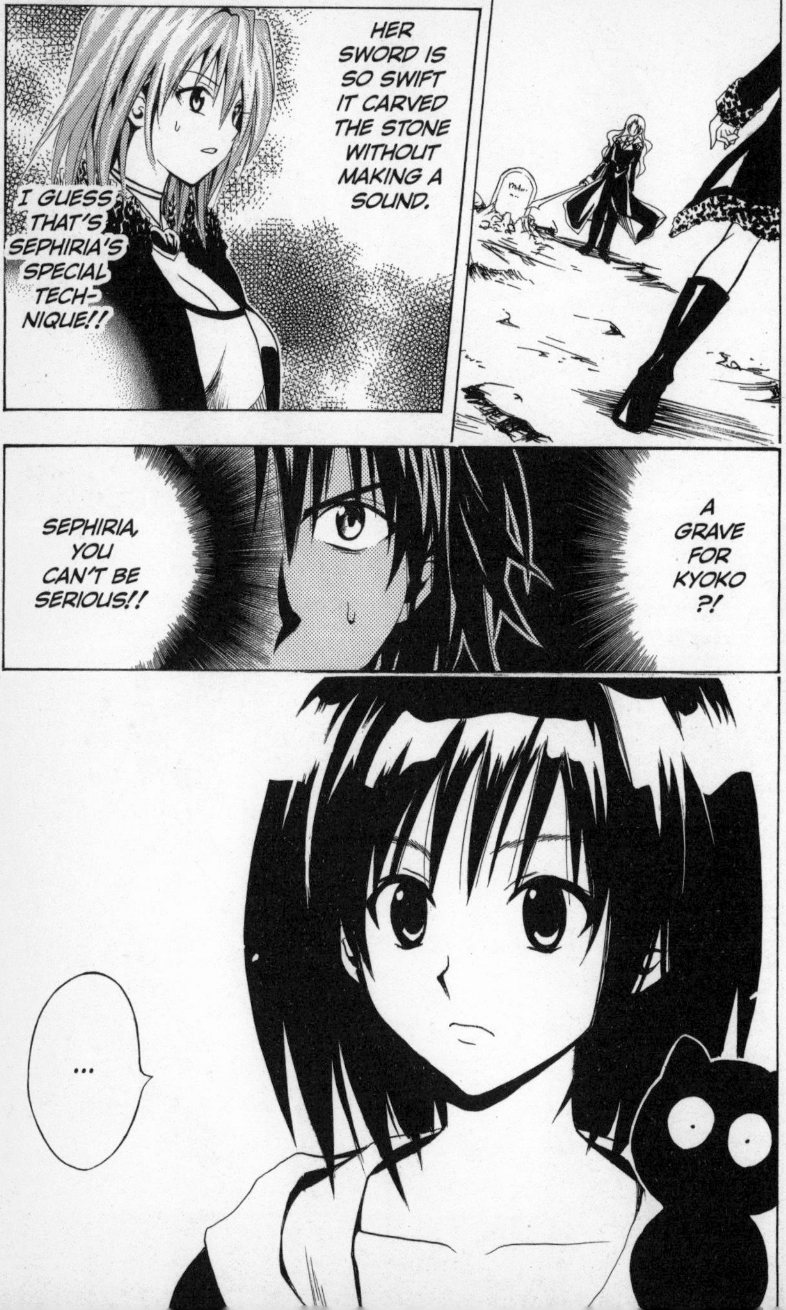
HER SWORD IS SO SWIFT IT CARVED THE STONE WITHOUT MAKING A SOUND.
I GUESS THAT'S SEPHIRIA'S SPECIAL TECH-NIQUE!!
A GRAVE FOR KYOKO ?!
SEPHIRIA, YOU CAN'T BE SERIOUS!!
...

BLACK CAT

CHAPTER 106: A HEART TESTED

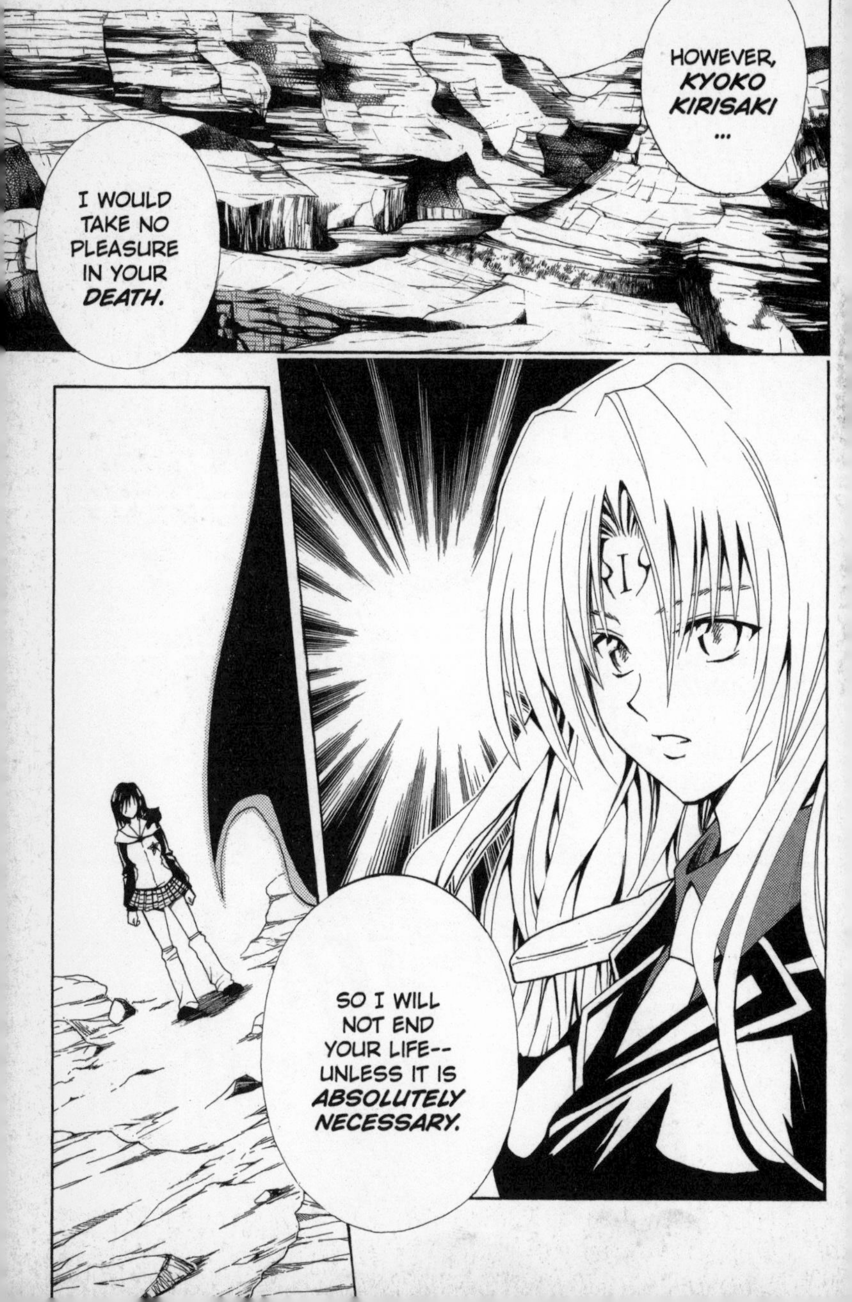
HOWEVER, KYOKO KIRISAKI ...
I WOULD TAKE NO PLEASURE IN YOUR DEATH.
SO I WILL NOT END YOUR LIFE-- UNLESS IT IS ABSOLUTELY NECESSARY.

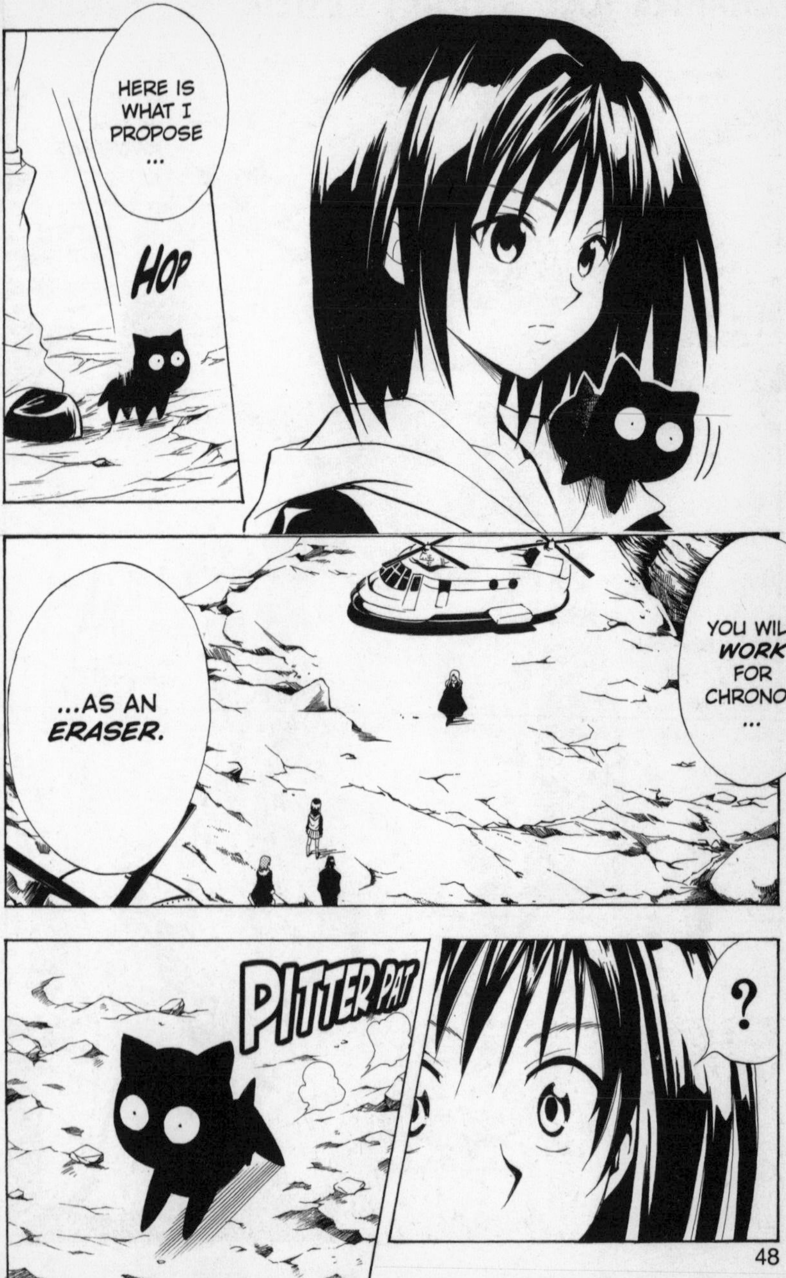
HERE IS WHAT I PROPOSE ...
HOP
YOU WILL **WORK** FOR CHRONOS ...
...AS AN **ERASER.**
?
PITTER PAT

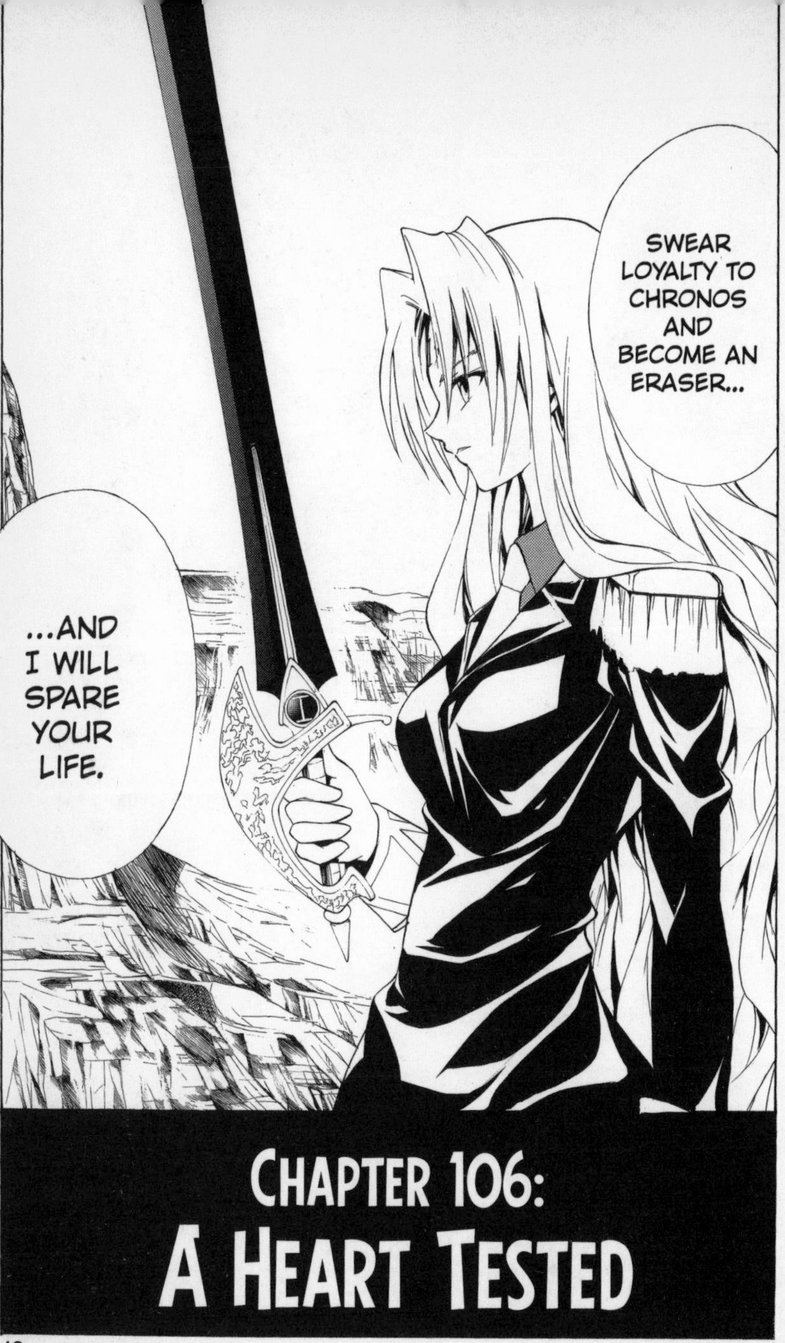
SWEAR LOYALTY TO CHRONOS AND BECOME AN ERASER...
...AND I WILL SPARE YOUR LIFE.

Chapter 106: A Heart Tested

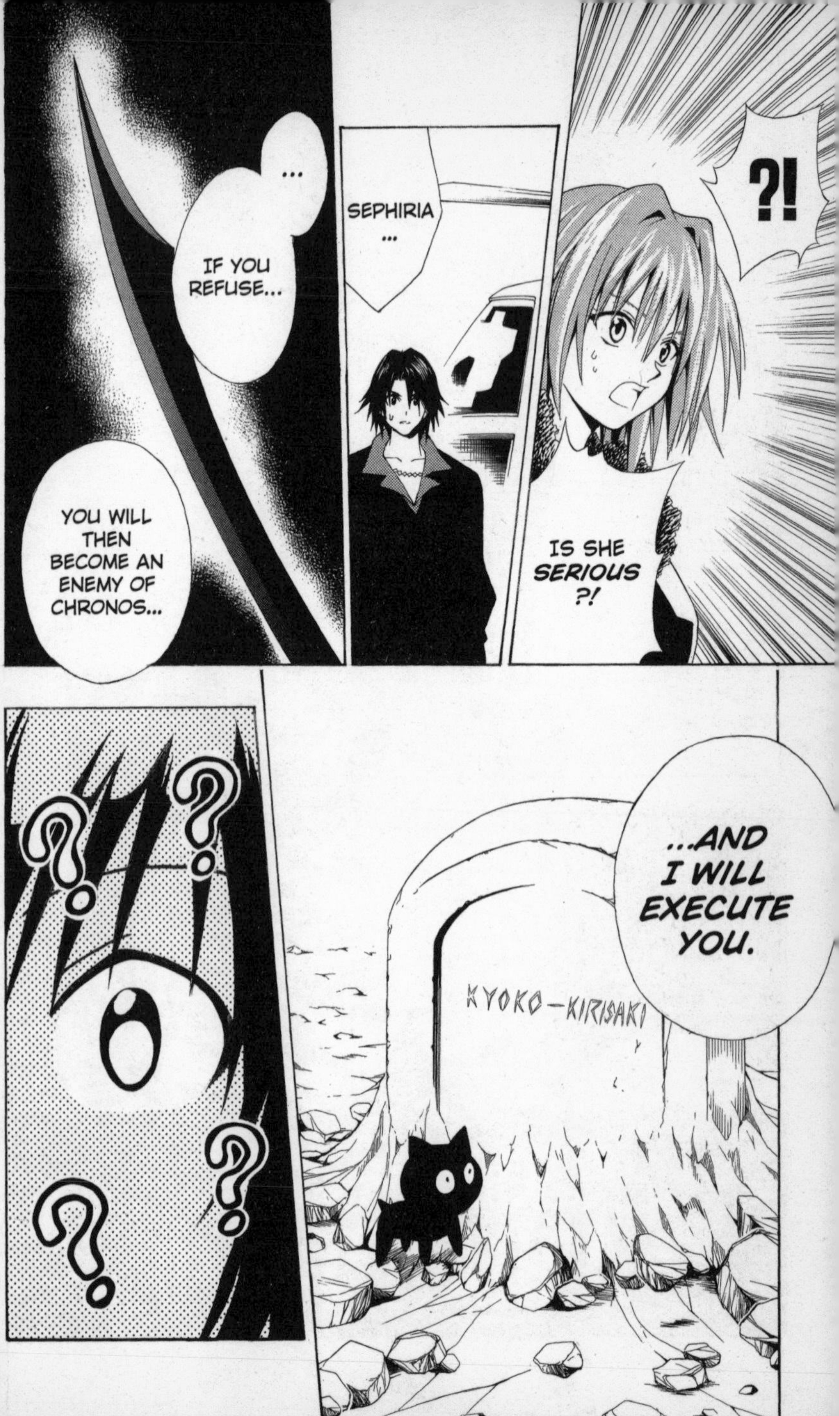
?!
IS SHE SERIOUS ?!
SEPHIRIA ...
...
IF YOU REFUSE...
YOU WILL THEN BECOME AN ENEMY OF CHRONOS...
...AND I WILL EXECUTE YOU.
KYOKO-KIRISAKI

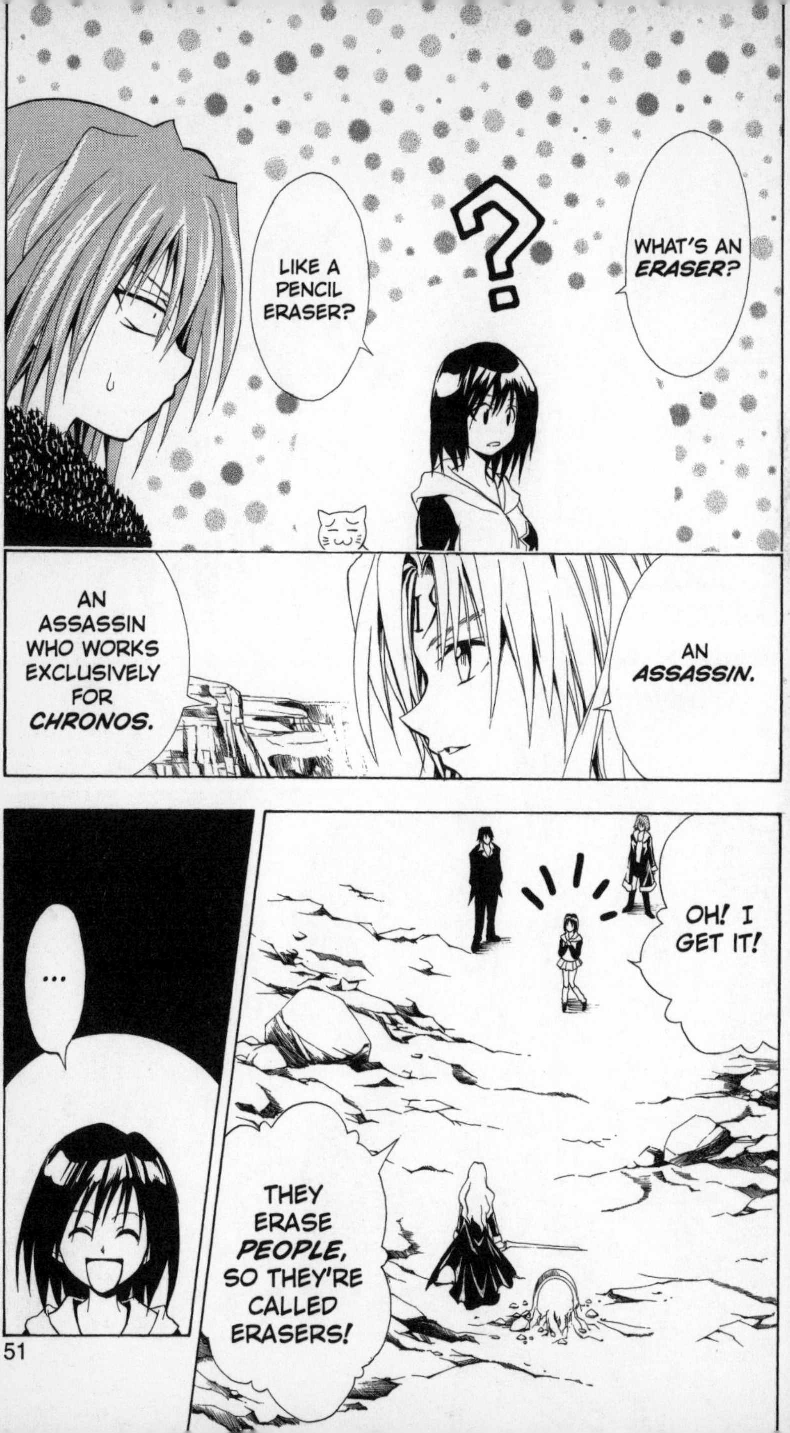
WHAT'S AN *ERASER?*
LIKE A PENCIL ERASER?
AN *ASSASSIN.*
AN ASSASSIN WHO WORKS EXCLUSIVELY FOR *CHRONOS.*
OH! I GET IT!
THEY ERASE *PEOPLE,* SO THEY'RE CALLED ERASERS!
...

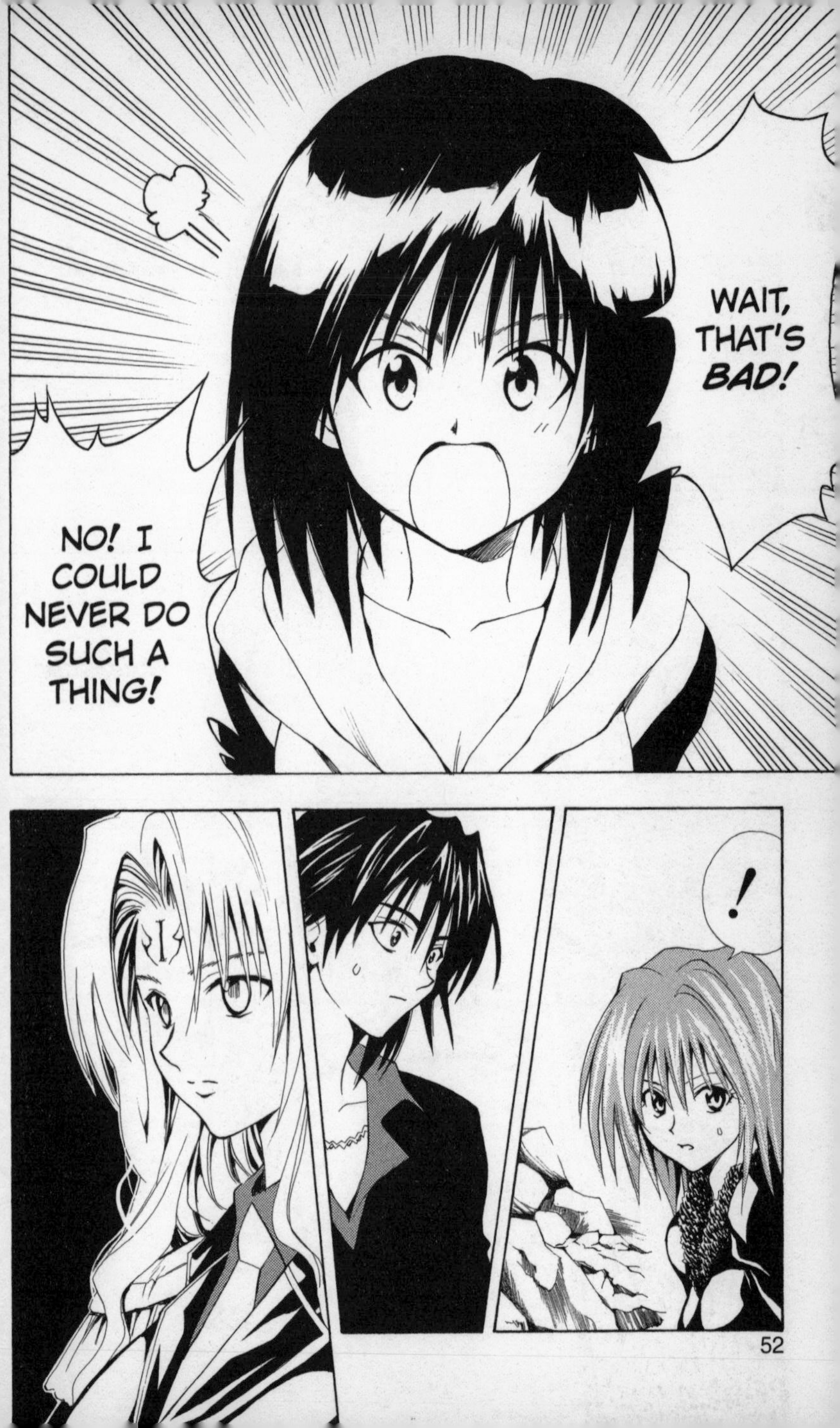
WAIT, THAT'S BAD!
NO! I COULD NEVER DO SUCH A THING!
!

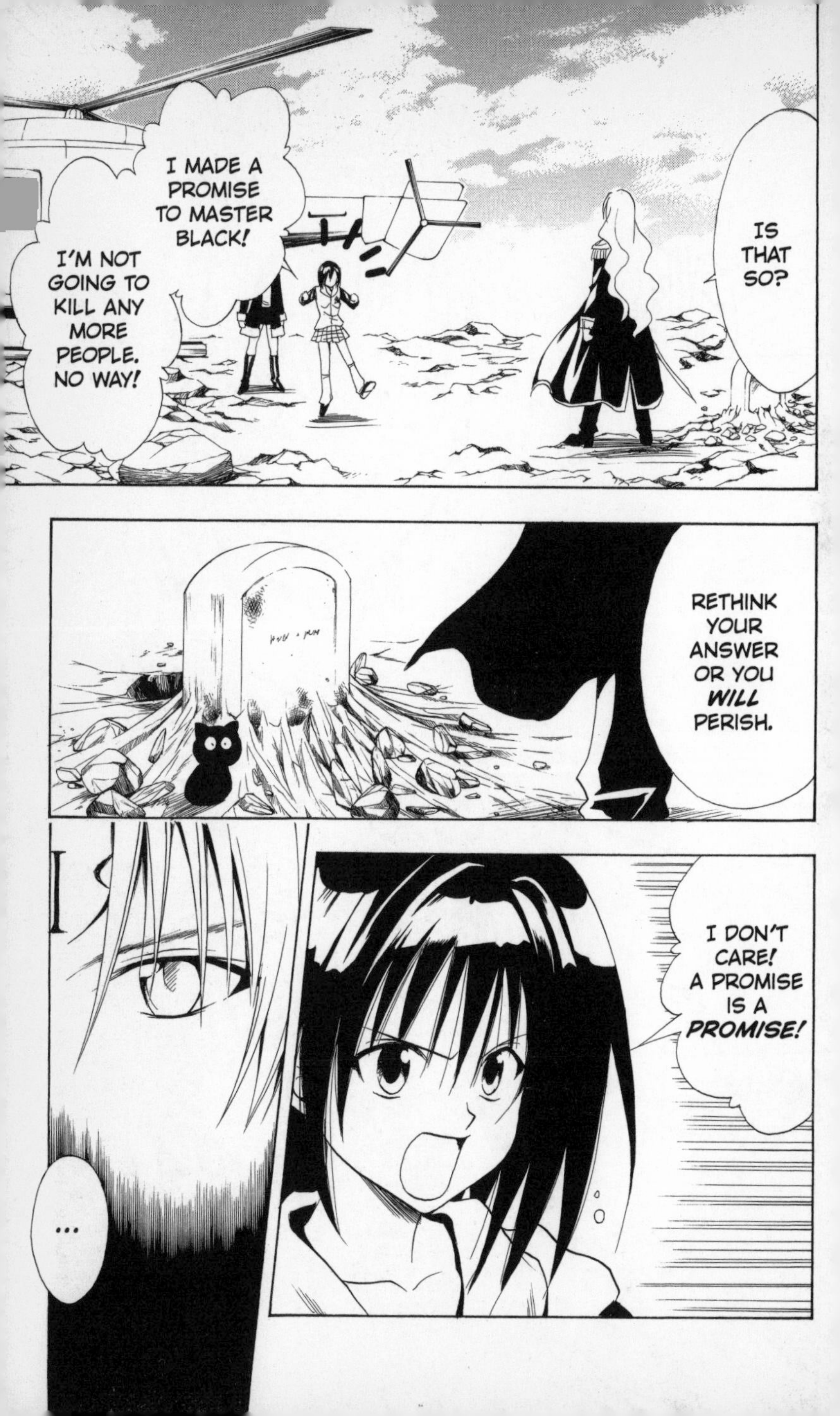
I MADE A PROMISE TO MASTER BLACK!
I'M NOT GOING TO KILL ANY MORE PEOPLE. NO WAY!
IS THAT SO?
RETHINK YOUR ANSWER OR YOU *WILL* PERISH.
I DON'T CARE! A PROMISE IS A *PROMISE!*
...

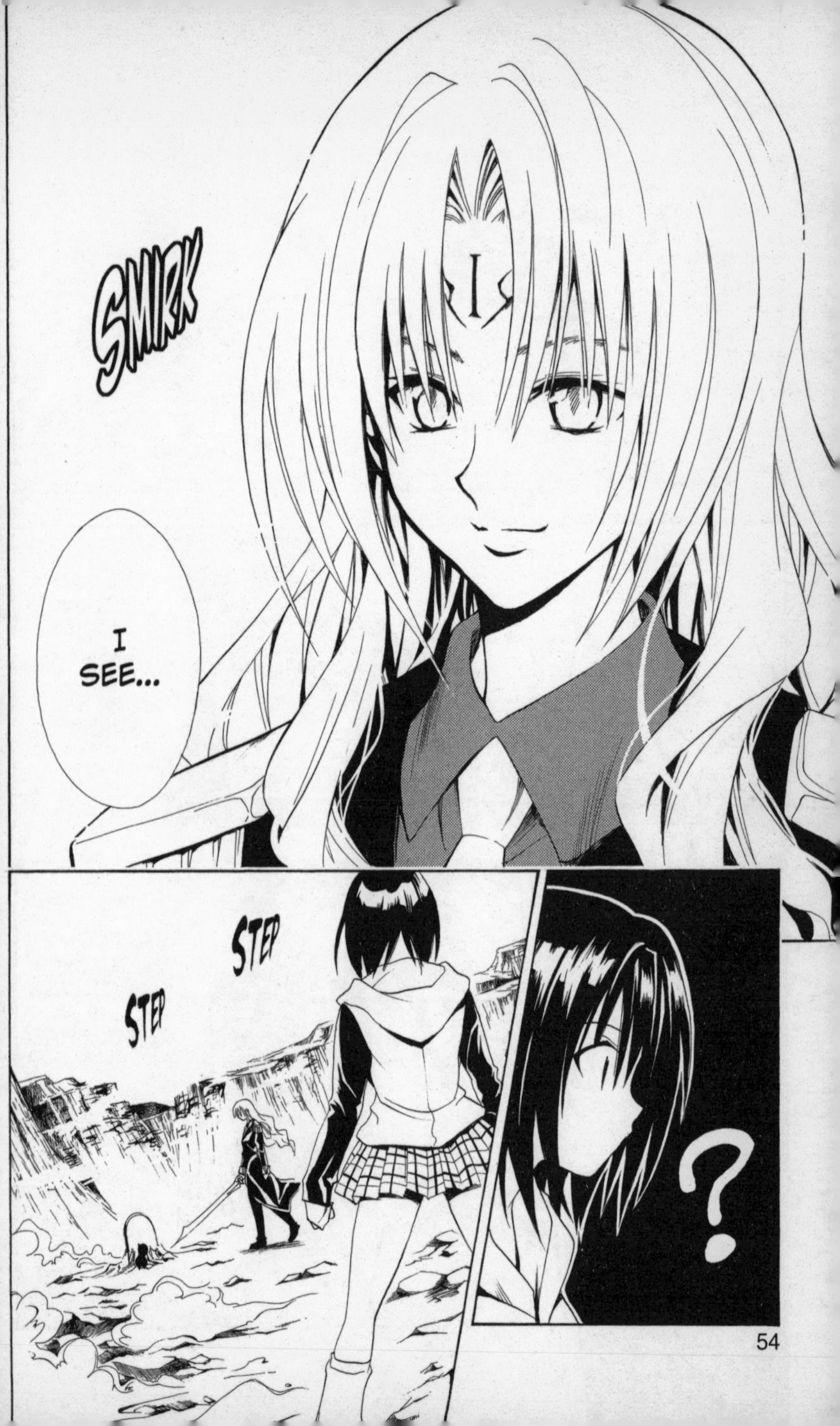
SMIRK
I SEE...
?
STEP
STEP

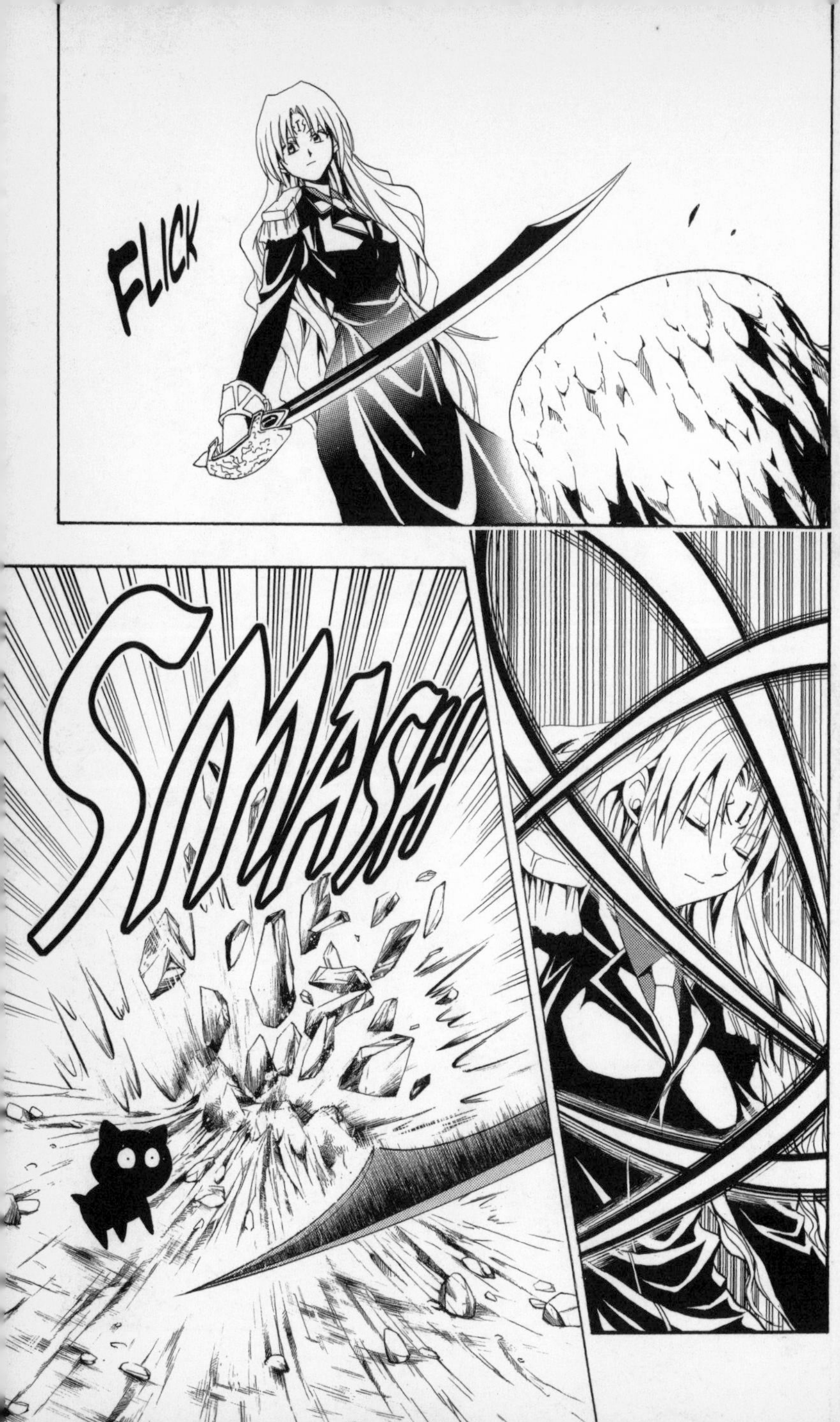
FLICK
SMASH

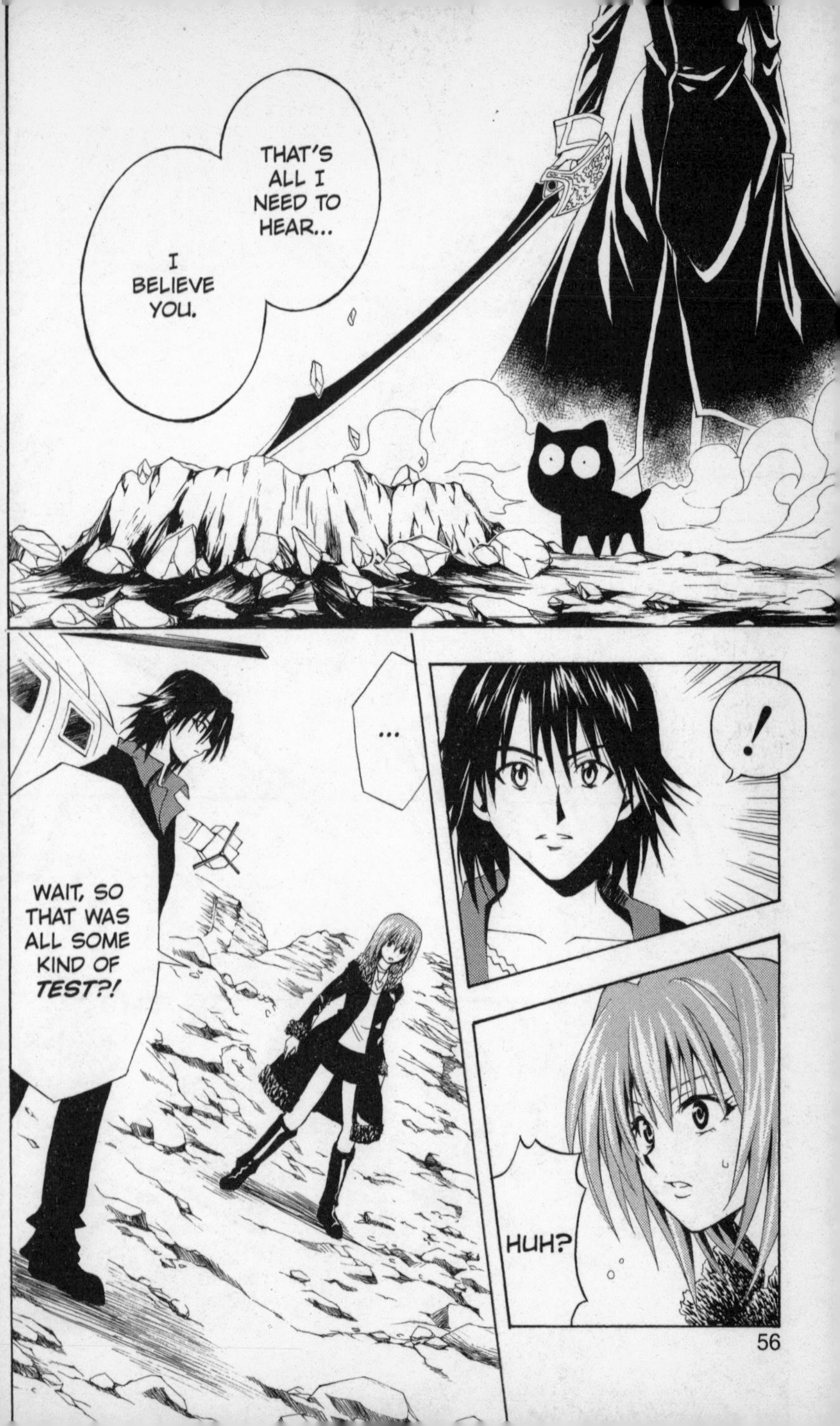

THAT'S ALL I NEED TO HEAR...
I BELIEVE YOU.
!
HUH?
...
WAIT, SO THAT WAS ALL SOME KIND OF *TEST?!*

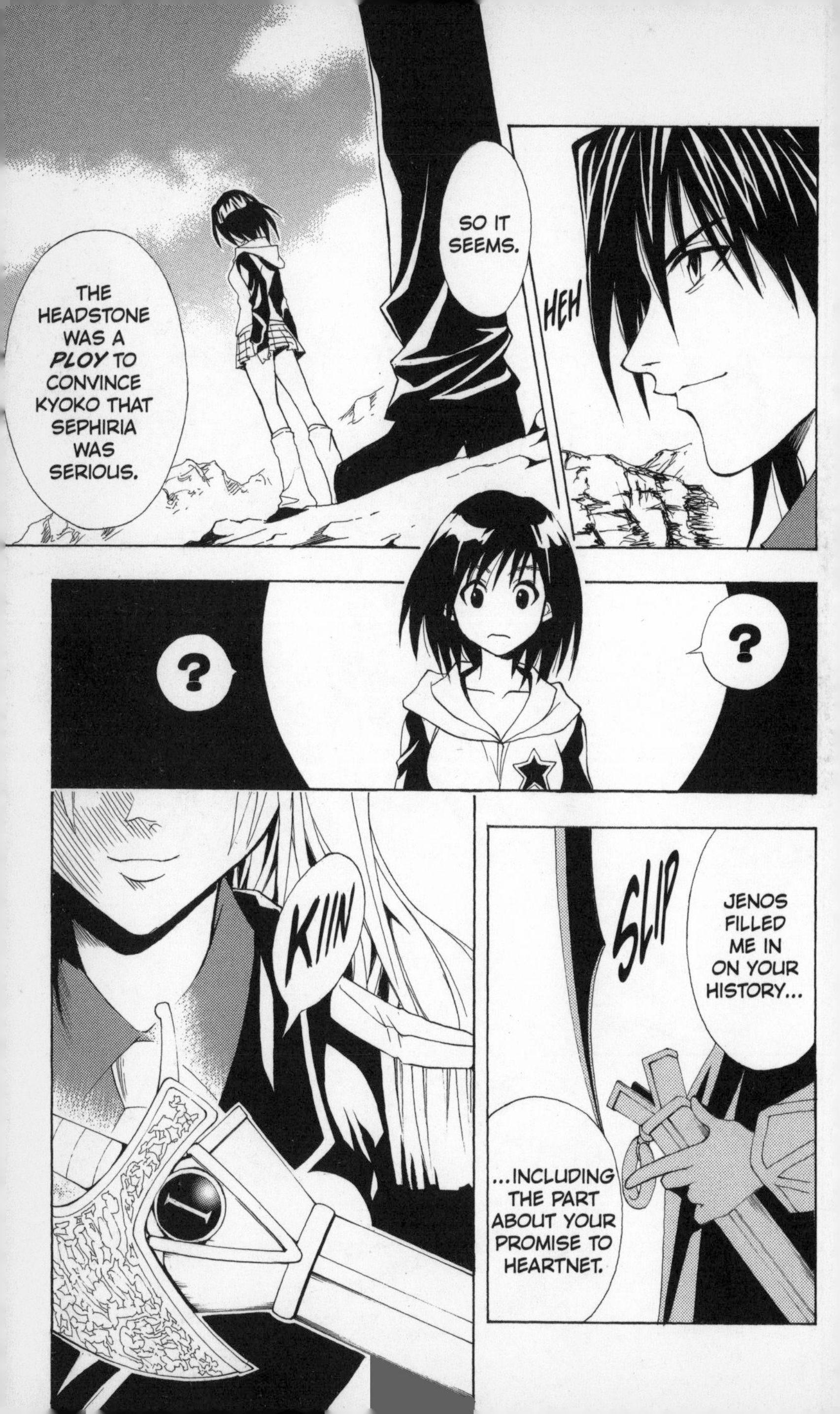

HEH
SO IT SEEMS.
THE HEADSTONE WAS A *PLOY* TO CONVINCE KYOKO THAT SEPHIRIA WAS SERIOUS.
?
?
SLIP
JENOS FILLED ME IN ON YOUR HISTORY...
...INCLUDING THE PART ABOUT YOUR PROMISE TO HEARTNET.
KIIN

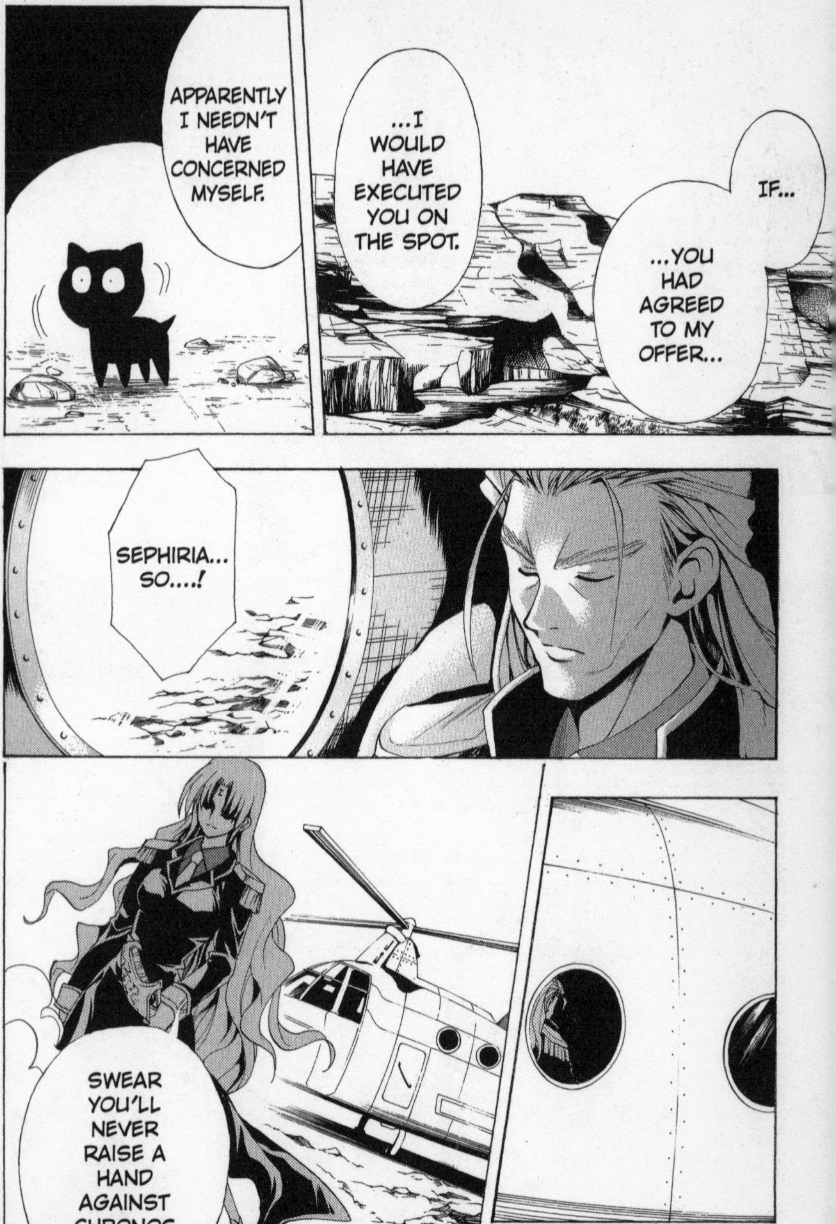
IF...
...YOU HAD AGREED TO MY OFFER...
...I WOULD HAVE EXECUTED YOU ON THE SPOT.
APPARENTLY I NEEDN'T HAVE CONCERNED MYSELF.
SEPHIRIA... SO....!
SWEAR YOU'LL NEVER RAISE A HAND AGAINST CHRONOS AGAIN...

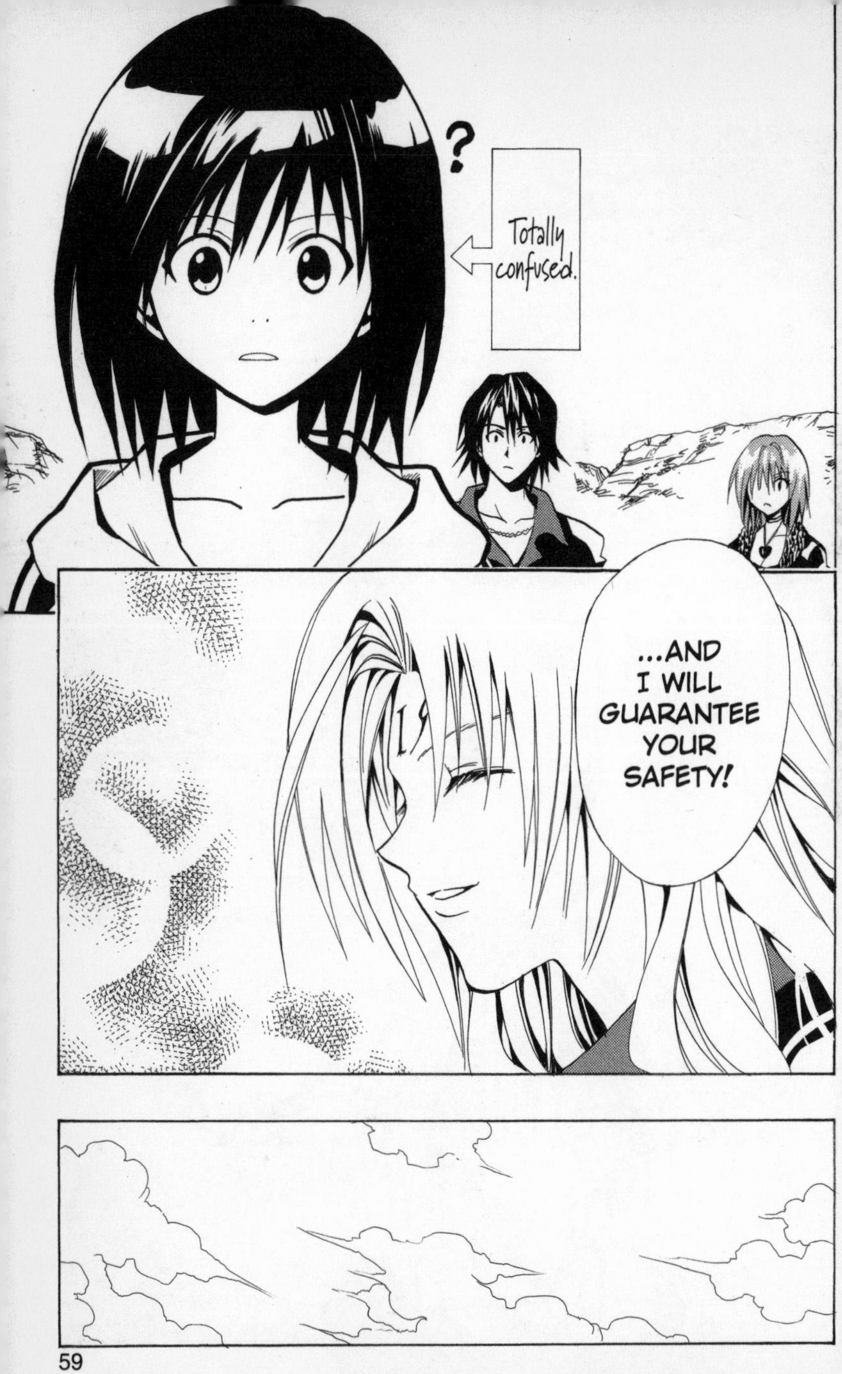
?
Totally confused.
...AND I WILL GUARANTEE YOUR SAFETY!

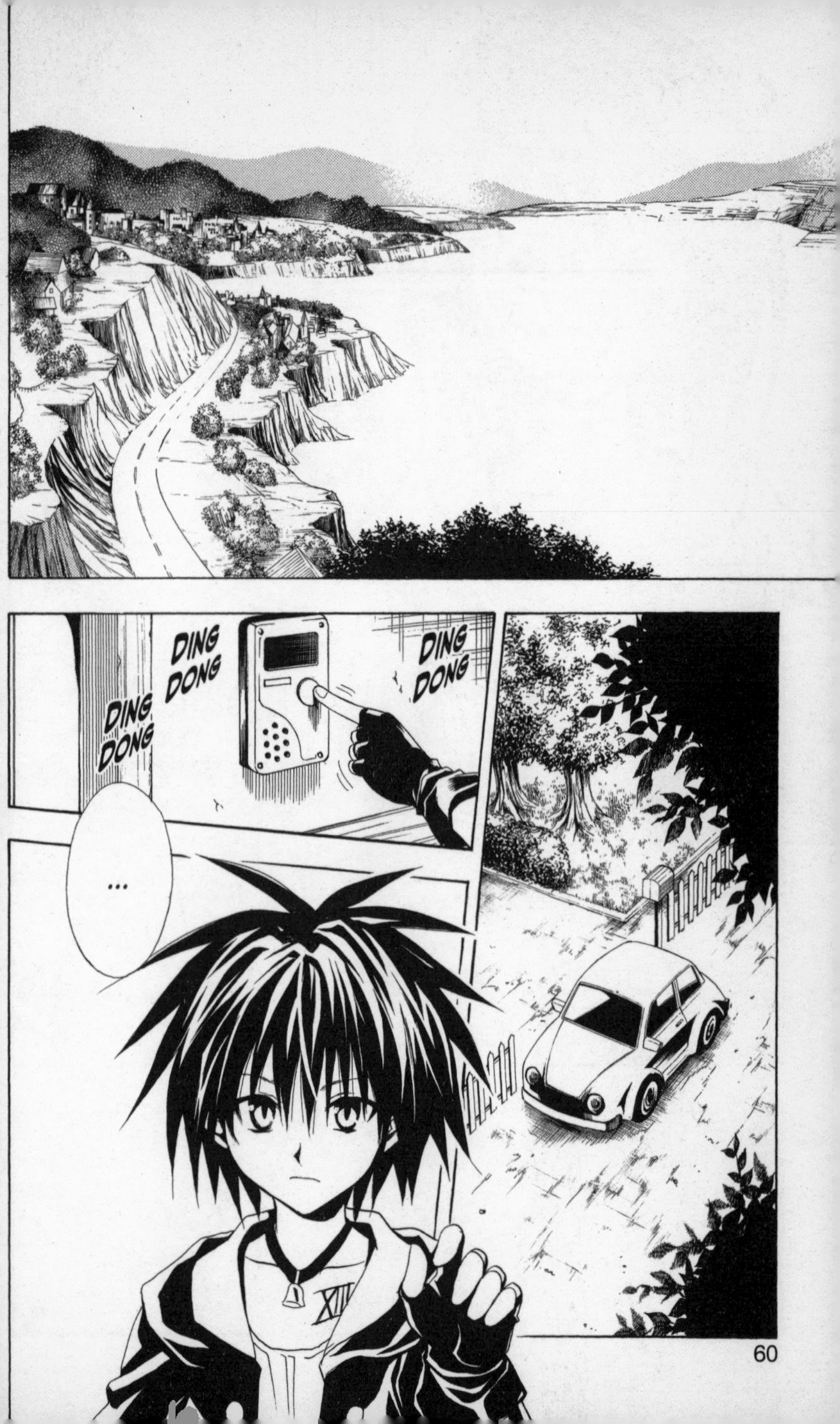
DING DONG
DING DONG
DING DONG
...

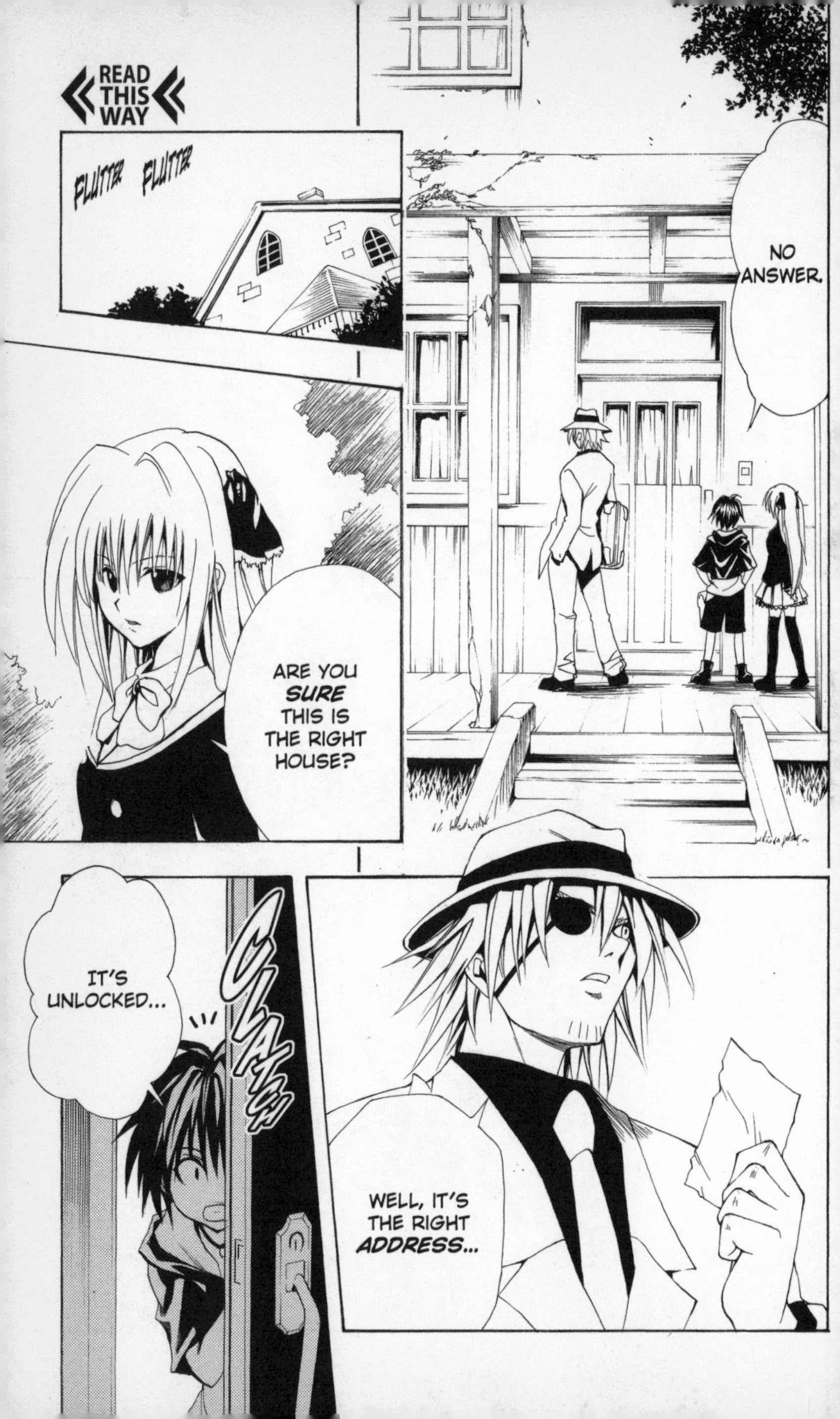
READ THIS WAY
NO ANSWER.
FLUTTER FLUTTER
ARE YOU SURE THIS IS THE RIGHT HOUSE?
WELL, IT'S THE RIGHT ADDRESS...
CLACK
IT'S UNLOCKED...

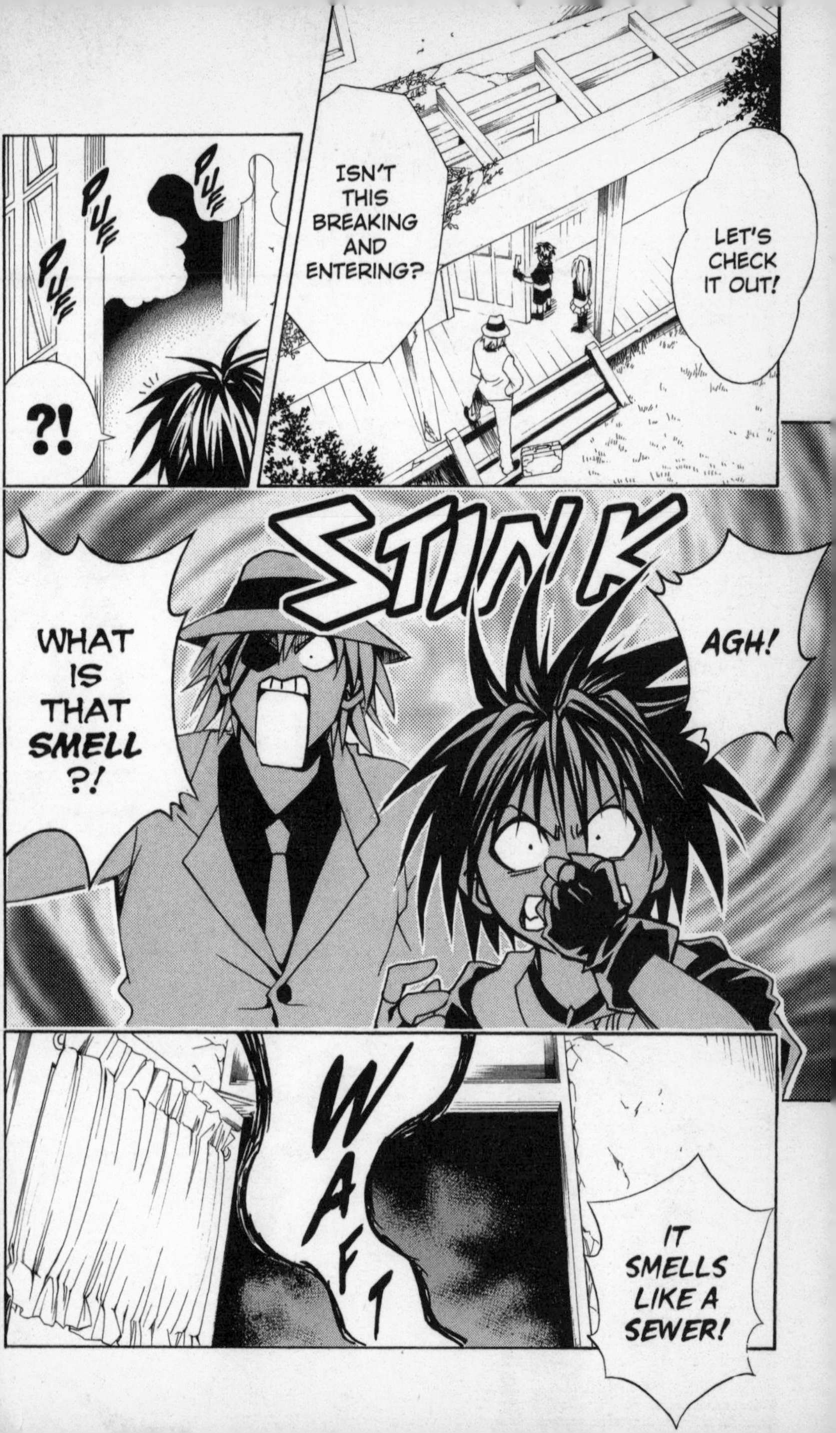
LET'S CHECK IT OUT!
ISN'T THIS BREAKING AND ENTERING?
PUFF PUFF
?!
STINK
AGH!
WHAT IS THAT SMELL?!
IT SMELLS LIKE A SEWER!
WAFT

READ THIS WAY

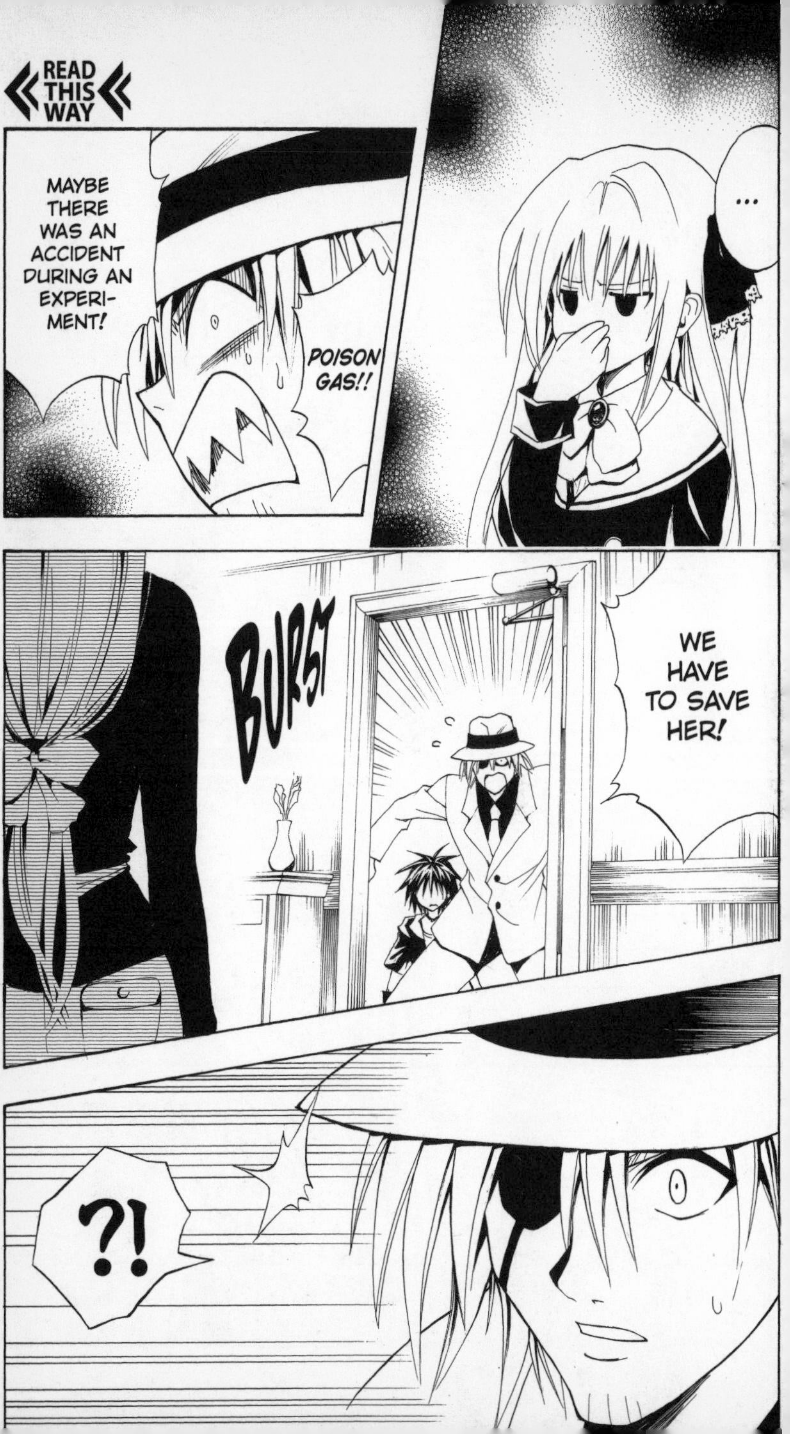
...
MAYBE THERE WAS AN ACCIDENT DURING AN EXPERI- MENT!
POISON GAS!!
WE HAVE TO SAVE HER!
BURST
?!

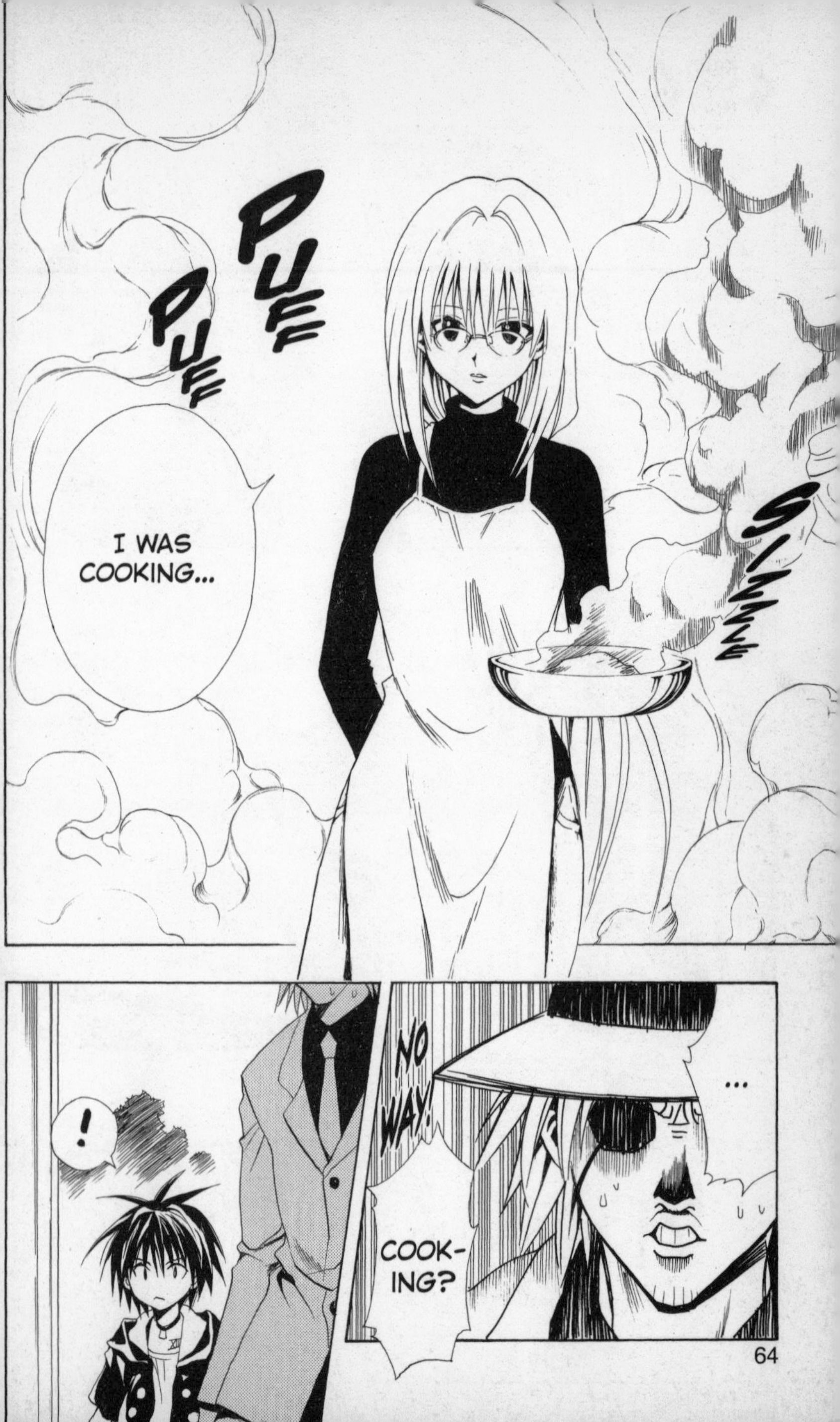
PUFF
PUFF
I WAS COOKING...
SIZZLE
...
NO WAY!
COOK-ING?
!

READ THIS WAY

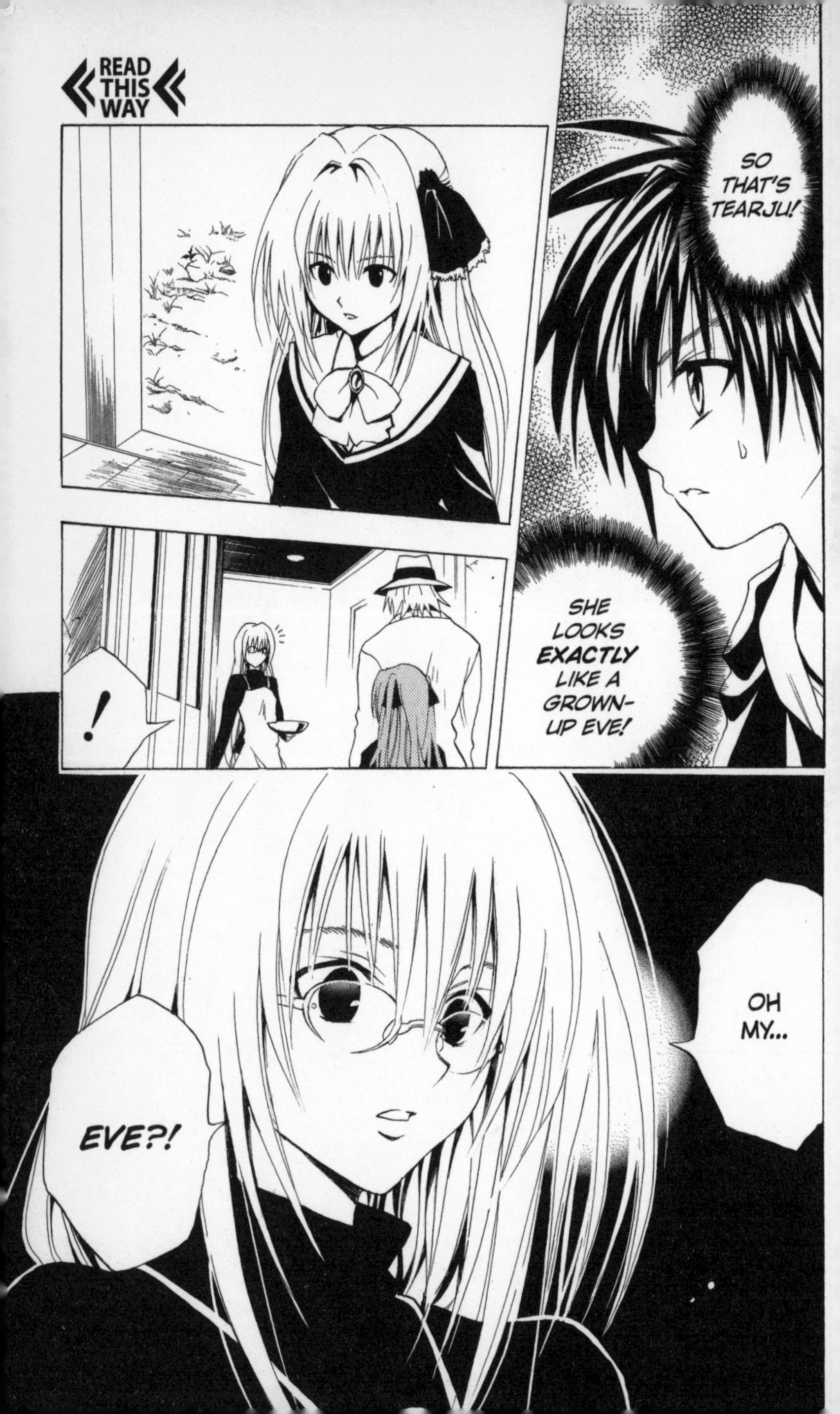
SO THAT'S TEARJU!
SHE LOOKS EXACTLY LIKE A GROWN-UP EVE!
!
OH MY...
EVE?!

Kyoko named him
〈Little Blackie〉

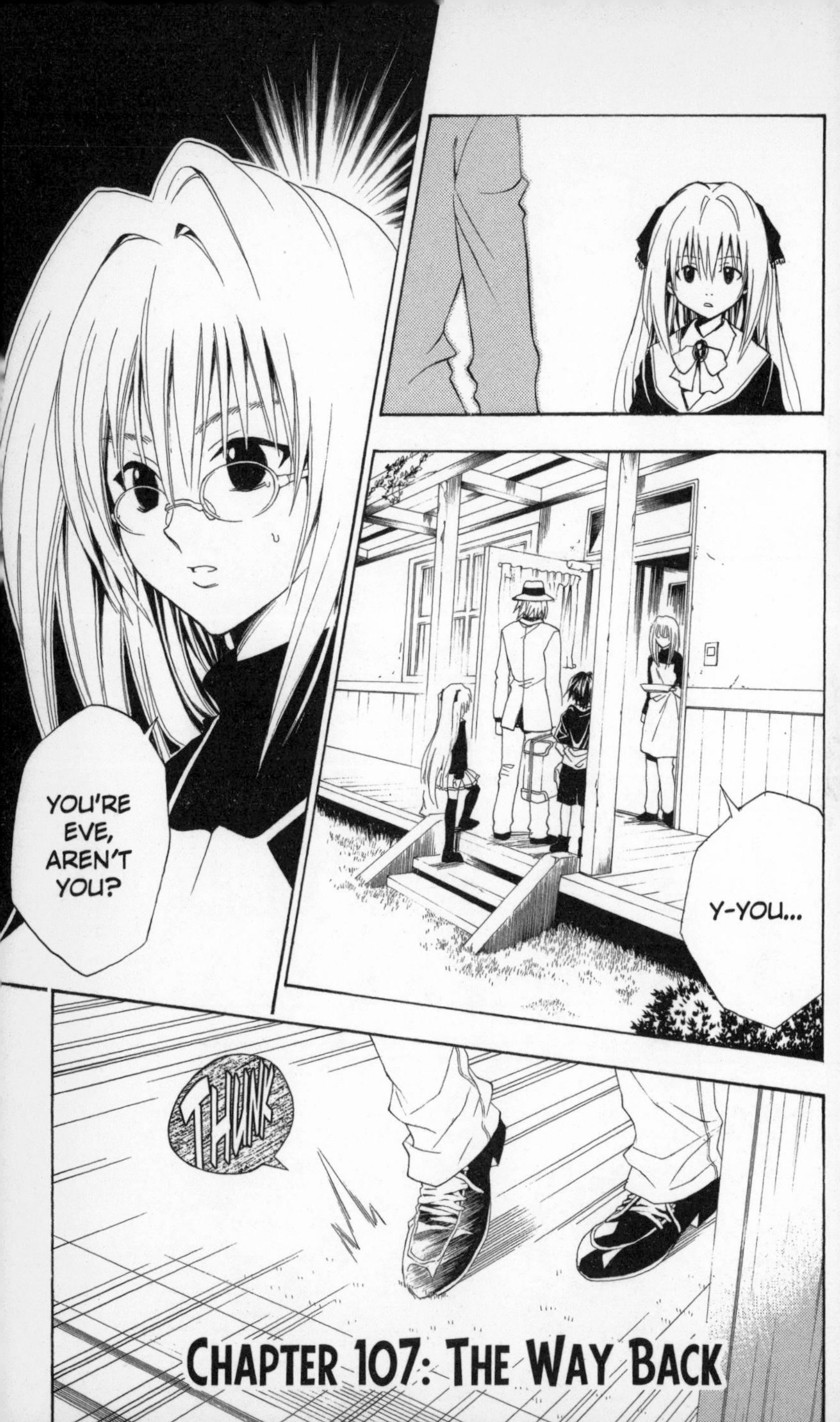
Y-YOU...
YOU'RE EVE, AREN'T YOU?
THUNK
CHAPTER 107: THE WAY BACK

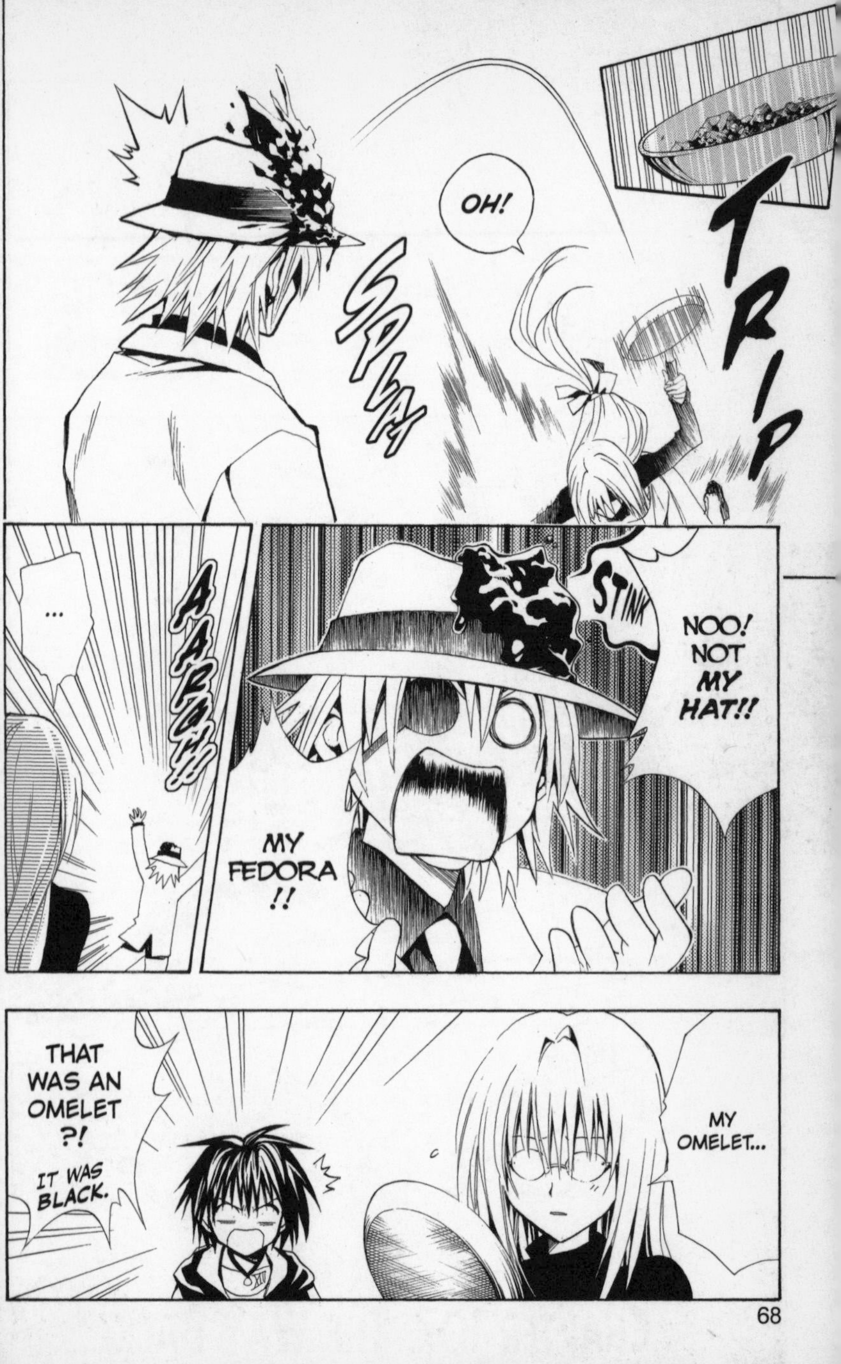
TRIP
OH!
SPLAT
STINK
NOO! NOT MY HAT!!
MY FEDORA!!
AAARGH!!
...
MY OMELET...
THAT WAS AN OMELET?!
IT WAS BLACK.

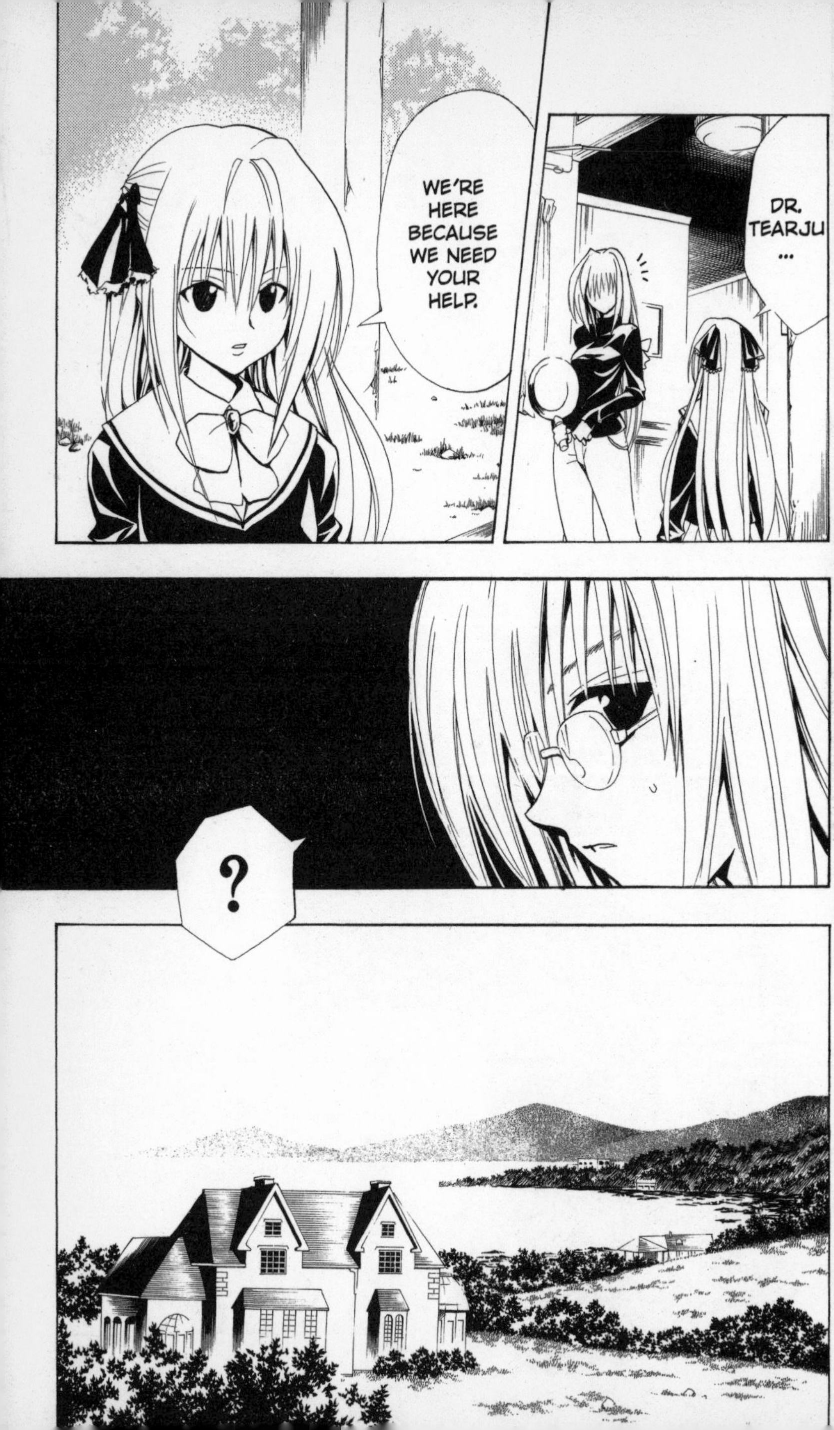
DR. TEARJU ...
WE'RE HERE BECAUSE WE NEED YOUR HELP.
?

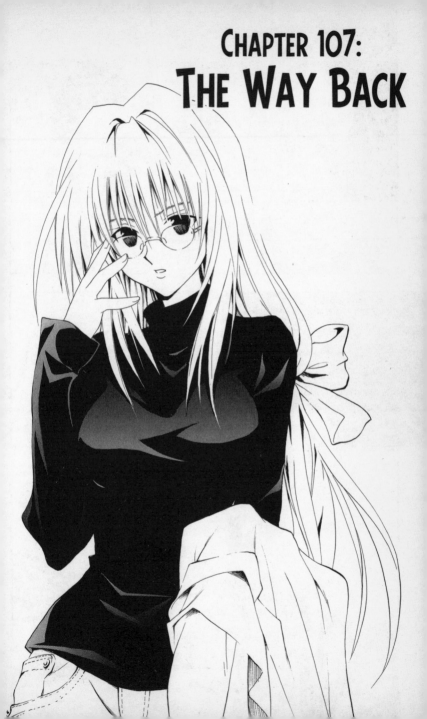

Chapter 107: The Way Back

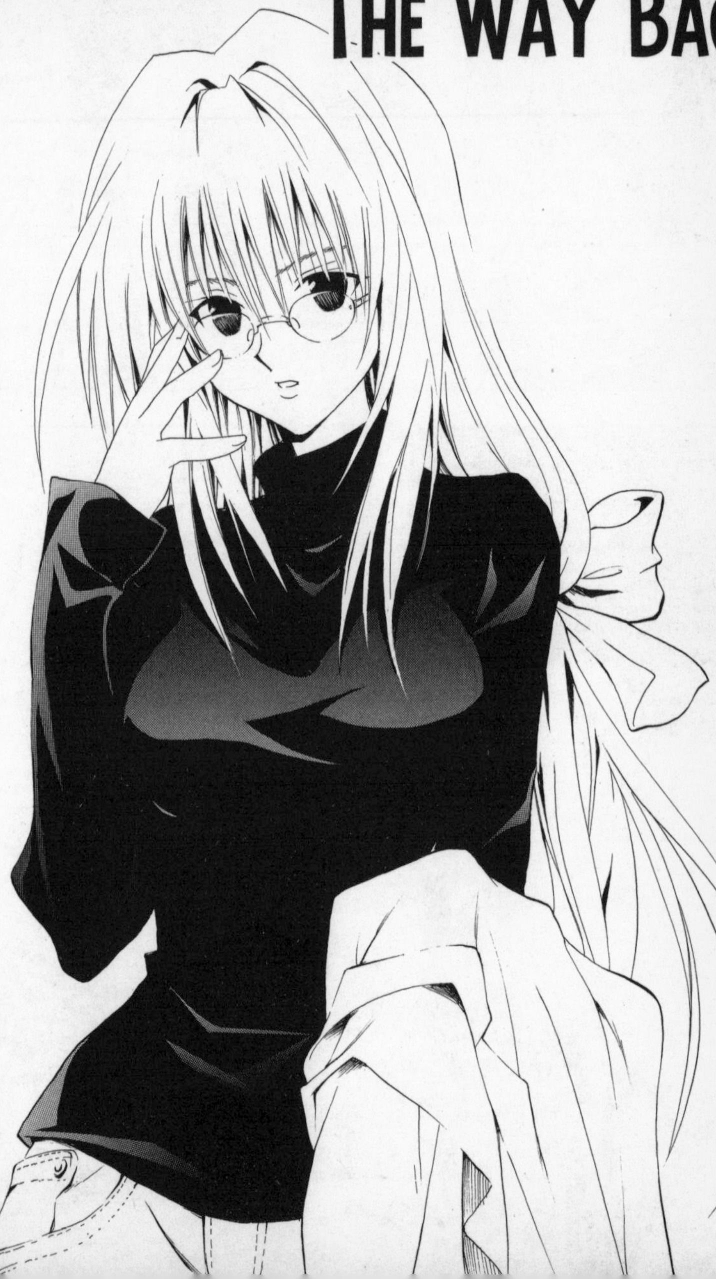

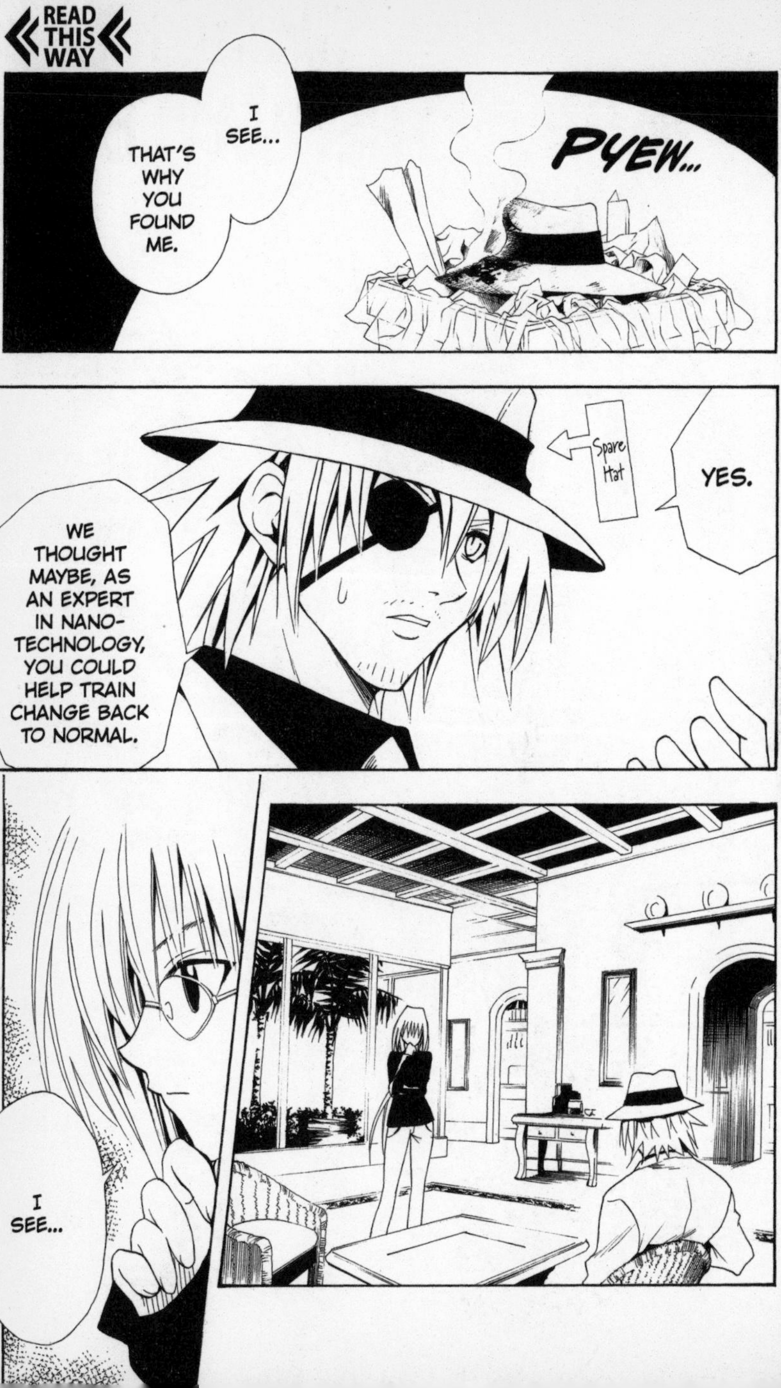
READ THIS WAY
PYEW...
I SEE... THAT'S WHY YOU FOUND ME.
YES.
Spare Hat
WE THOUGHT MAYBE, AS AN EXPERT IN NANO-TECHNOLOGY, YOU COULD HELP TRAIN CHANGE BACK TO NORMAL.
I SEE...

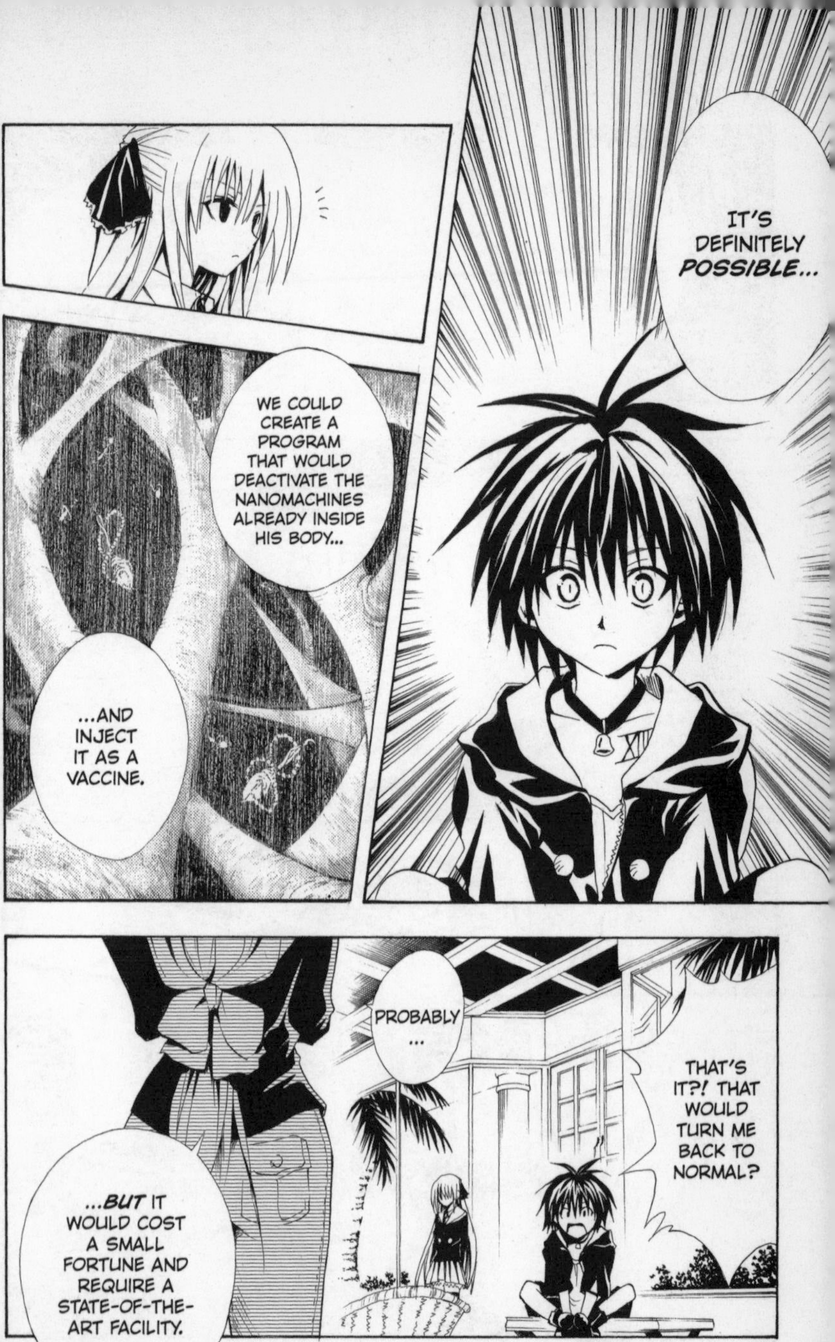
IT'S DEFINITELY *POSSIBLE...*
WE COULD CREATE A PROGRAM THAT WOULD DEACTIVATE THE NANOMACHINES ALREADY INSIDE HIS BODY...
...AND INJECT IT AS A VACCINE.
THAT'S IT?! THAT WOULD TURN ME BACK TO NORMAL?
PROBABLY ...
...BUT IT WOULD COST A SMALL FORTUNE AND REQUIRE A STATE-OF-THE-ART FACILITY.

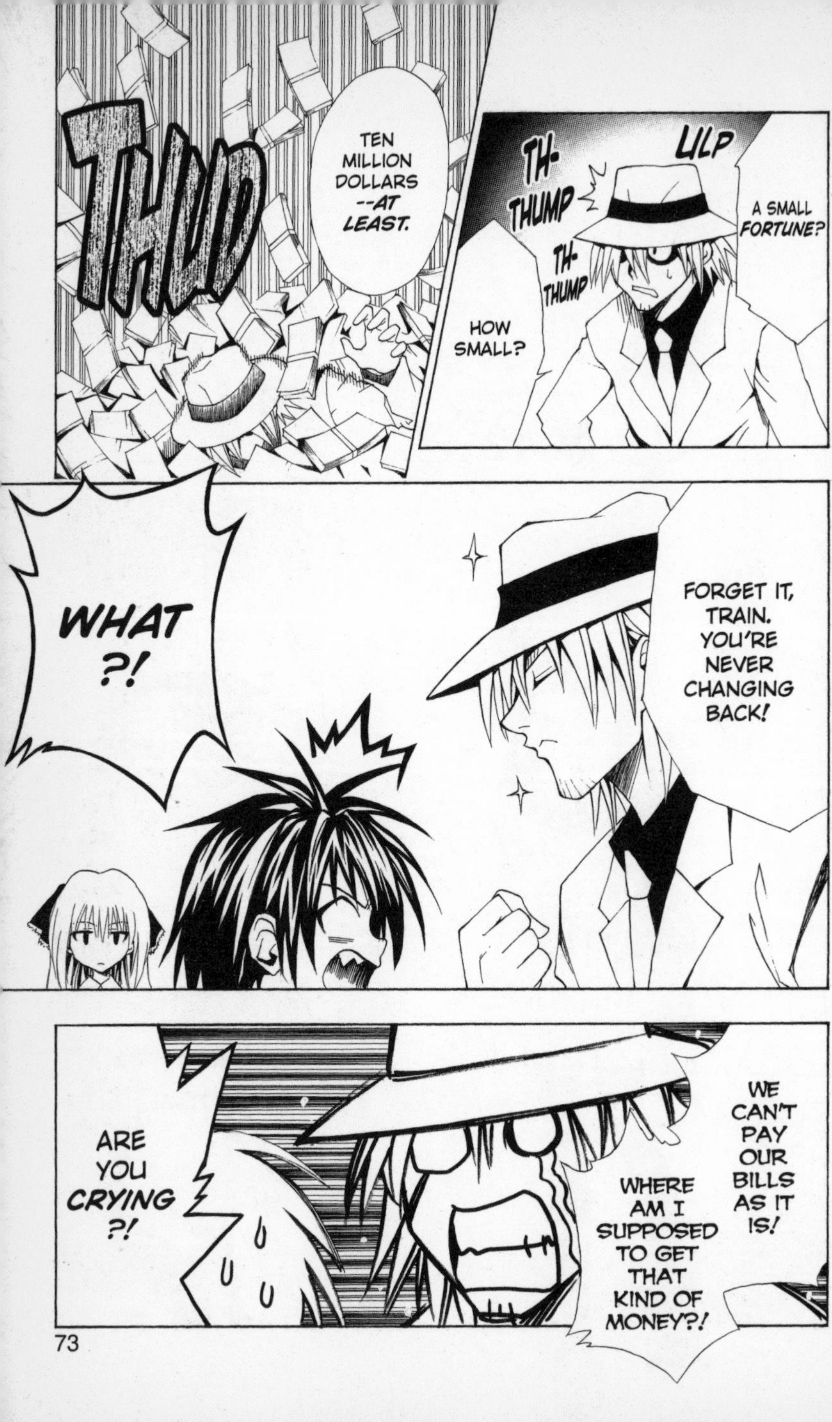
ULP
TH-THUMP
TH-THUMP
A SMALL *FORTUNE?*
HOW SMALL?
TEN MILLION DOLLARS --*AT LEAST.*
THUD
FORGET IT, TRAIN. YOU'RE NEVER CHANGING BACK!
WHAT ?!
WE CAN'T PAY OUR BILLS AS IT IS!
WHERE AM I SUPPOSED TO GET THAT KIND OF MONEY?!
ARE YOU *CRYING* ?!

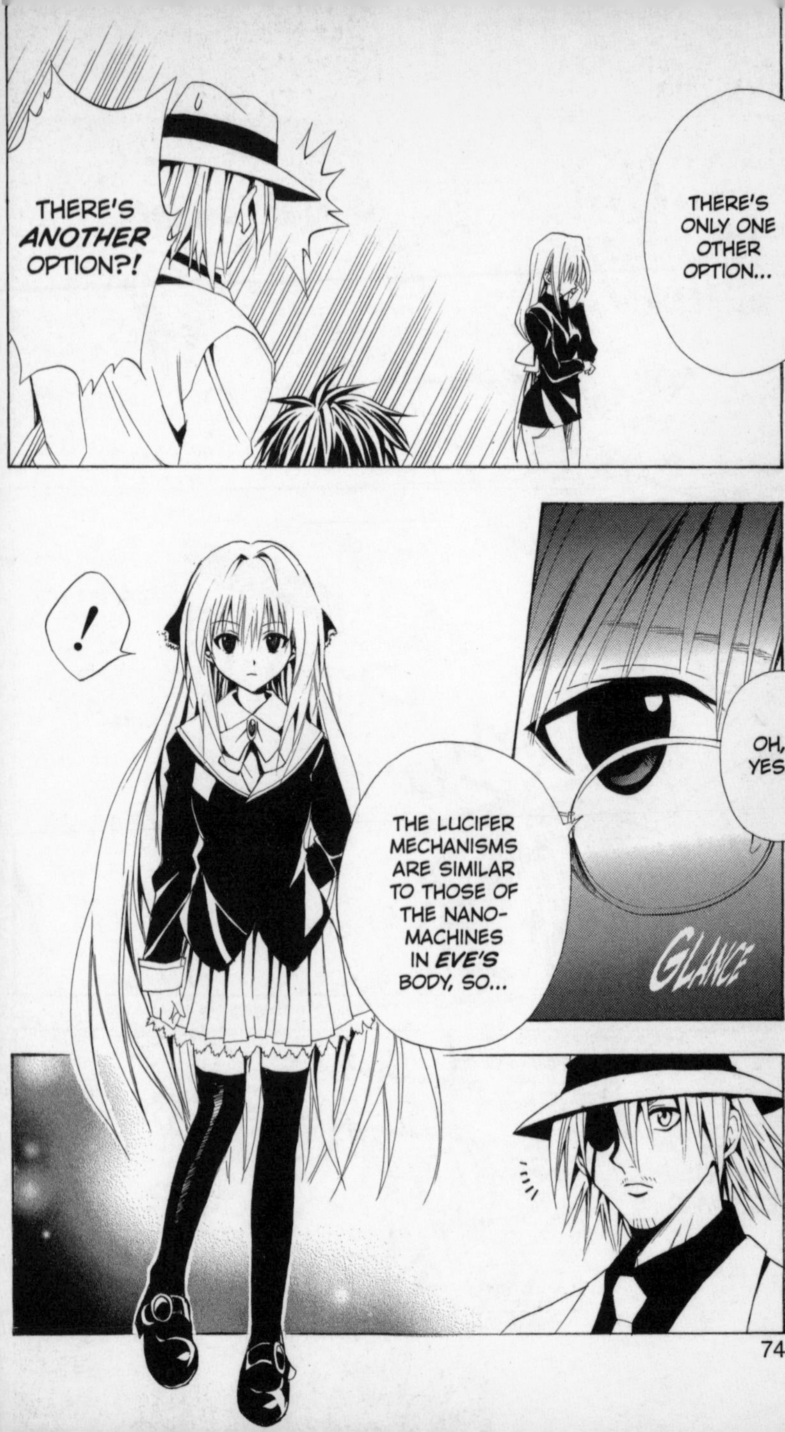
THERE'S ONLY ONE OTHER OPTION...
THERE'S ANOTHER OPTION?!
OH, YES.
GLANCE
THE LUCIFER MECHANISMS ARE SIMILAR TO THOSE OF THE NANO-MACHINES IN EVE'S BODY, SO...
!

READ THIS WAY

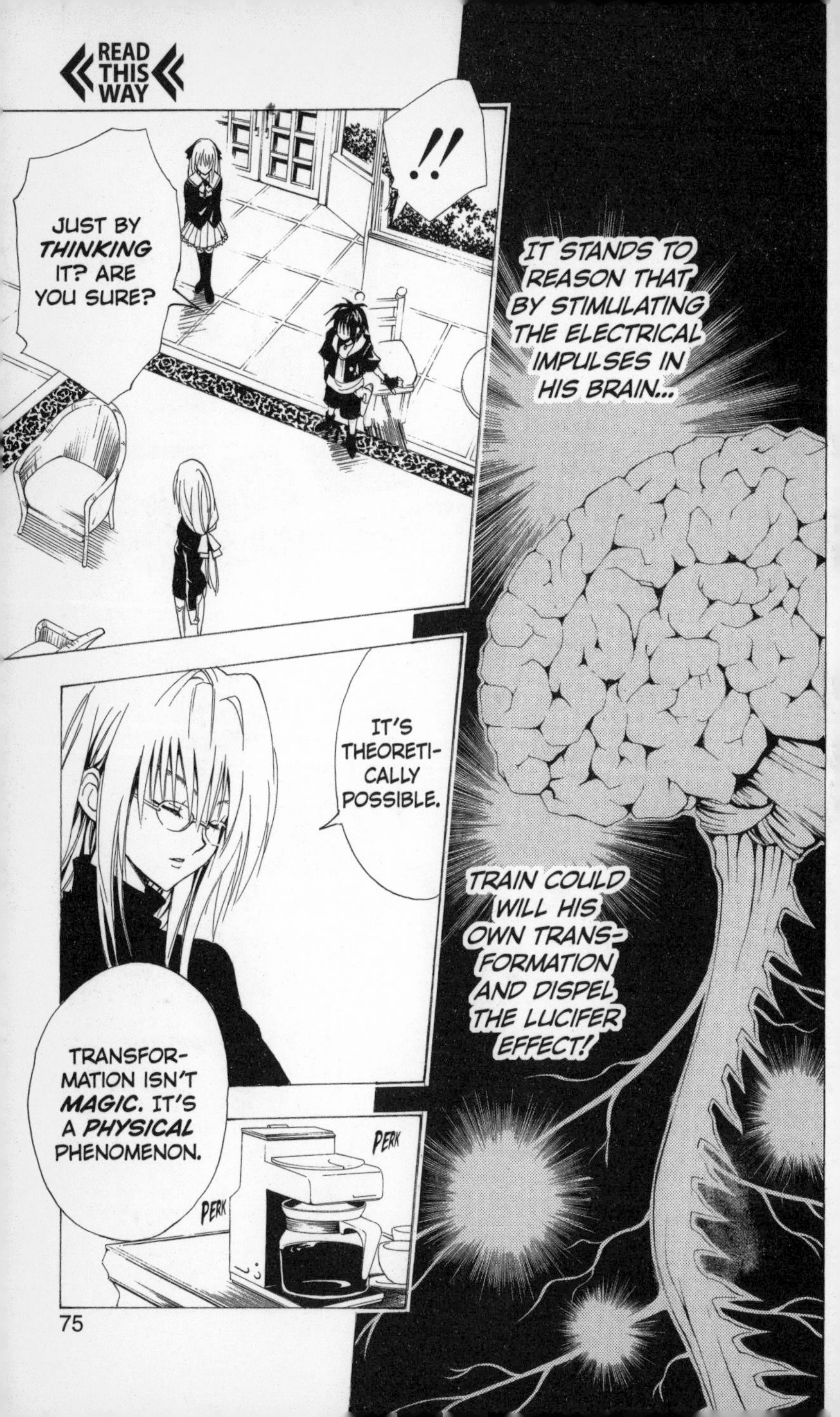

IT STANDS TO REASON THAT BY STIMULATING THE ELECTRICAL IMPULSES IN HIS BRAIN...
TRAIN COULD WILL HIS OWN TRANS-FORMATION AND DISPEL THE LUCIFER EFFECT!
!!
JUST BY *THINKING* IT? ARE YOU SURE?
IT'S THEORETI-CALLY POSSIBLE.
TRANSFOR-MATION ISN'T *MAGIC*. IT'S A *PHYSICAL* PHENOMENON.
PERK
PERK

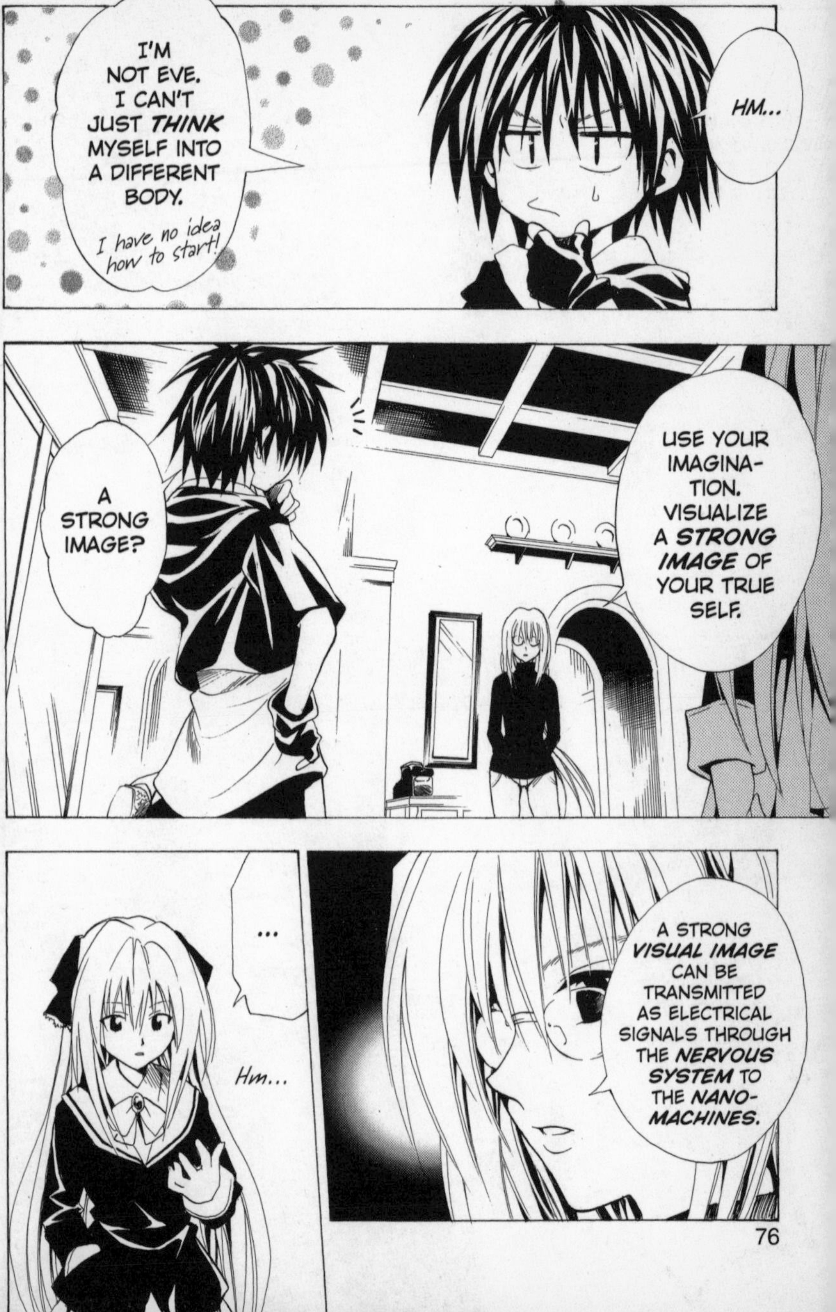
HM...
I'M NOT EVE. I CAN'T JUST *THINK* MYSELF INTO A DIFFERENT BODY.
I have no idea how to start!
USE YOUR IMAGINATION. VISUALIZE A *STRONG IMAGE* OF YOUR TRUE SELF.
A STRONG IMAGE?
A STRONG *VISUAL IMAGE* CAN BE TRANSMITTED AS ELECTRICAL SIGNALS THROUGH THE *NERVOUS SYSTEM* TO THE *NANO-MACHINES*.
...
Hm...

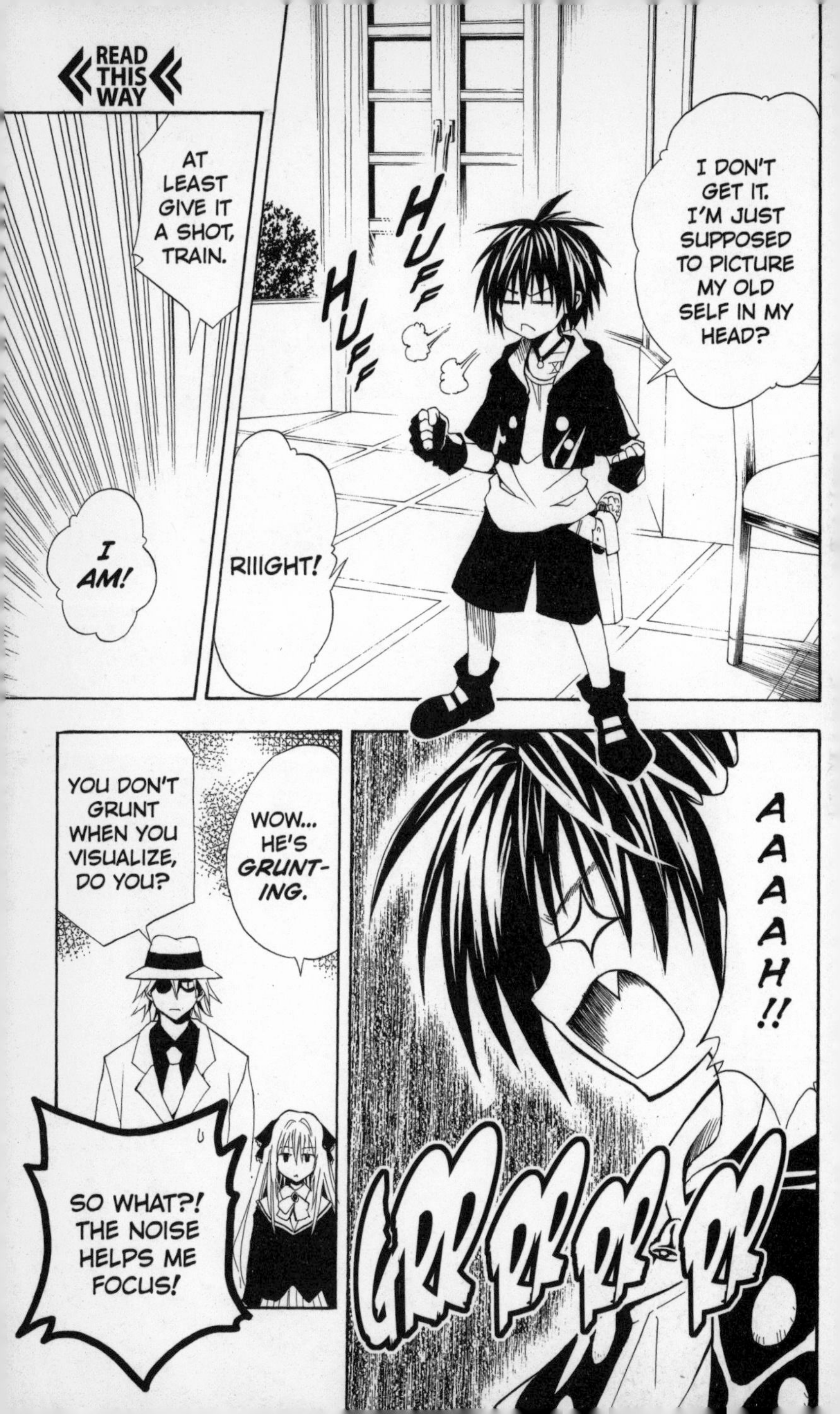
READ THIS WAY
I DON'T GET IT. I'M JUST SUPPOSED TO PICTURE MY OLD SELF IN MY HEAD?
HUFF
HUFF
RIIIGHT!
AT LEAST GIVE IT A SHOT, TRAIN.
I AM!
AAAAAH!!
WOW... HE'S GRUNTING.
YOU DON'T GRUNT WHEN YOU VISUALIZE, DO YOU?
SO WHAT?! THE NOISE HELPS ME FOCUS!

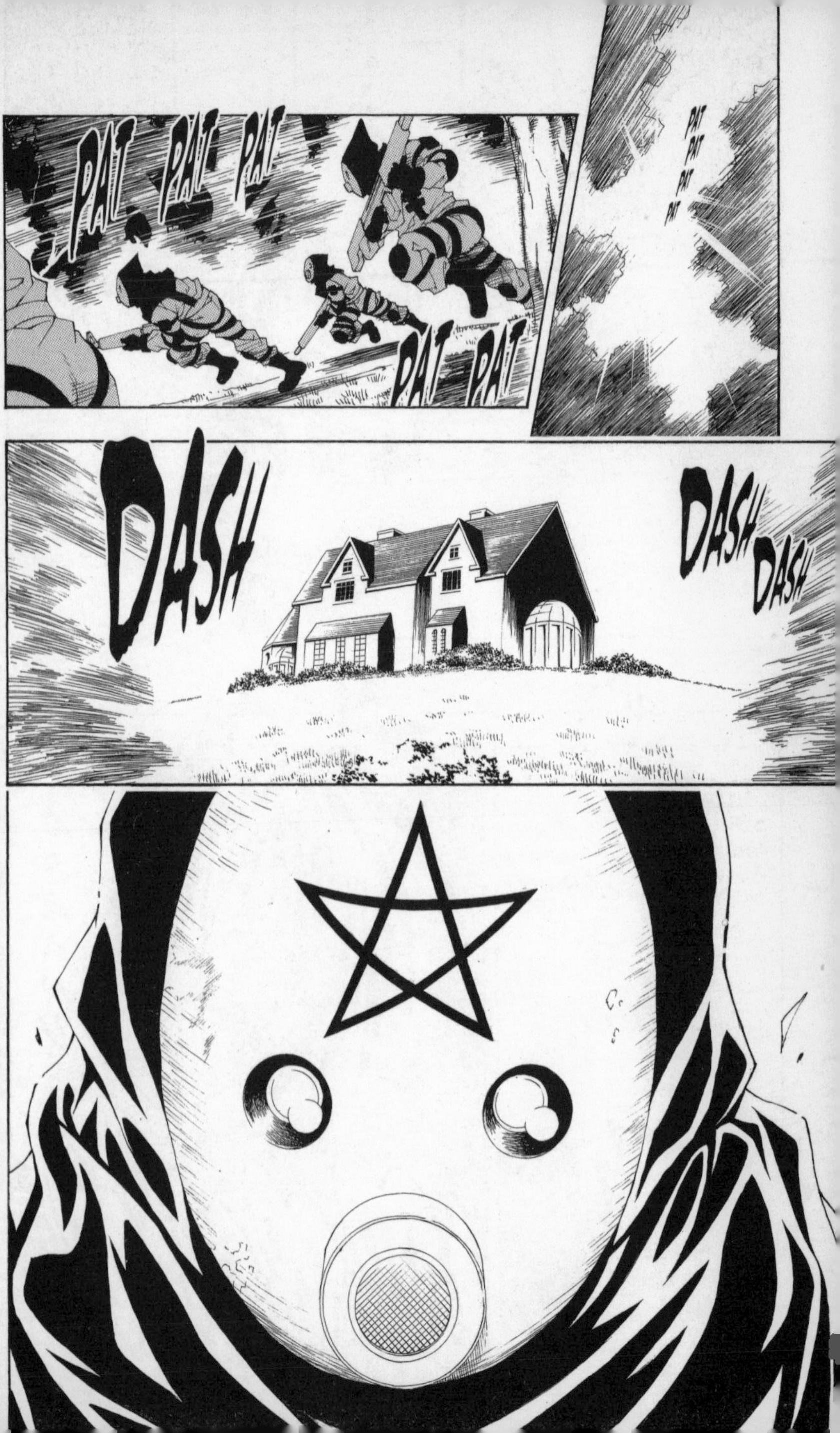
PAT PAT PAT PAT
PAT PAT PAT
PAT PAT
DASH DASH
DASH

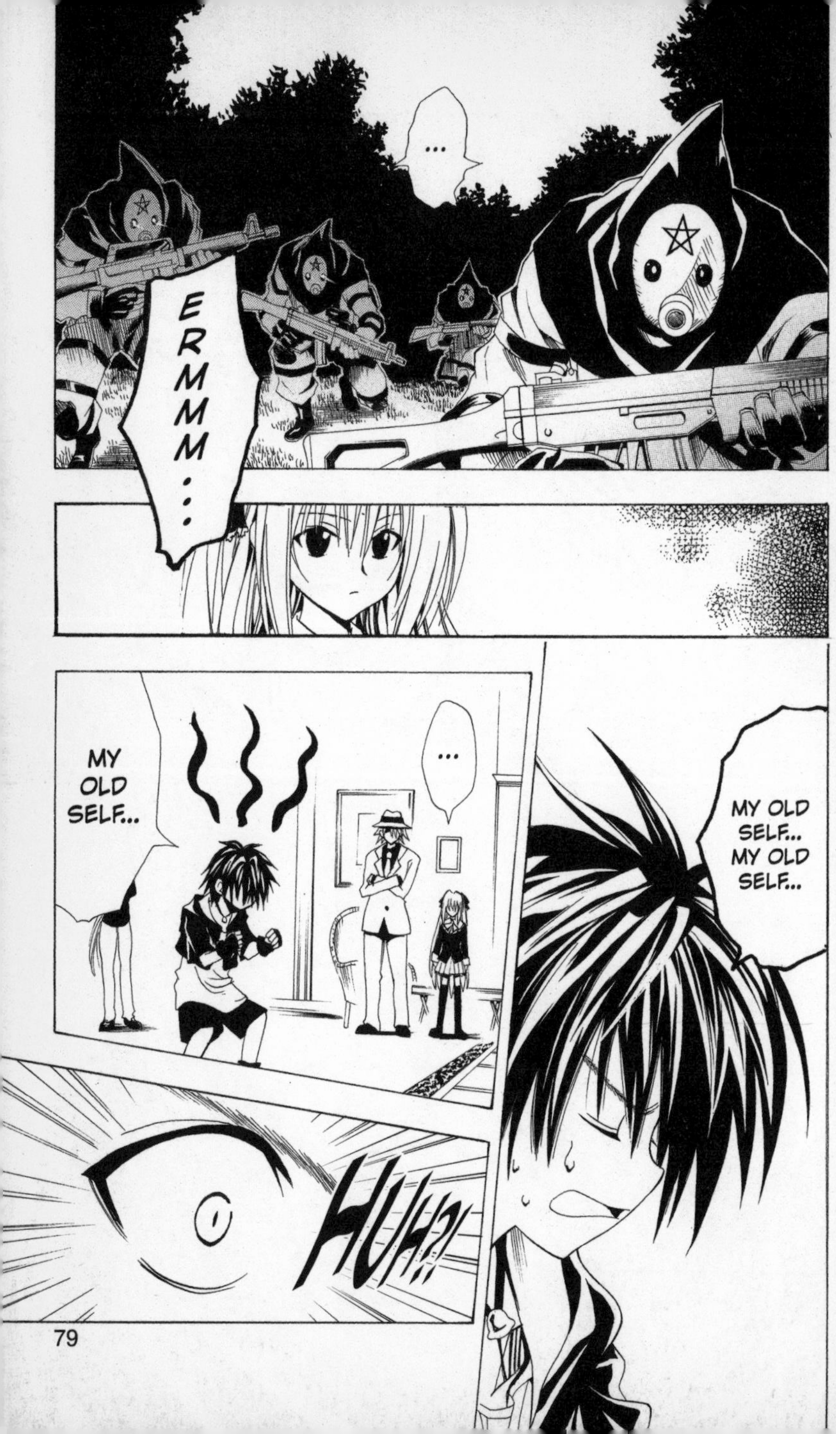
...
ERMMM...
MY OLD SELF... MY OLD SELF...
...
MY OLD SELF...
HUH?!

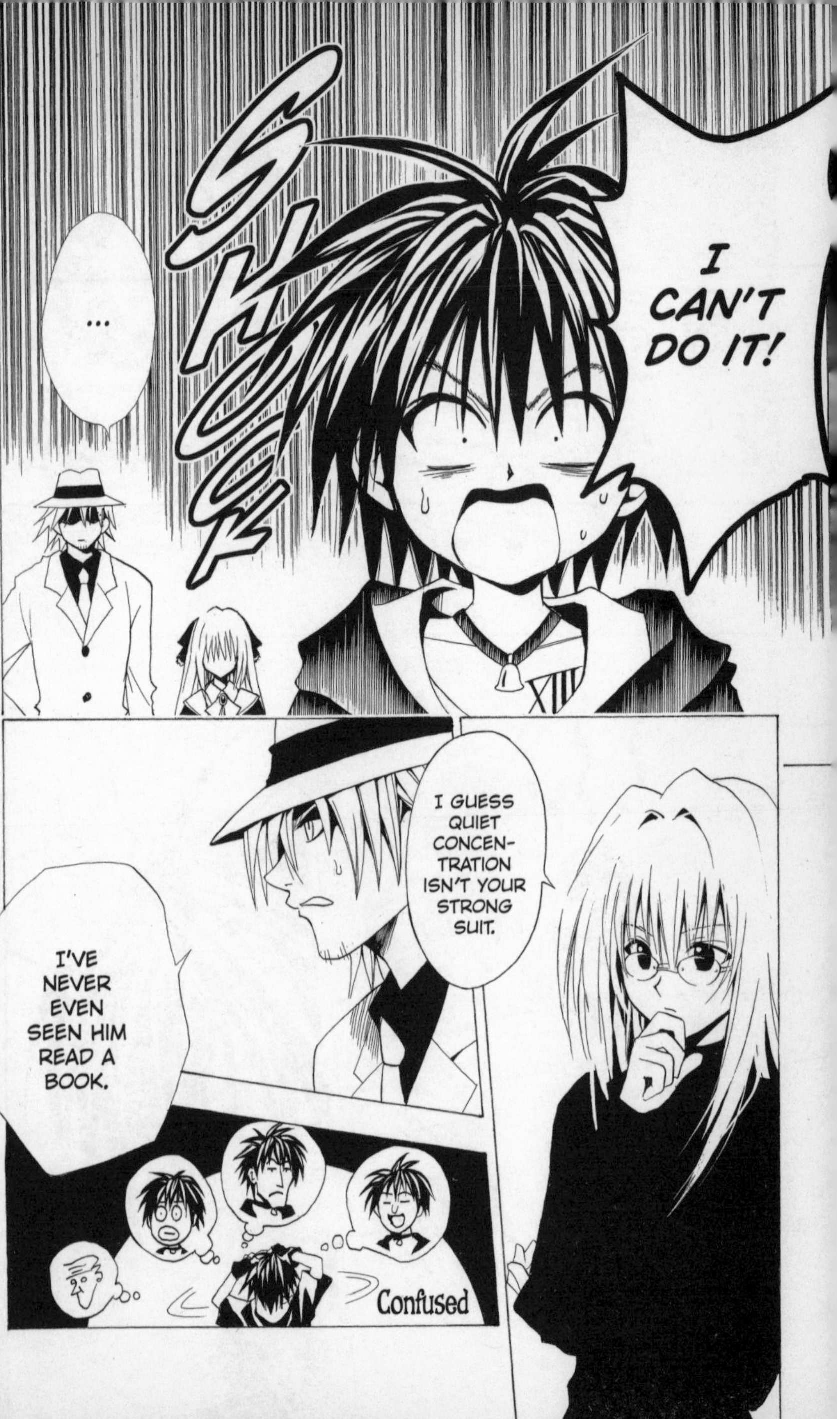
I CAN'T DO IT!
...
I GUESS QUIET CONCEN-TRATION ISN'T YOUR STRONG SUIT.
I'VE NEVER EVEN SEEN HIM READ A BOOK.
Confused

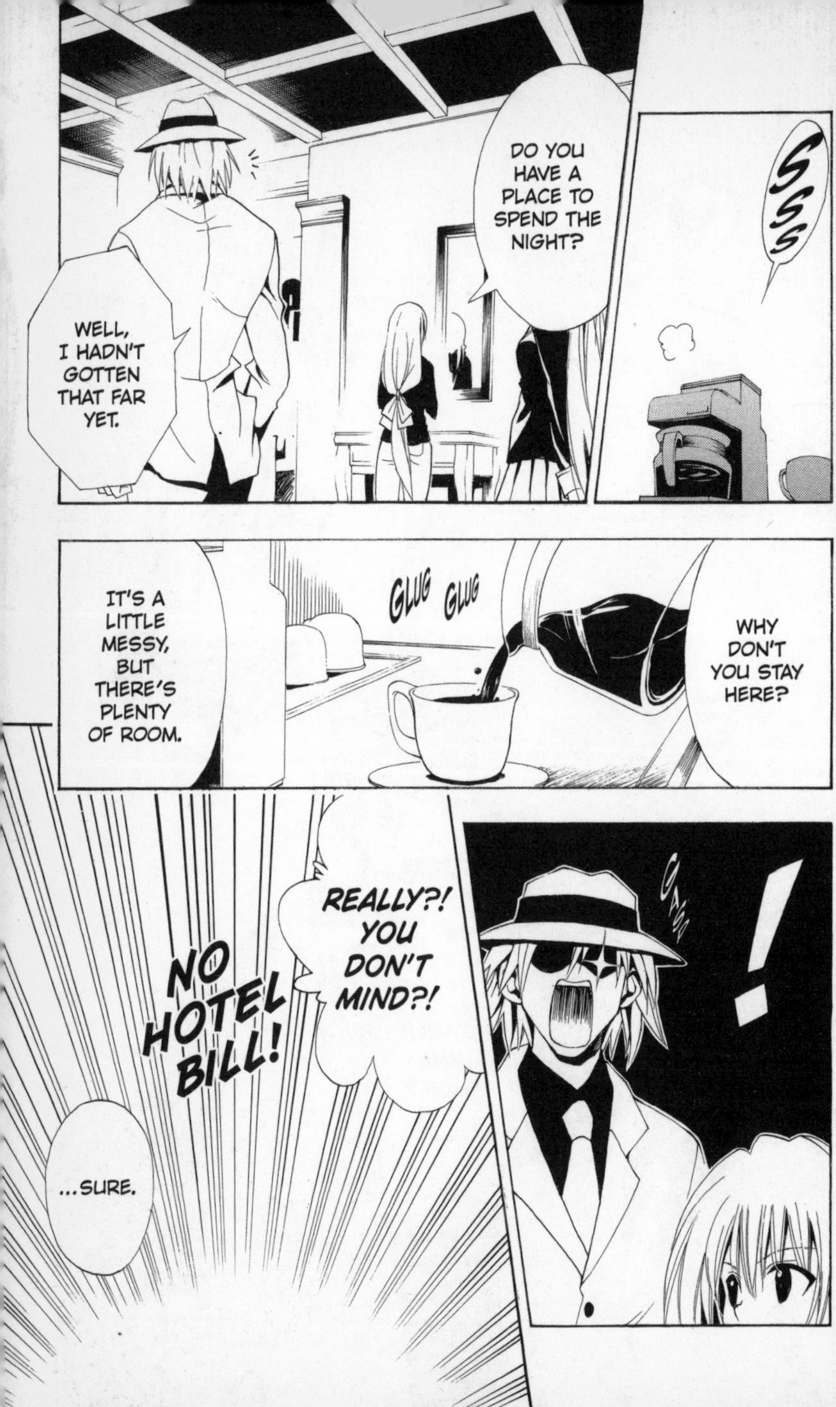
SSS
DO YOU HAVE A PLACE TO SPEND THE NIGHT?
WELL, I HADN'T GOTTEN THAT FAR YET.
WHY DON'T YOU STAY HERE?
GLUG GLUG
IT'S A LITTLE MESSY, BUT THERE'S PLENTY OF ROOM.
!
REALLY?! YOU DON'T MIND?!
NO HOTEL BILL!
...SURE.

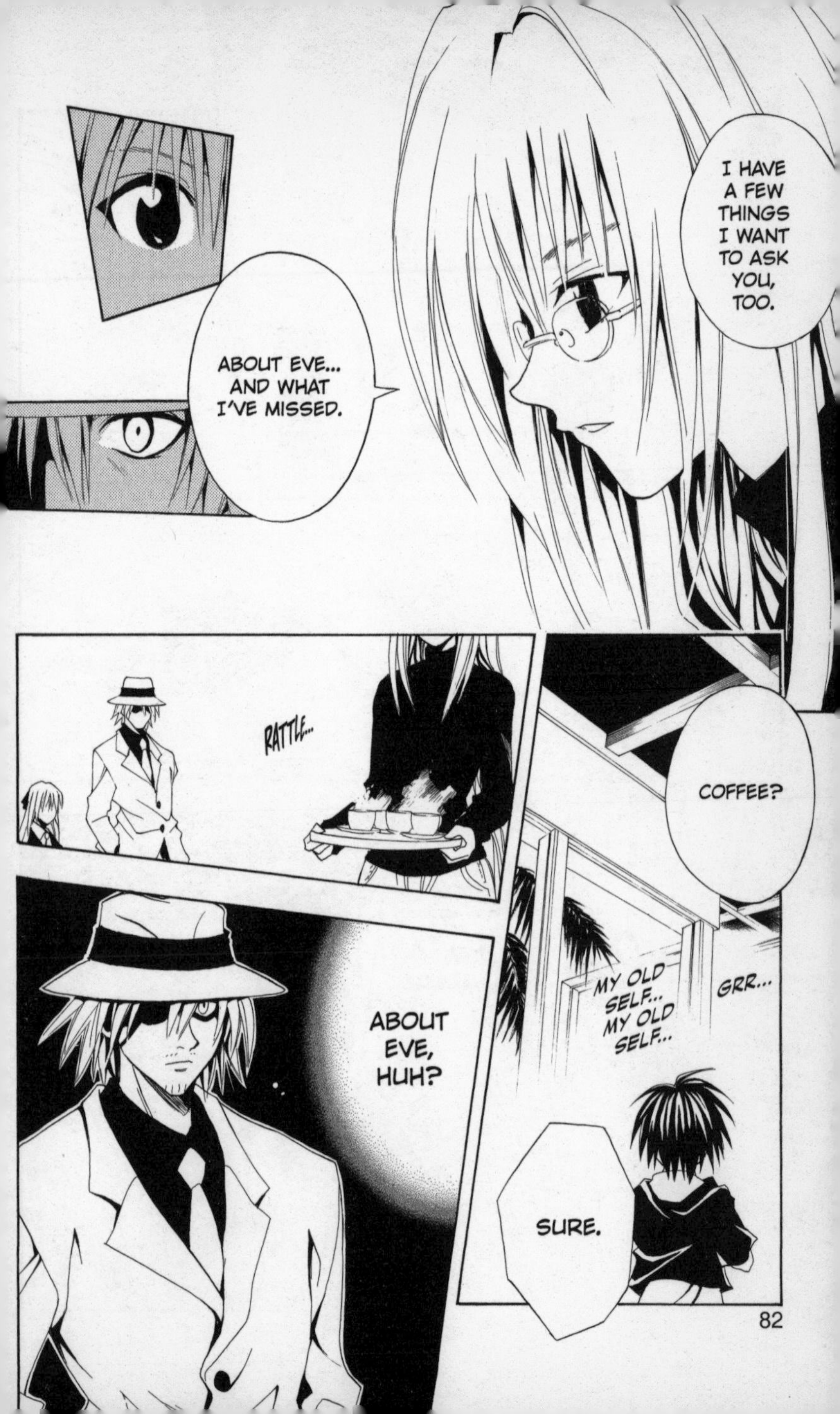
I HAVE A FEW THINGS I WANT TO ASK YOU, TOO.
ABOUT EVE... AND WHAT I'VE MISSED.
COFFEE?
GRR...
MY OLD SELF... MY OLD SELF...
SURE.
RATTLE...
ABOUT EVE, HUH?

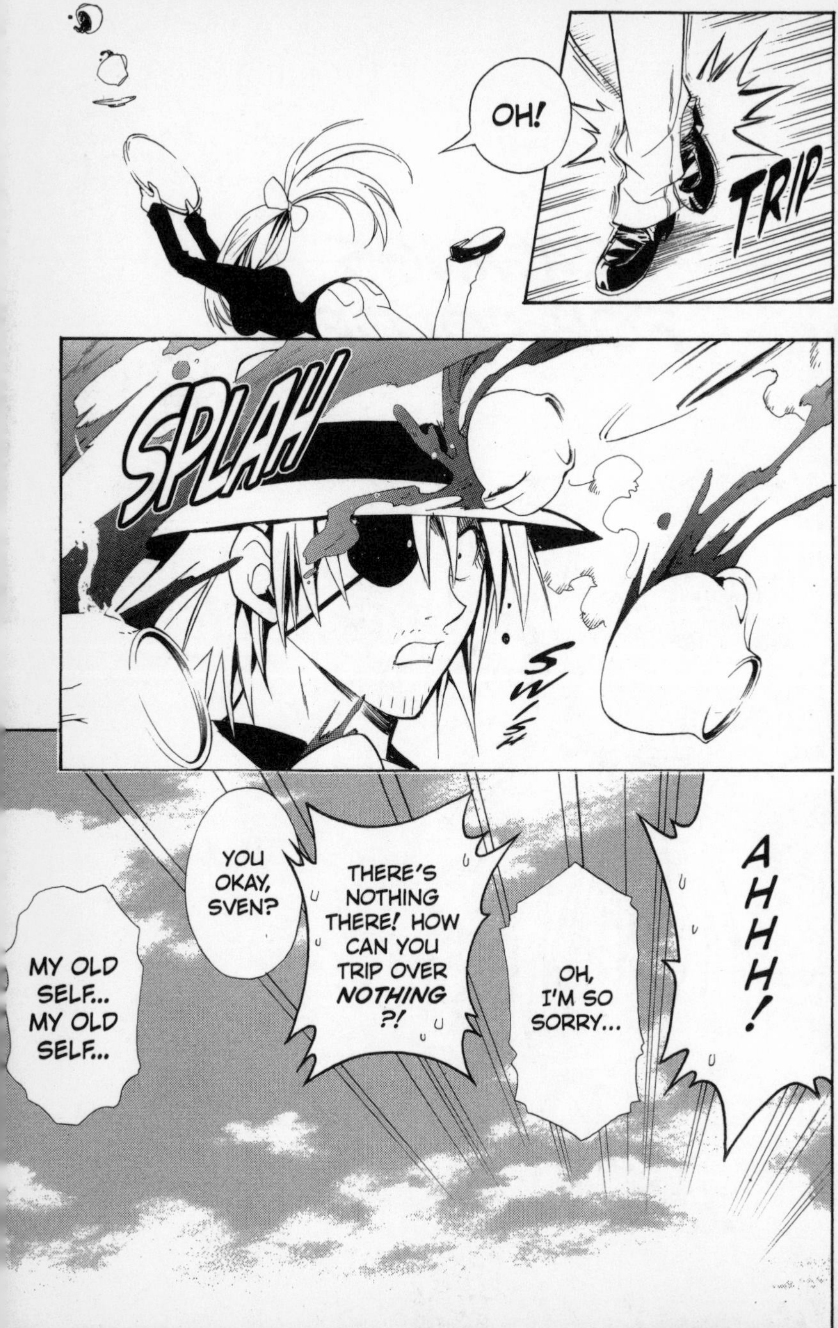
TRIP
OH!
SPLAH
SWISH
AHHH!
OH, I'M SO SORRY...
THERE'S NOTHING THERE! HOW CAN YOU TRIP OVER NOTHING ?!
YOU OKAY, SVEN?
MY OLD SELF... MY OLD SELF...

DRAWINGS FOR COLOR

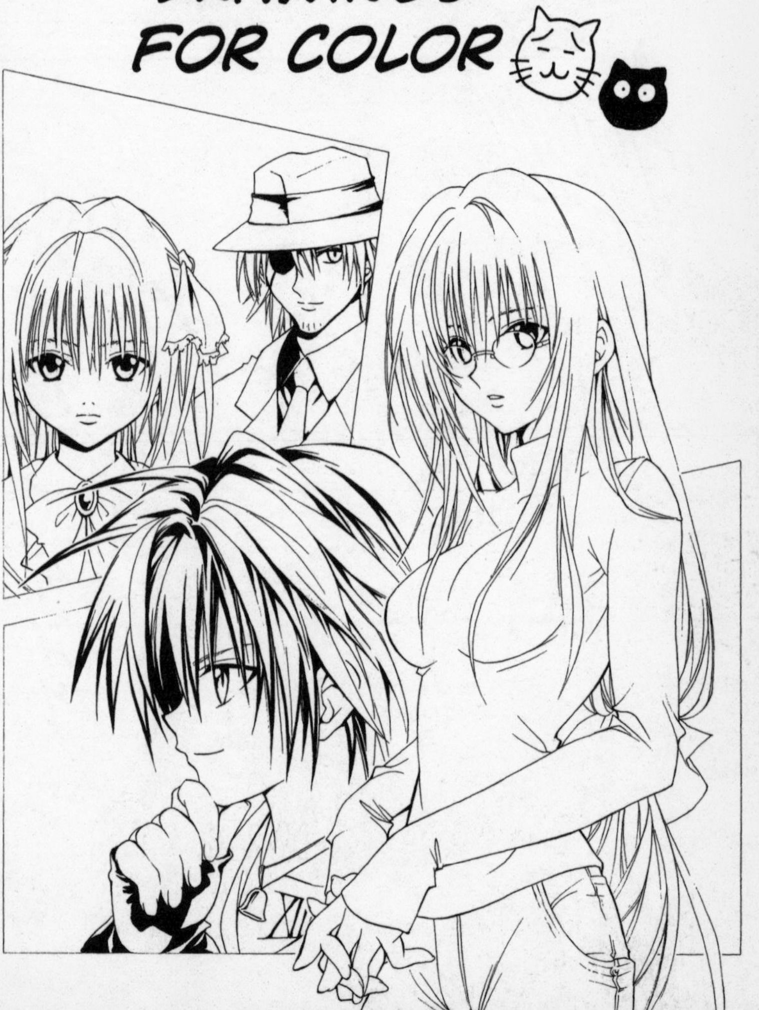

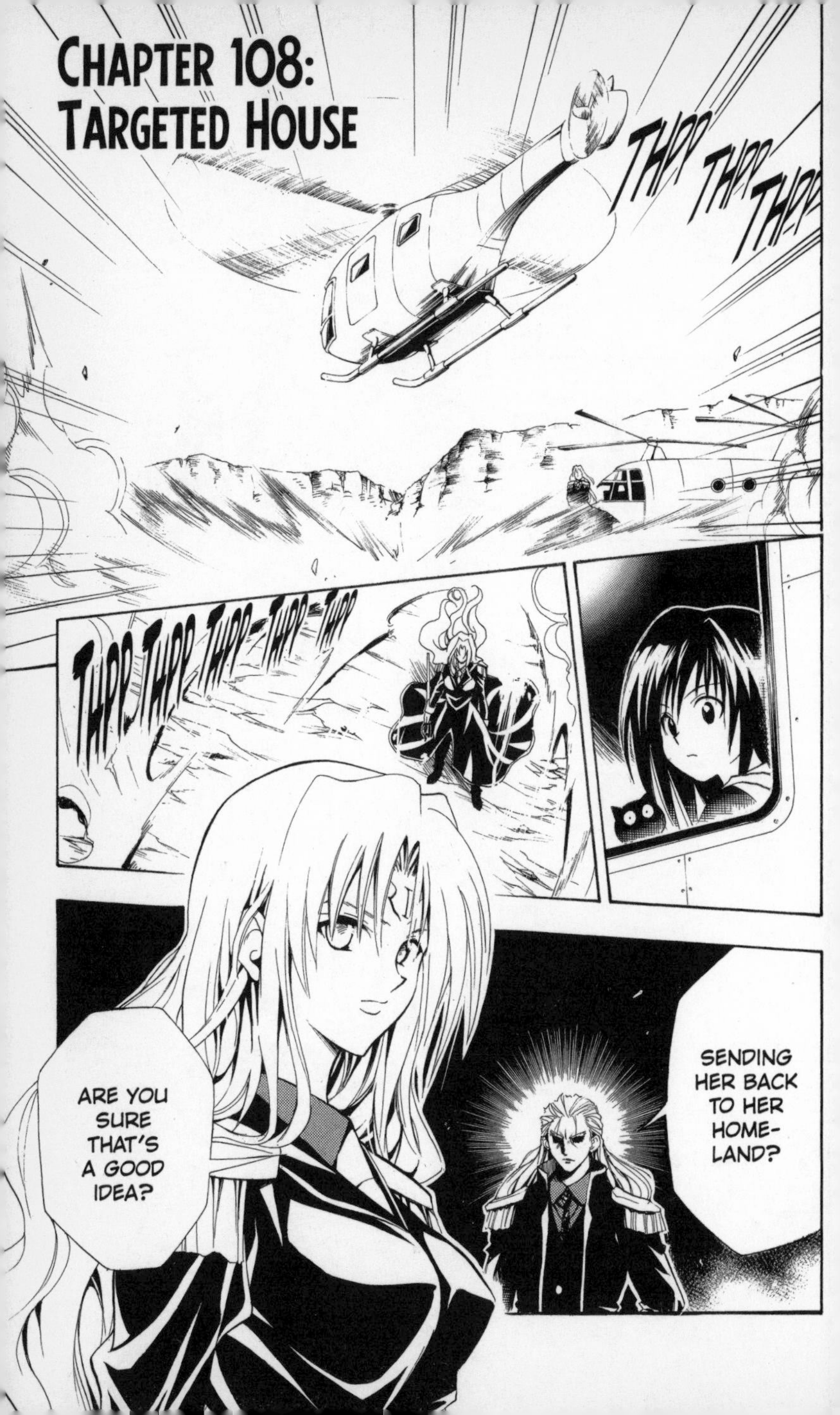
CHAPTER 108:
TARGETED HOUSE
THPP THPP THPP
THPP THPP THPP-THPP-THPP
SENDING HER BACK TO HER HOME-LAND?
ARE YOU SURE THAT'S A GOOD IDEA?

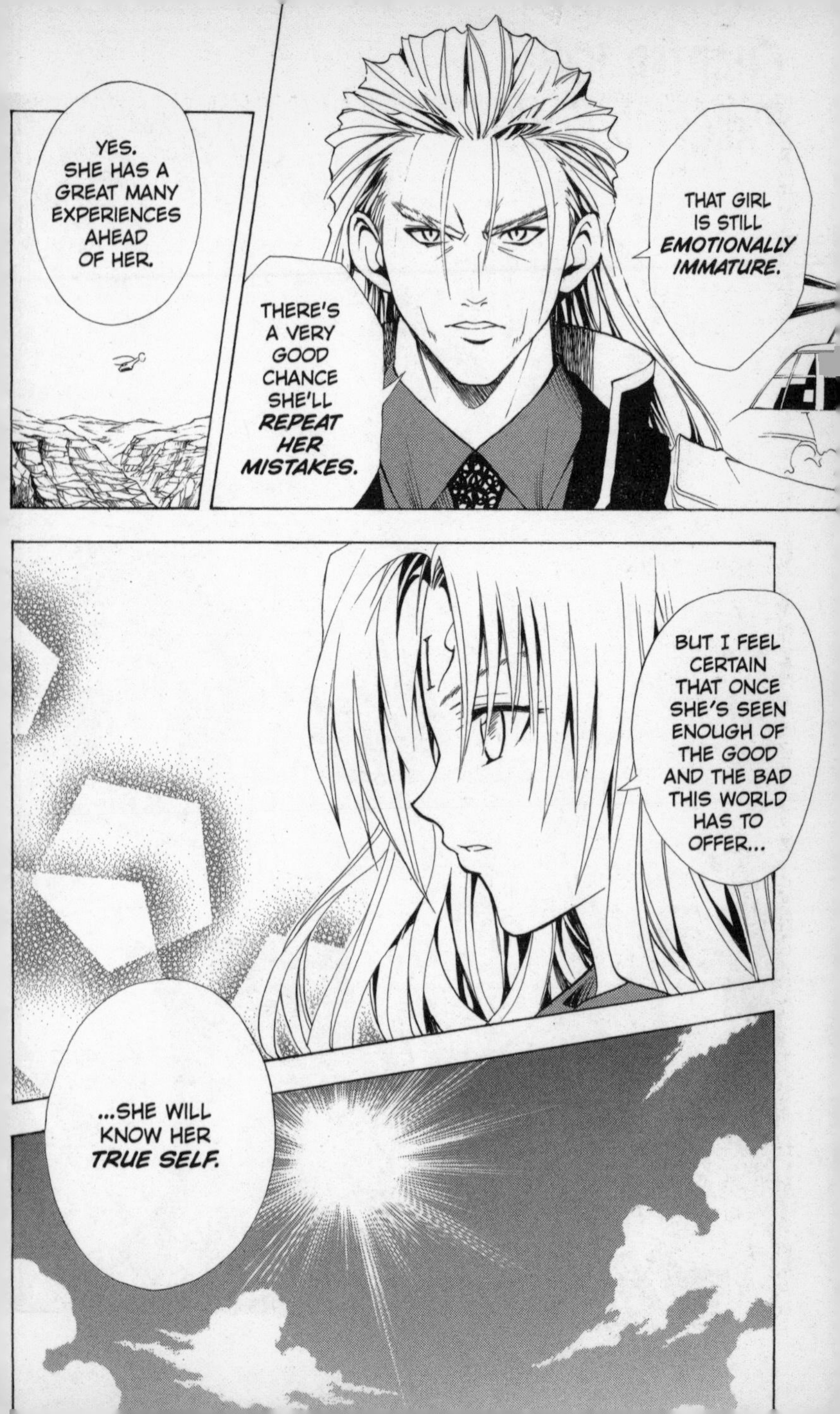
THAT GIRL IS STILL *EMOTIONALLY IMMATURE.*
THERE'S A VERY GOOD CHANCE SHE'LL *REPEAT HER MISTAKES.*
YES. SHE HAS A GREAT MANY EXPERIENCES AHEAD OF HER.
BUT I FEEL CERTAIN THAT ONCE SHE'S SEEN ENOUGH OF THE GOOD AND THE BAD THIS WORLD HAS TO OFFER...
...SHE WILL KNOW HER *TRUE SELF.*

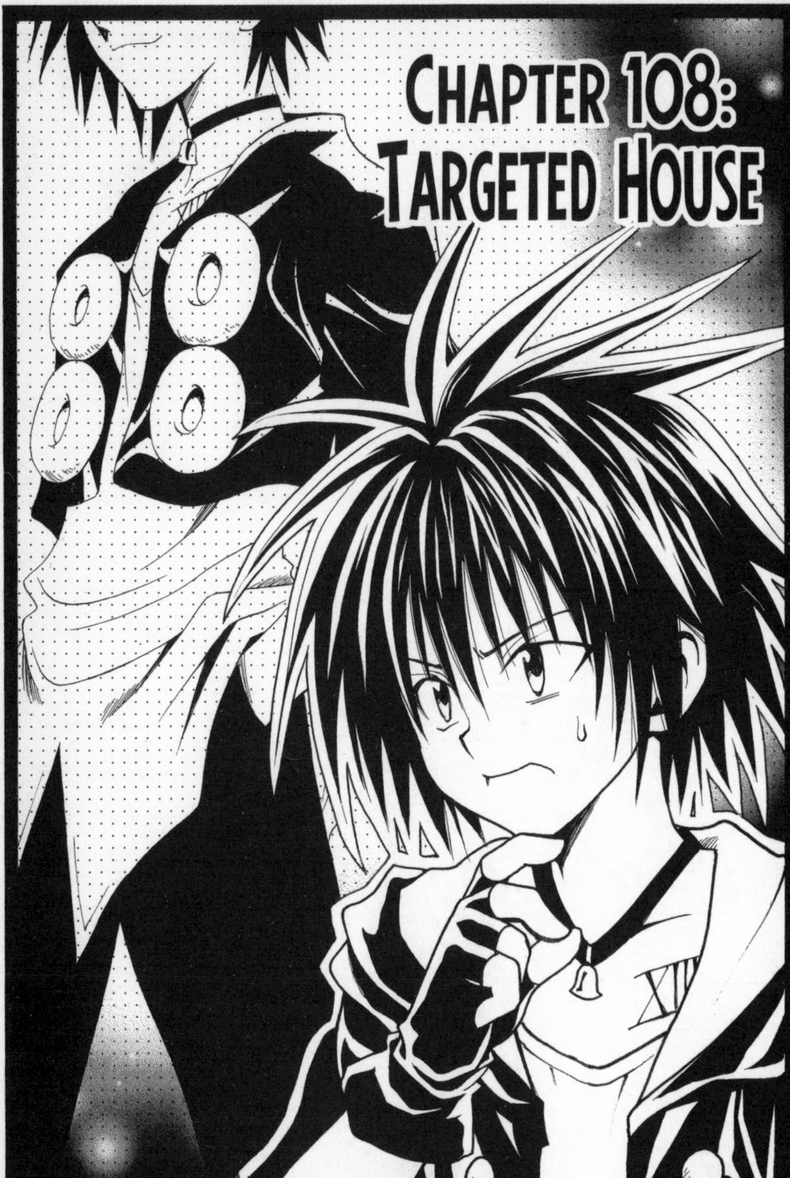
CHAPTER 108:
TARGETED HOUSE

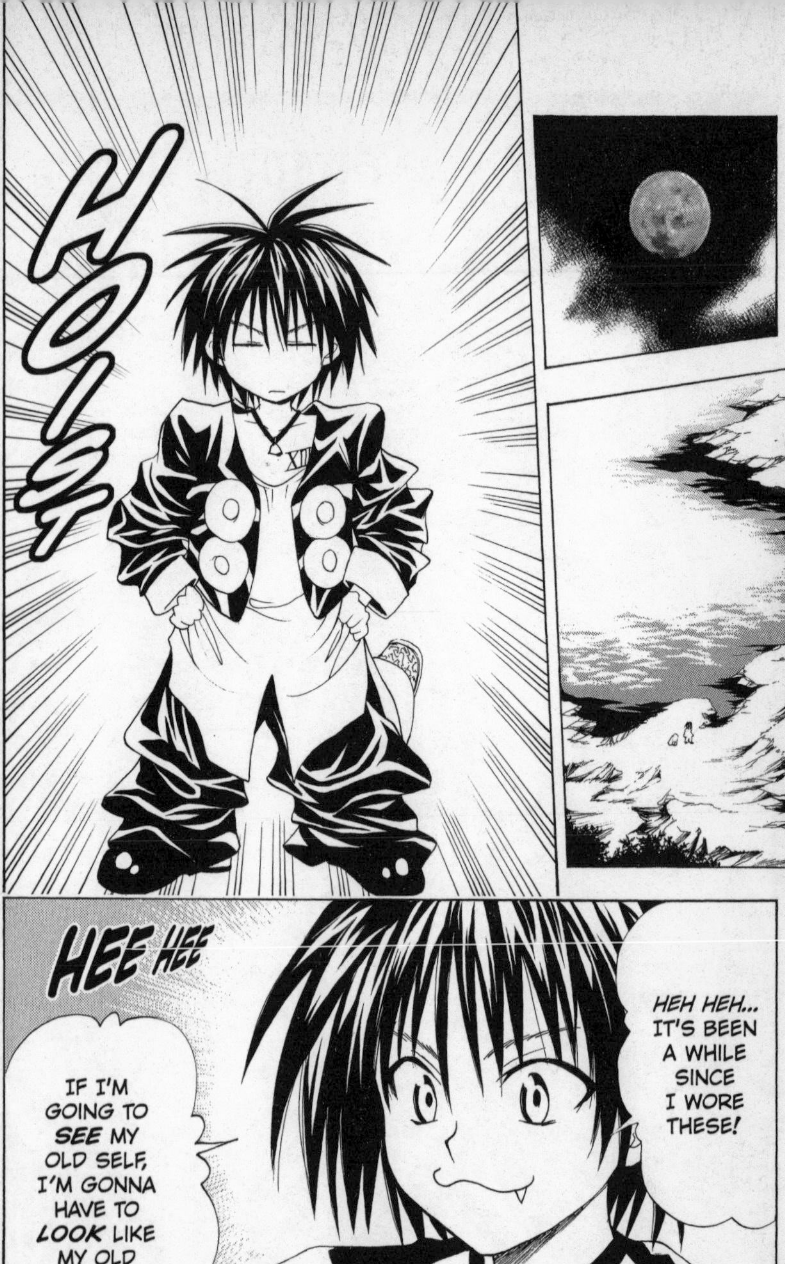
HOIST
HEH HEH... IT'S BEEN A WHILE SINCE I WORE THESE!
HEE HEE
IF I'M GOING TO SEE MY OLD SELF, I'M GONNA HAVE TO LOOK LIKE MY OLD SELF!

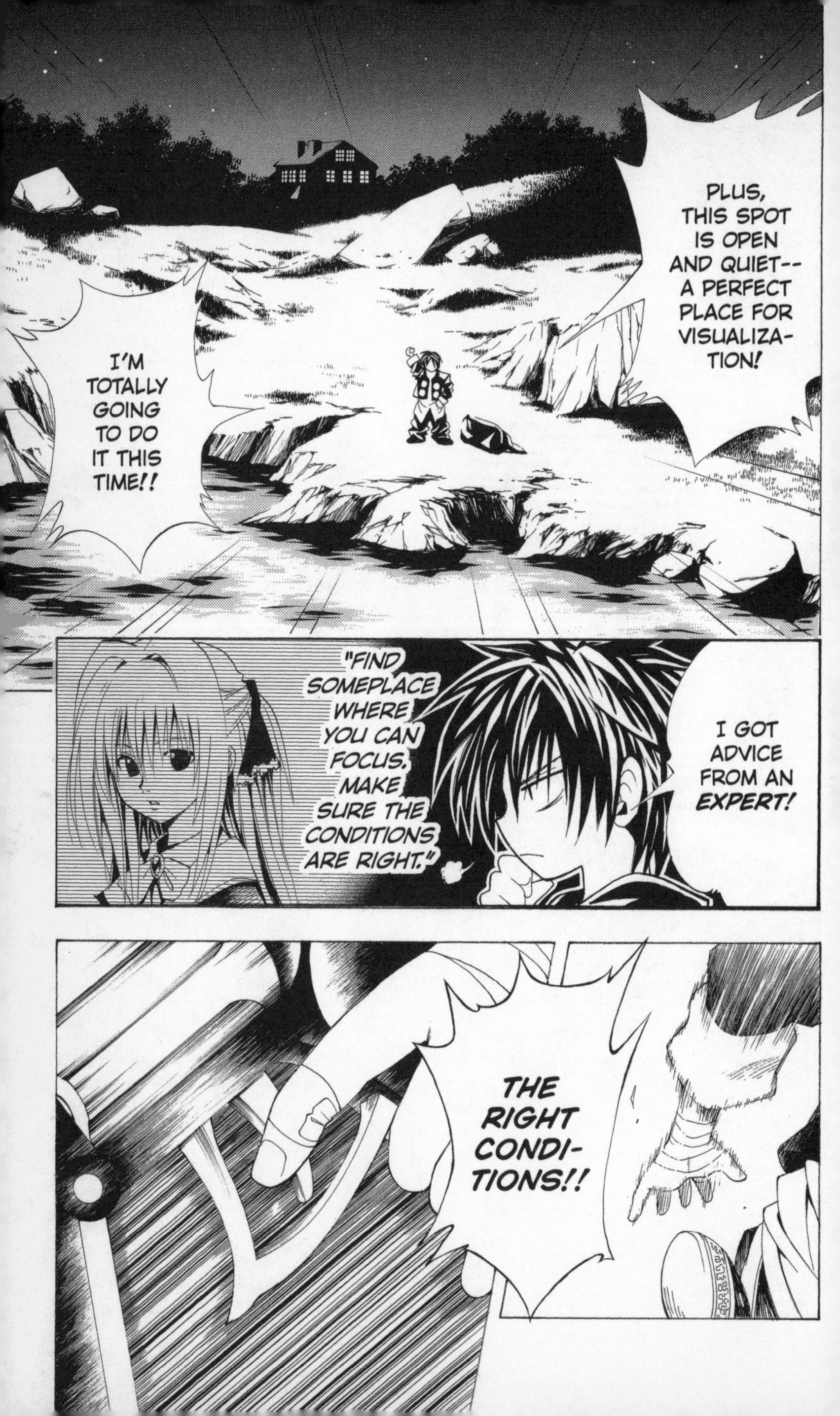
PLUS, THIS SPOT IS OPEN AND QUIET-- A PERFECT PLACE FOR VISUALIZA-TION!
I'M TOTALLY GOING TO DO IT THIS TIME!!
I GOT ADVICE FROM AN *EXPERT!*
"FIND SOMEPLACE WHERE YOU CAN FOCUS. MAKE SURE THE CONDITIONS ARE RIGHT."
THE RIGHT CONDI-TIONS!!

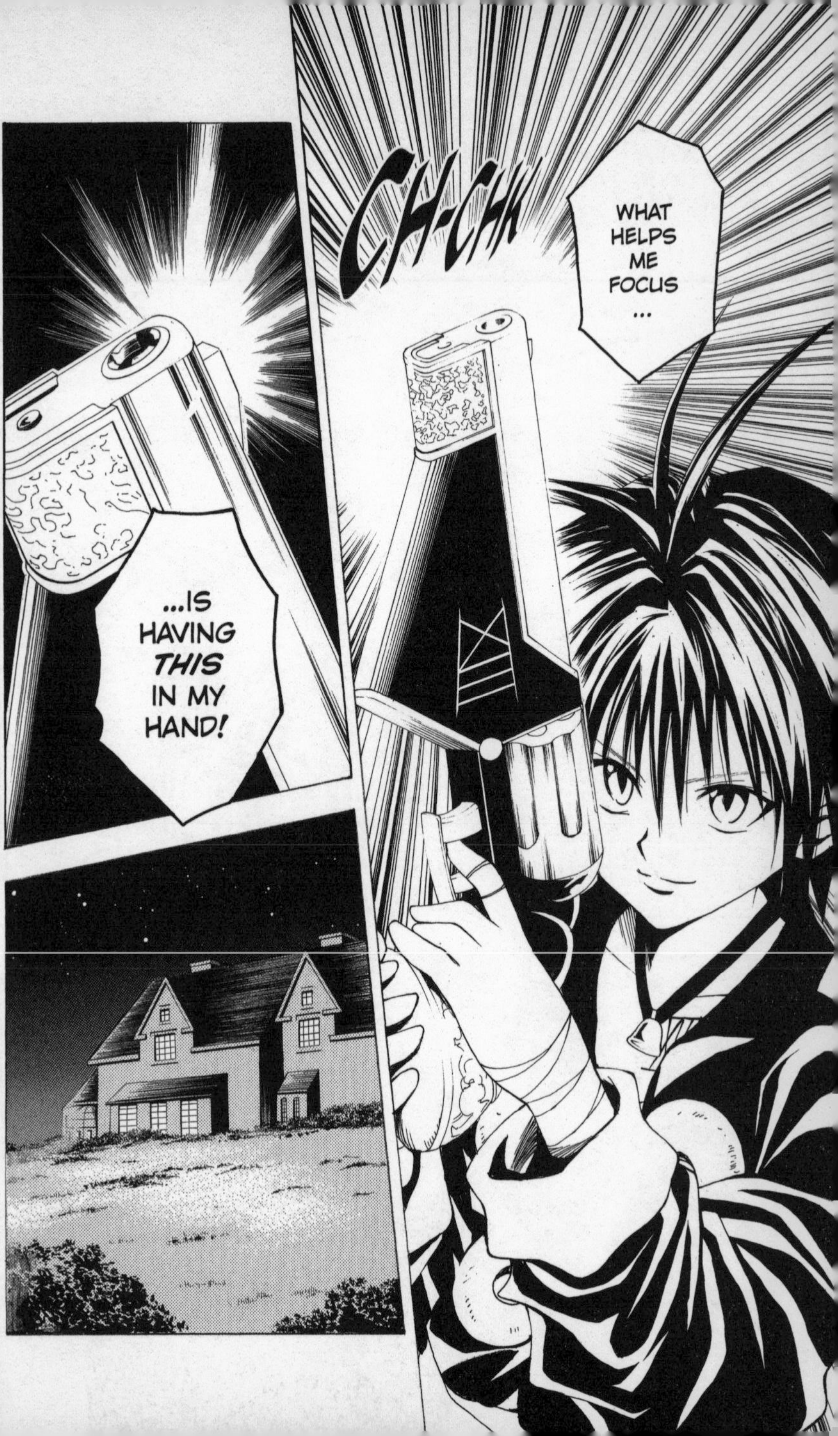
CH-CHK
WHAT HELPS ME FOCUS ...
...IS HAVING *THIS* IN MY HAND!

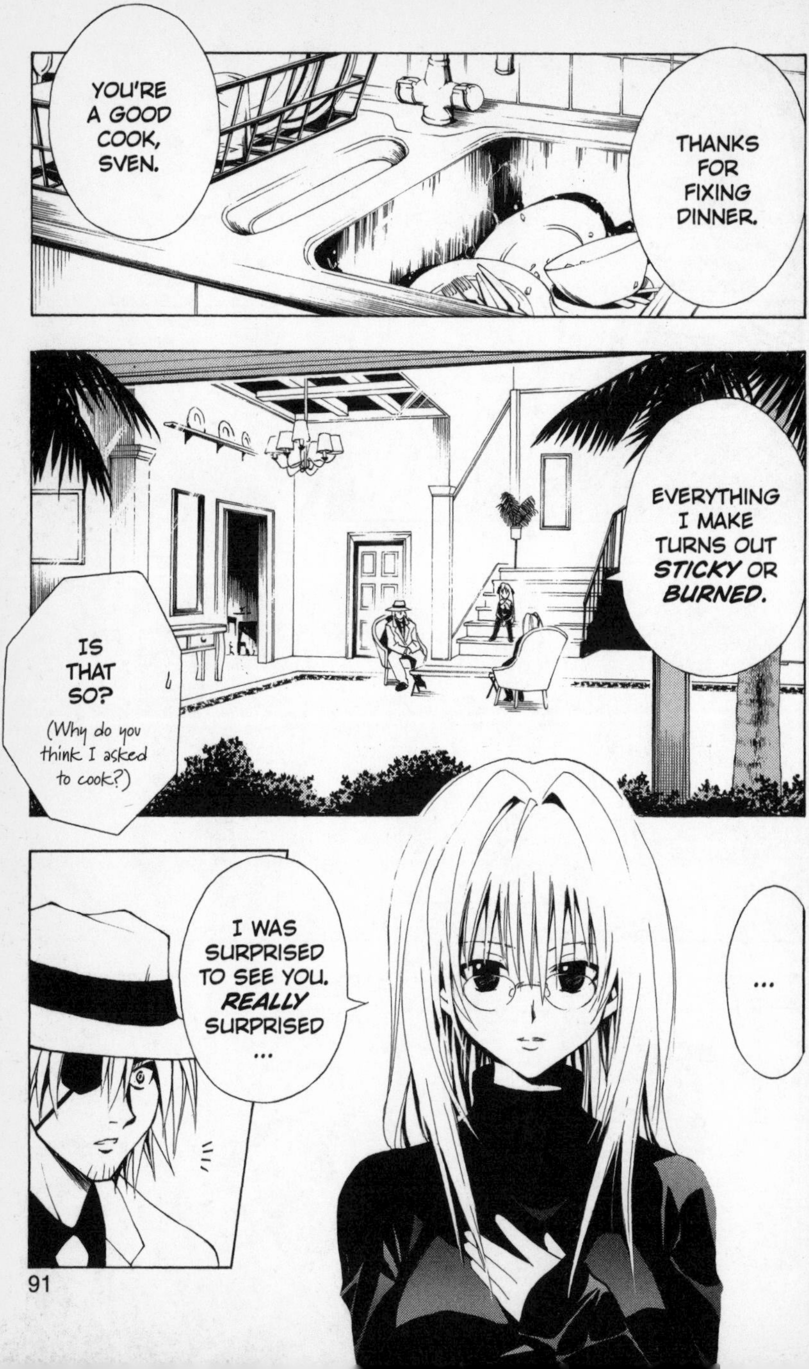
THANKS FOR FIXING DINNER.
YOU'RE A GOOD COOK, SVEN.
EVERYTHING I MAKE TURNS OUT *STICKY* OR *BURNED*.
IS THAT SO?
(Why do you think I asked to cook?)
...
I WAS SURPRISED TO SEE YOU. *REALLY* SURPRISED ...

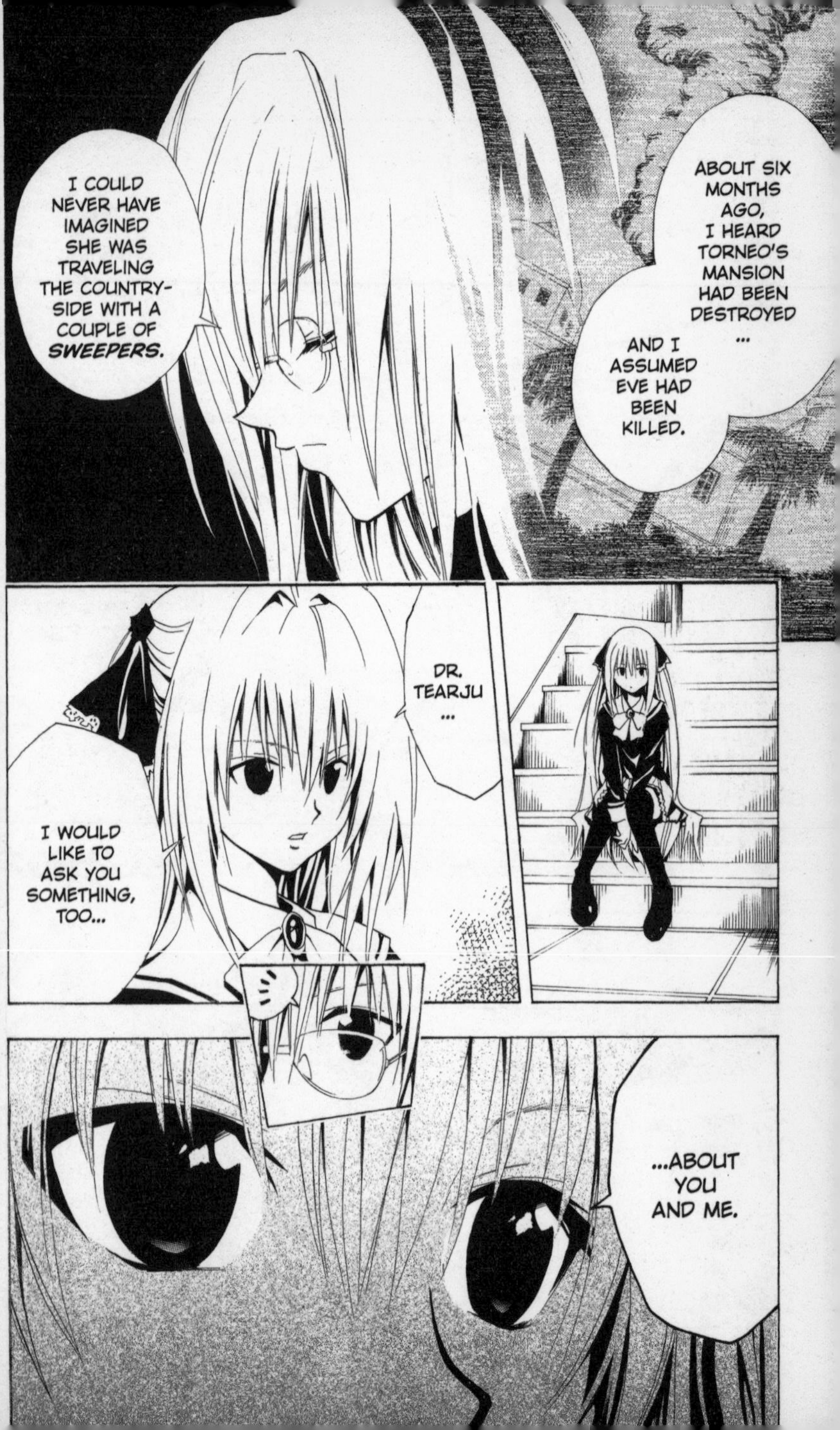
ABOUT SIX MONTHS AGO, I HEARD TORNEO'S MANSION HAD BEEN DESTROYED...
AND I ASSUMED EVE HAD BEEN KILLED.
I COULD NEVER HAVE IMAGINED SHE WAS TRAVELING THE COUNTRY-SIDE WITH A COUPLE OF *SWEEPERS*.
DR. TEARJU...
I WOULD LIKE TO ASK YOU SOMETHING, TOO...
...ABOUT YOU AND ME.

READ THIS WAY

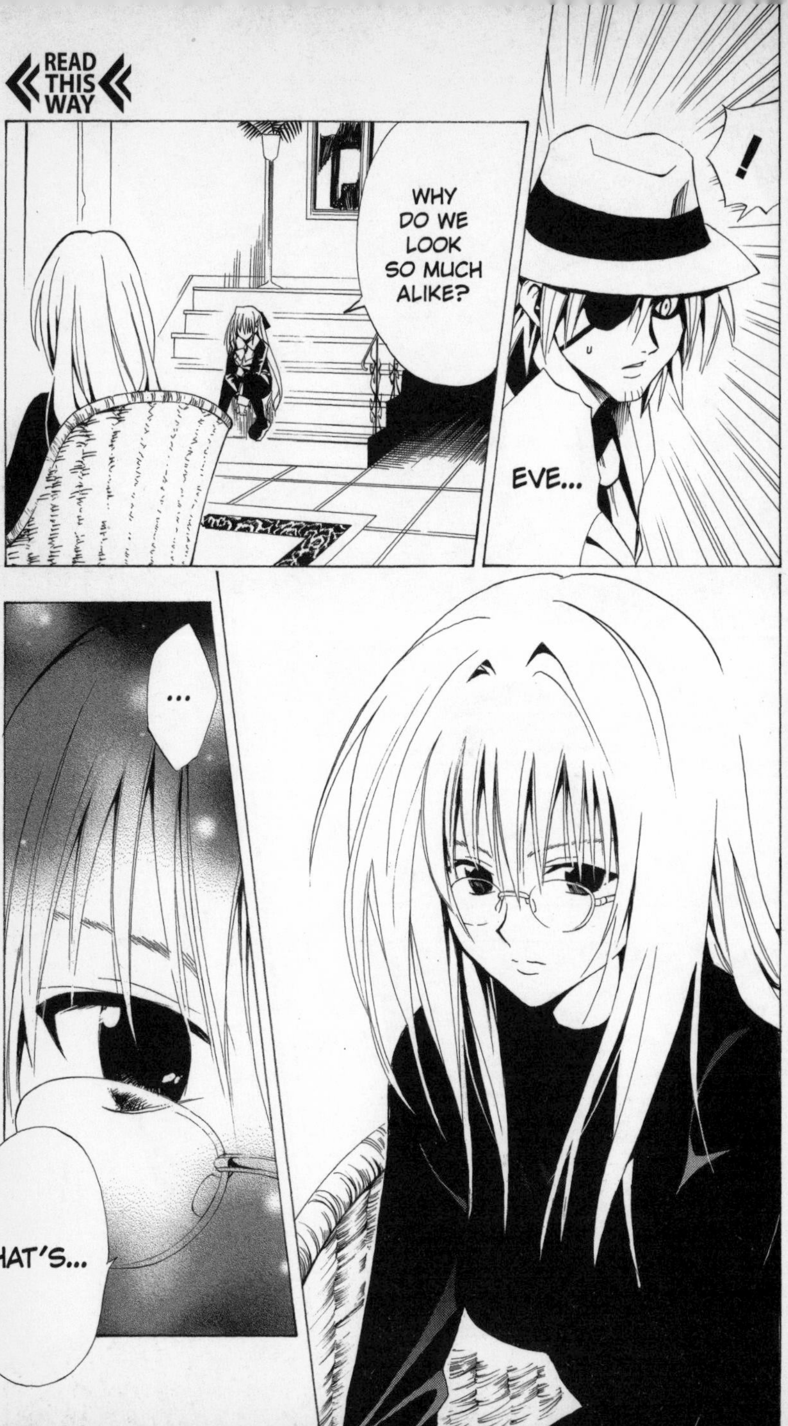
!
EVE...
WHY DO WE LOOK SO MUCH ALIKE?
...
THAT'S...

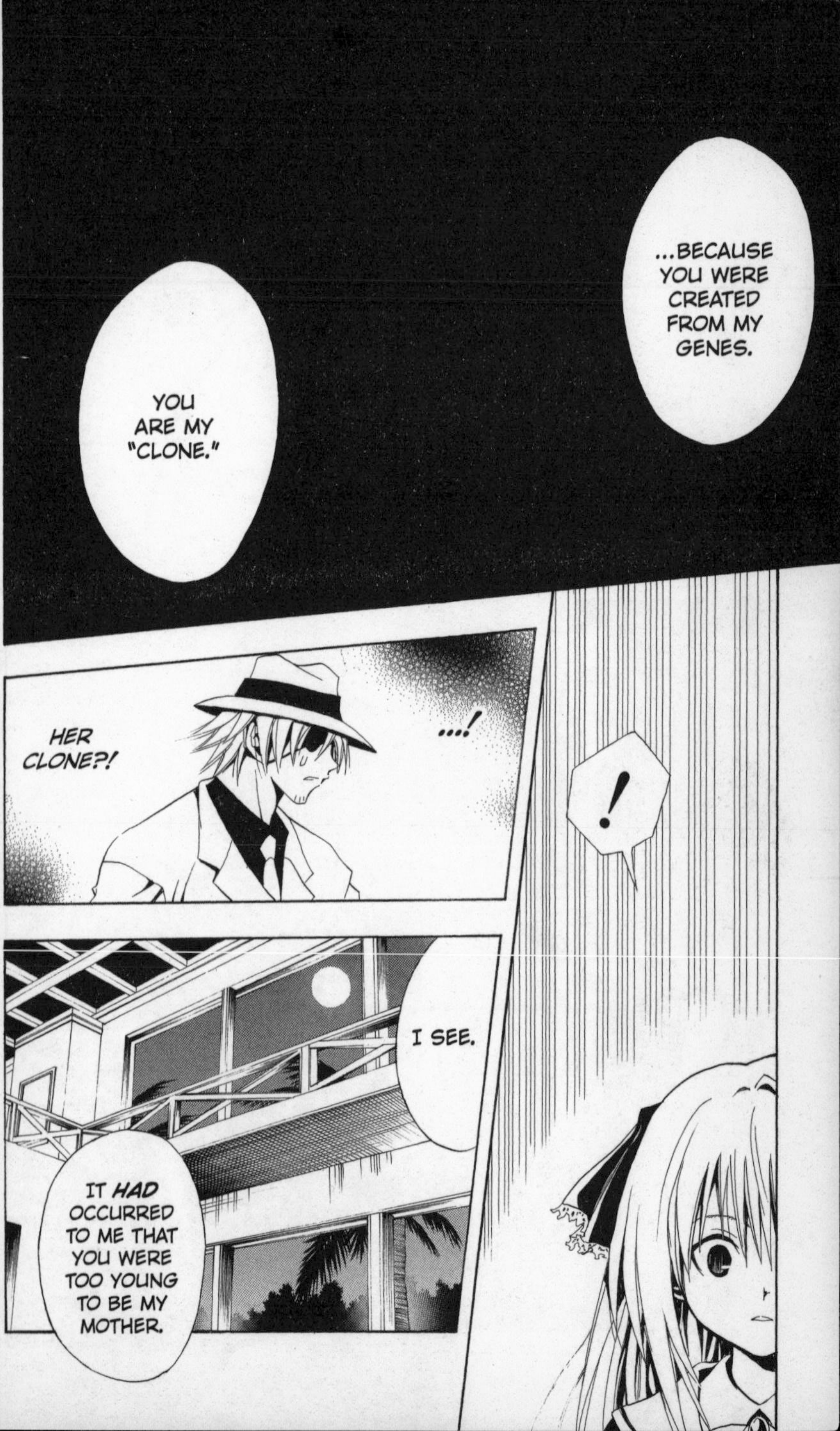

...BECAUSE YOU WERE CREATED FROM MY GENES.
YOU ARE MY "CLONE."
!
...!
HER CLONE?!
I SEE.
IT *HAD* OCCURRED TO ME THAT YOU WERE TOO YOUNG TO BE MY MOTHER.

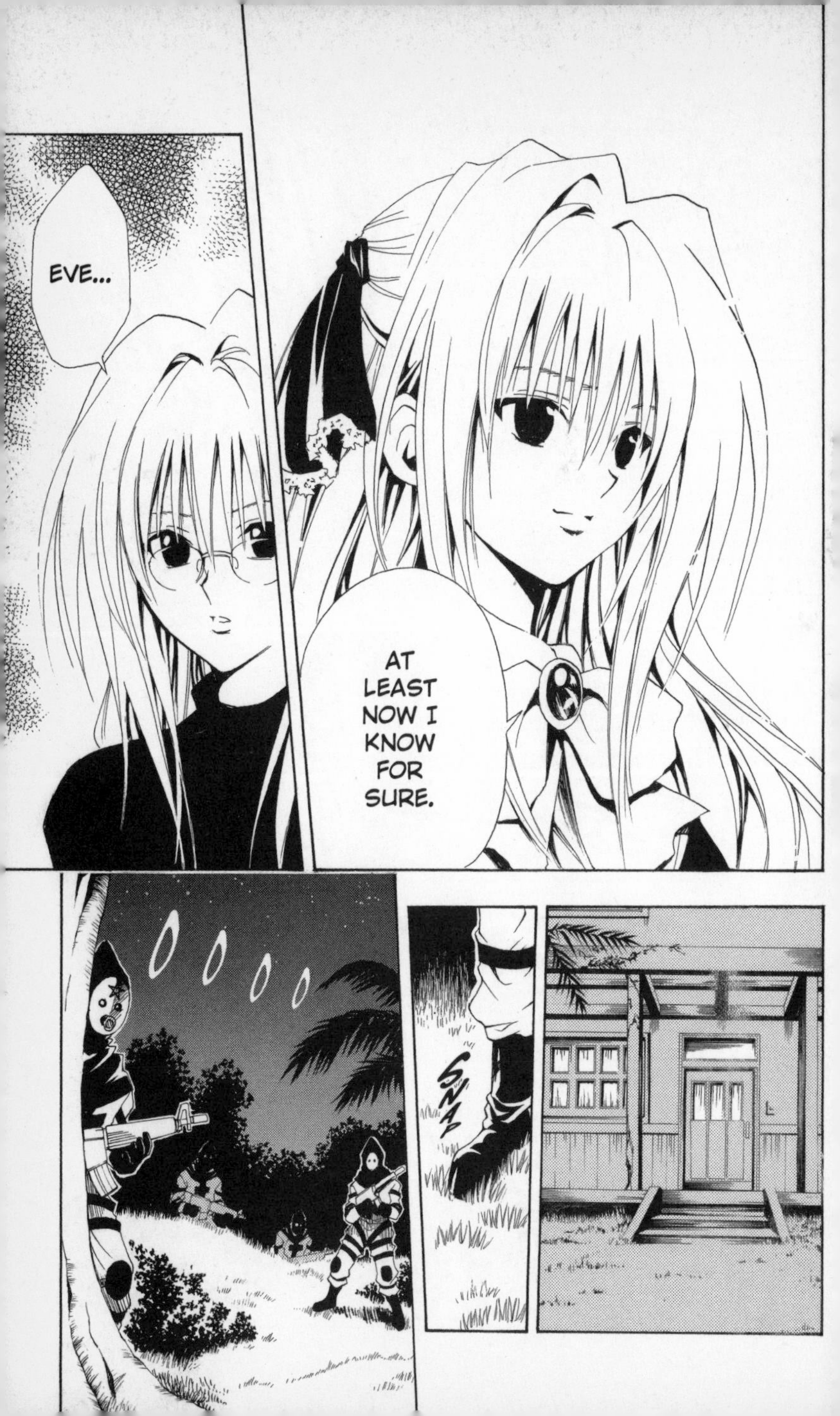
AT LEAST NOW I KNOW FOR SURE.
EVE...
SNAP

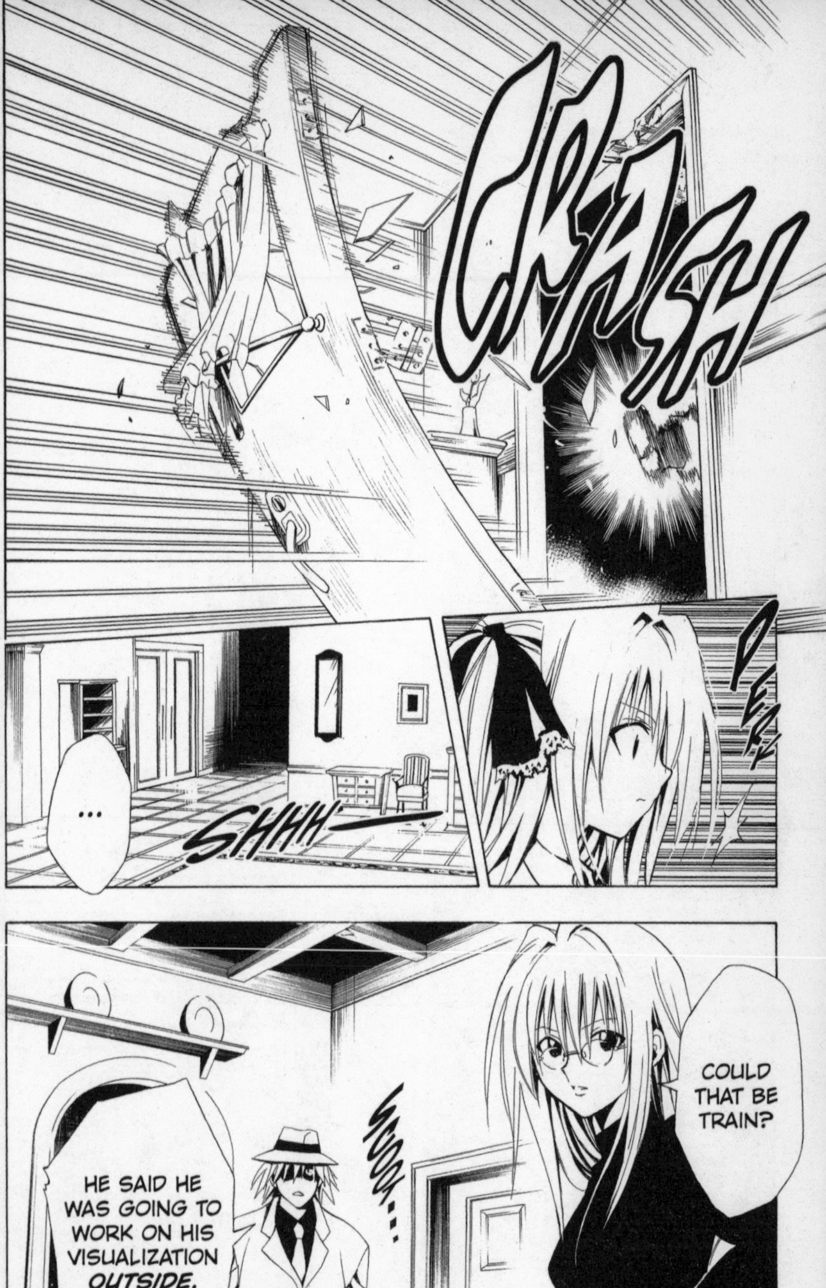
CRASH
...
SHHH
COULD THAT BE TRAIN?
HE SAID HE WAS GOING TO WORK ON HIS VISUALIZATION *OUTSIDE*.

READ THIS WAY

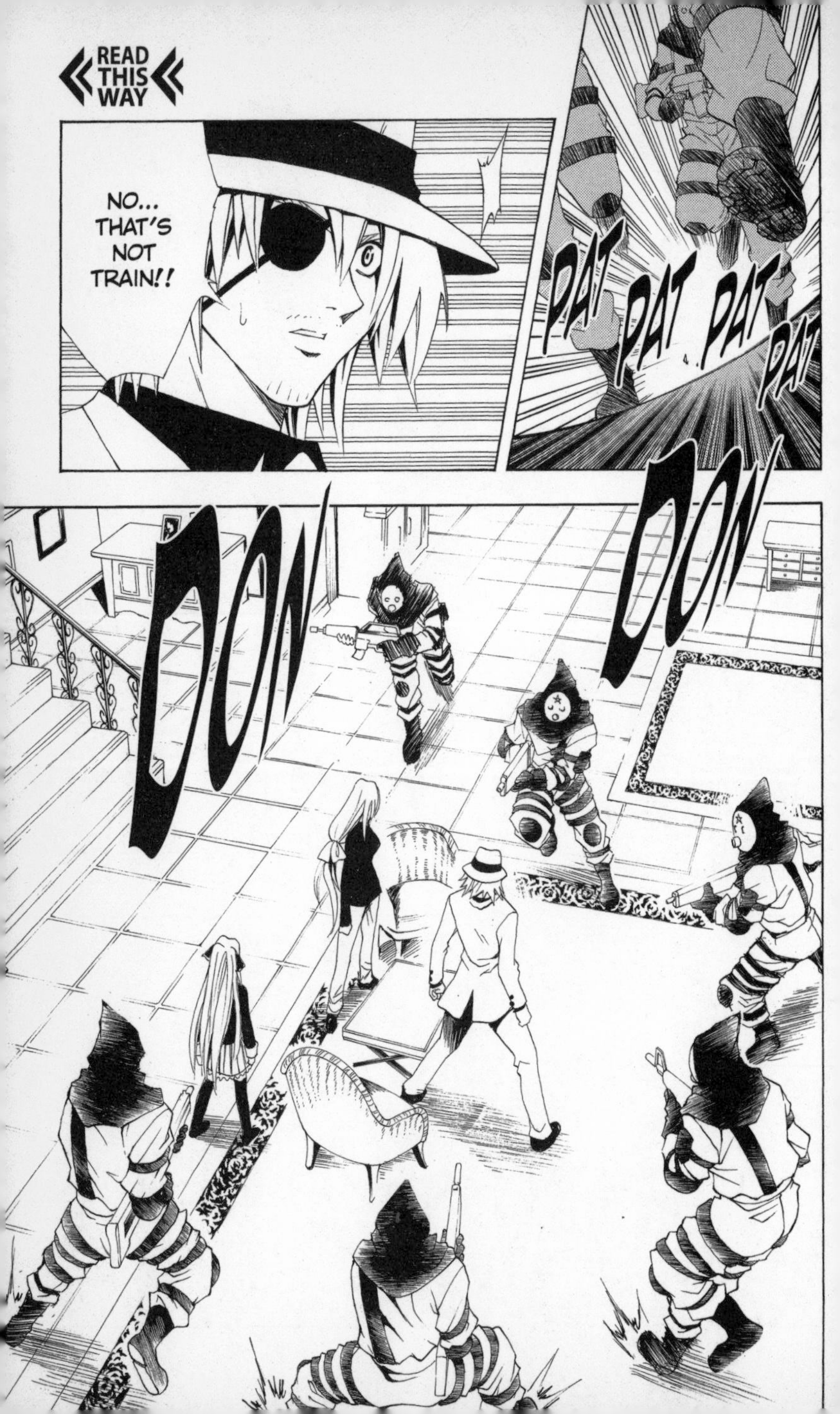

PAT PAT PAT PAT
NO... THAT'S NOT TRAIN!!
DON
DON

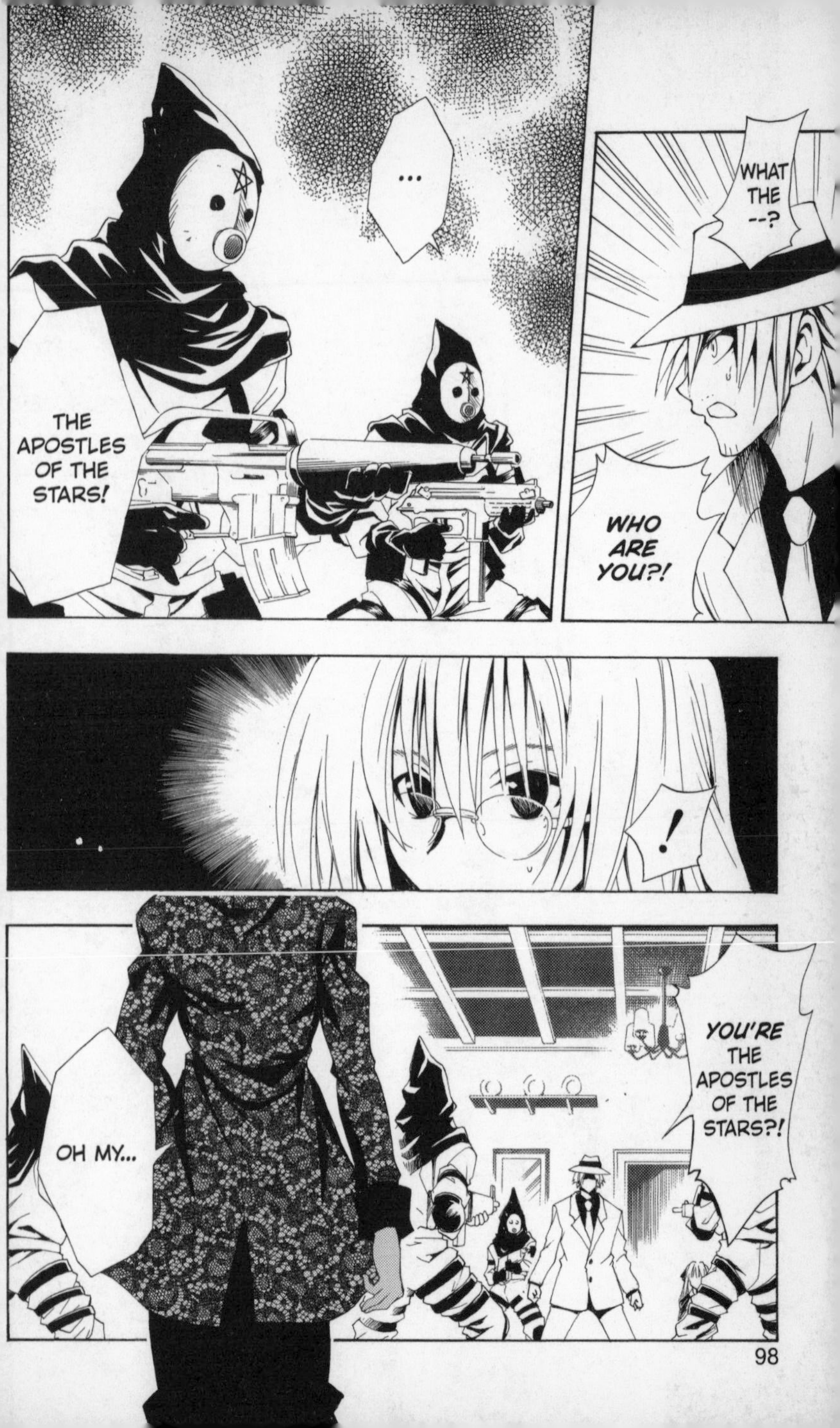
WHAT THE --?
WHO ARE YOU?!
...
THE APOSTLES OF THE STARS!
!
YOU'RE THE APOSTLES OF THE STARS?!
OH MY...

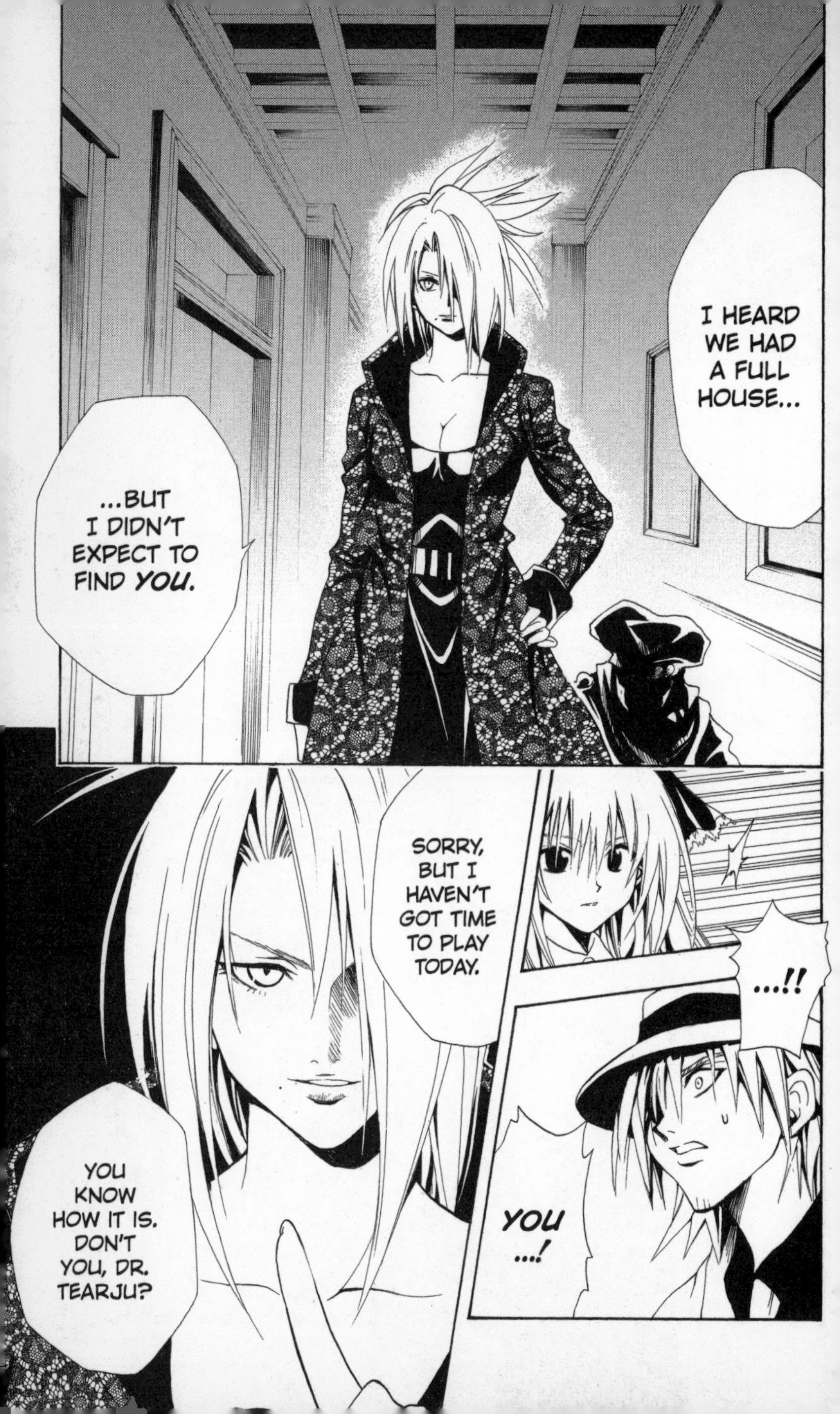
I HEARD WE HAD A FULL HOUSE...
...BUT I DIDN'T EXPECT TO FIND *YOU*.
...!!
YOU ...!
SORRY, BUT I HAVEN'T GOT TIME TO PLAY TODAY.
YOU KNOW HOW IT IS. DON'T YOU, DR. TEARJU?

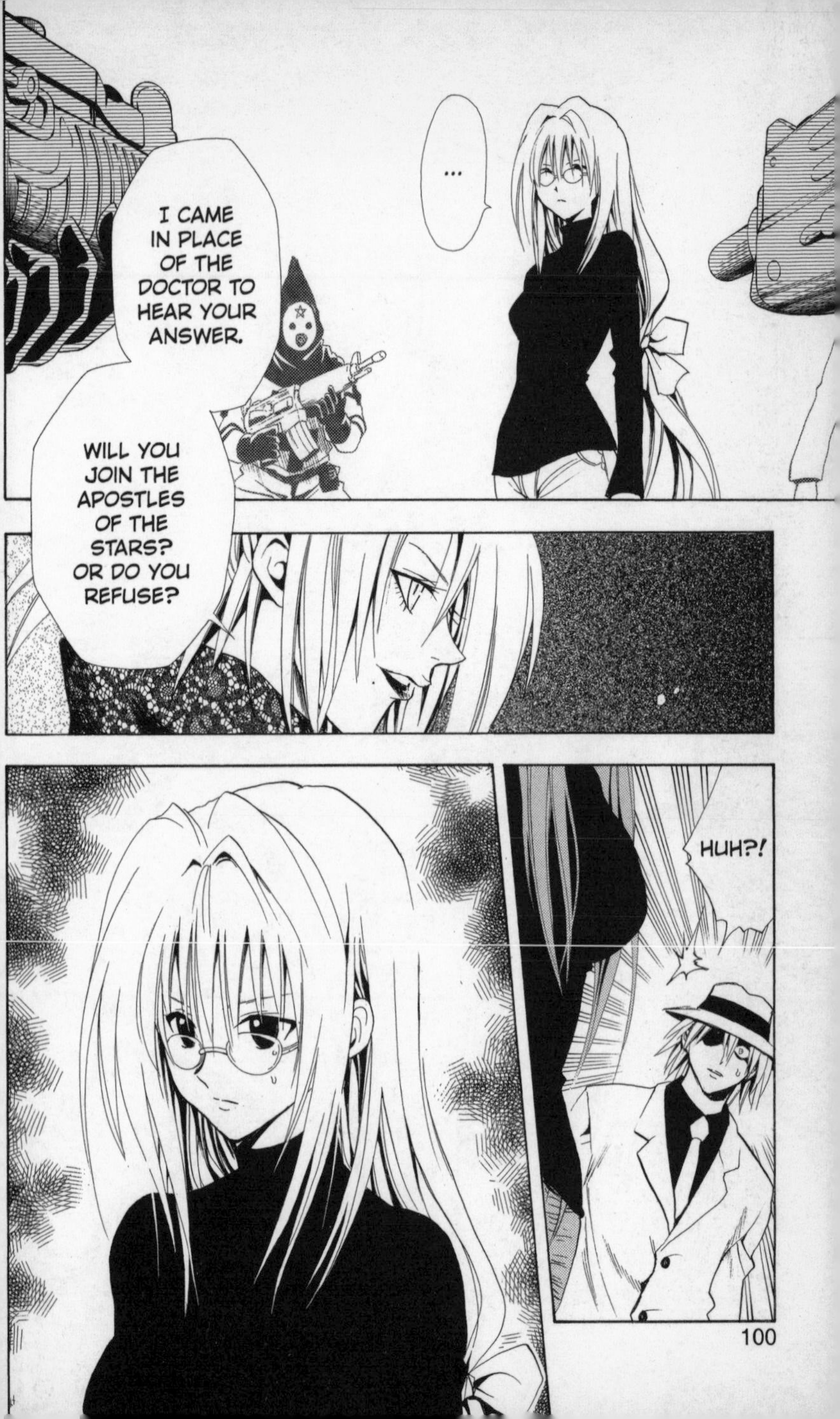
...
I CAME IN PLACE OF THE DOCTOR TO HEAR YOUR ANSWER.
WILL YOU JOIN THE APOSTLES OF THE STARS? OR DO YOU REFUSE?
HUH?!

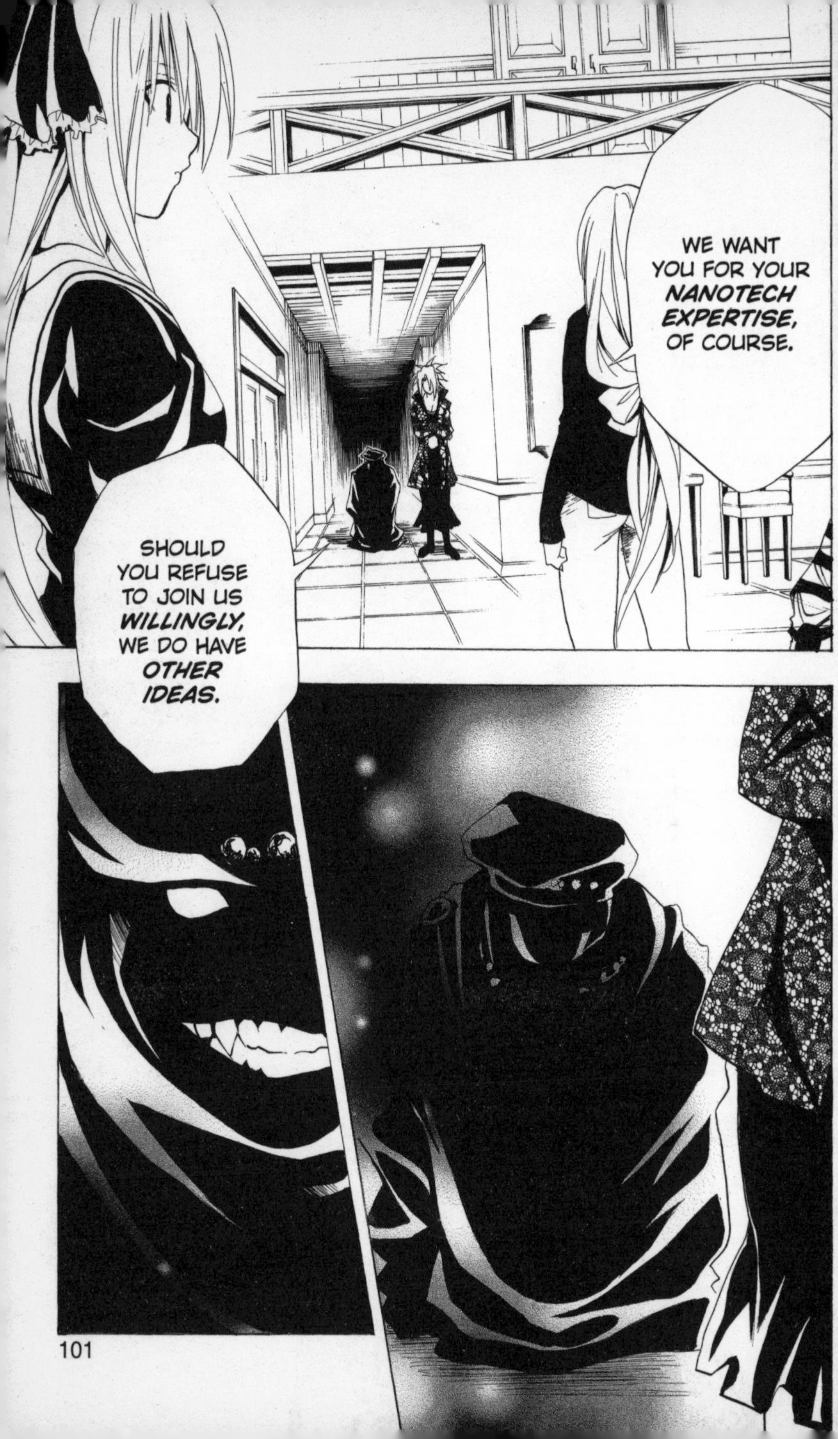
WE WANT YOU FOR YOUR *NANOTECH EXPERTISE,* OF COURSE.
SHOULD YOU REFUSE TO JOIN US *WILLINGLY,* WE DO HAVE *OTHER IDEAS.*

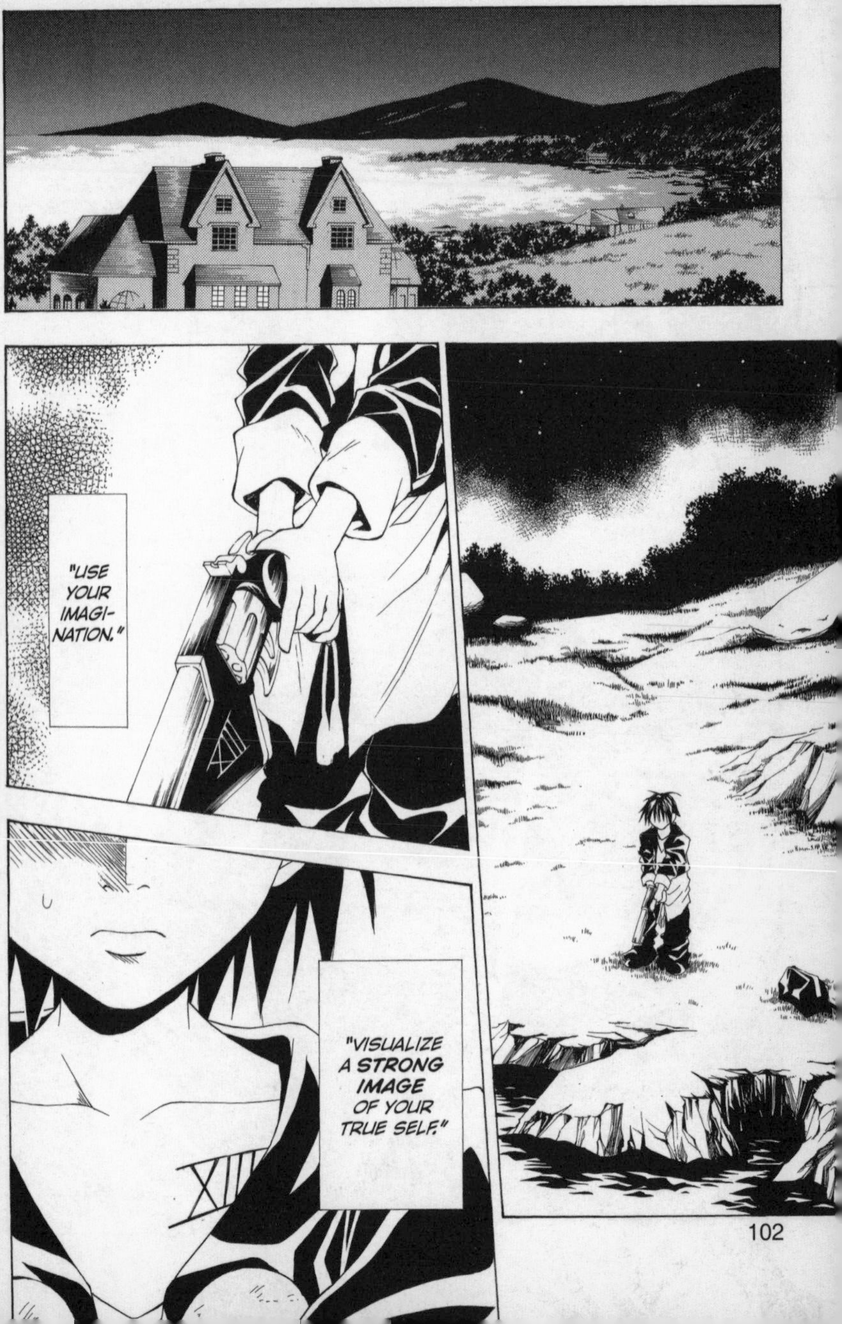
"USE YOUR IMAGI-NATION."
"VISUALIZE A STRONG IMAGE OF YOUR TRUE SELF."

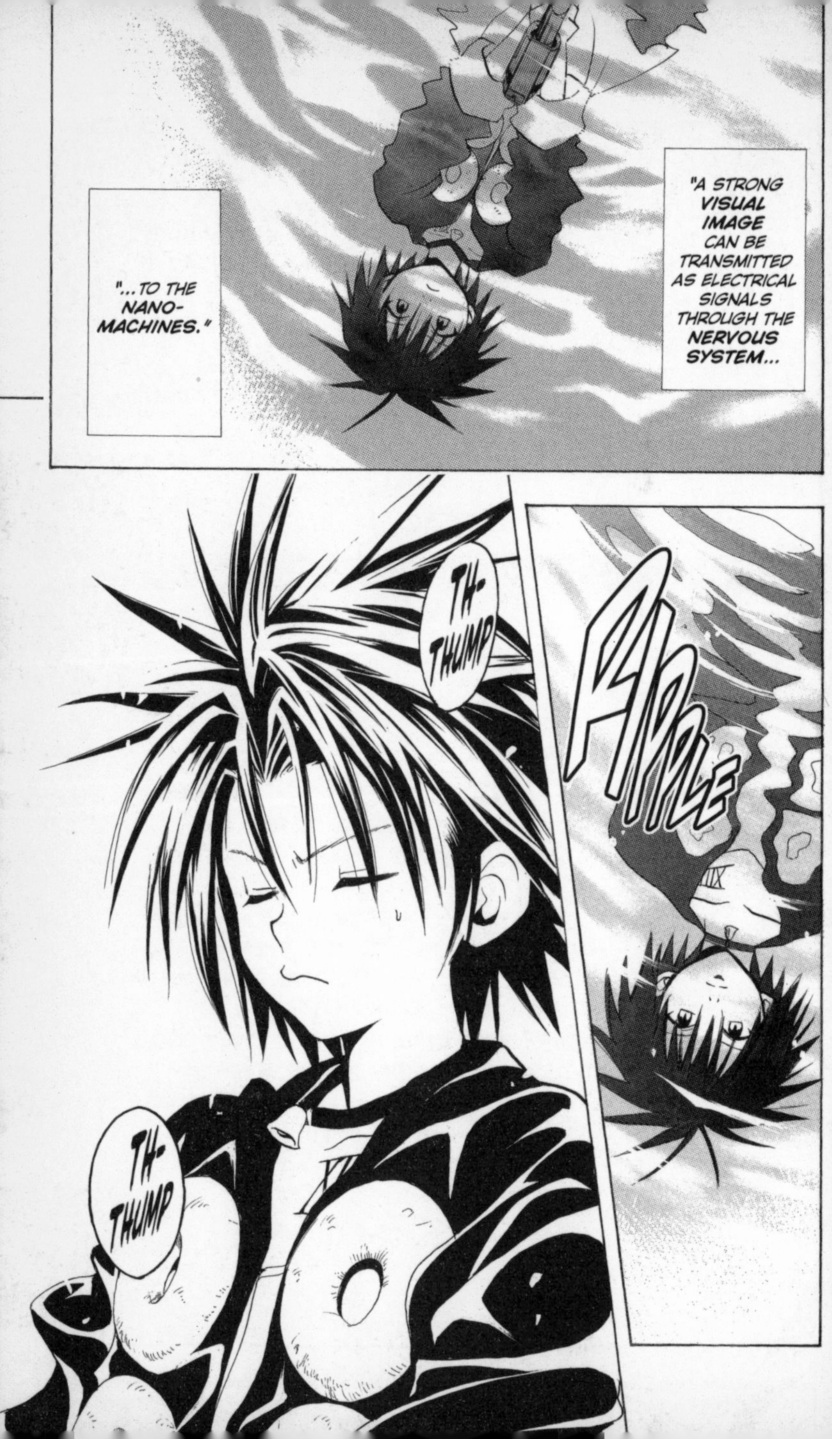
"A STRONG VISUAL IMAGE CAN BE TRANSMITTED AS ELECTRICAL SIGNALS THROUGH THE NERVOUS SYSTEM...
"...TO THE NANO-MACHINES."
TH-THUMP
TH-THUMP

BLACK CAT

profile

TEARJU LUNATIQUE

DATA	
BIRTHDATE:	MAY 26
AGE:	27
BLOOD TYPE:	AB
HEIGHT:	155CM
WEIGHT:	42 KG
PERSONALITY:	CALM AND COMPOSED, BUT SCATTERBRAINED.
INTERESTS:	READING COOKBOOKS AND TRYING OUT RECIPES. GARDENING. READING.
SPECIAL SKILLS (?):	ANYTHING SHE COOKS TURNS OUT MUSHY OR GOOEY. (ACCORDING TO HER, "THEY TASTE BETTER THAN THEY LOOK.") SHE ALSO HAS AN UNCANNY ABILITY TO TRIP OVER NOTHING.
COMMENTS:	GENIUS-LEVEL INTELLIGENCE; IQ OVER 200. RANKS AS ONE OF THE WORLD'S TOP AUTHORITIES ON NANOTECHNOLOGY. TEARJU USED HER OWN DNA TO CREATE EVE, BUT THE EXACT DETAILS OF THAT EXPERIMENT ARE UNKNOWN.

CHAPTER 109: A NEW APOSTLE

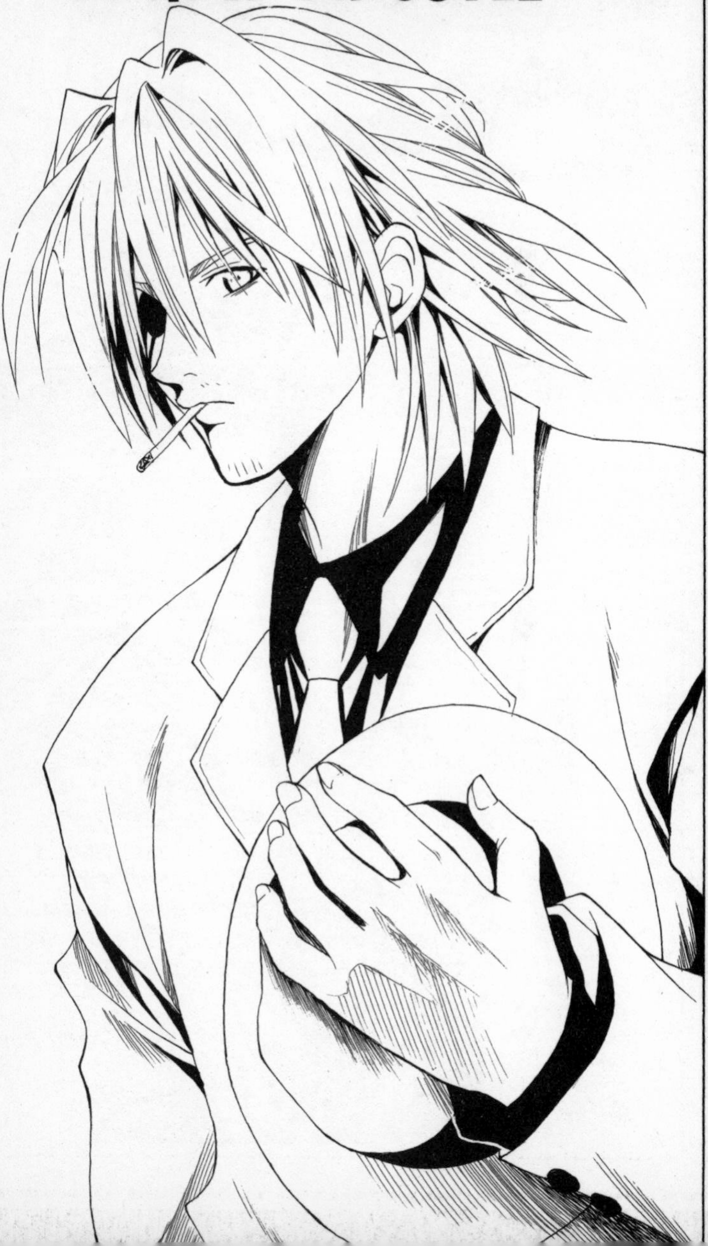

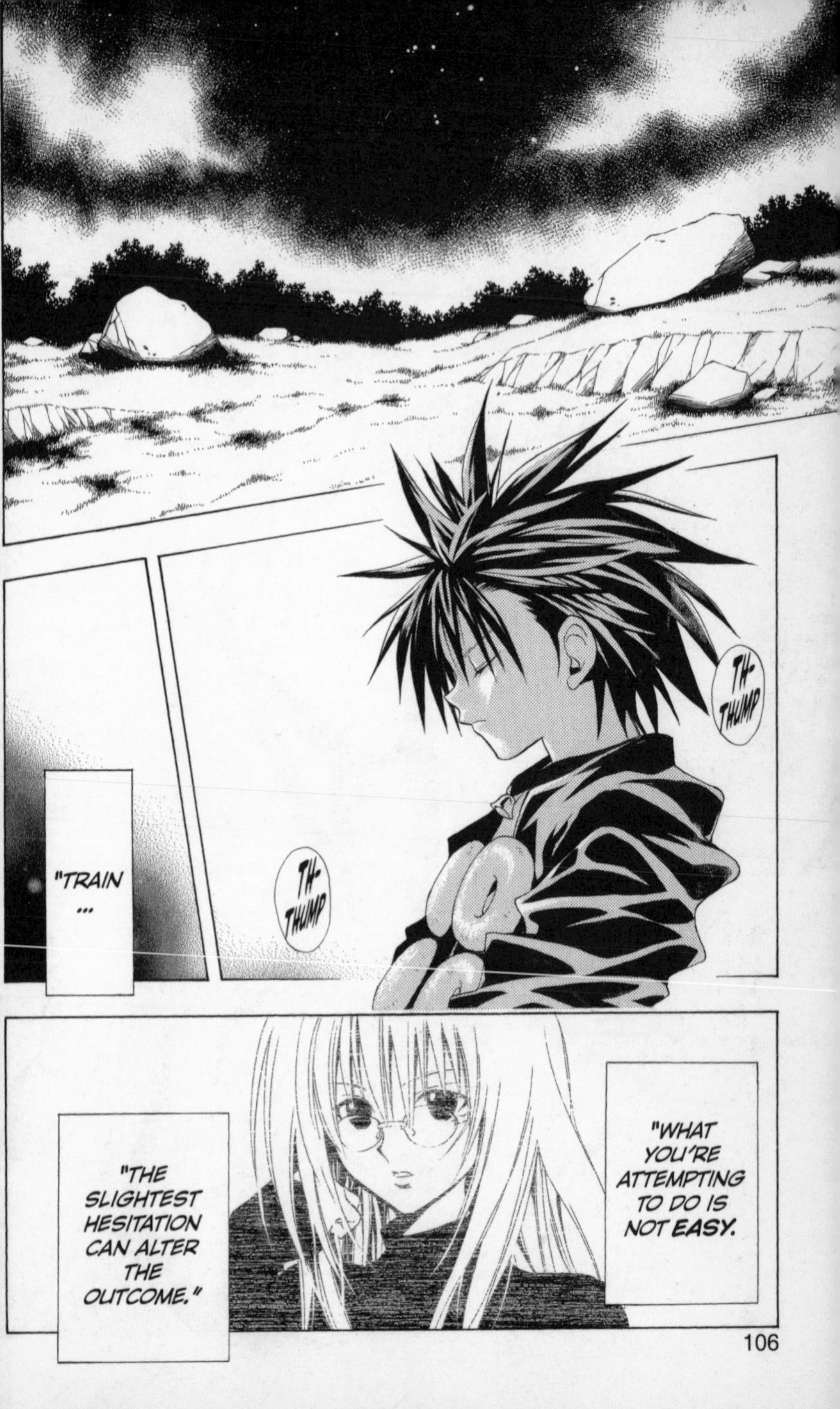
TH-THUMP
TH-THUMP
"TRAIN ...
"WHAT YOU'RE ATTEMPTING TO DO IS NOT EASY.
"THE SLIGHTEST HESITATION CAN ALTER THE OUTCOME."

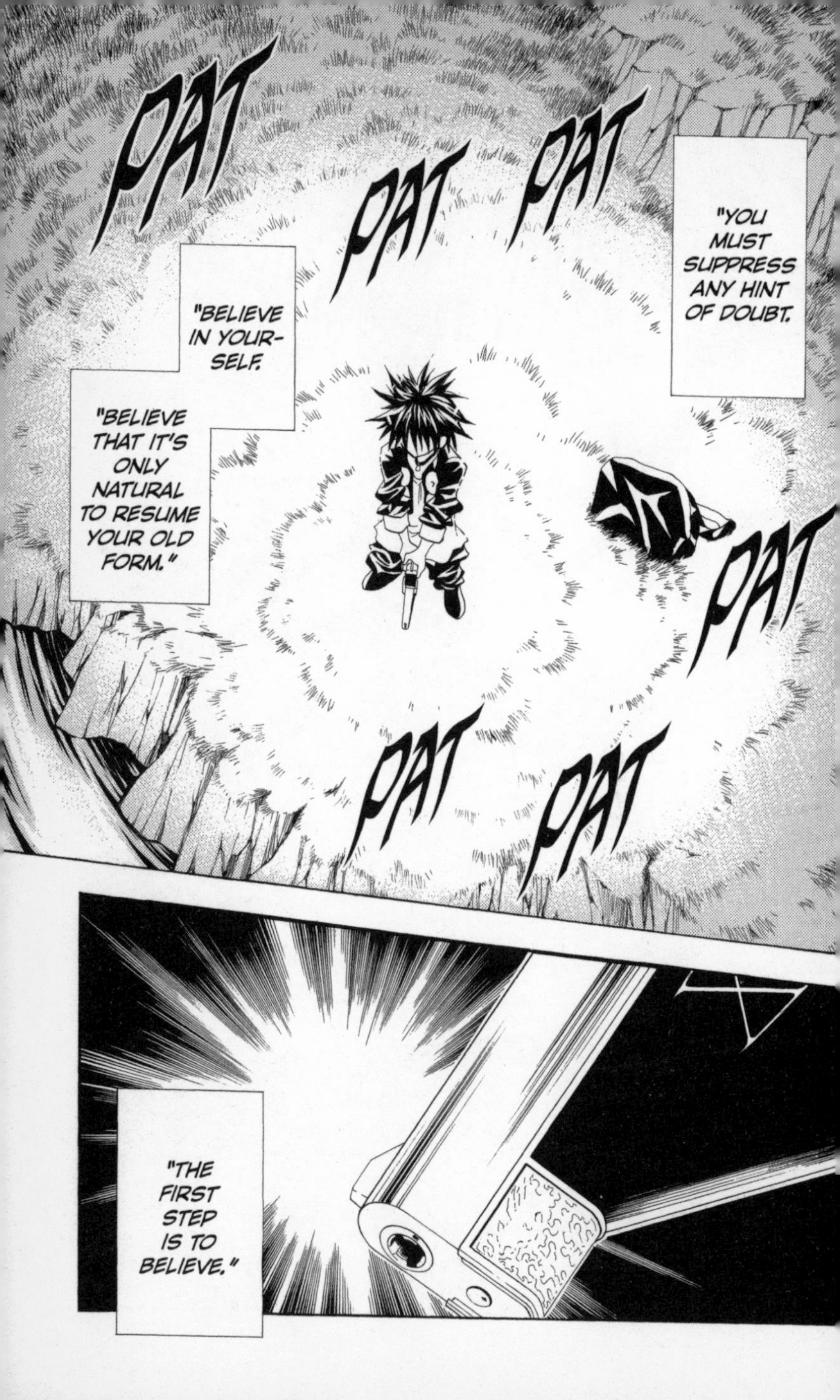
PAT
PAT
"YOU MUST SUPPRESS ANY HINT OF DOUBT.
PAT
"BELIEVE IN YOUR-SELF.
"BELIEVE THAT IT'S ONLY NATURAL TO RESUME YOUR OLD FORM."
PAT
PAT
PAT
"THE FIRST STEP IS TO BELIEVE."

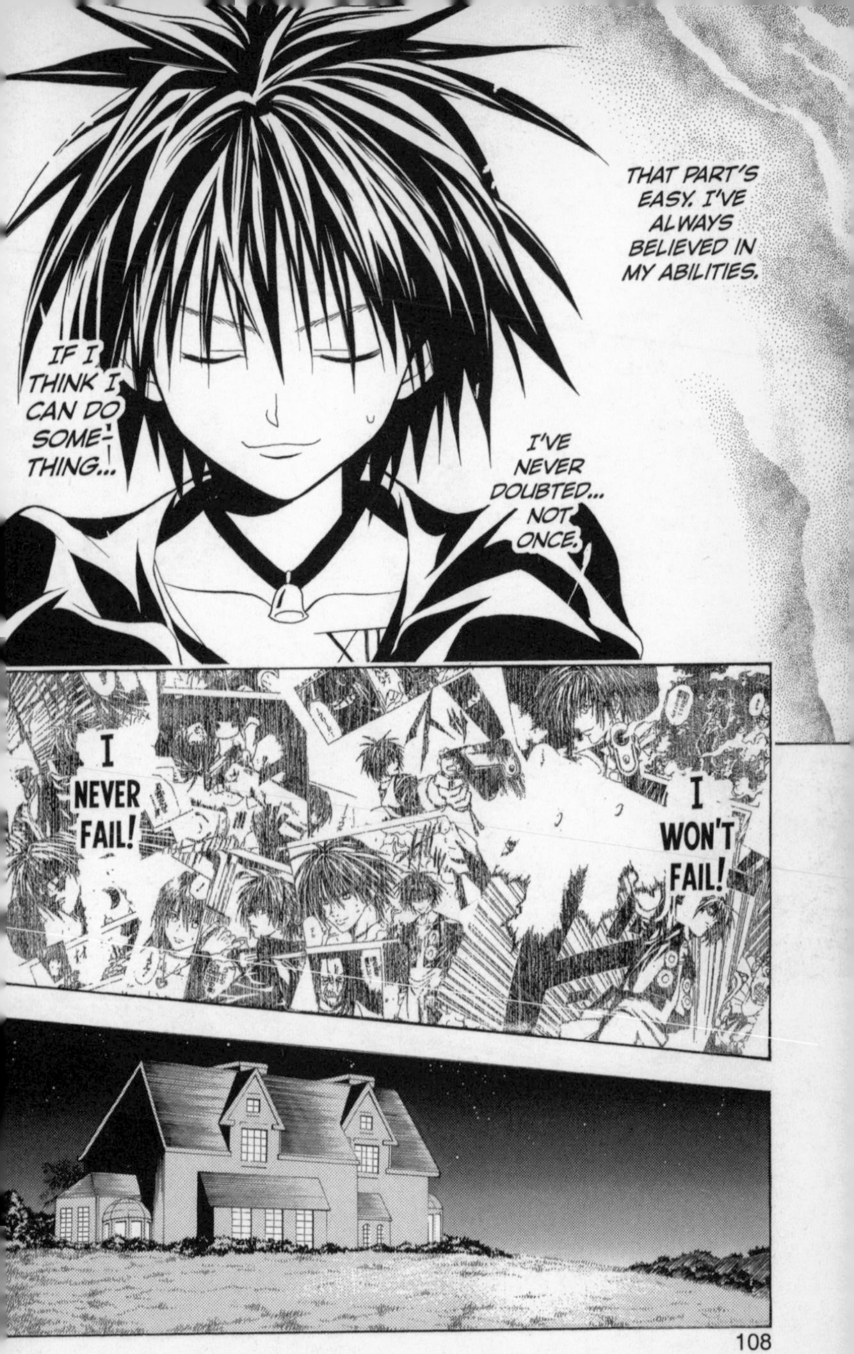
THAT PART'S EASY. I'VE ALWAYS BELIEVED IN MY ABILITIES.
I'VE NEVER DOUBTED... NOT ONCE.
IF I THINK I CAN DO SOME-THING...
I WON'T FAIL!
I NEVER FAIL!

READ THIS WAY

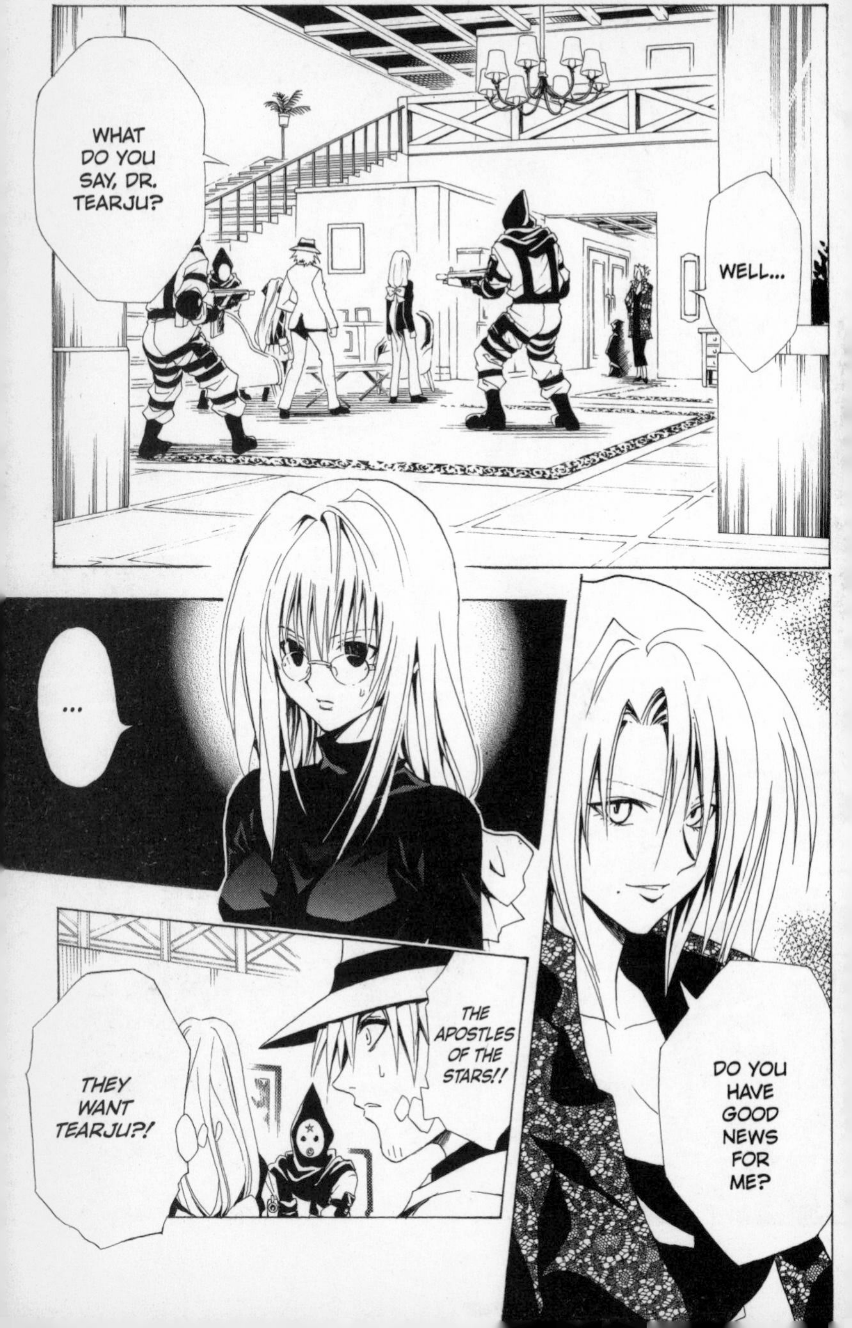
WHAT DO YOU SAY, DR. TEARJU?
WELL...
DO YOU HAVE GOOD NEWS FOR ME?
...
THE APOSTLES OF THE STARS!!
THEY WANT TEARJU?!

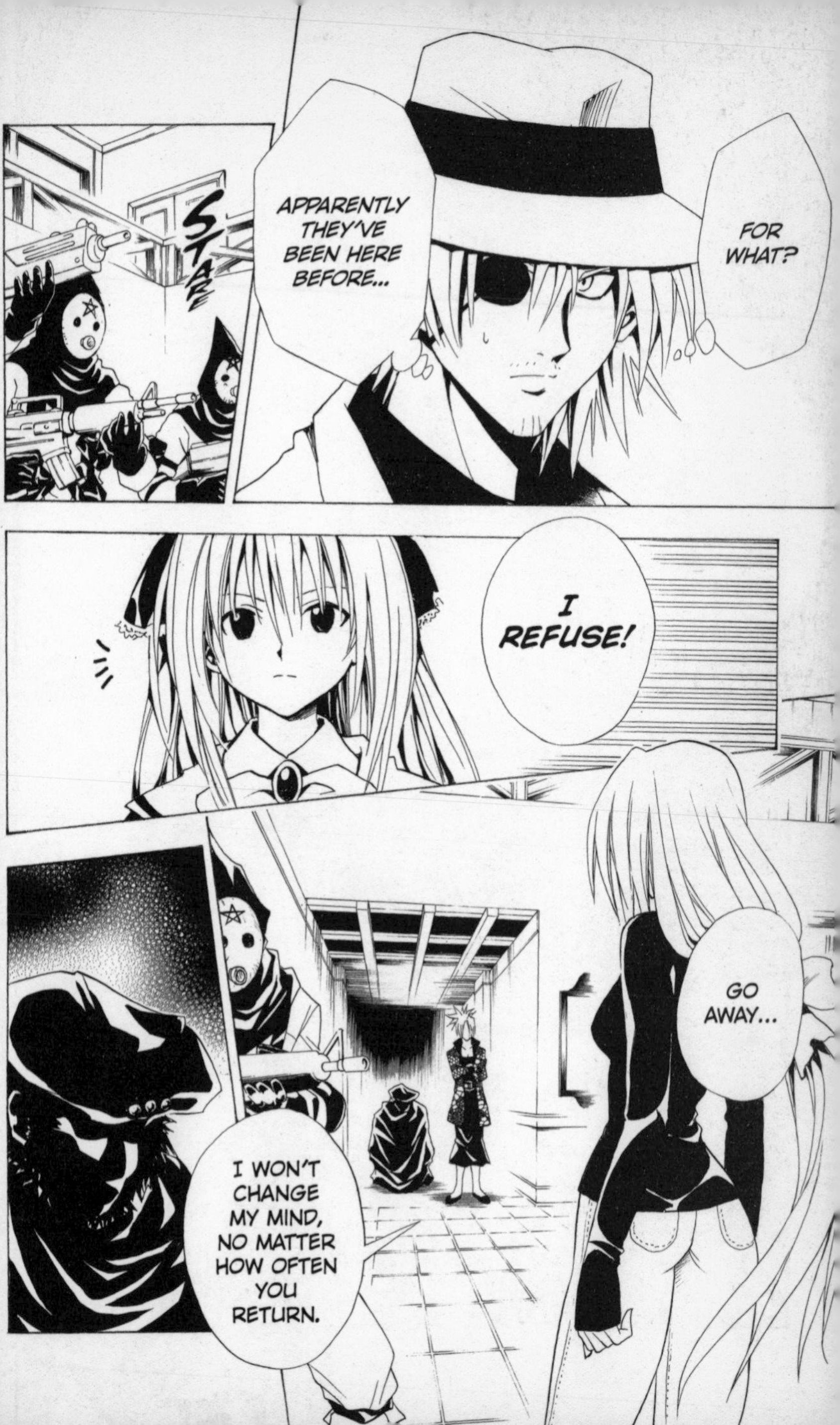
FOR WHAT?
APPARENTLY THEY'VE BEEN HERE BEFORE...
STARE
I REFUSE!
GO AWAY...
I WON'T CHANGE MY MIND, NO MATTER HOW OFTEN YOU RETURN.

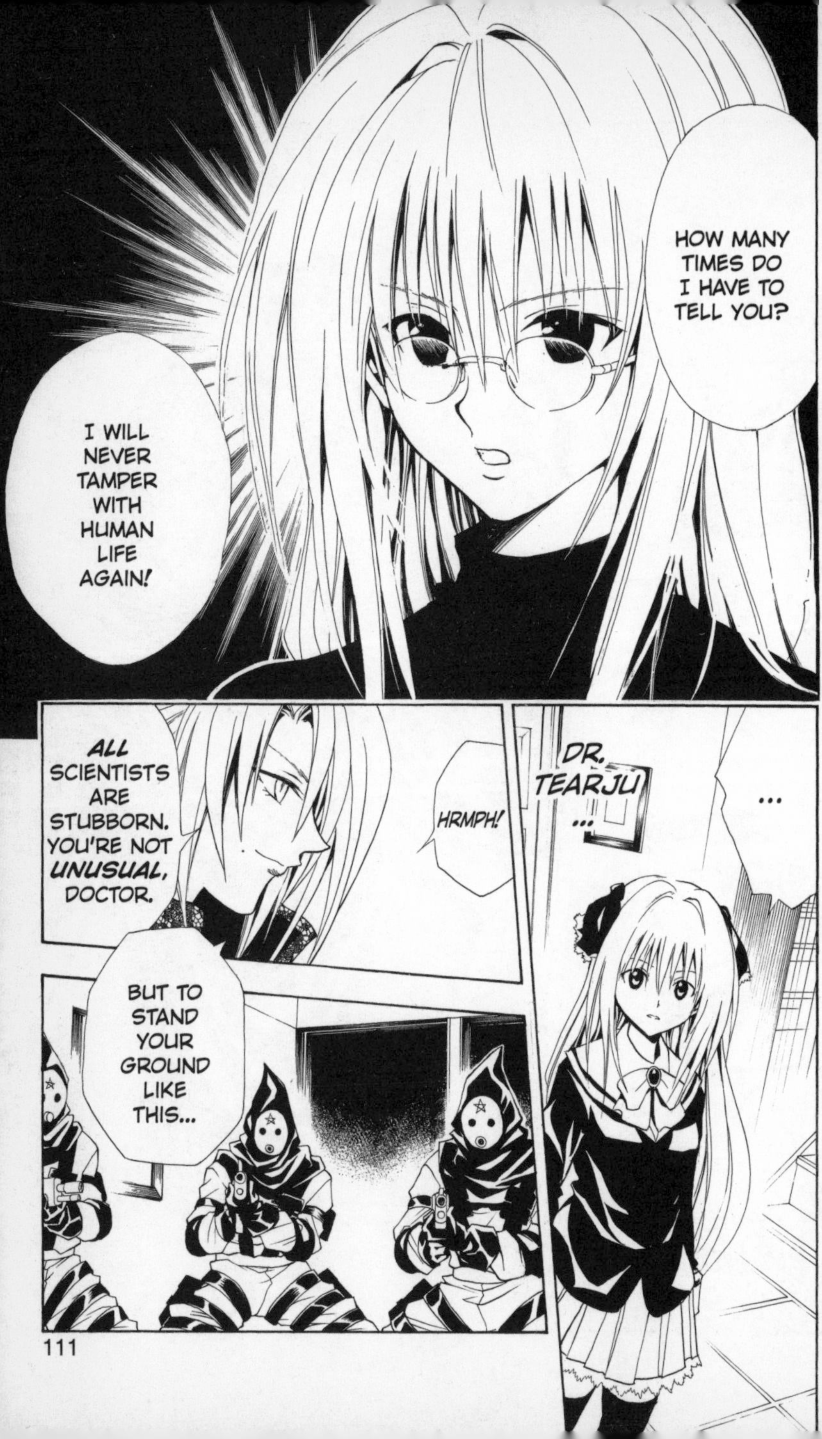
HOW MANY TIMES DO I HAVE TO TELL YOU?
I WILL NEVER TAMPER WITH HUMAN LIFE AGAIN!
...
DR. TEARJU ...
HRMPH!
ALL SCIENTISTS ARE STUBBORN. YOU'RE NOT *UNUSUAL,* DOCTOR.
BUT TO STAND YOUR GROUND LIKE THIS...

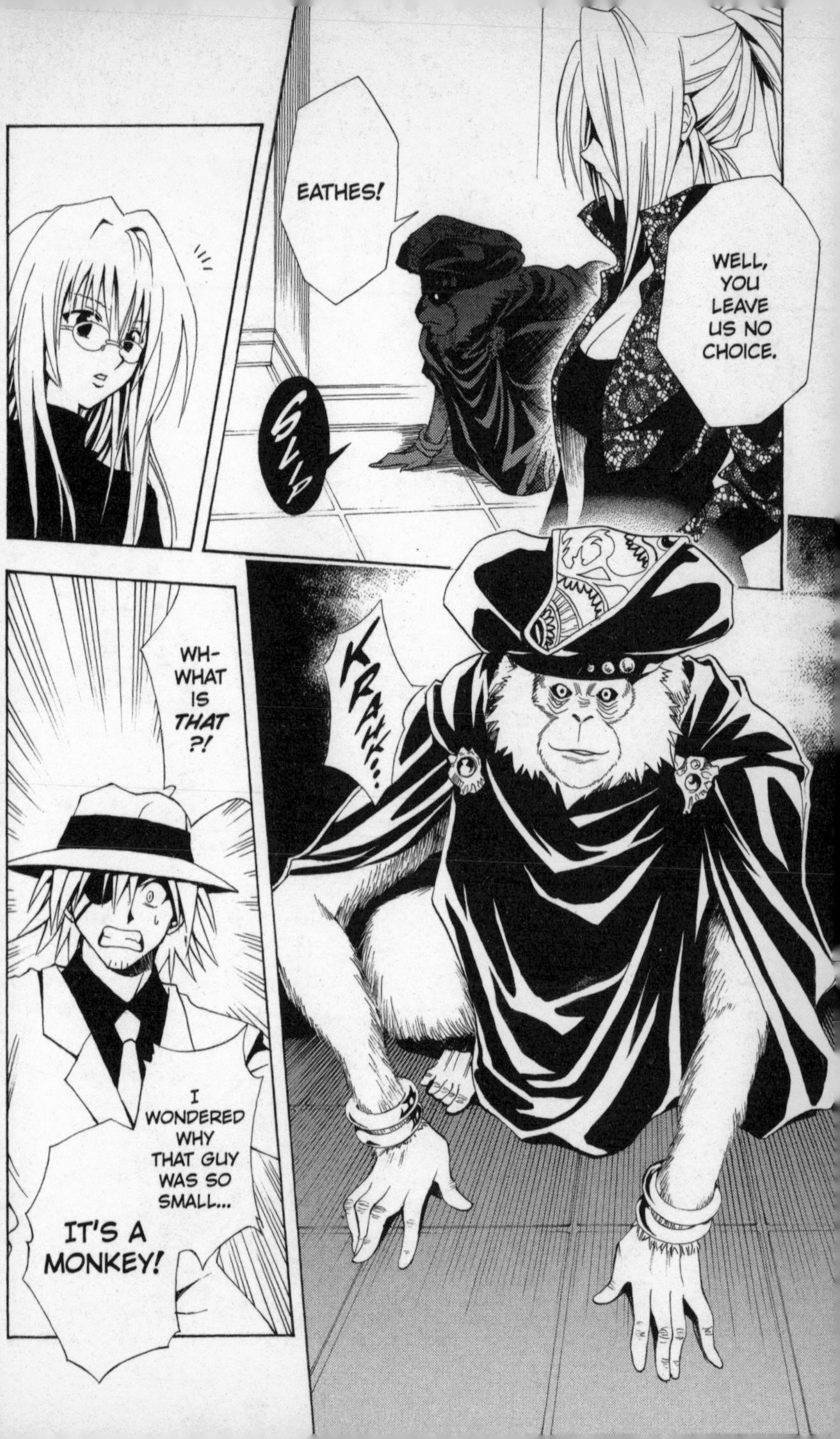
WELL, YOU LEAVE US NO CHOICE.
EATHES!
SLIP
KRAAK...
WH-WHAT IS THAT?!
I WONDERED WHY THAT GUY WAS SO SMALL...
IT'S A MONKEY!

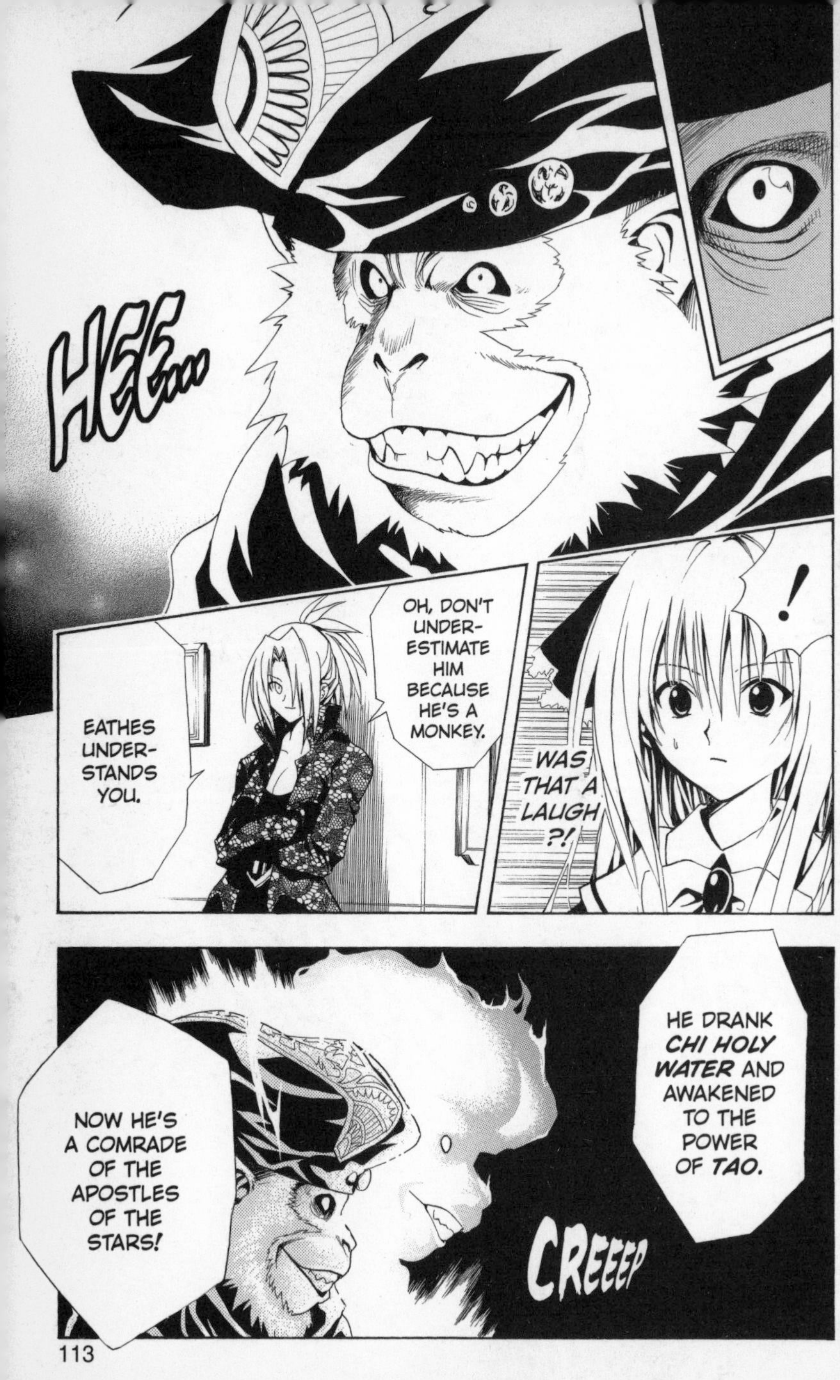
HEE...
!
WAS THAT A LAUGH?!
OH, DON'T UNDERESTIMATE HIM BECAUSE HE'S A MONKEY.
EATHES UNDERSTANDS YOU.
HE DRANK *CHI HOLY WATER* AND AWAKENED TO THE POWER OF *TAO*.
CREEEP
NOW HE'S A COMRADE OF THE APOSTLES OF THE STARS!

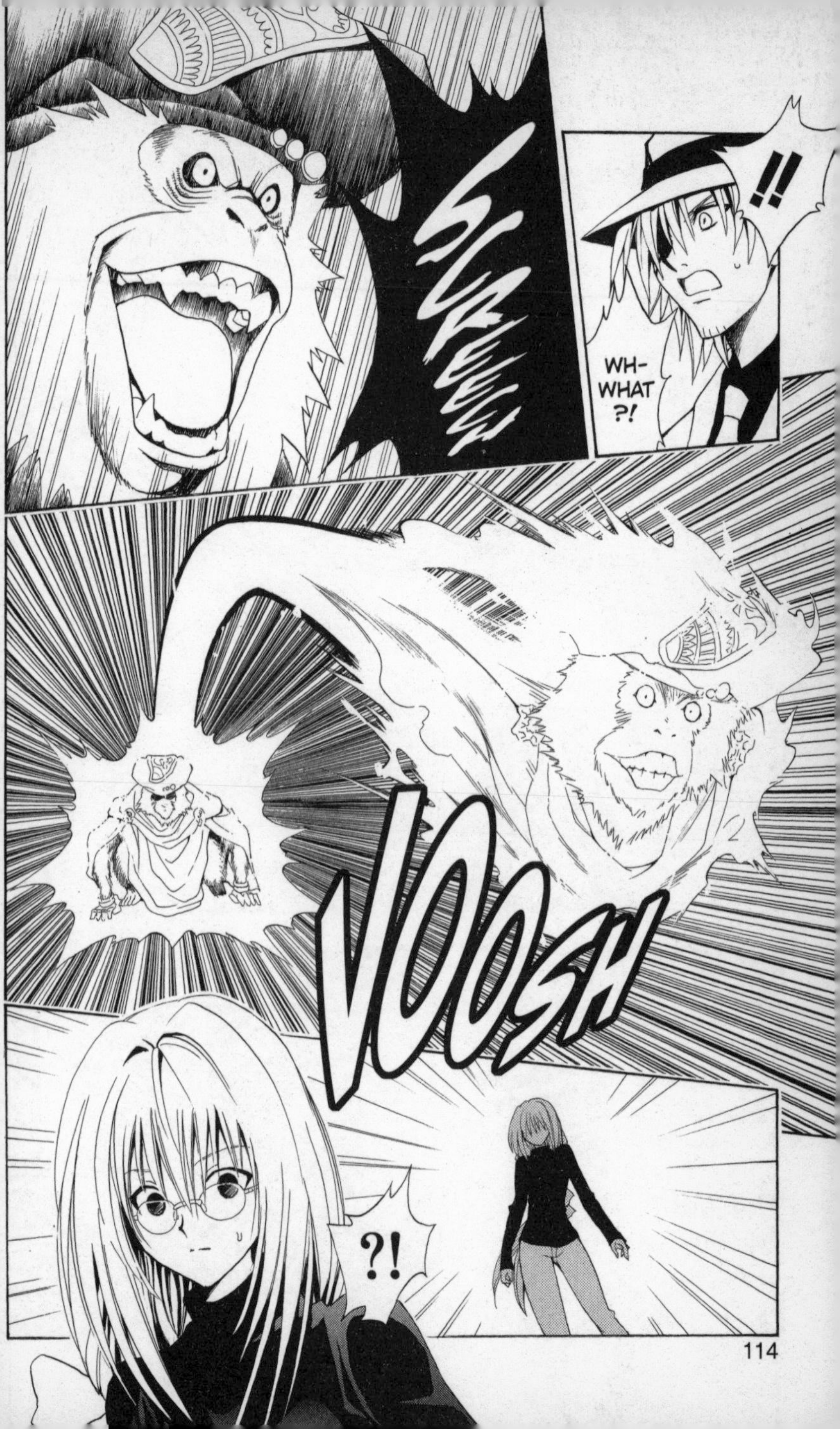
!!
WH-WHAT ?!
JOOSH
?!

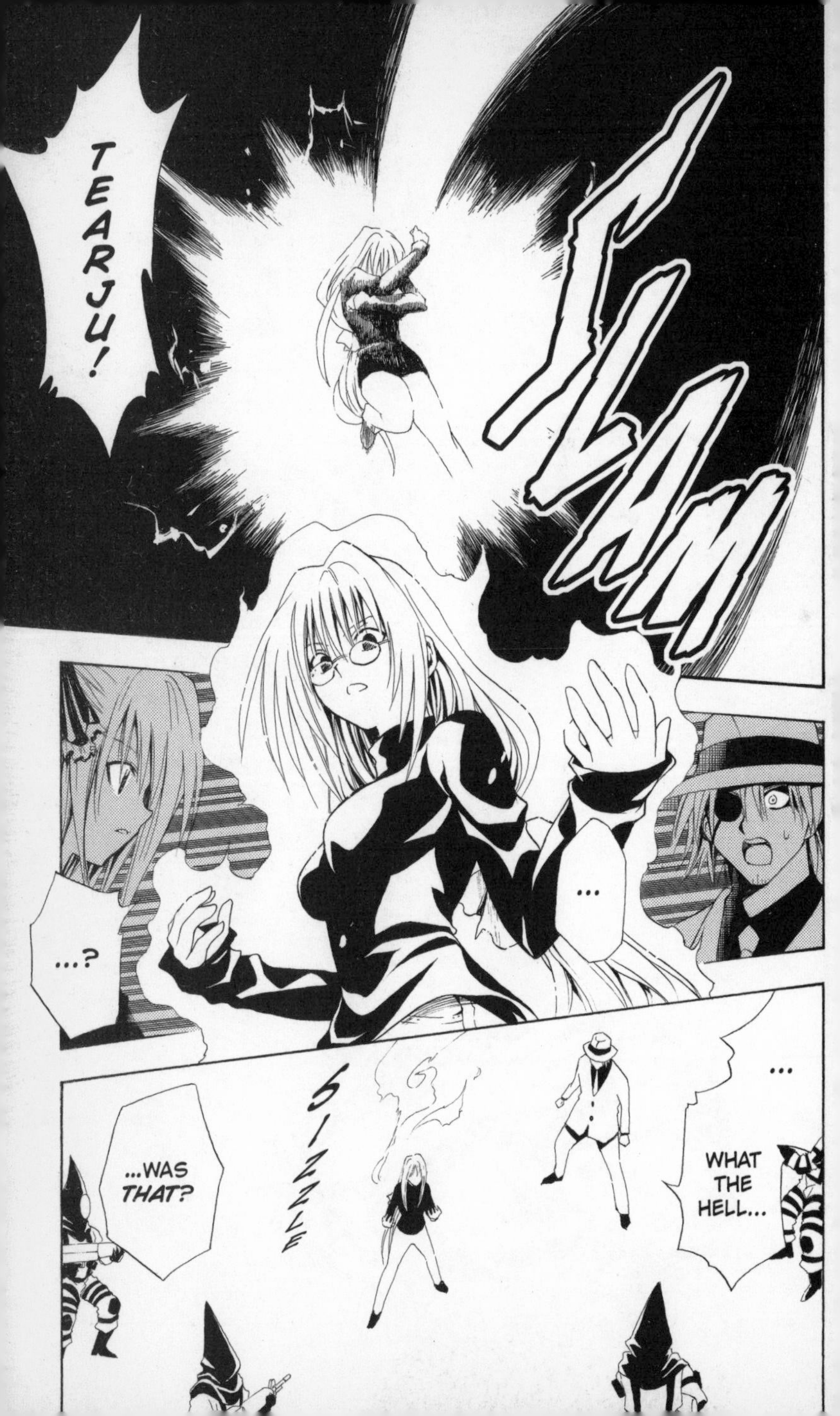
TEARJU!
...
...?
...
WHAT THE HELL...
SIZZLE
...WAS *THAT*?

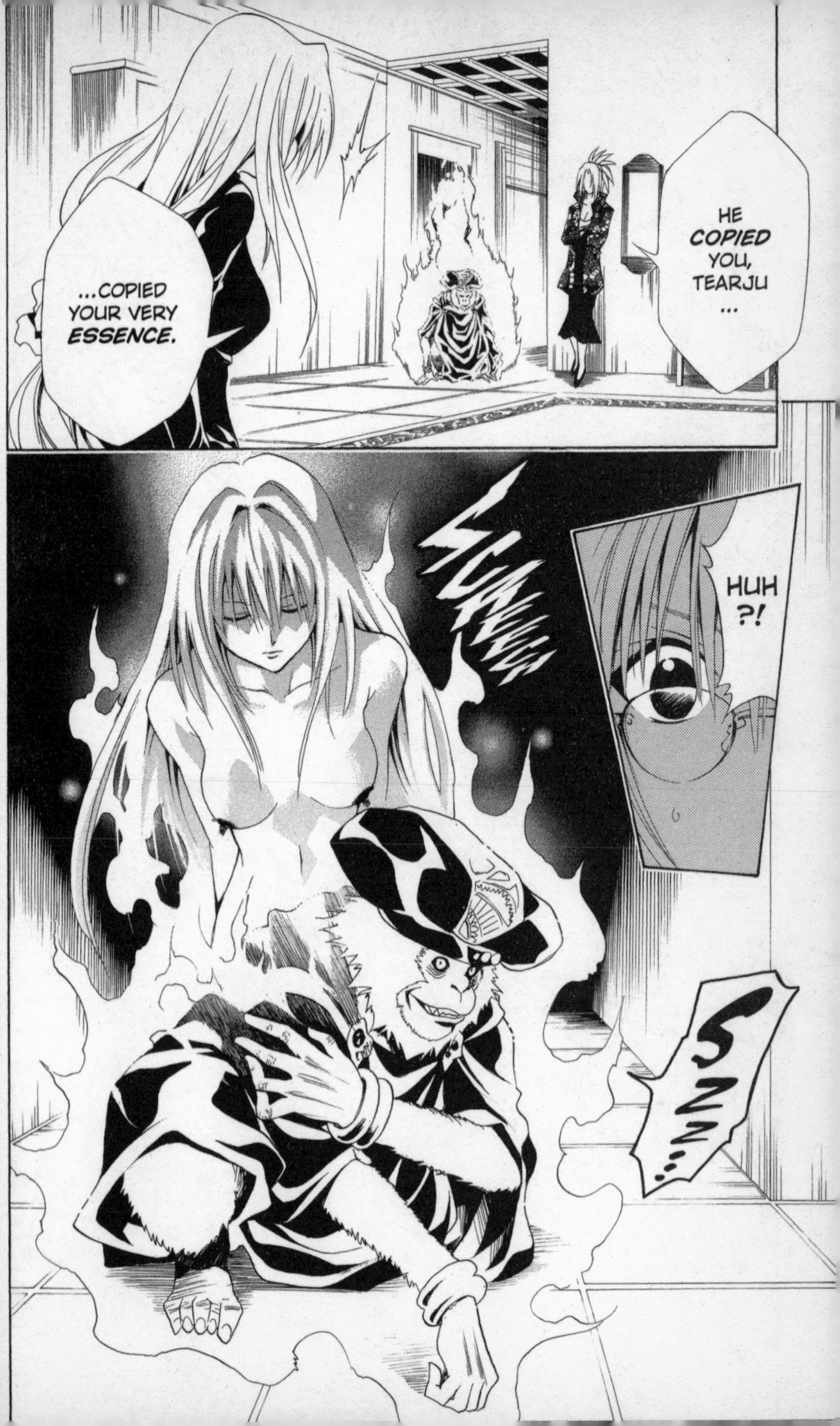
HE COPIED YOU, TEARJU ...
...COPIED YOUR VERY ESSENCE.
HUH ?!
SZZZ...

READ THIS WAY

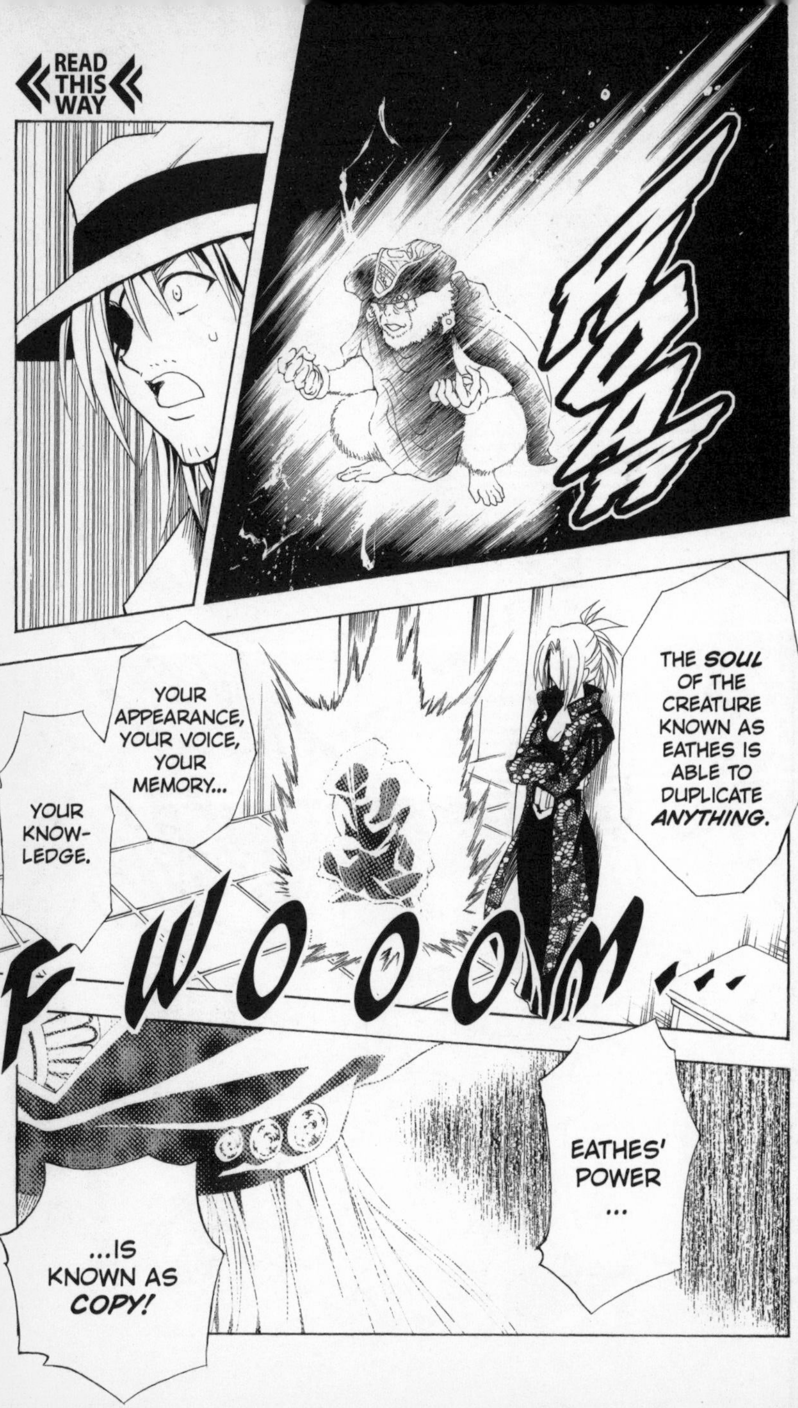
THE *SOUL* OF THE CREATURE KNOWN AS EATHES IS ABLE TO DUPLICATE *ANYTHING*.
YOUR APPEARANCE, YOUR VOICE, YOUR MEMORY...
YOUR KNOW-LEDGE.
FWOOOM...
EATHES' POWER ...
...IS KNOWN AS *COPY!*

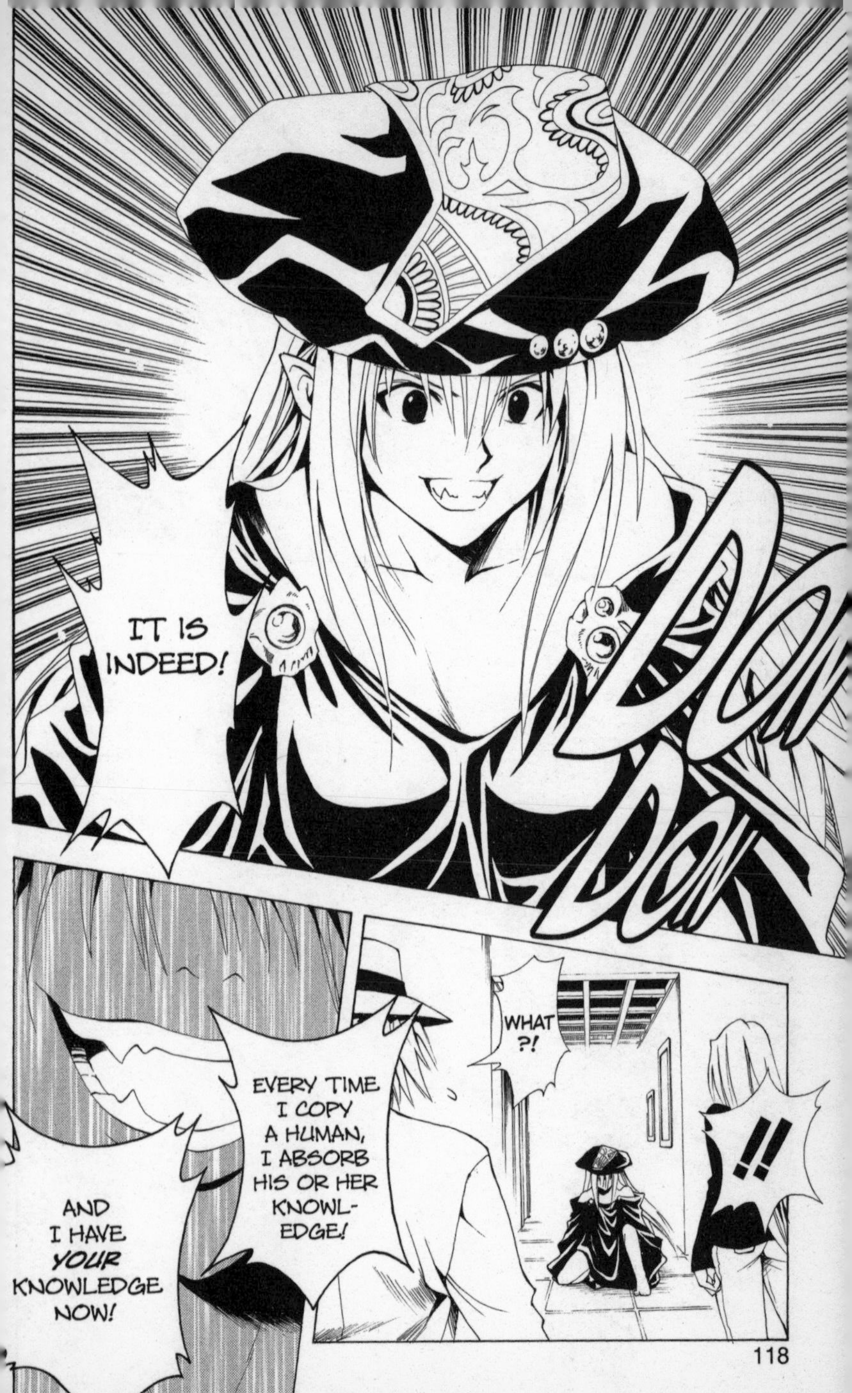
IT IS INDEED!
WHAT?!
!!
EVERY TIME I COPY A HUMAN, I ABSORB HIS OR HER KNOWL-EDGE!
AND I HAVE *YOUR* KNOWLEDGE NOW!

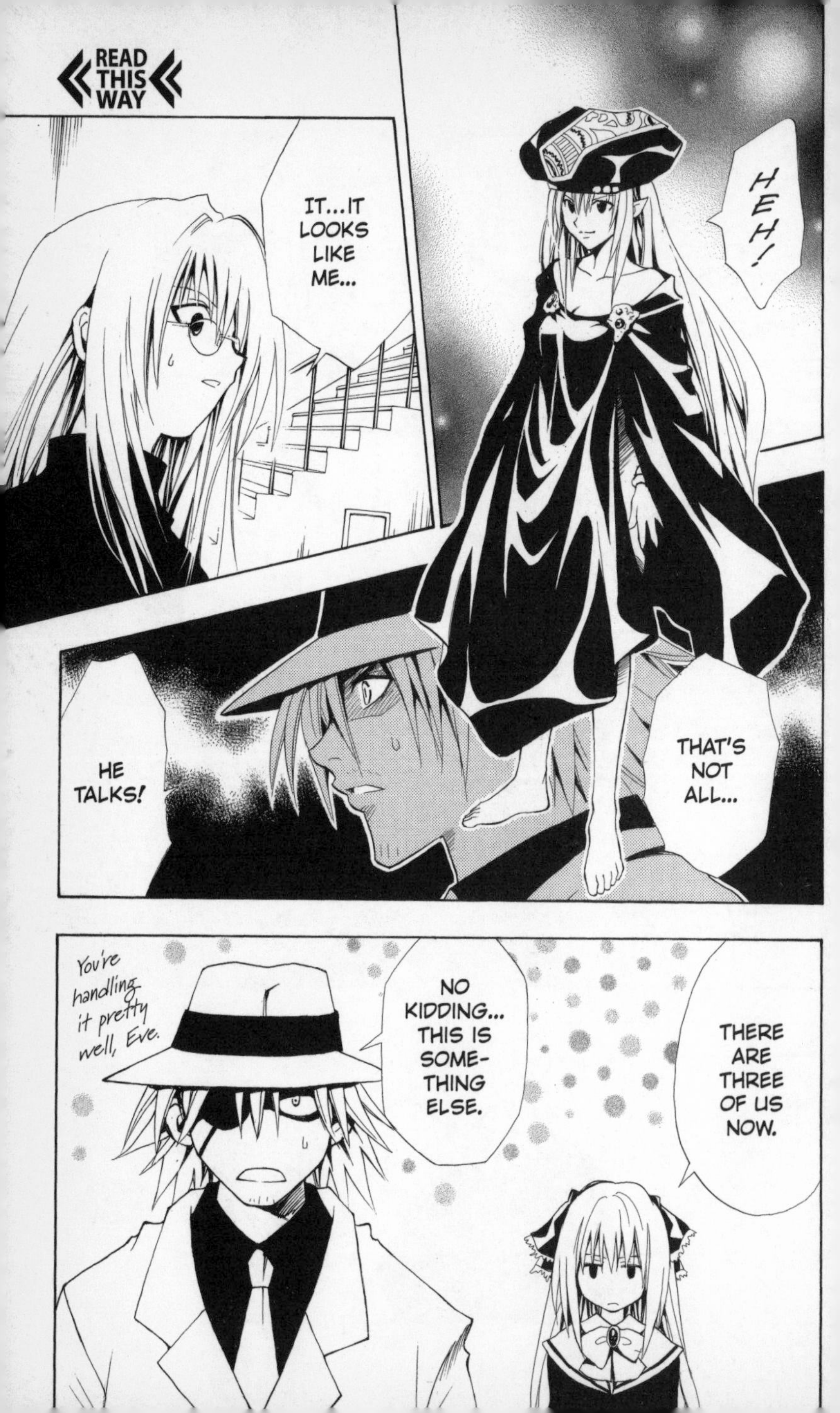
READ THIS WAY
HEH!
IT...IT LOOKS LIKE ME...
THAT'S NOT ALL...
HE TALKS!
THERE ARE THREE OF US NOW.
NO KIDDING... THIS IS SOME-THING ELSE.
You're handling it pretty well, Eve.

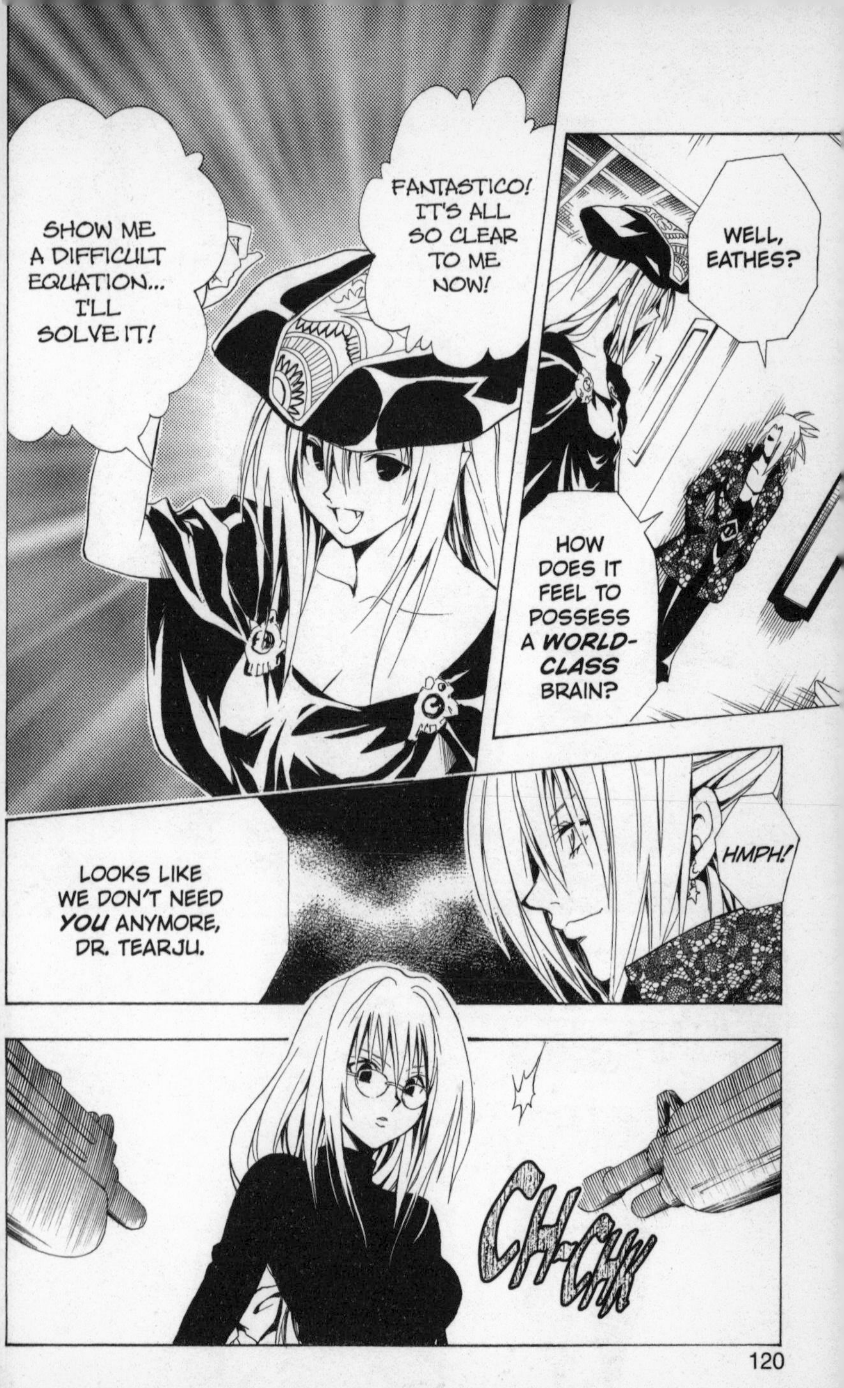
WELL, EATHES?
HOW DOES IT FEEL TO POSSESS A **WORLD-CLASS** BRAIN?
FANTASTICO! IT'S ALL SO CLEAR TO ME NOW!
SHOW ME A DIFFICULT EQUATION... I'LL SOLVE IT!
HMPH!
LOOKS LIKE WE DON'T NEED **YOU** ANYMORE, DR. TEARJU.
CH-CHK

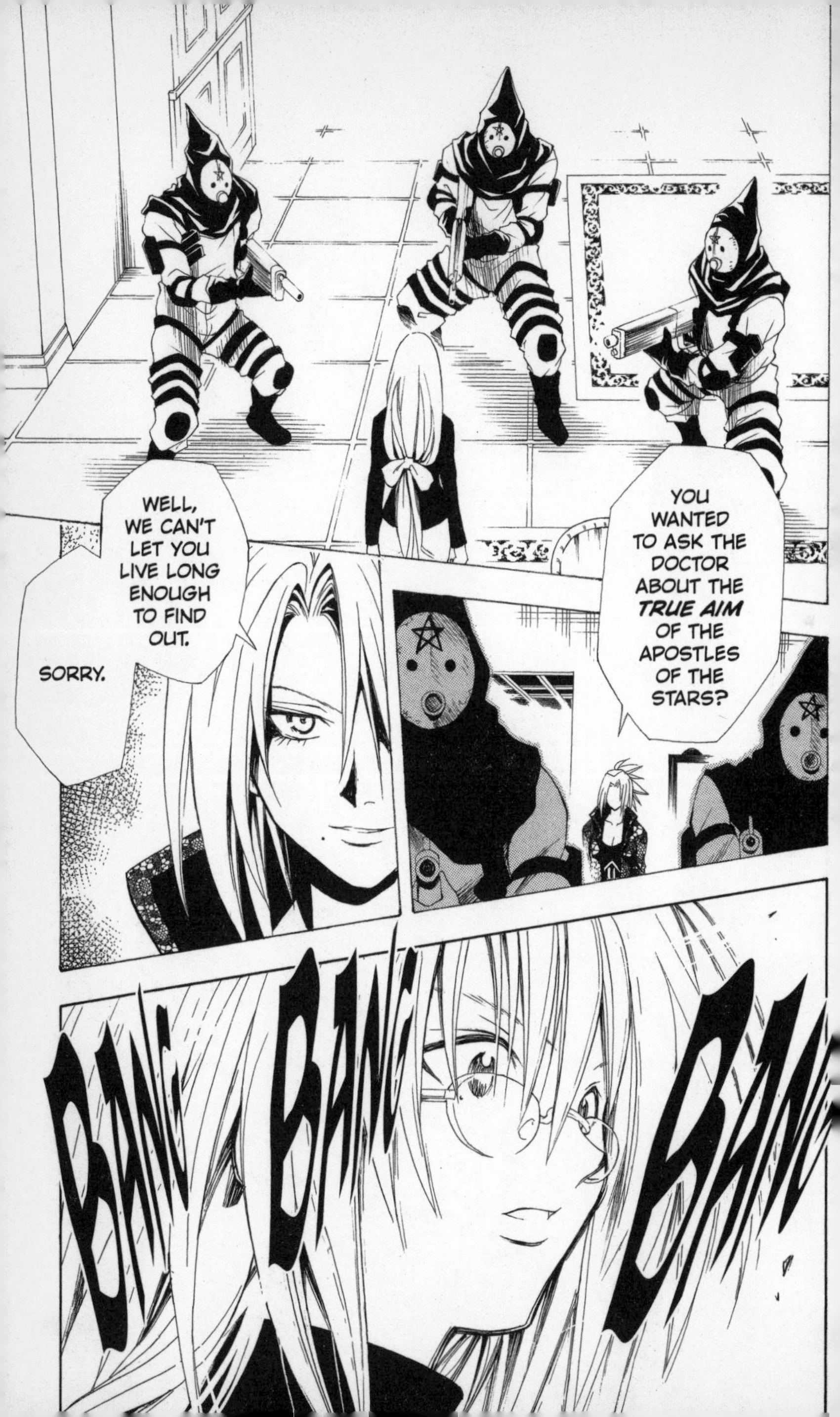
YOU WANTED TO ASK THE DOCTOR ABOUT THE ***TRUE AIM*** OF THE APOSTLES OF THE STARS?
WELL, WE CAN'T LET YOU LIVE LONG ENOUGH TO FIND OUT.
SORRY.
BAN
BANG
BANG

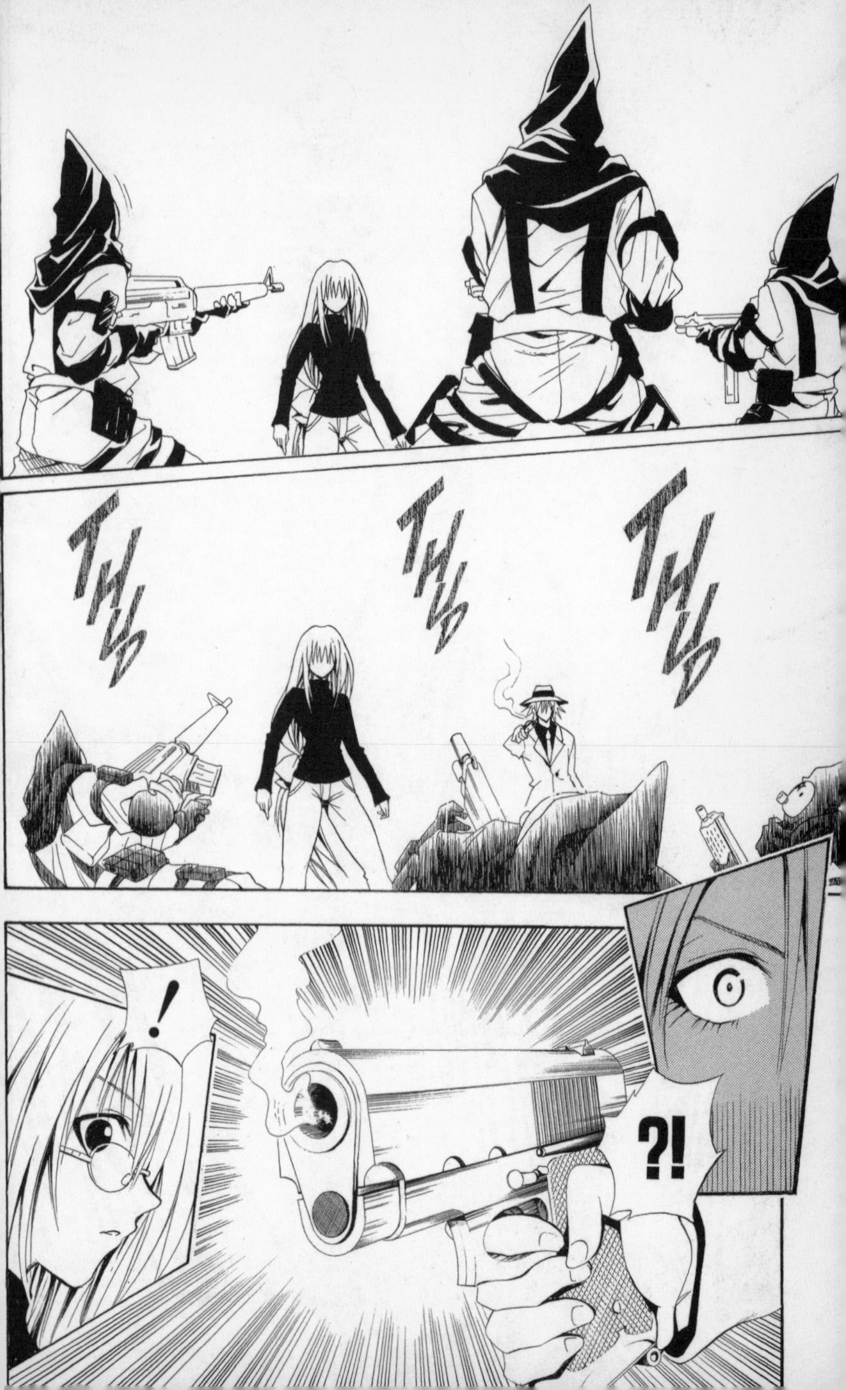
THUD
THUD
THUD
?!
!

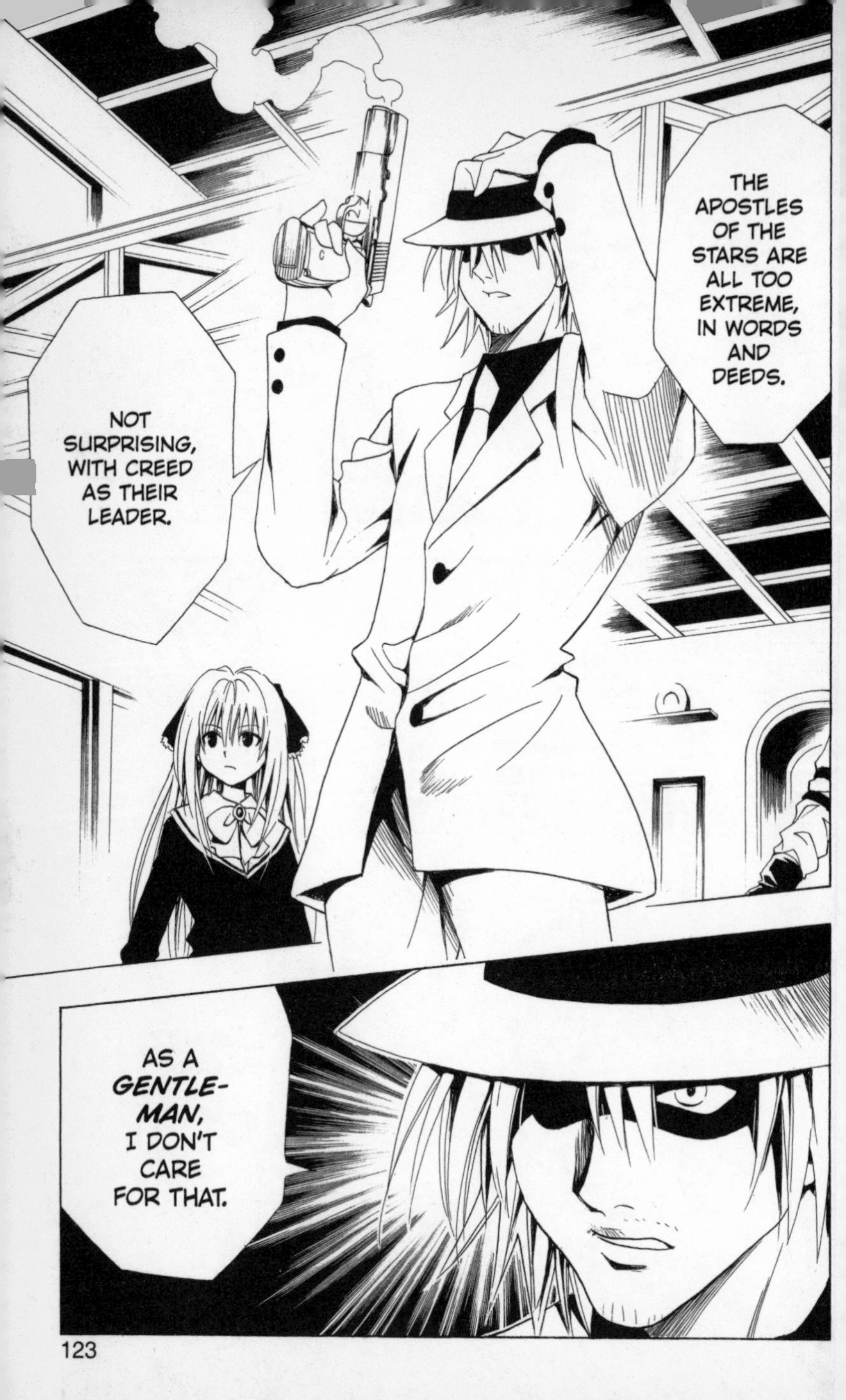
THE APOSTLES OF THE STARS ARE ALL TOO EXTREME, IN WORDS AND DEEDS.
NOT SURPRISING, WITH CREED AS THEIR LEADER.
AS A *GENTLEMAN*, I DON'T CARE FOR THAT.

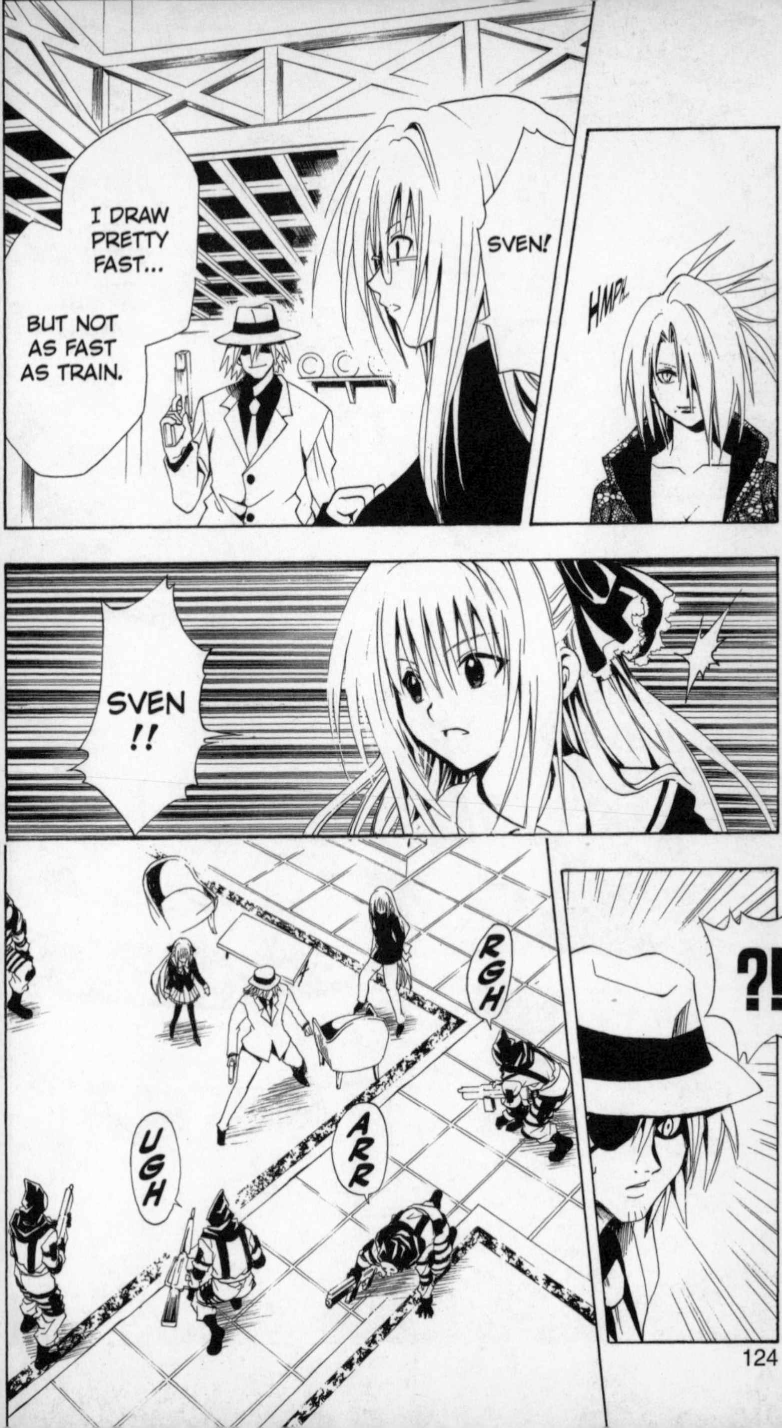
HMPH...
SVEN!
I DRAW PRETTY FAST...
BUT NOT AS FAST AS TRAIN.
SVEN !!
?!
RGH
ARR
UGH

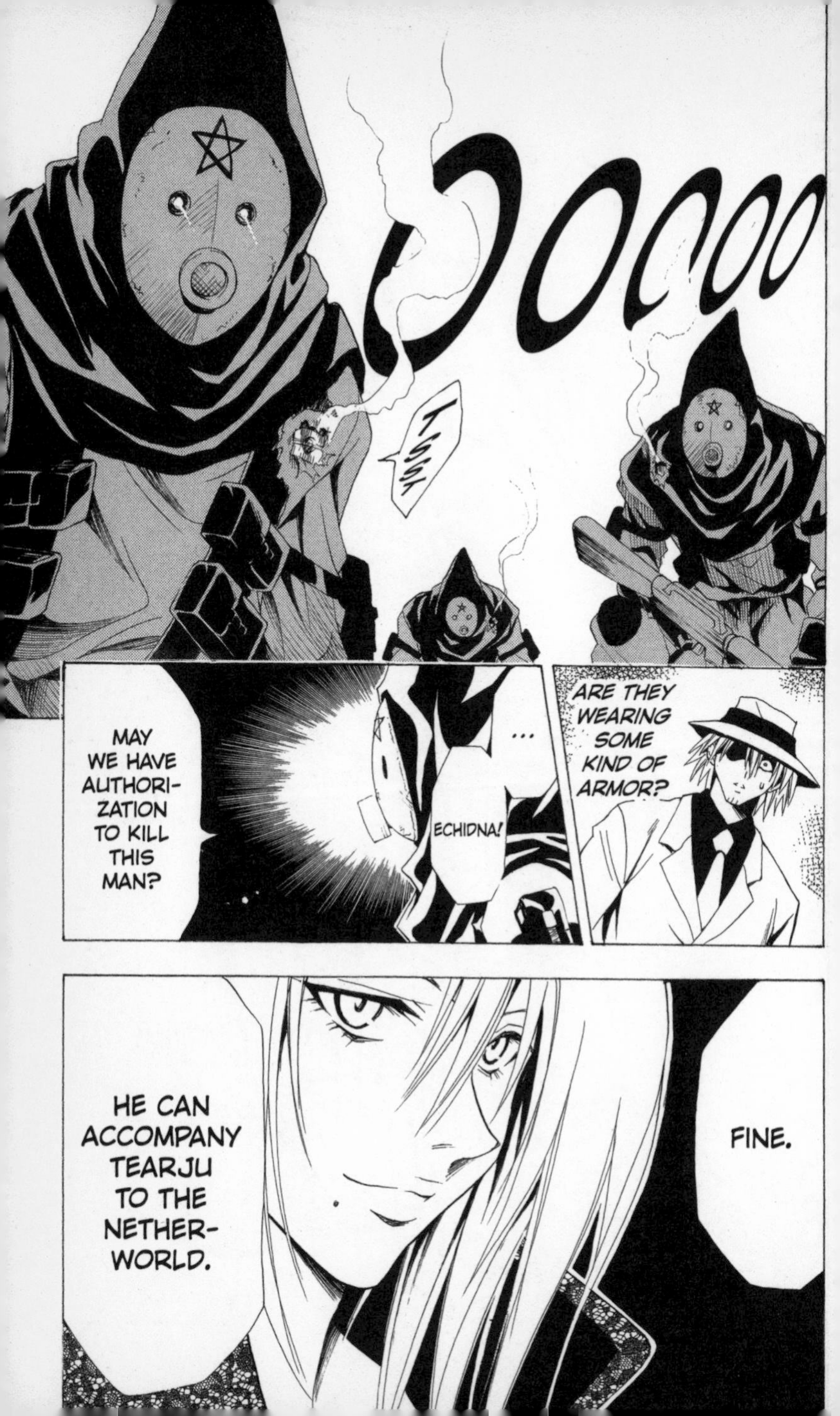
OOOOO
TSSK
ARE THEY WEARING SOME KIND OF ARMOR?
...
ECHIDNA!
MAY WE HAVE AUTHORI-ZATION TO KILL THIS MAN?
FINE.
HE CAN ACCOMPANY TEARJU TO THE NETHER-WORLD.

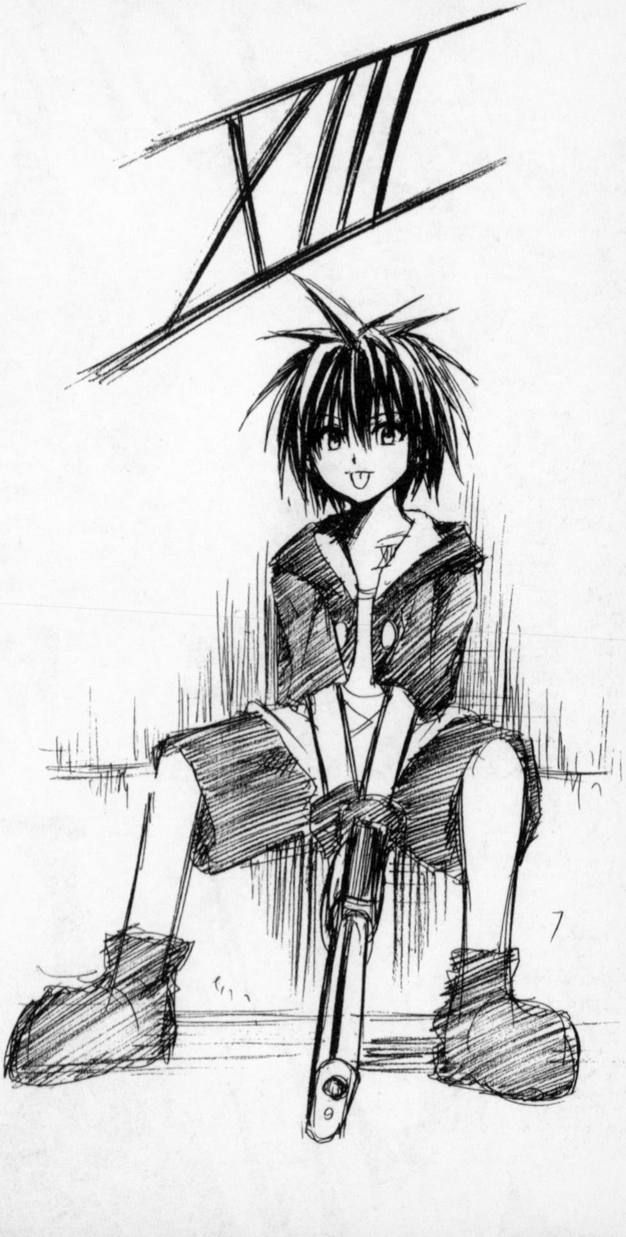

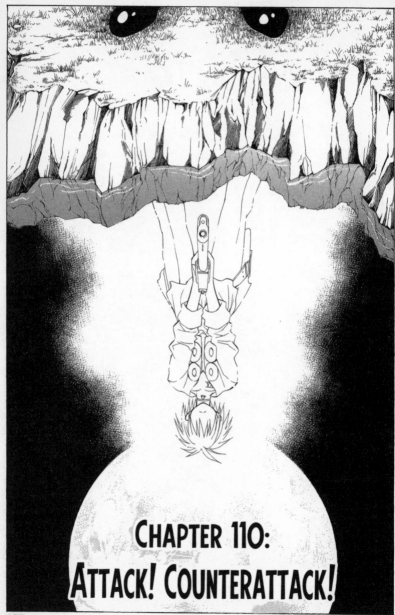

CHAPTER 110: ATTACK! COUNTERATTACK!

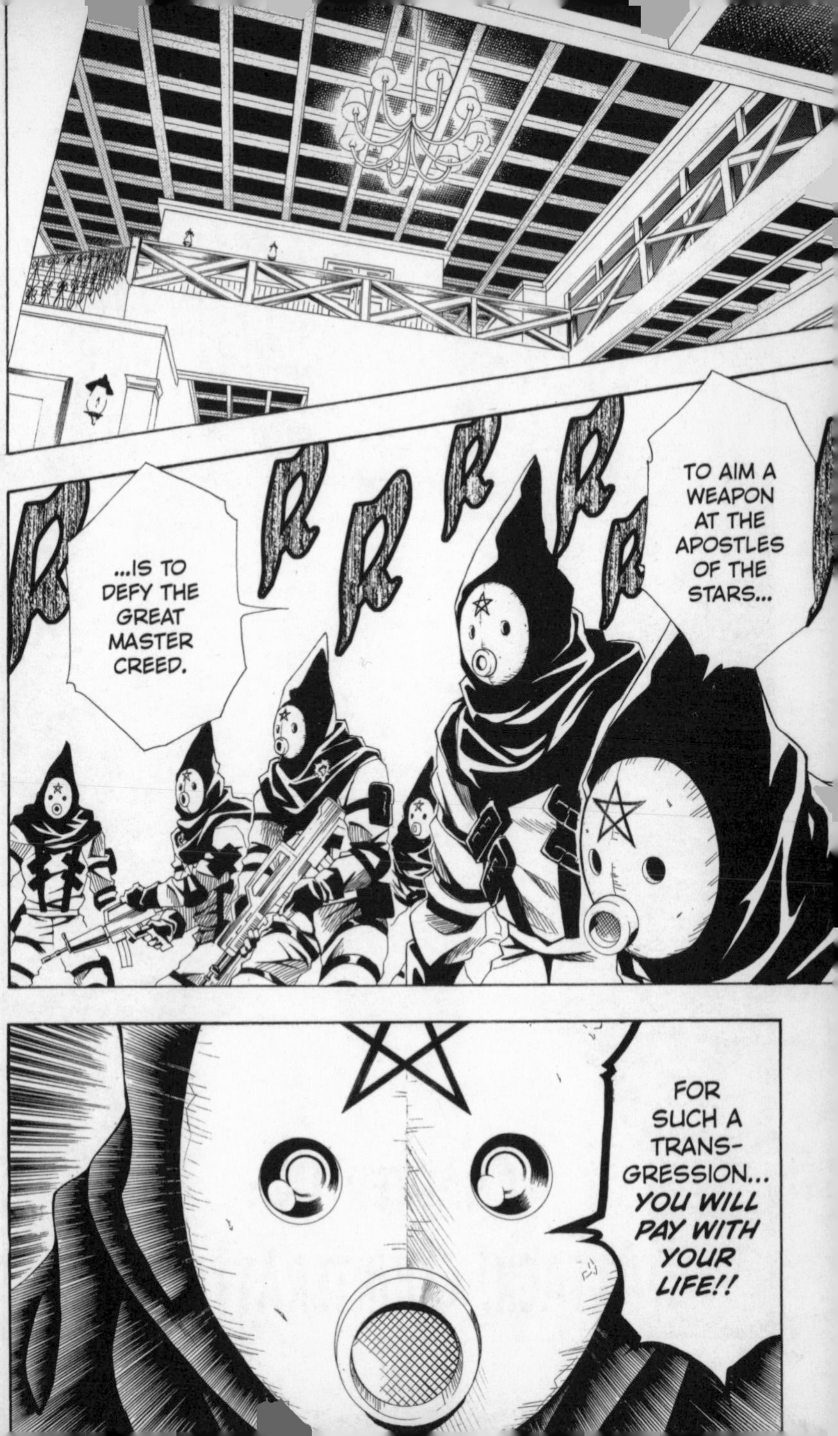
TO AIM A WEAPON AT THE APOSTLES OF THE STARS...
...IS TO DEFY THE GREAT MASTER CREED.
FOR SUCH A TRANS-GRESSION... *YOU WILL PAY WITH YOUR LIFE!!*

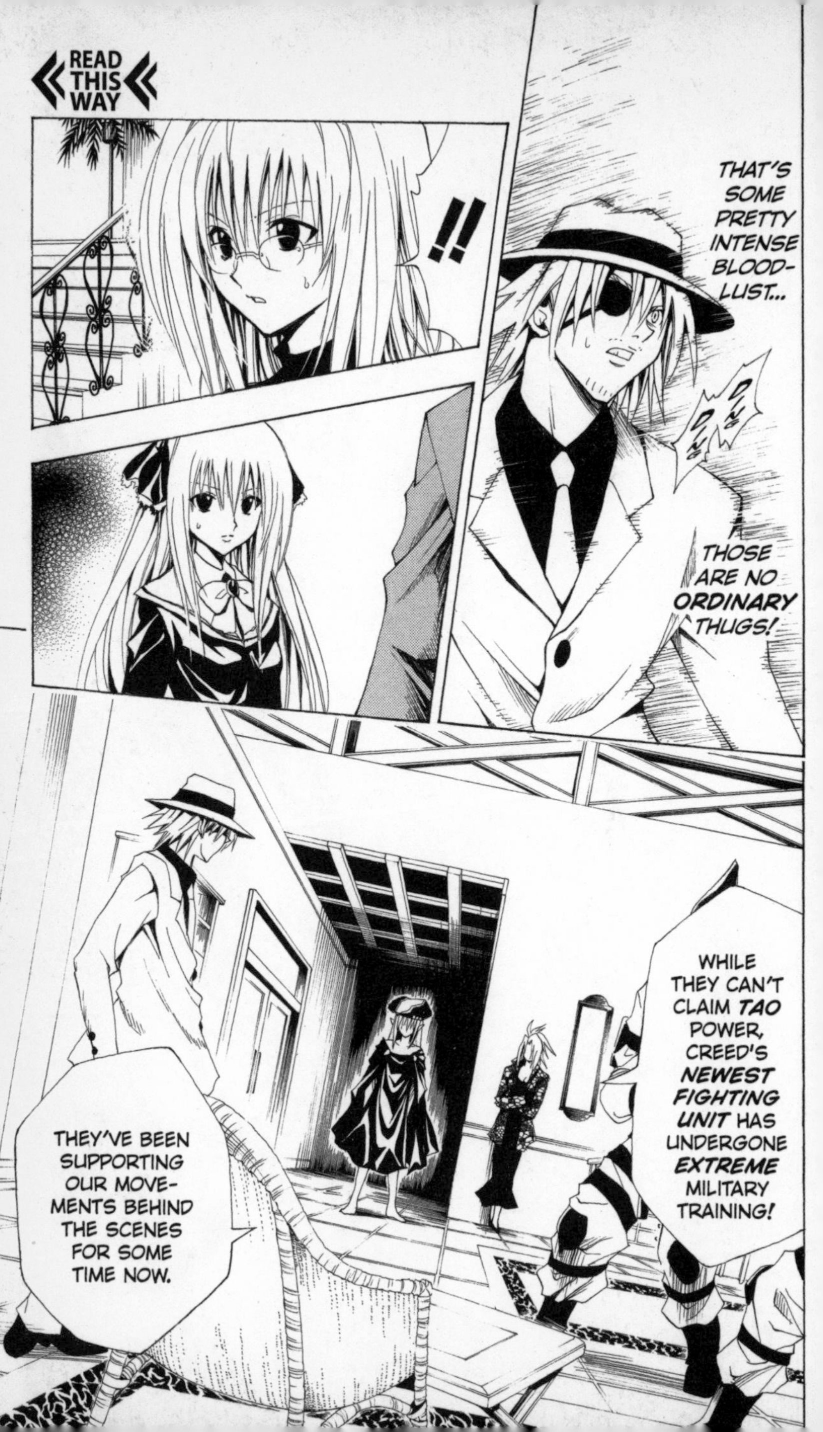
READ THIS WAY
THAT'S SOME PRETTY INTENSE BLOOD-LUST...
!!
DIN DIN
THOSE ARE NO ORDINARY THUGS!
WHILE THEY CAN'T CLAIM TAO POWER, CREED'S NEWEST FIGHTING UNIT HAS UNDERGONE EXTREME MILITARY TRAINING!
THEY'VE BEEN SUPPORTING OUR MOVE-MENTS BEHIND THE SCENES FOR SOME TIME NOW.

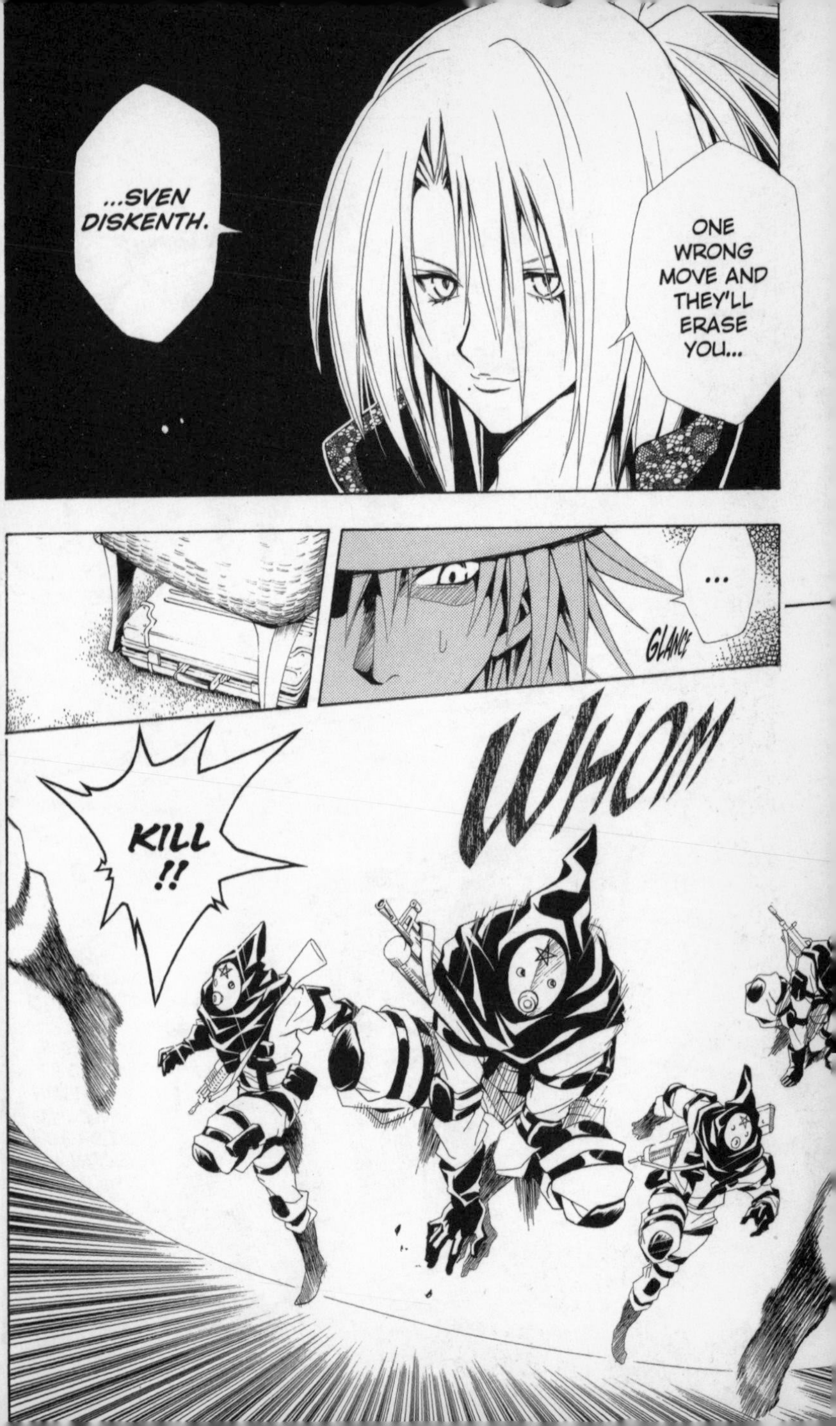
ONE WRONG MOVE AND THEY'LL ERASE YOU...
...SVEN DISKENTH.
...
GLANCE
WHOM
KILL!!

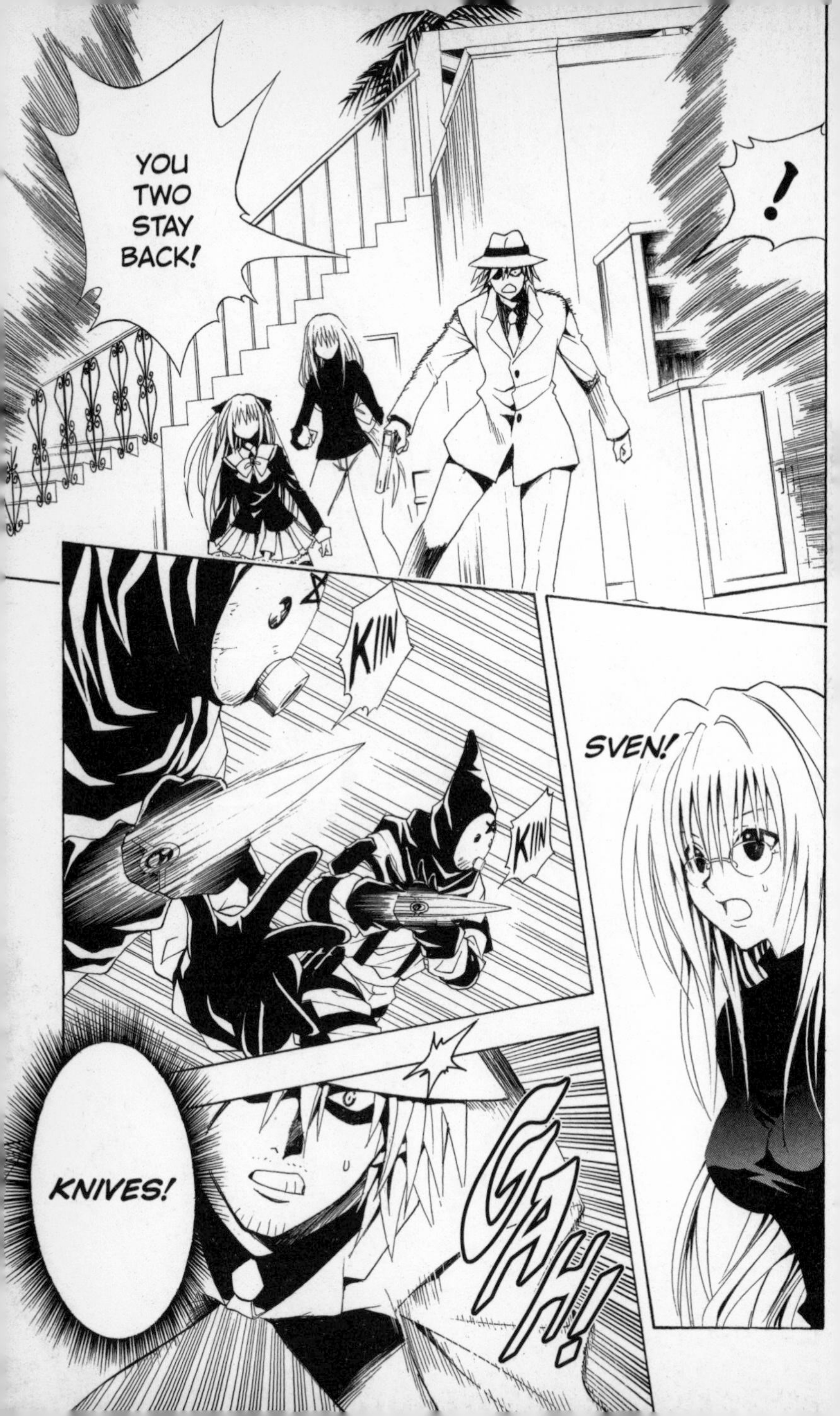
!
YOU TWO STAY BACK!
SVEN!
KIIN
KIIN
GAHH!
KNIVES!

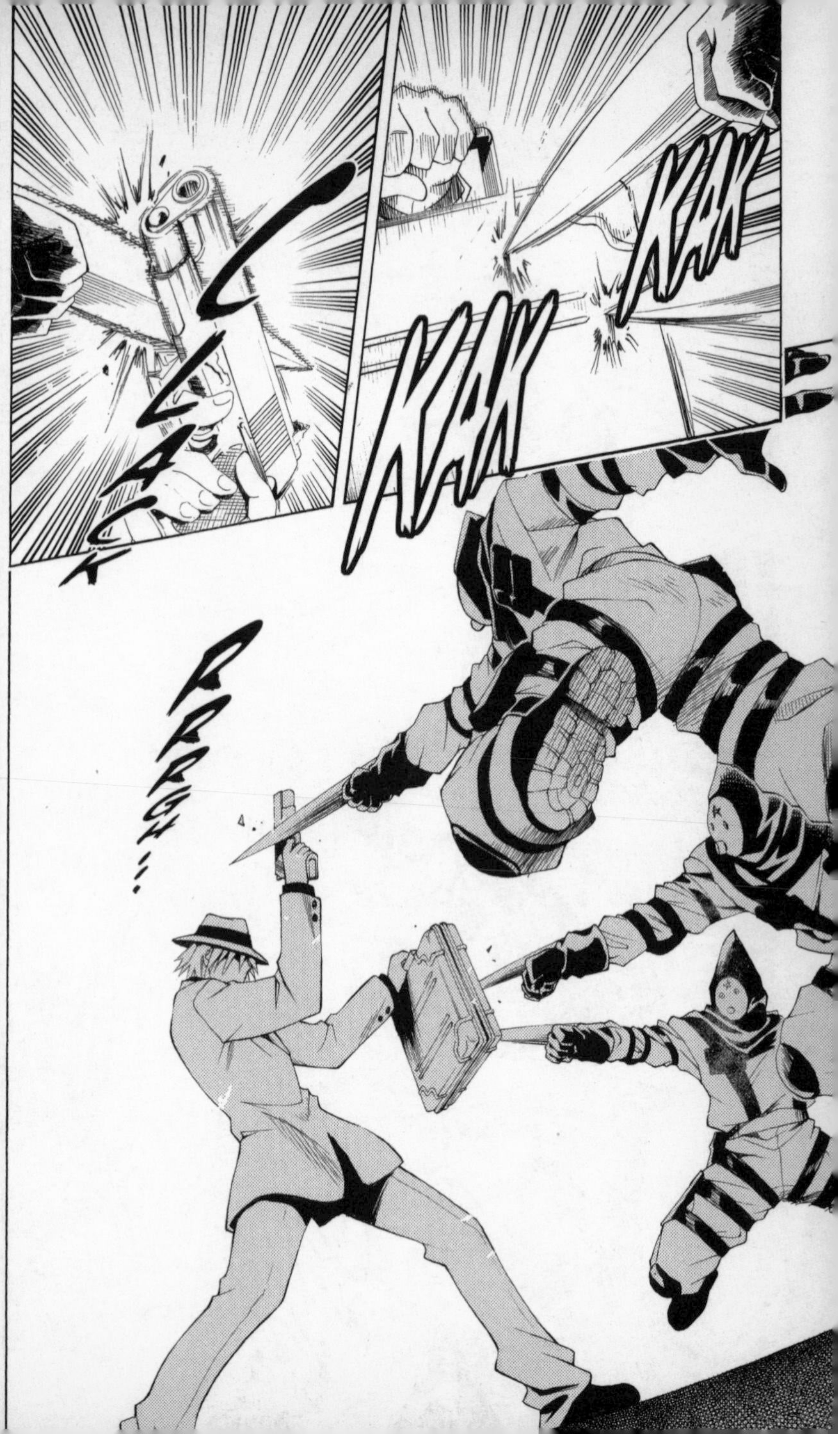
KAK KAK
CLACK
RRRGH!!

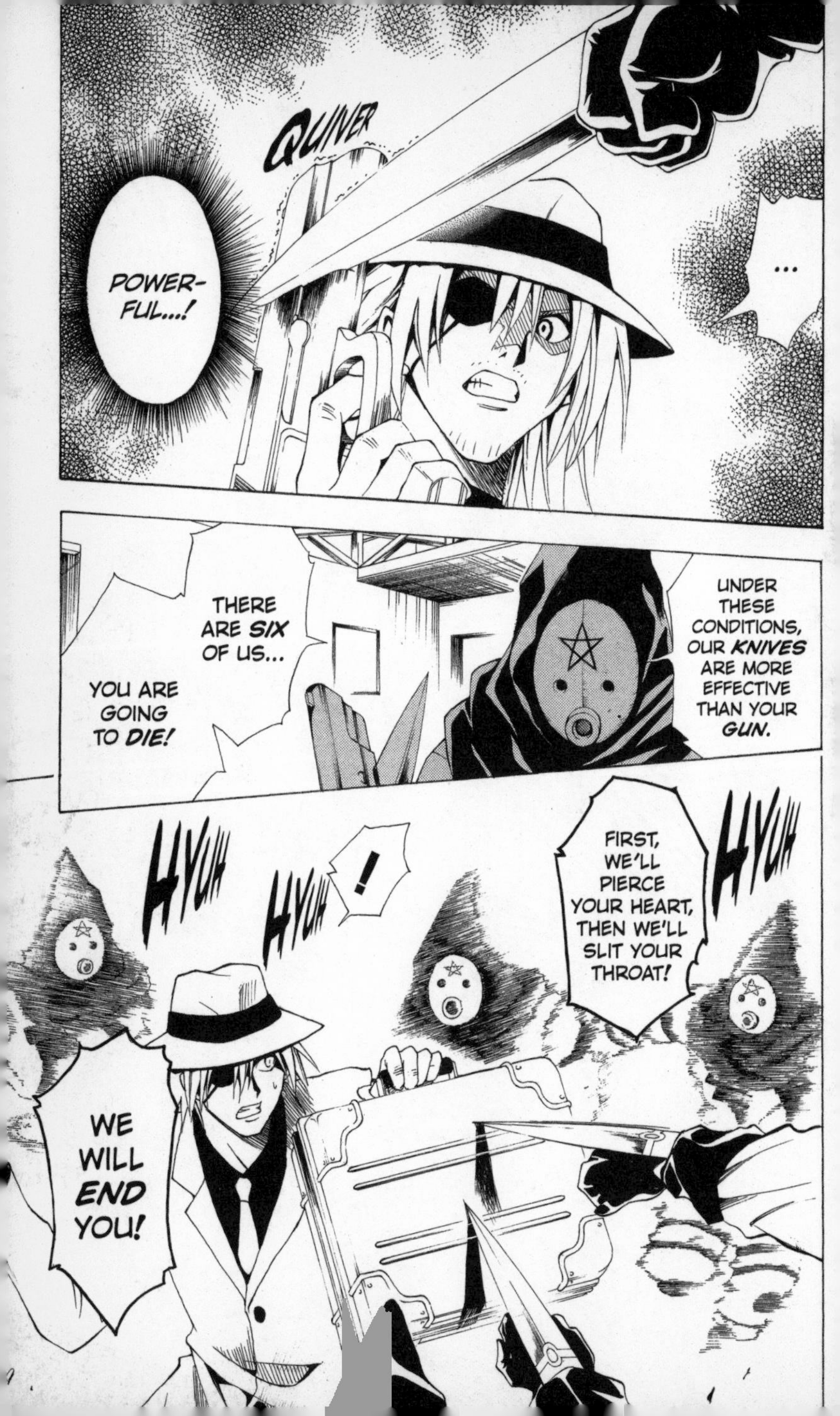
...
QUIVER
POWER-FUL...!
UNDER THESE CONDITIONS, OUR KNIVES ARE MORE EFFECTIVE THAN YOUR GUN.
THERE ARE SIX OF US...
YOU ARE GOING TO DIE!
HYUH
FIRST, WE'LL PIERCE YOUR HEART, THEN WE'LL SLIT YOUR THROAT!
!
HYUH
HYUH
WE WILL END YOU!

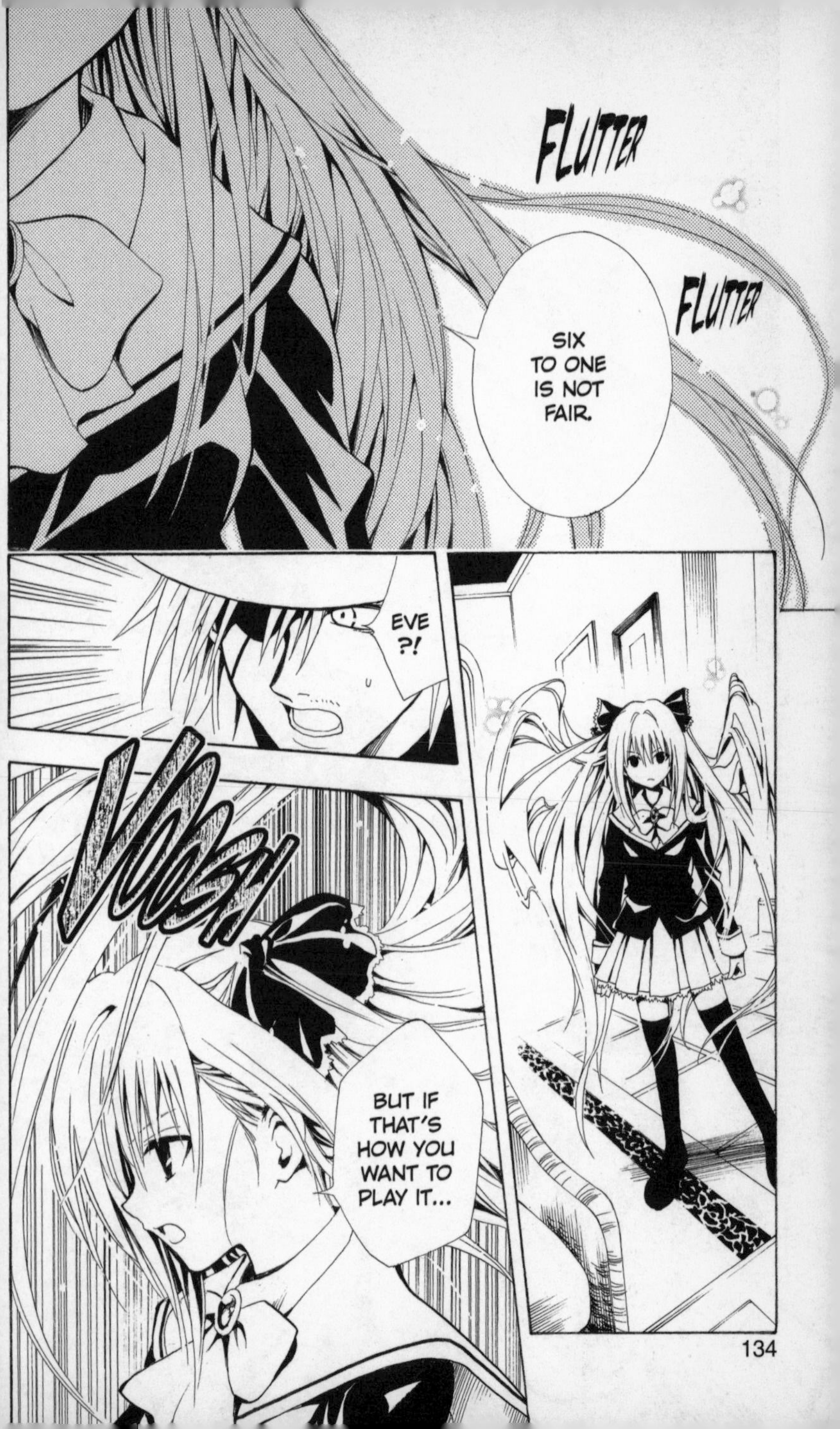
FLUTTER
FLUTTER
SIX TO ONE IS NOT FAIR.
EVE ?!
VWSH
BUT IF THAT'S HOW YOU WANT TO PLAY IT...

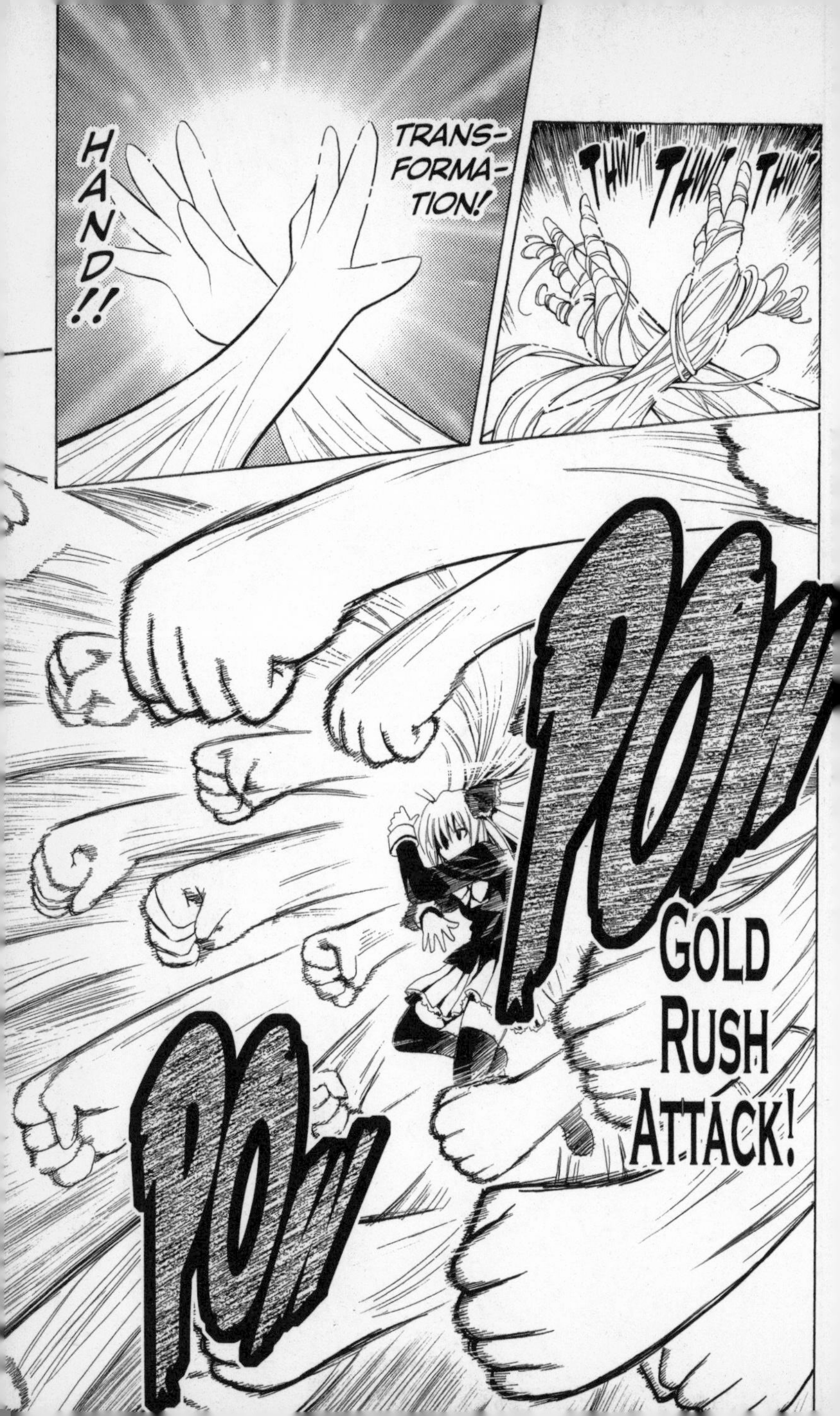
THWI THWI THWI
TRANS-
FORMA-
TION!
HAND!!
POW
GOLD
RUSH
ATTACK!
POW

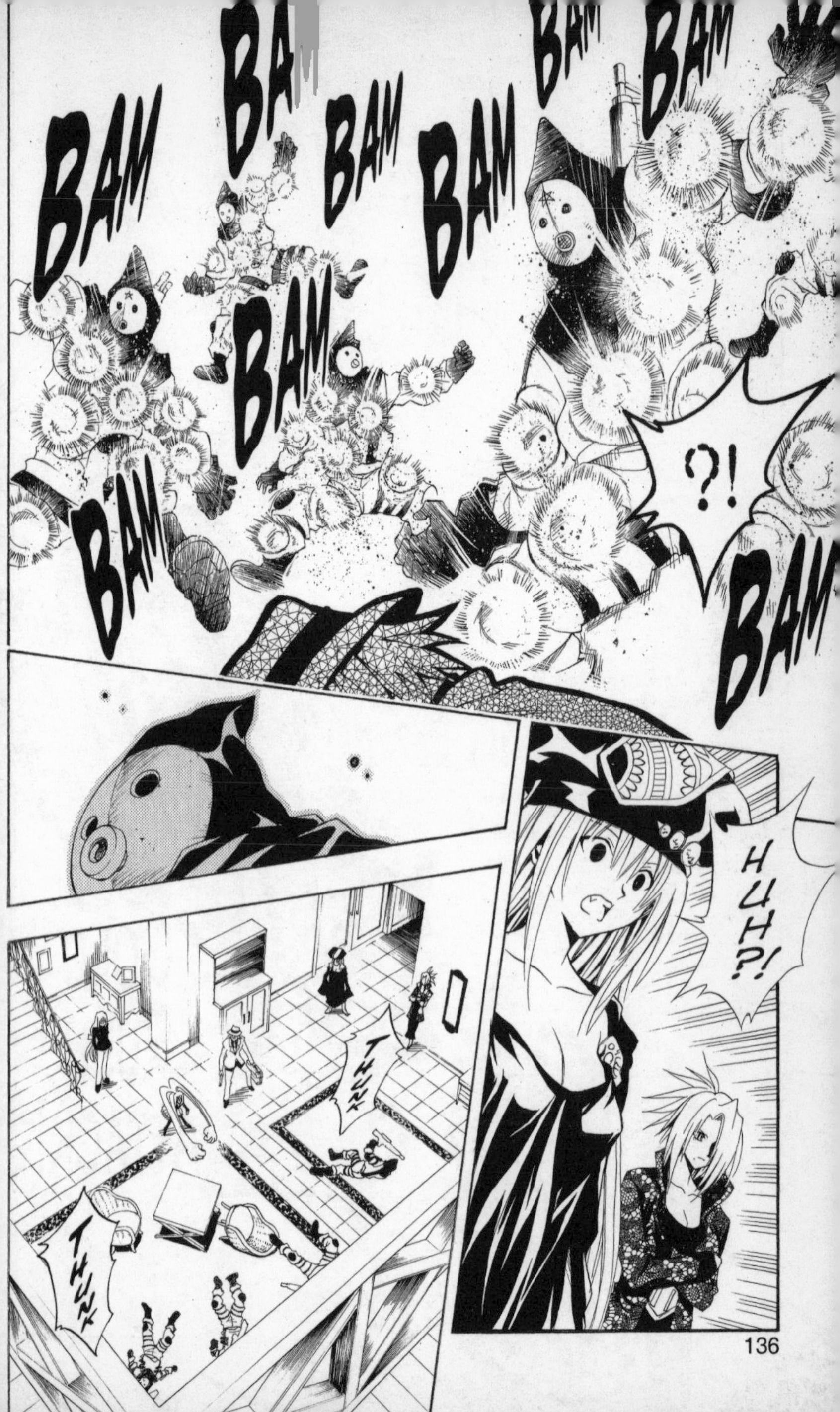
BAM
BAM
BAM
BAM
BAM
BAM
BAM
BAM
?!
BAM
HUH?!
THUNK
THUNK

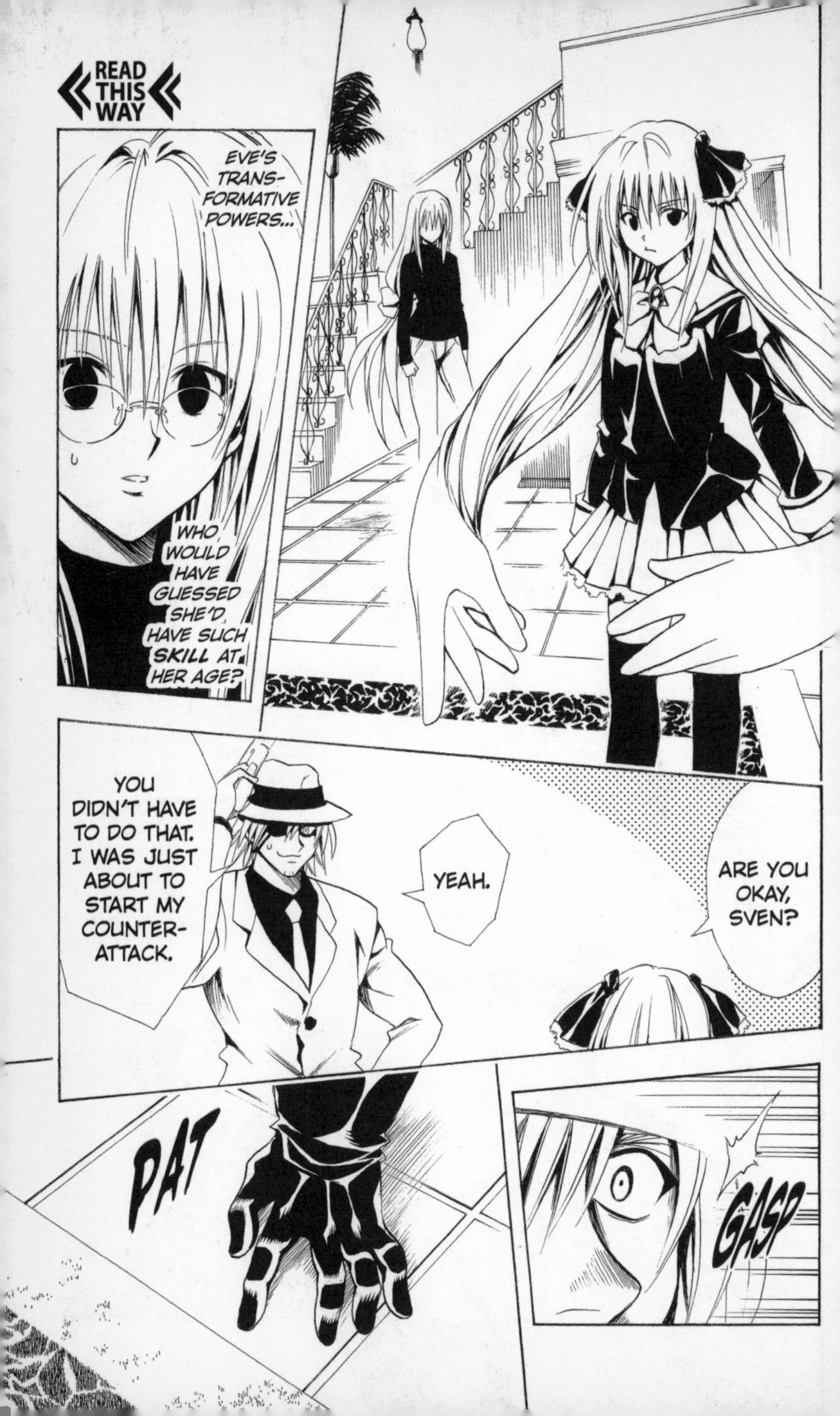
READ THIS WAY
EVE'S TRANS-FORMATIVE POWERS...
WHO WOULD HAVE GUESSED SHE'D HAVE SUCH SKILL AT HER AGE?
ARE YOU OKAY, SVEN?
YEAH.
YOU DIDN'T HAVE TO DO THAT. I WAS JUST ABOUT TO START MY COUNTER-ATTACK.
GASP
PAT

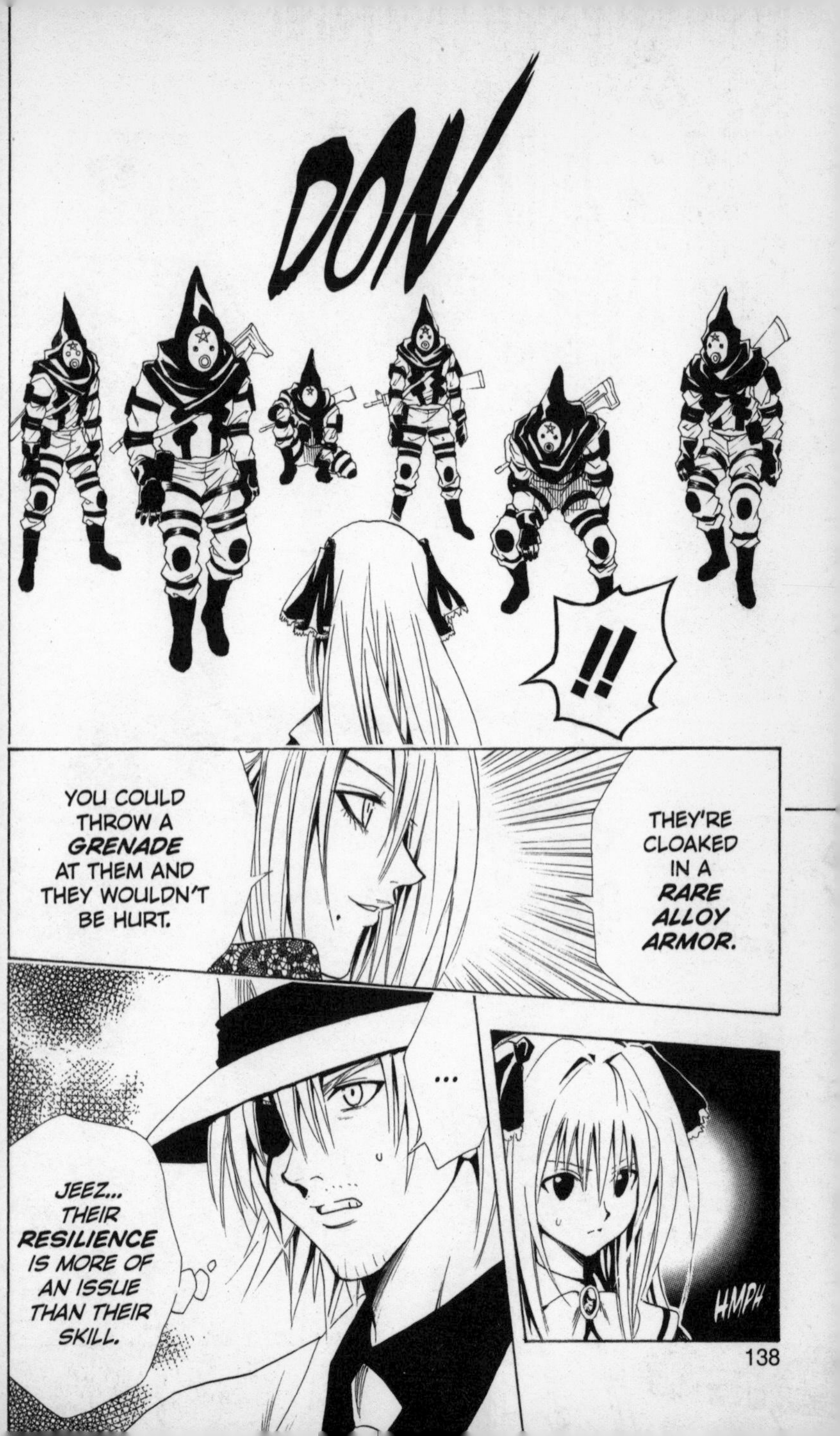
DON
!!
THEY'RE CLOAKED IN A *RARE ALLOY* ARMOR.
YOU COULD THROW A *GRENADE* AT THEM AND THEY WOULDN'T BE HURT.
HMPH
...
JEEZ... THEIR **RESILIENCE** IS MORE OF AN ISSUE THAN THEIR SKILL.

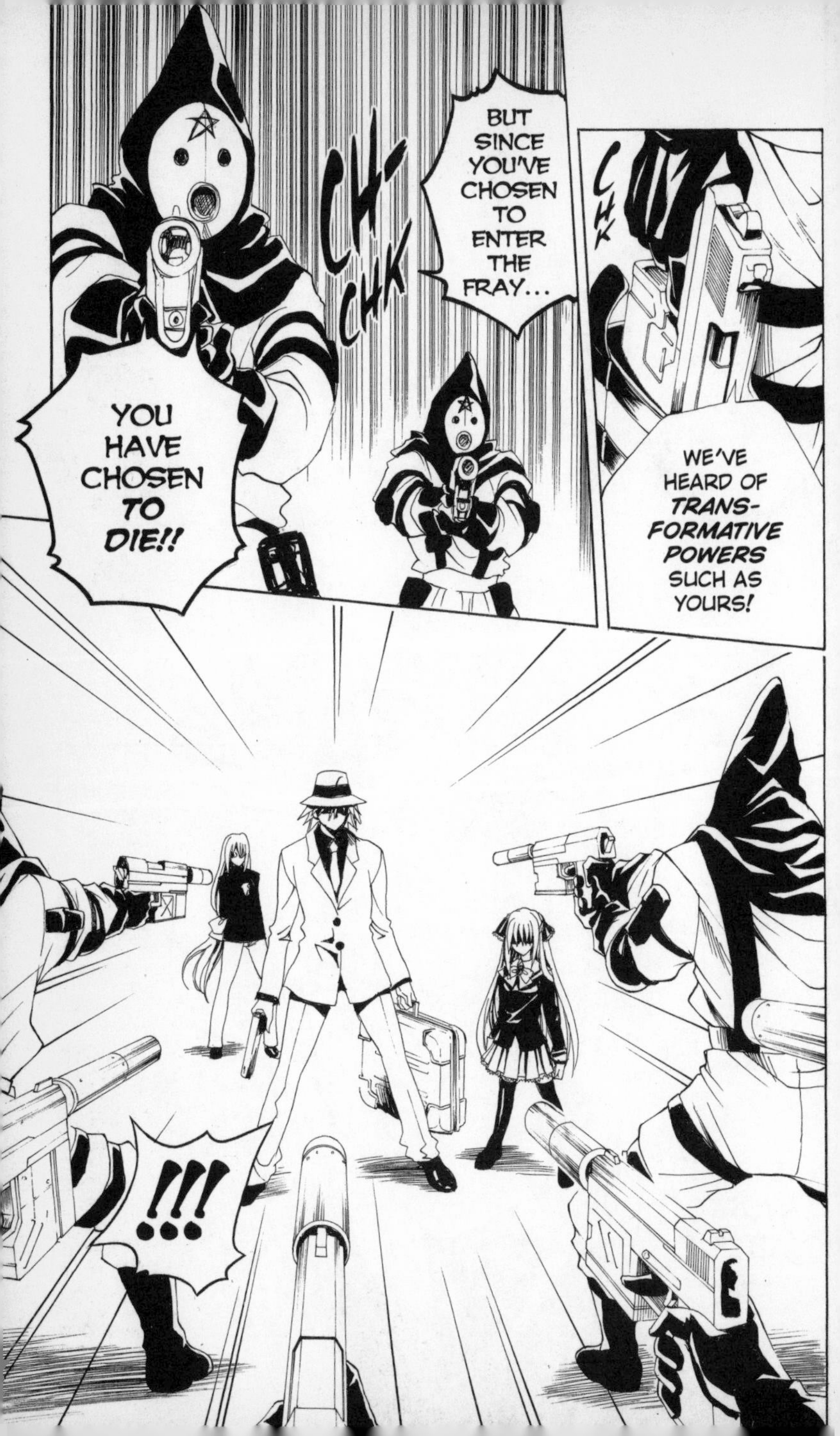
CHK
WE'VE HEARD OF TRANSFORMATIVE POWERS SUCH AS YOURS!
BUT SINCE YOU'VE CHOSEN TO ENTER THE FRAY...
CH-CHK
YOU HAVE CHOSEN TO DIE!!
!!!

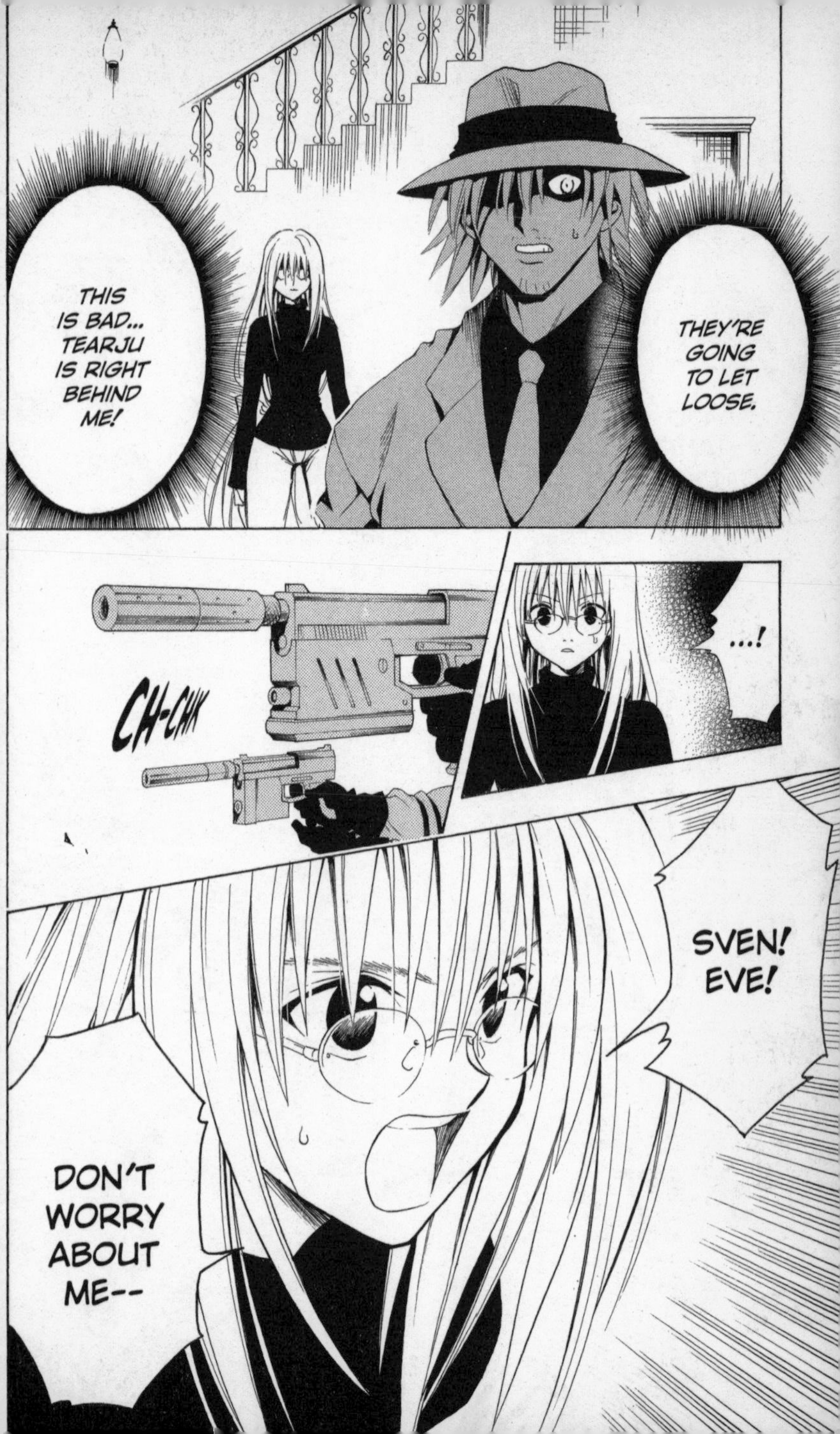
THEY'RE GOING TO LET LOOSE.
THIS IS BAD... TEARJU IS RIGHT BEHIND ME!
...!
CH-CHK
SVEN! EVE!
DON'T WORRY ABOUT ME--

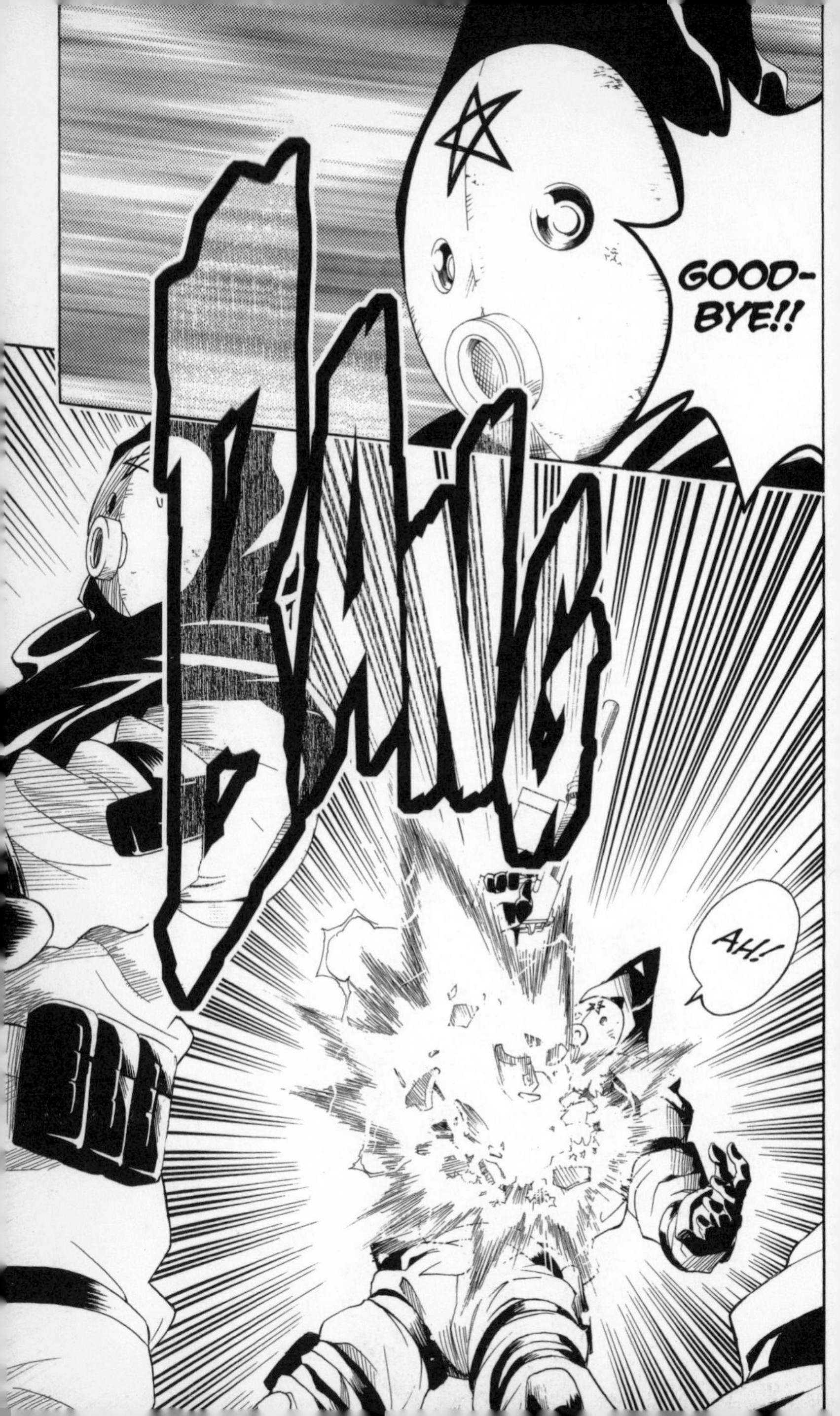
GOOD-BYE!!
AH!

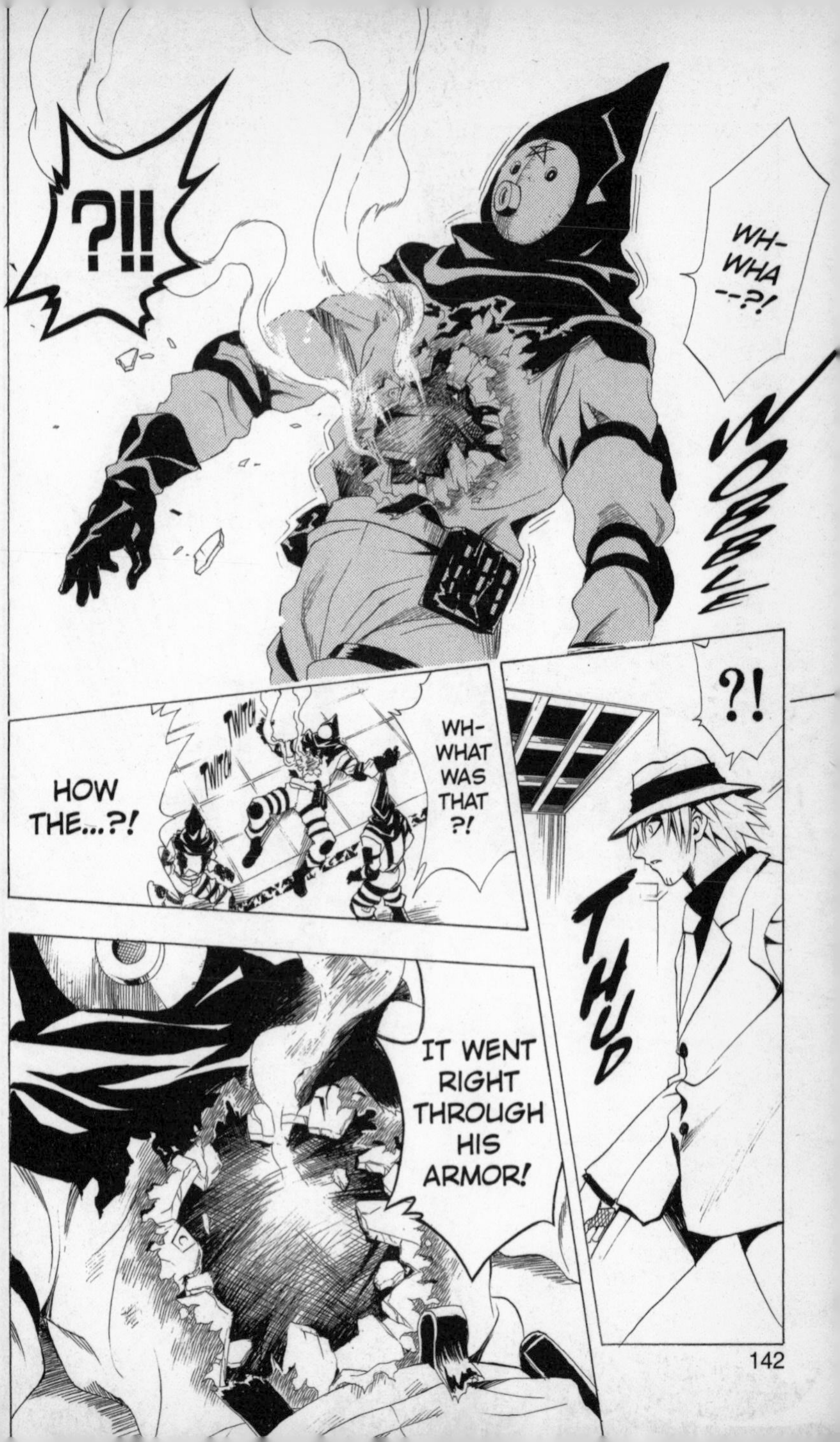
WH-WHA--?!
?!!
?!
THUD
WH-WHAT WAS THAT?!
TWITCH
TWITCH
HOW THE...?!
IT WENT RIGHT THROUGH HIS ARMOR!

READ THIS WAY

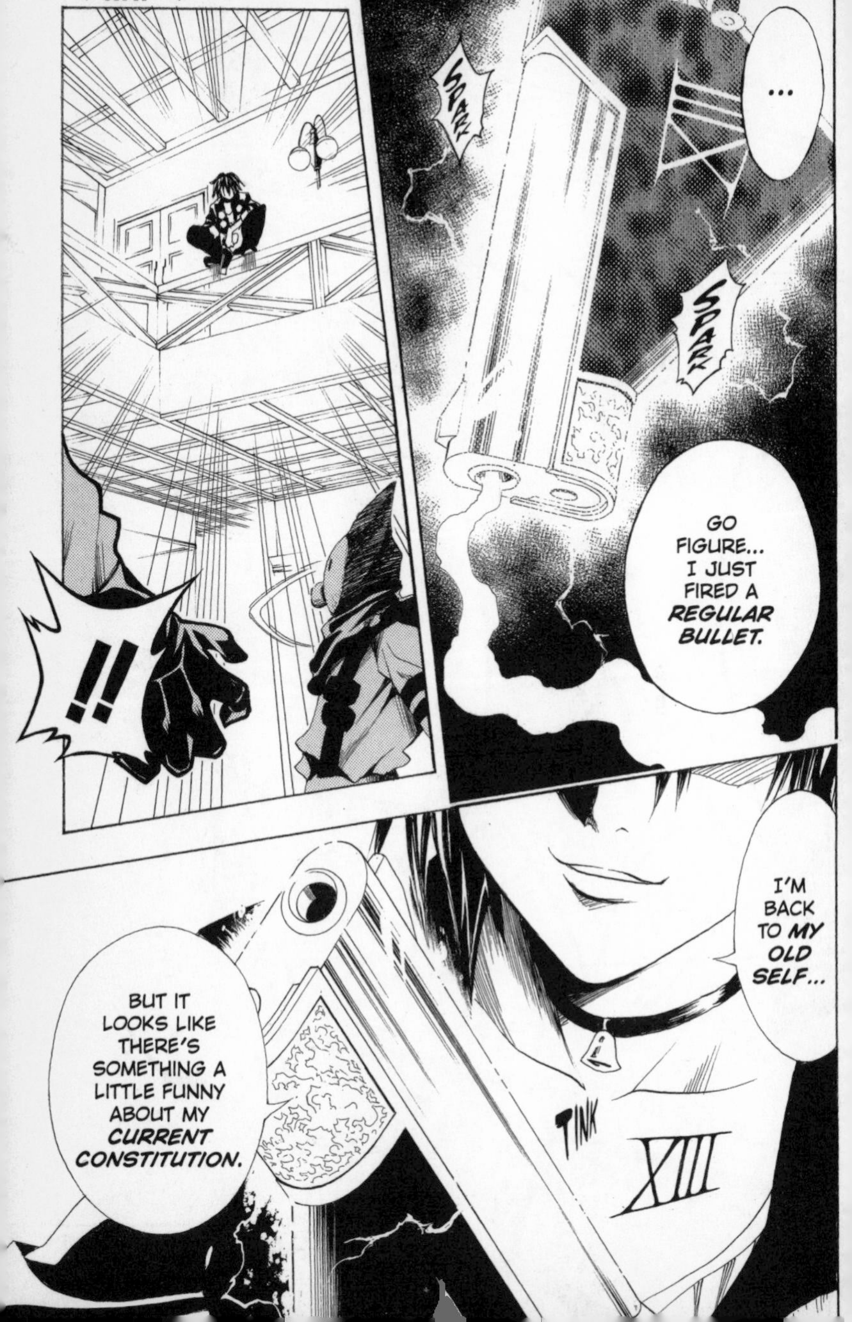

...
SPARK
SPARK
GO FIGURE... I JUST FIRED A *REGULAR BULLET.*
!!
I'M BACK TO *MY OLD SELF...*
BUT IT LOOKS LIKE THERE'S SOMETHING A LITTLE FUNNY ABOUT MY *CURRENT CONSTITUTION.*
TINK
XIII

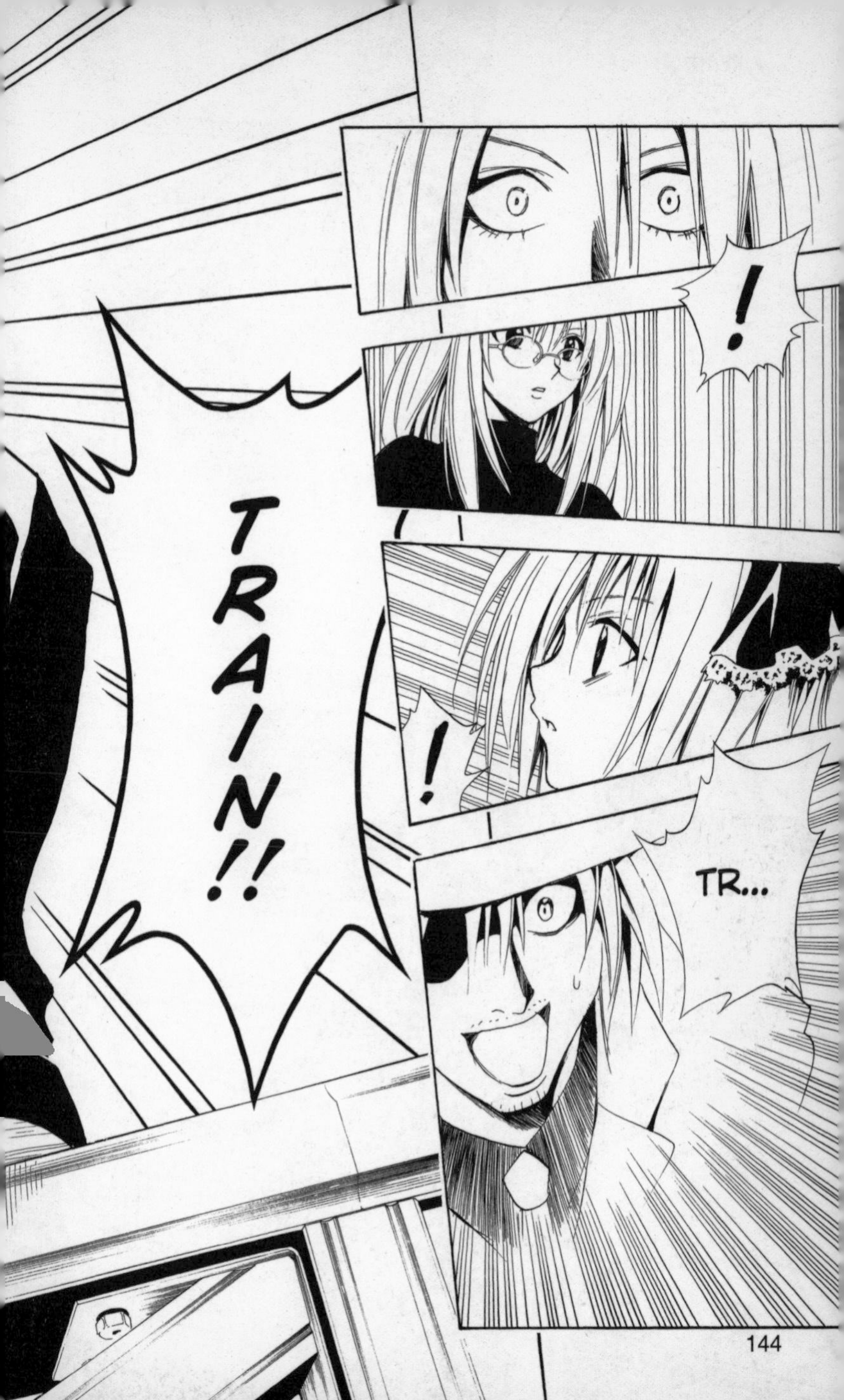
!
!
TR...
TRAIN!!

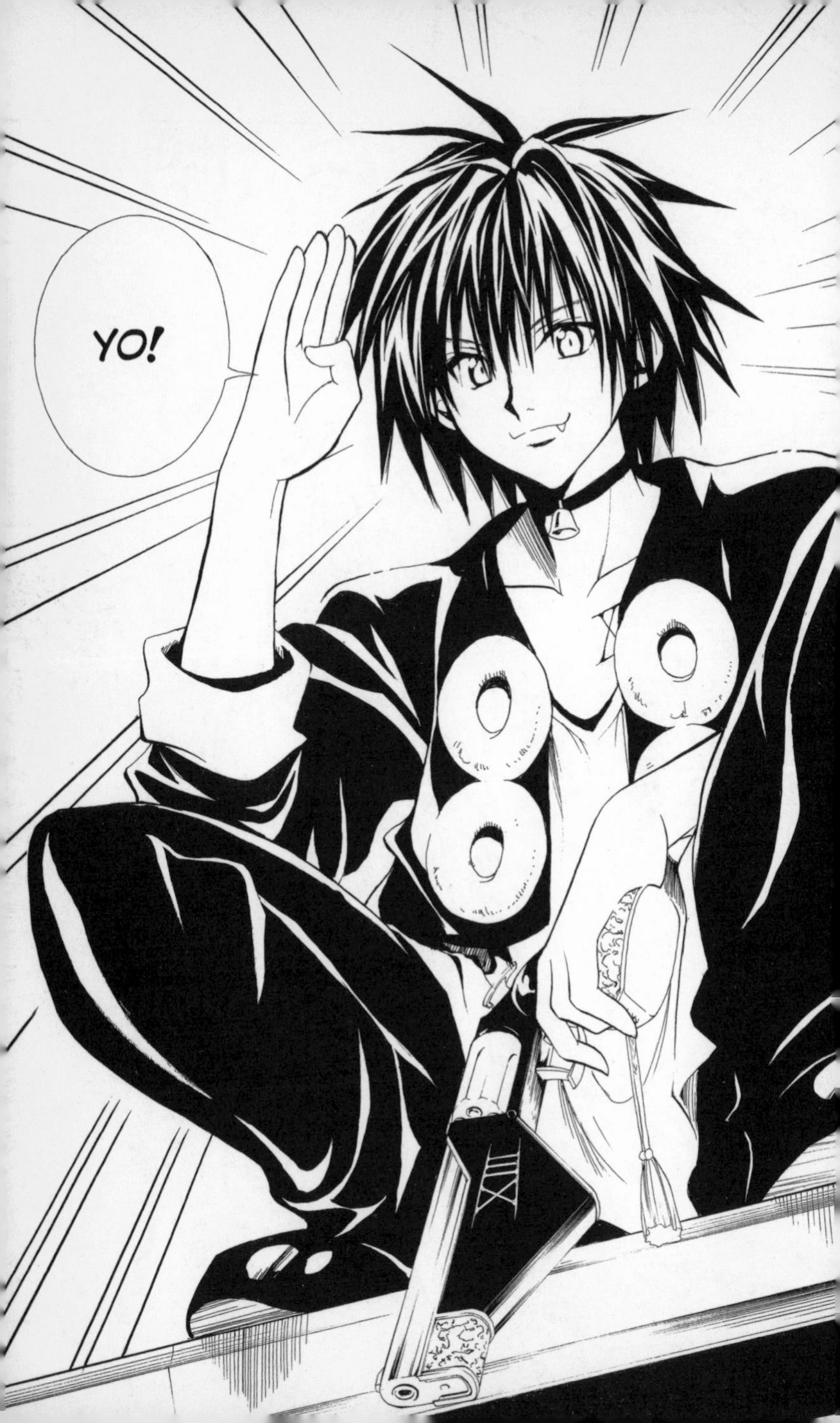
YO!

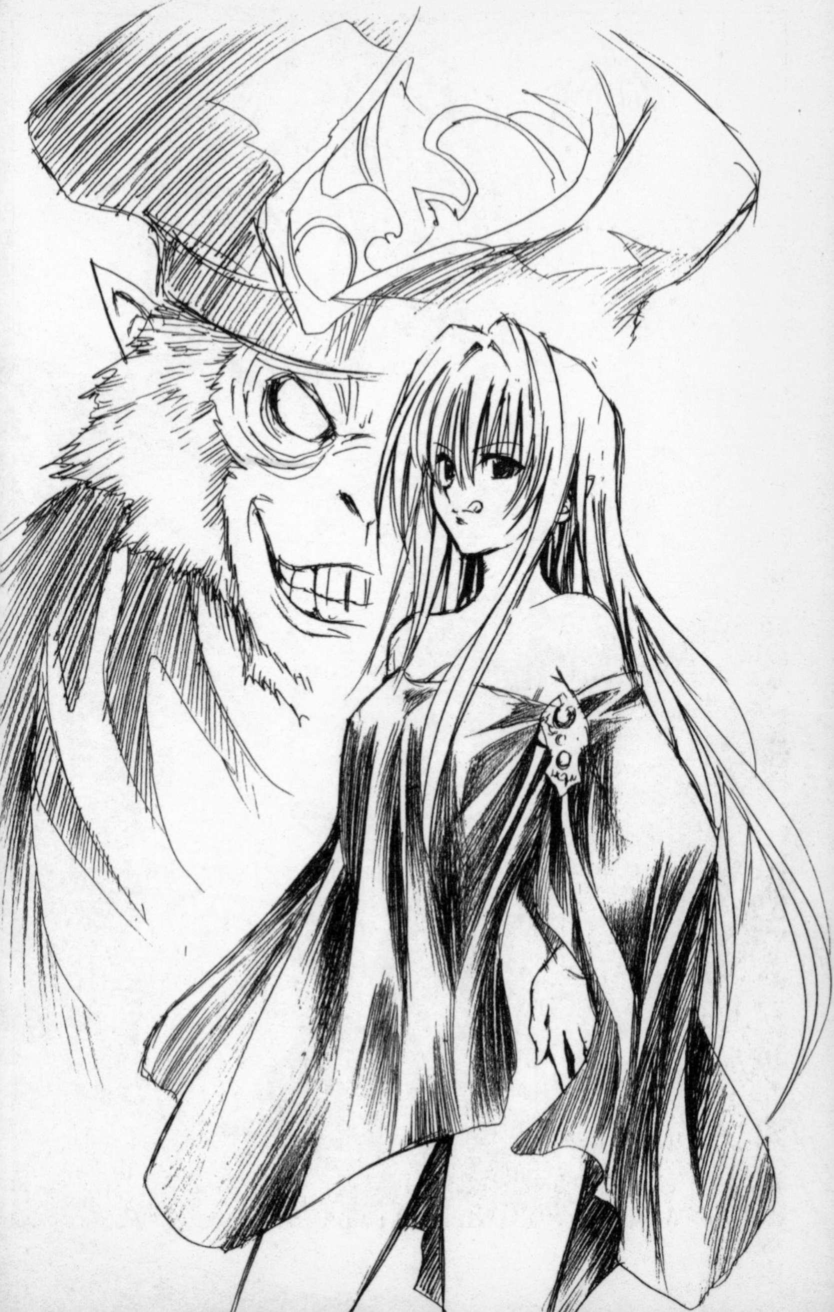

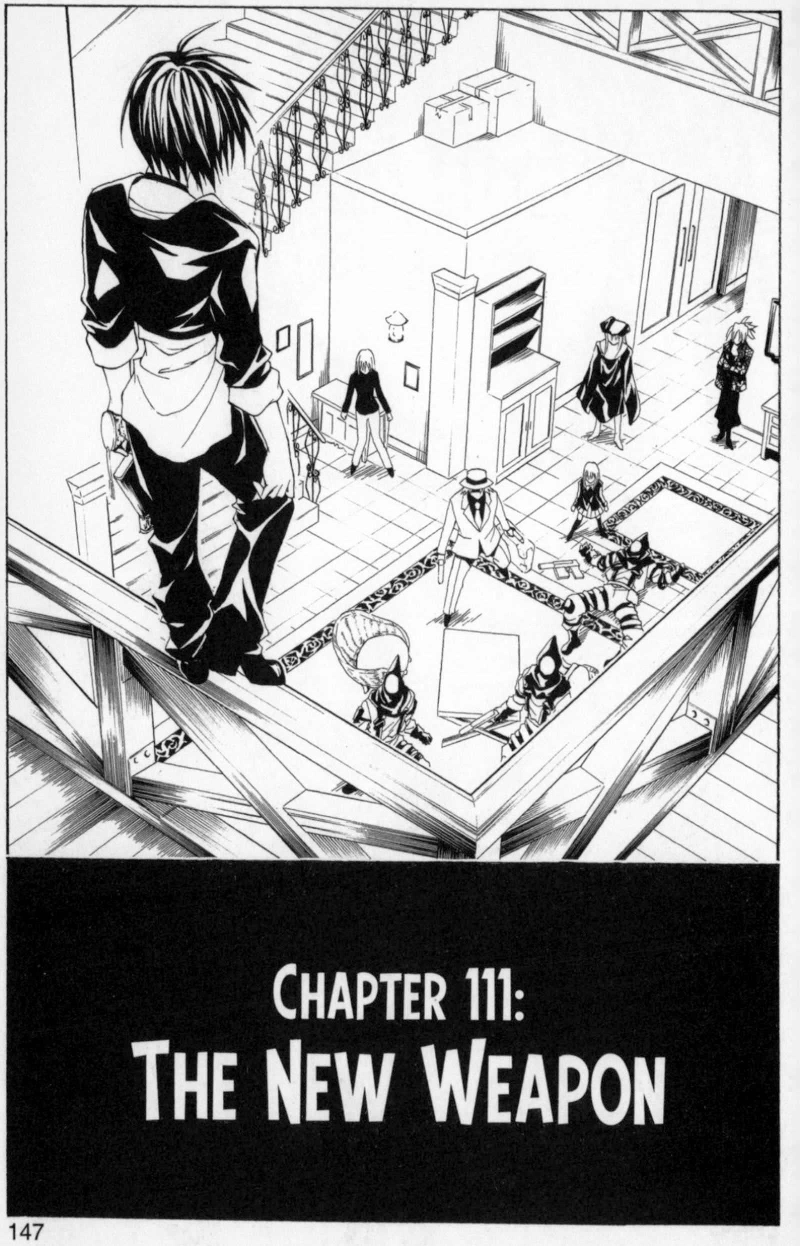

Chapter 111: The New Weapon

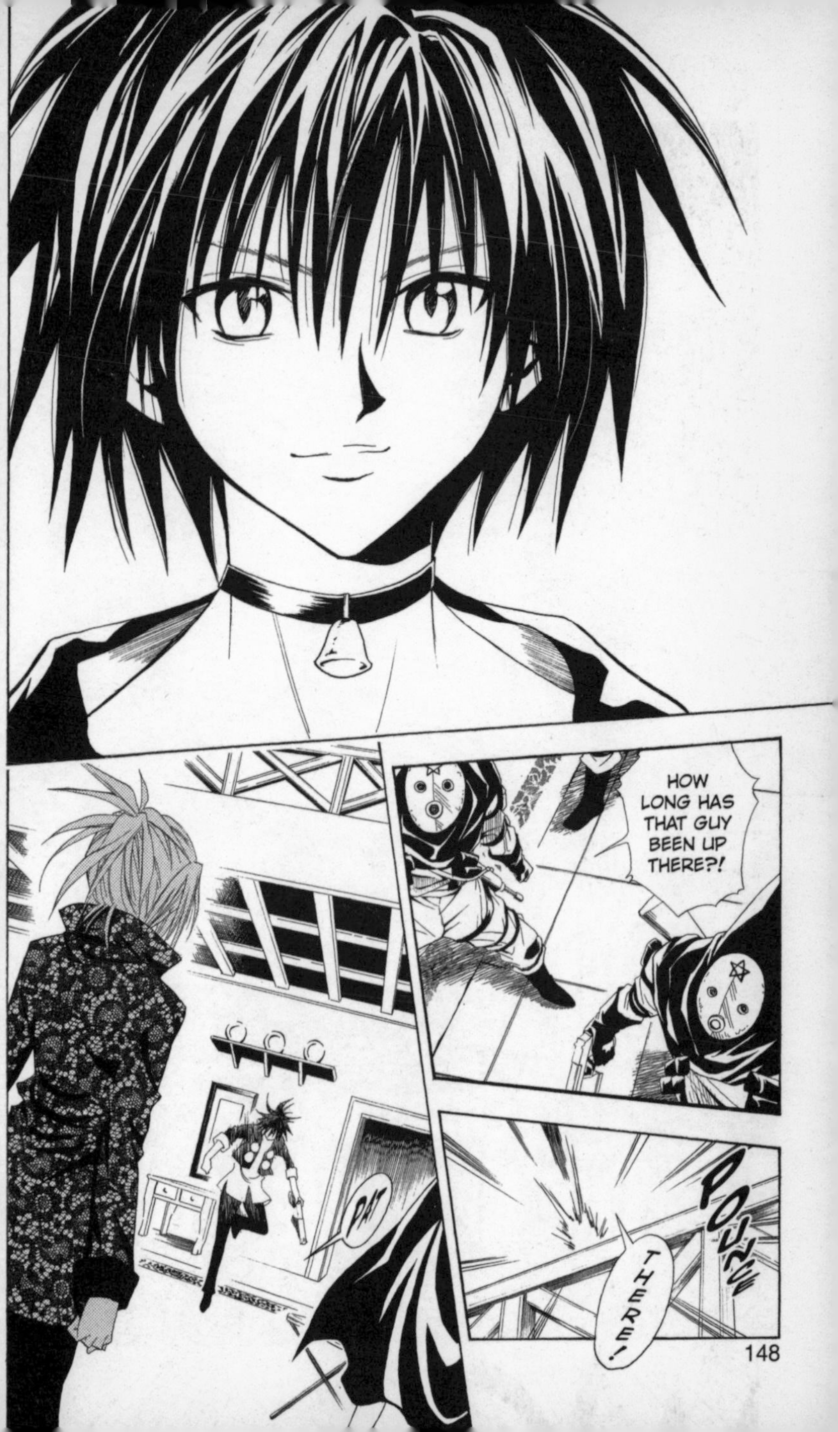
HOW LONG HAS THAT GUY BEEN UP THERE?!
PAT
POUNCE
THERE!

READ THIS WAY

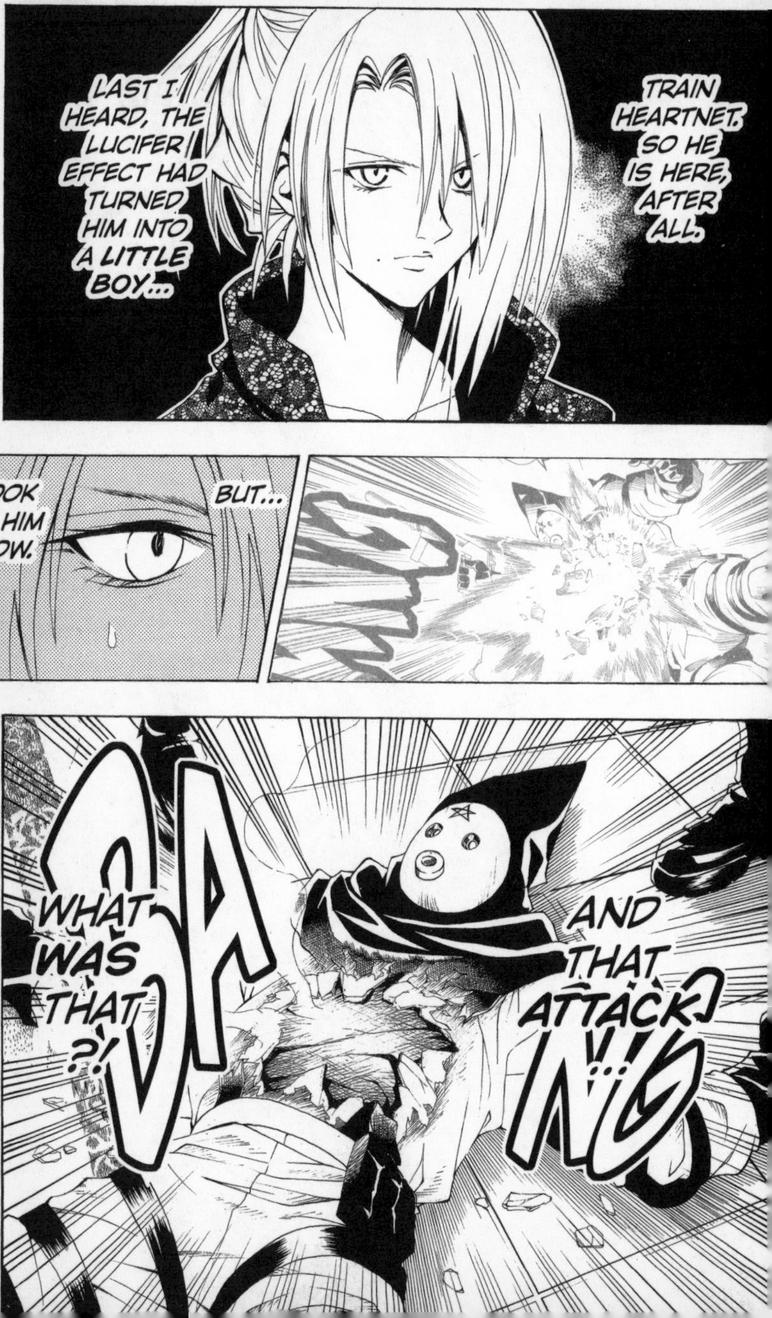
TRAIN HEARTNET. SO HE IS HERE, AFTER ALL.
LAST I HEARD, THE LUCIFER EFFECT HAD TURNED HIM INTO A LITTLE BOY...
BUT...
LOOK AT HIM NOW.
AND THAT ATTACK...
WHAT WAS THAT?!
GA
NG

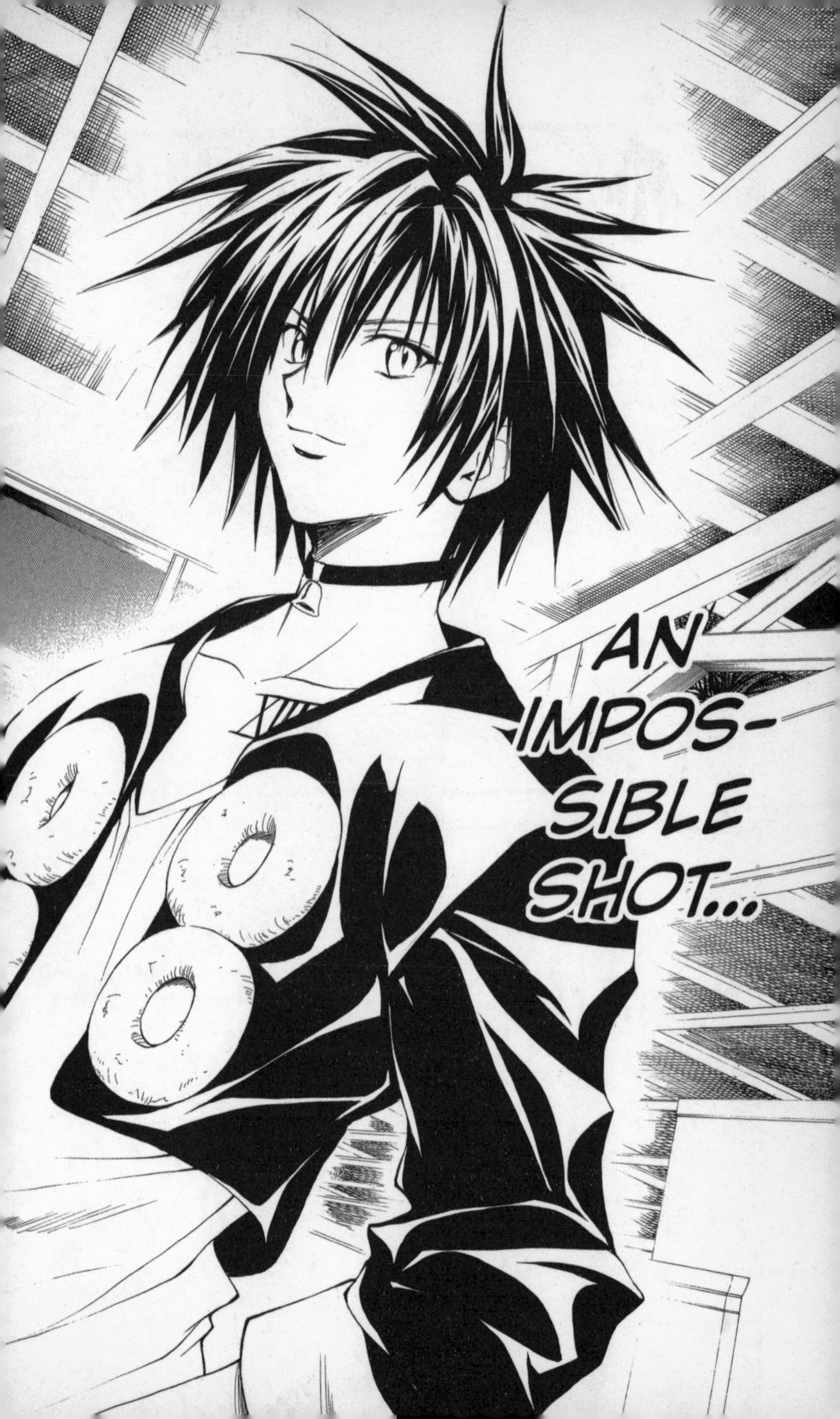
AN IMPOS-SIBLE SHOT...

READ THIS WAY

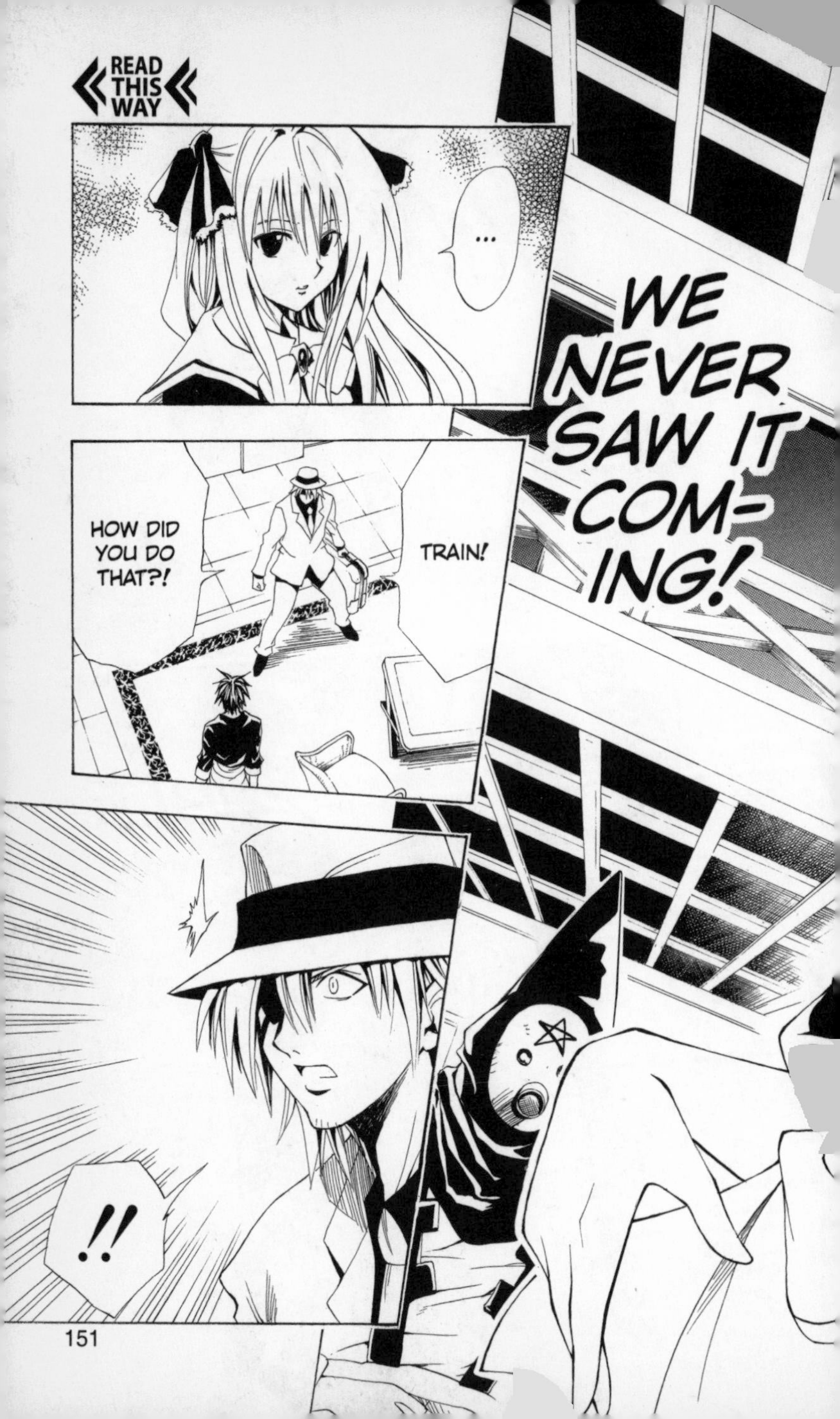
WE NEVER SAW IT COMING!
...
TRAIN!
HOW DID YOU DO THAT?!
!!

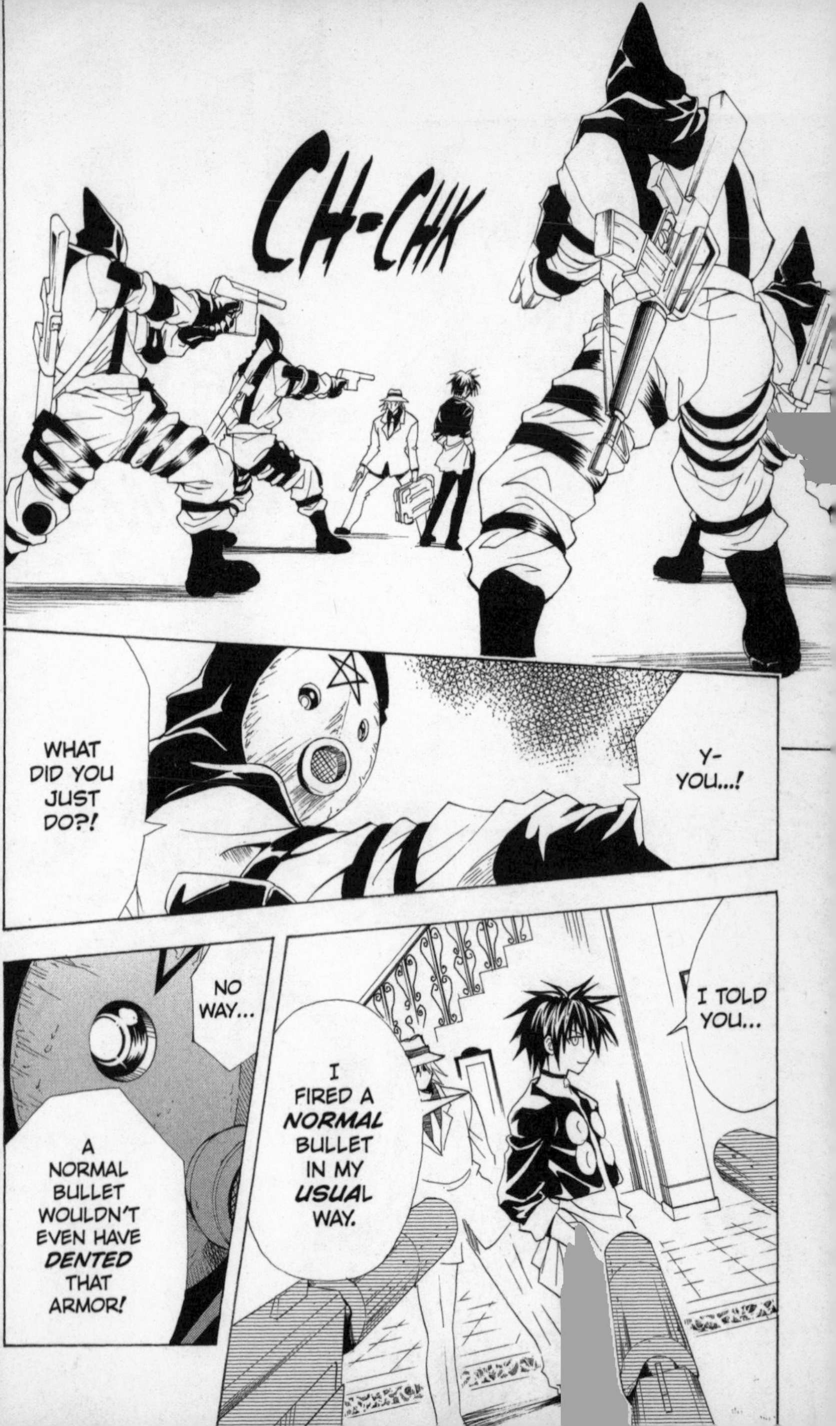
CH-CHK
Y- YOU...!
WHAT DID YOU JUST DO?!
I TOLD YOU...
I FIRED A *NORMAL* BULLET IN MY *USUAL* WAY.
NO WAY...
A NORMAL BULLET WOULDN'T EVEN HAVE *DENTED* THAT ARMOR!

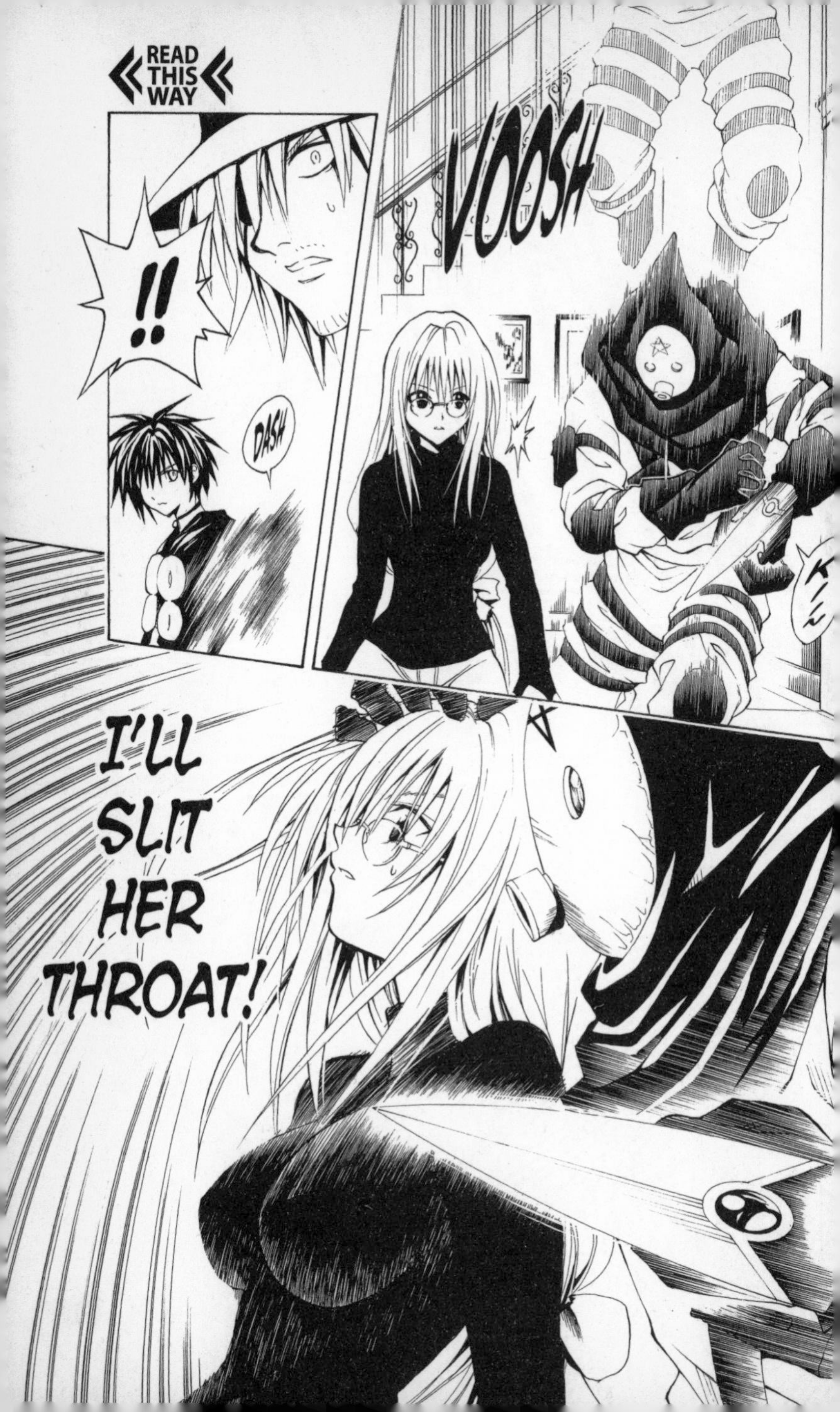
READ THIS WAY
VOOSH
!!
DASH
I'LL SLIT HER THROAT!

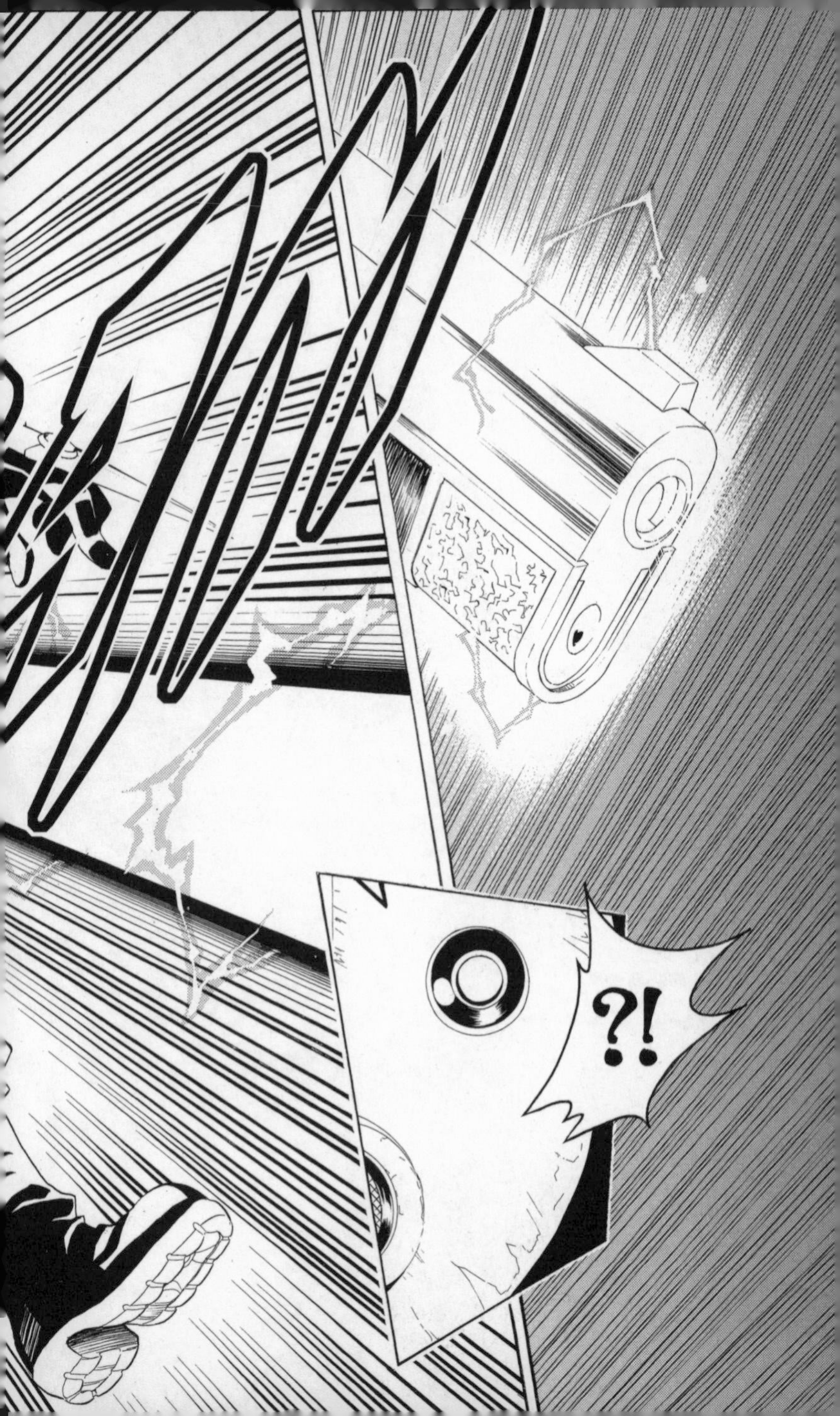
?!

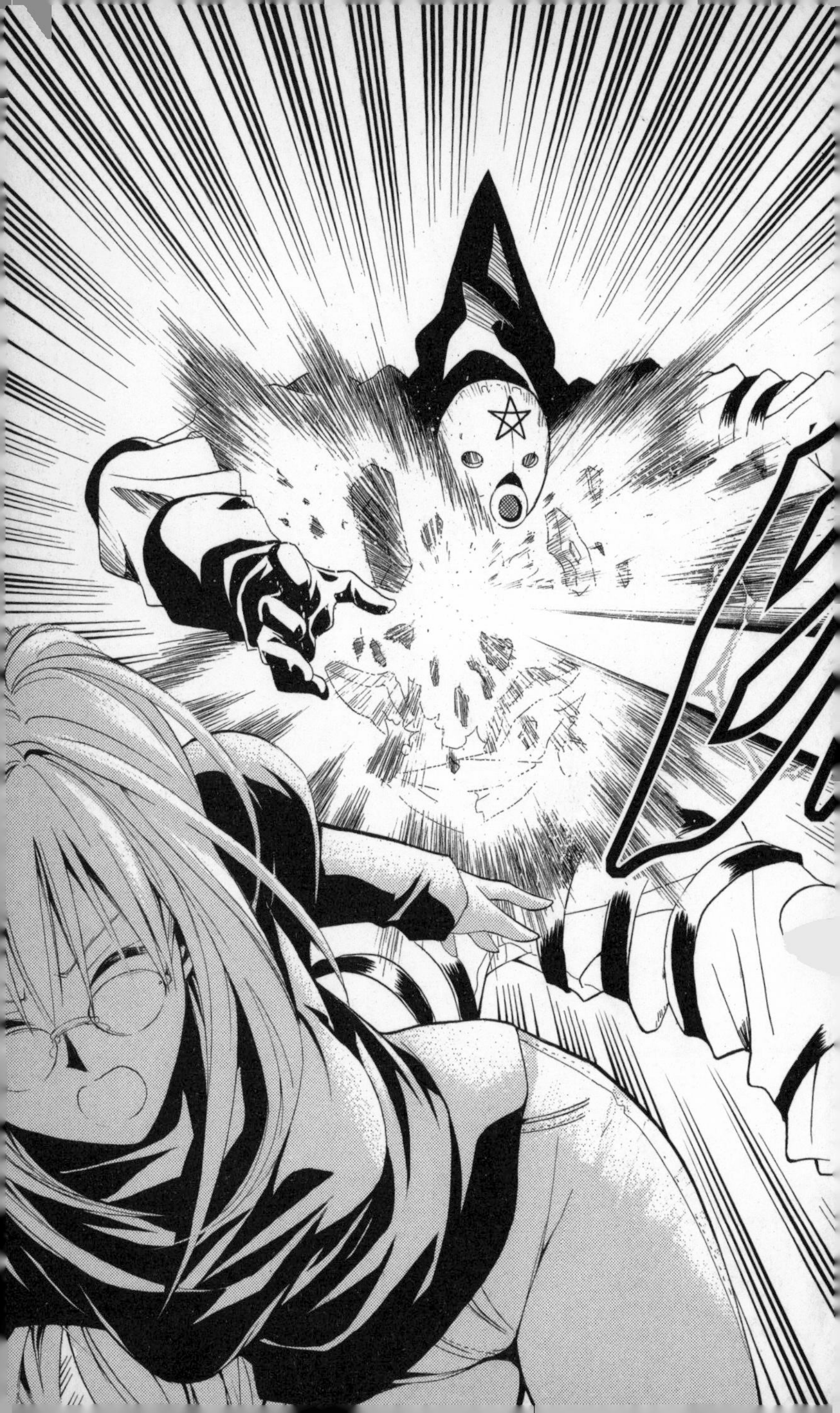

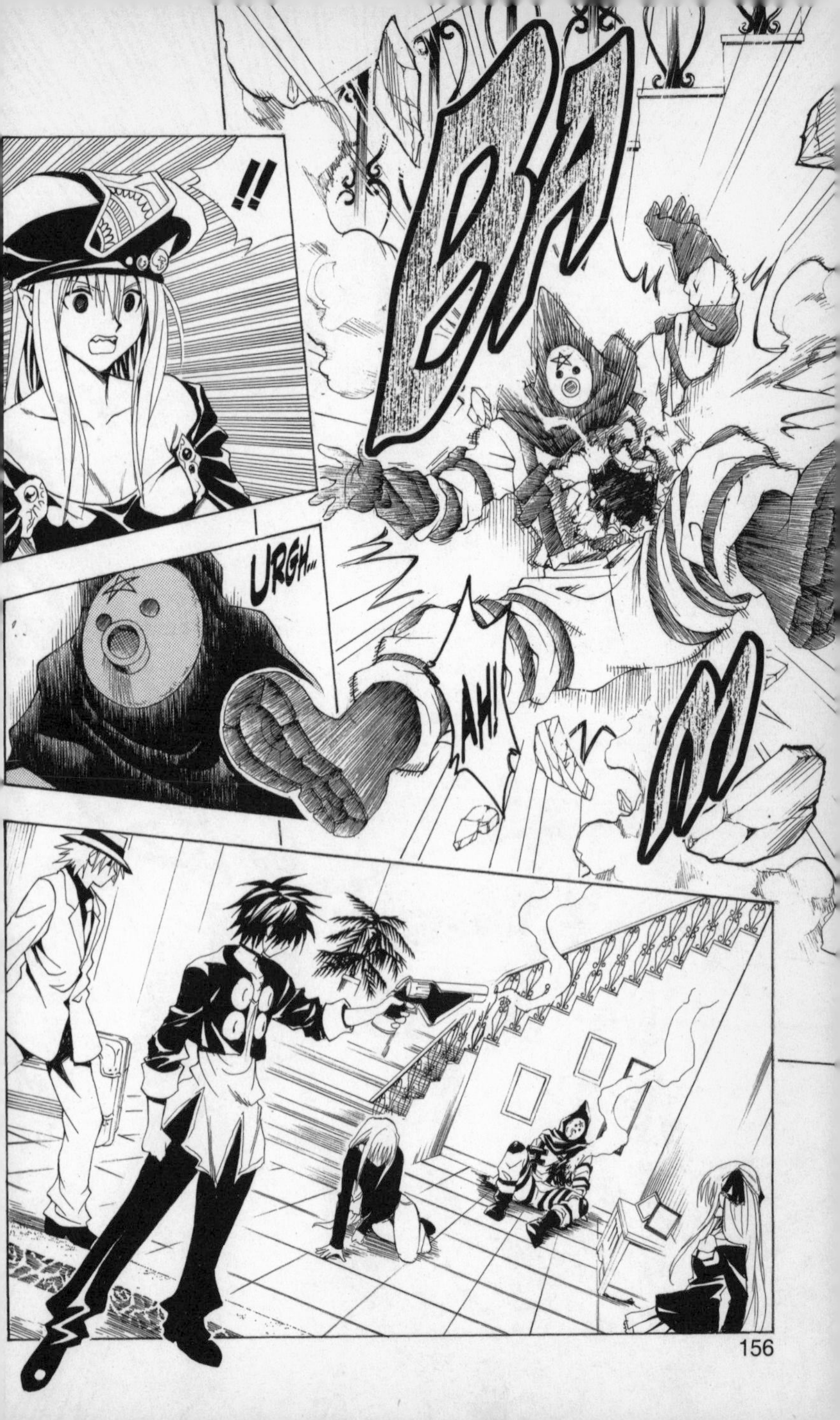
!!
URGH...
AH!

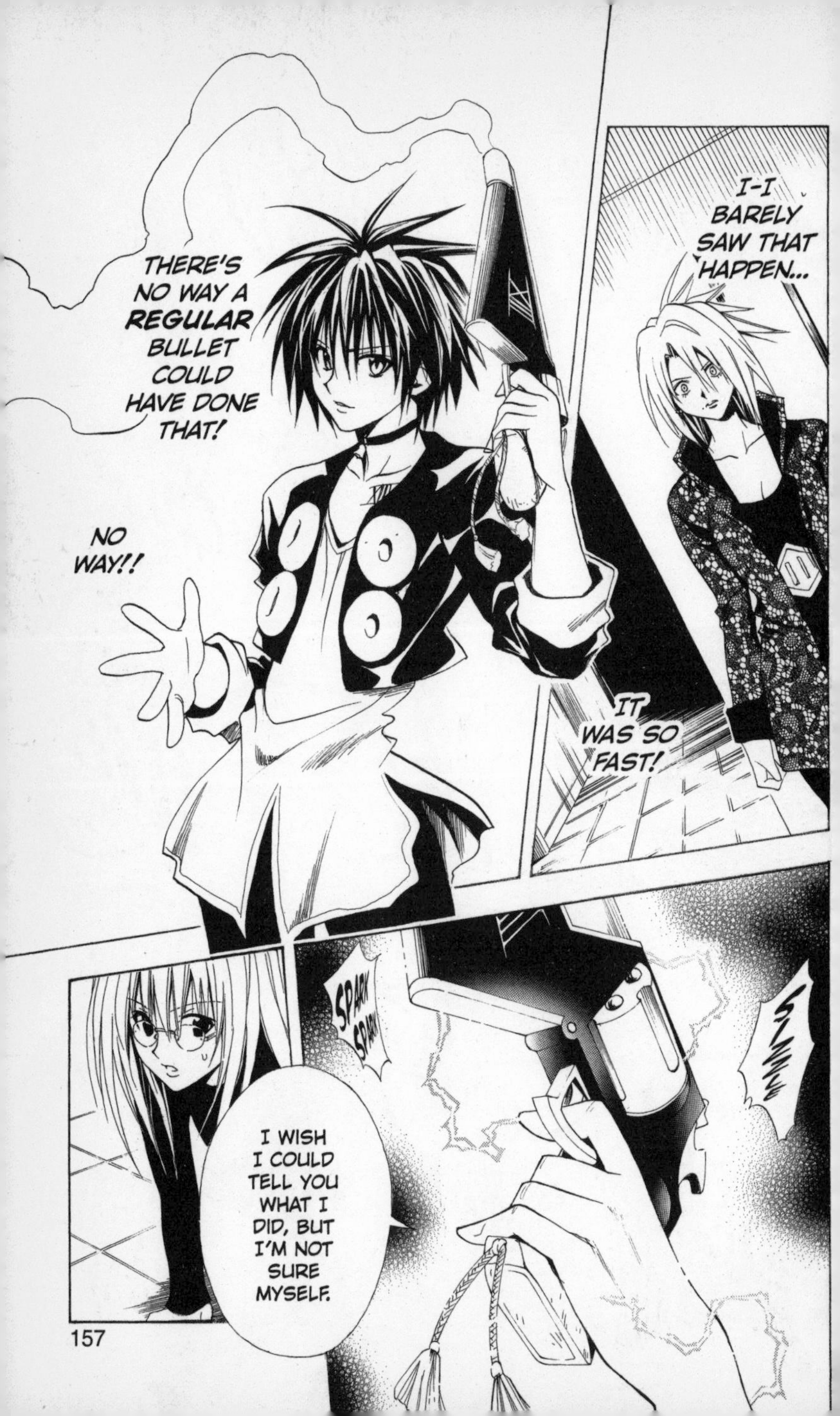
I-I BARELY SAW THAT HAPPEN...
IT WAS SO FAST!
THERE'S NO WAY A REGULAR BULLET COULD HAVE DONE THAT!
NO WAY!!
SPARK SPARK
I WISH I COULD TELL YOU WHAT I DID, BUT I'M NOT SURE MYSELF.

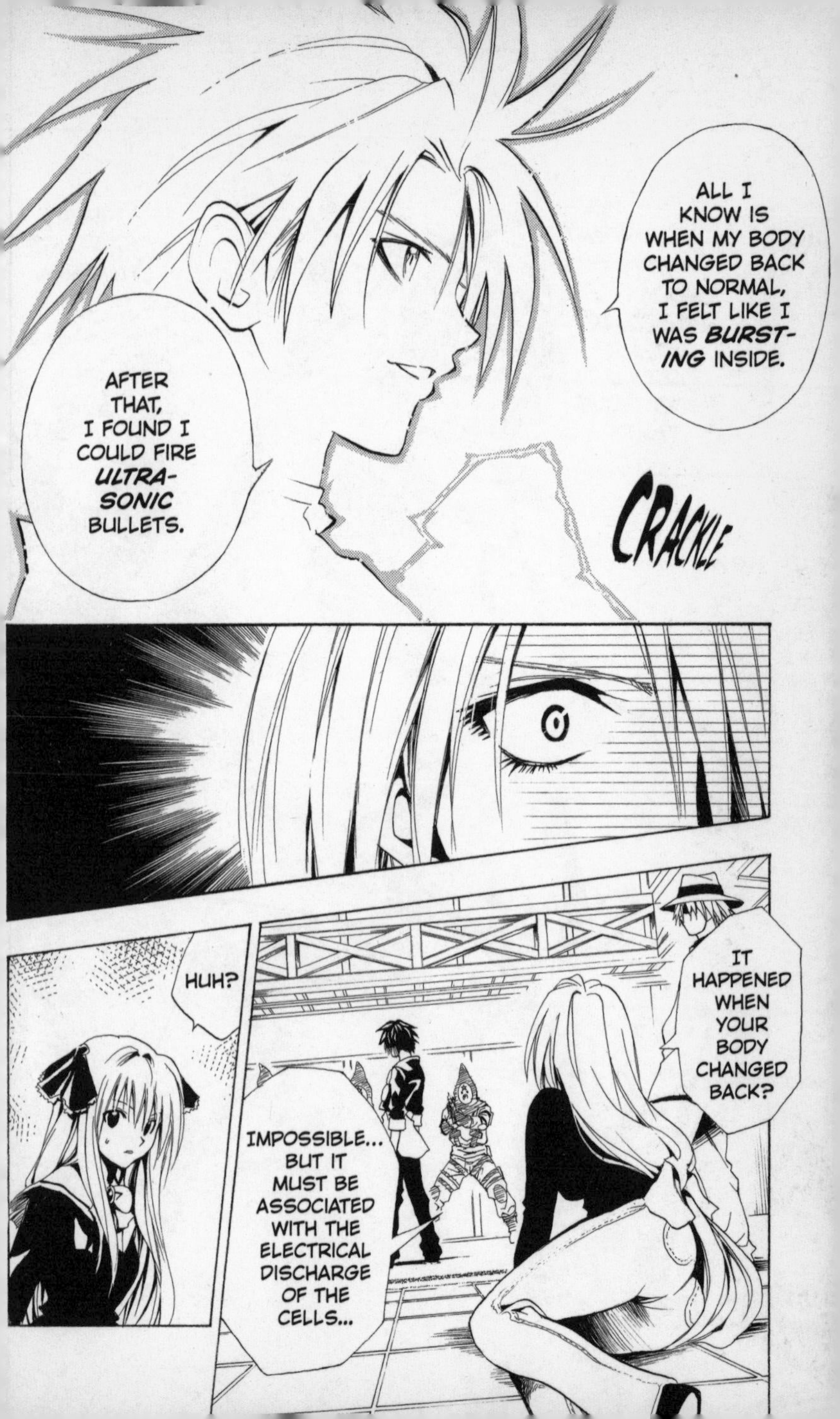
ALL I KNOW IS WHEN MY BODY CHANGED BACK TO NORMAL, I FELT LIKE I WAS *BURSTING* INSIDE.
AFTER THAT, I FOUND I COULD FIRE *ULTRASONIC* BULLETS.
CRACKLE
IT HAPPENED WHEN YOUR BODY CHANGED BACK?
IMPOSSIBLE... BUT IT MUST BE ASSOCIATED WITH THE ELECTRICAL DISCHARGE OF THE CELLS...
HUH?

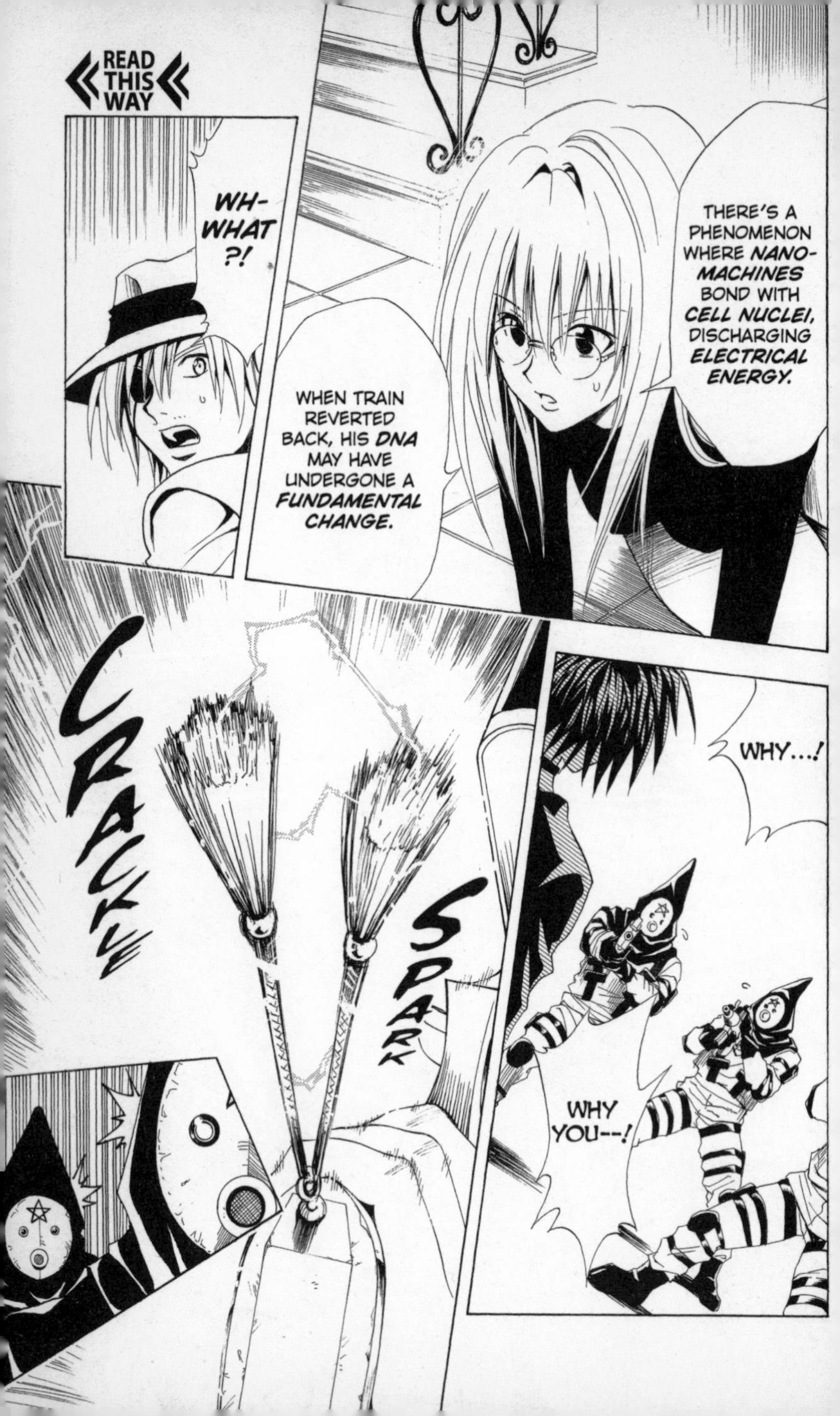
READ THIS WAY
THERE'S A PHENOMENON WHERE NANO-MACHINES BOND WITH CELL NUCLEI, DISCHARGING ELECTRICAL ENERGY.
WHEN TRAIN REVERTED BACK, HIS DNA MAY HAVE UNDERGONE A FUNDAMENTAL CHANGE.
WH-WHAT ?!
WHY...!
WHY YOU--!
CRACKLE
SPARK

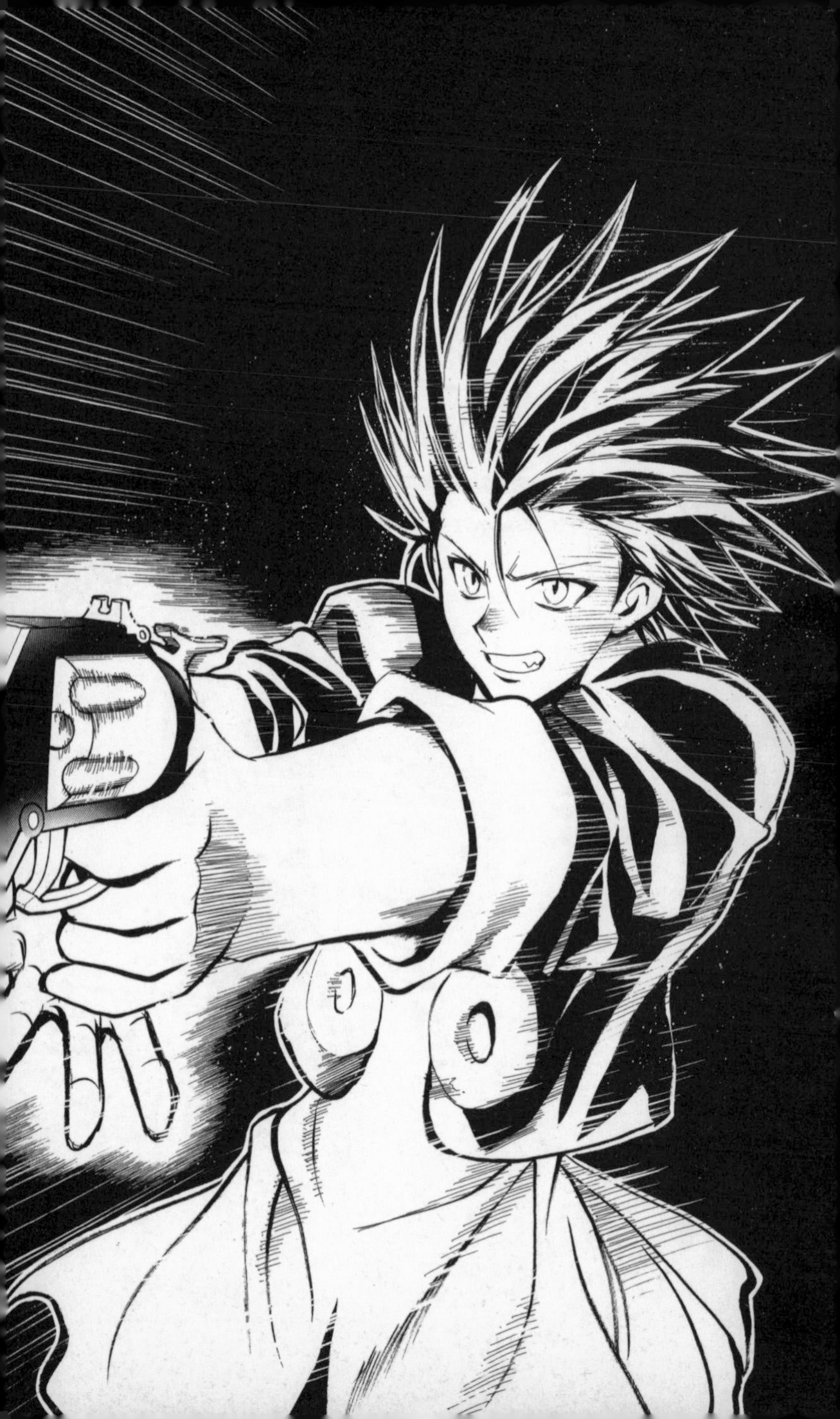

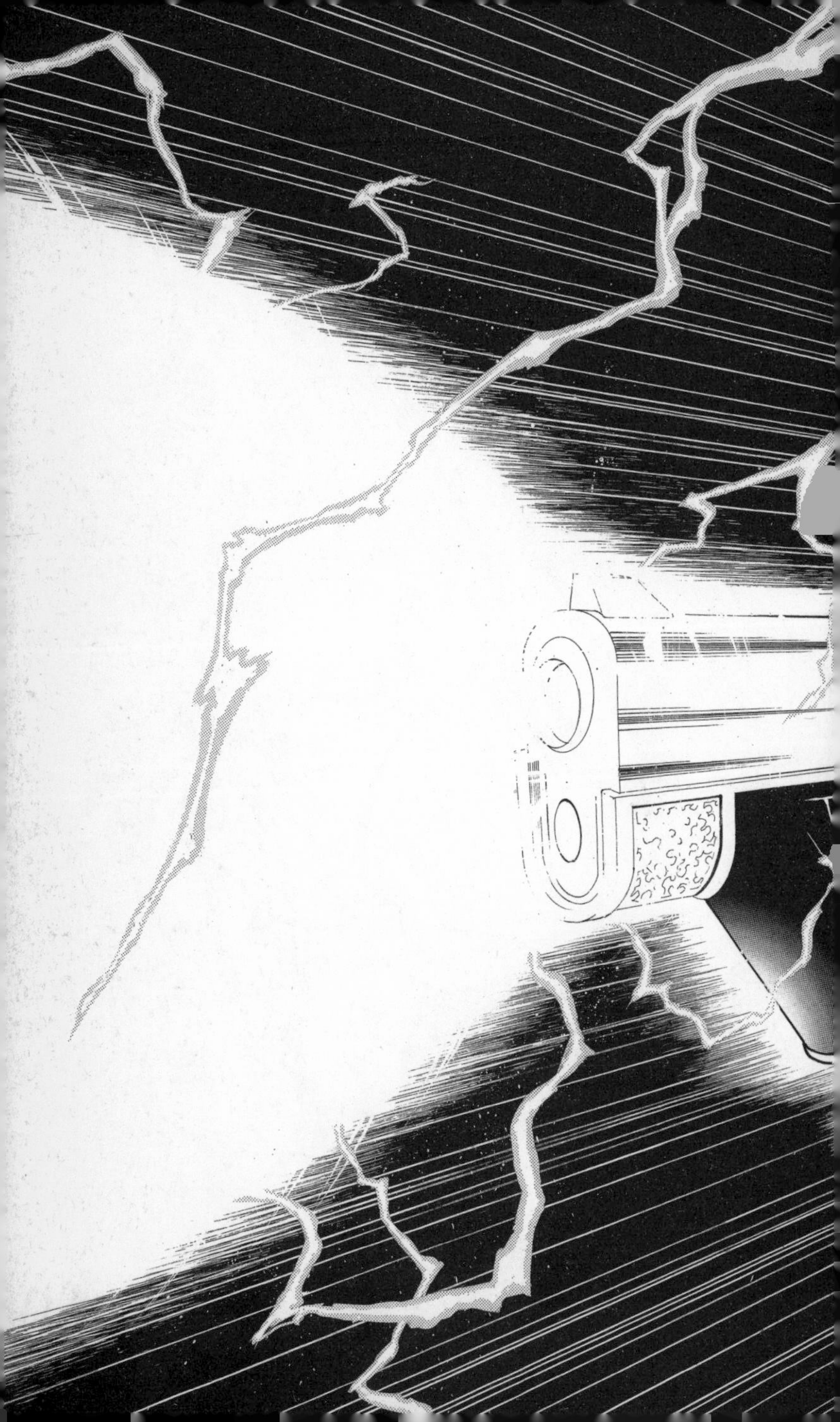

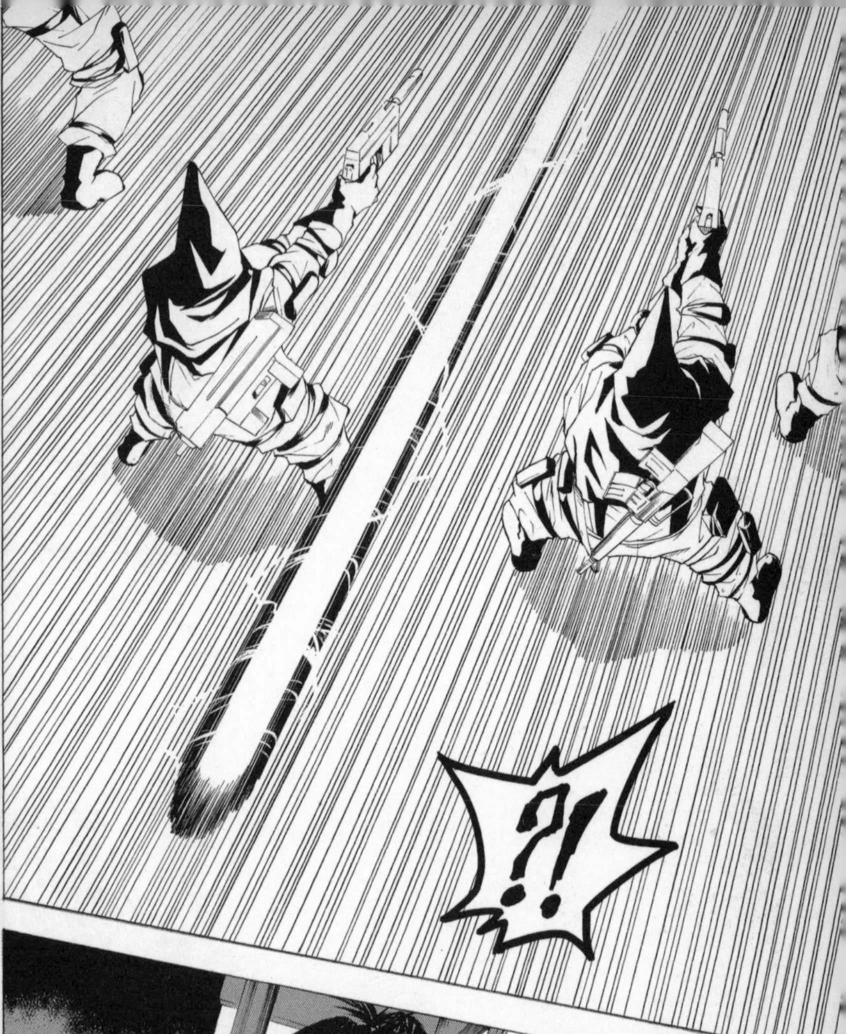
?!
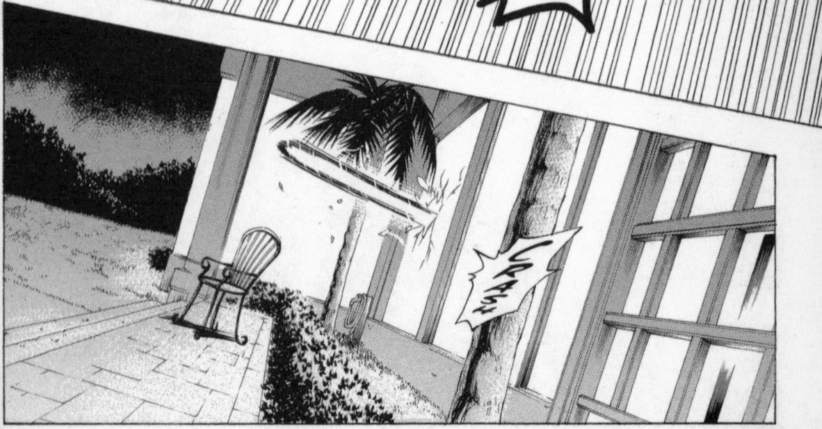
CRASH

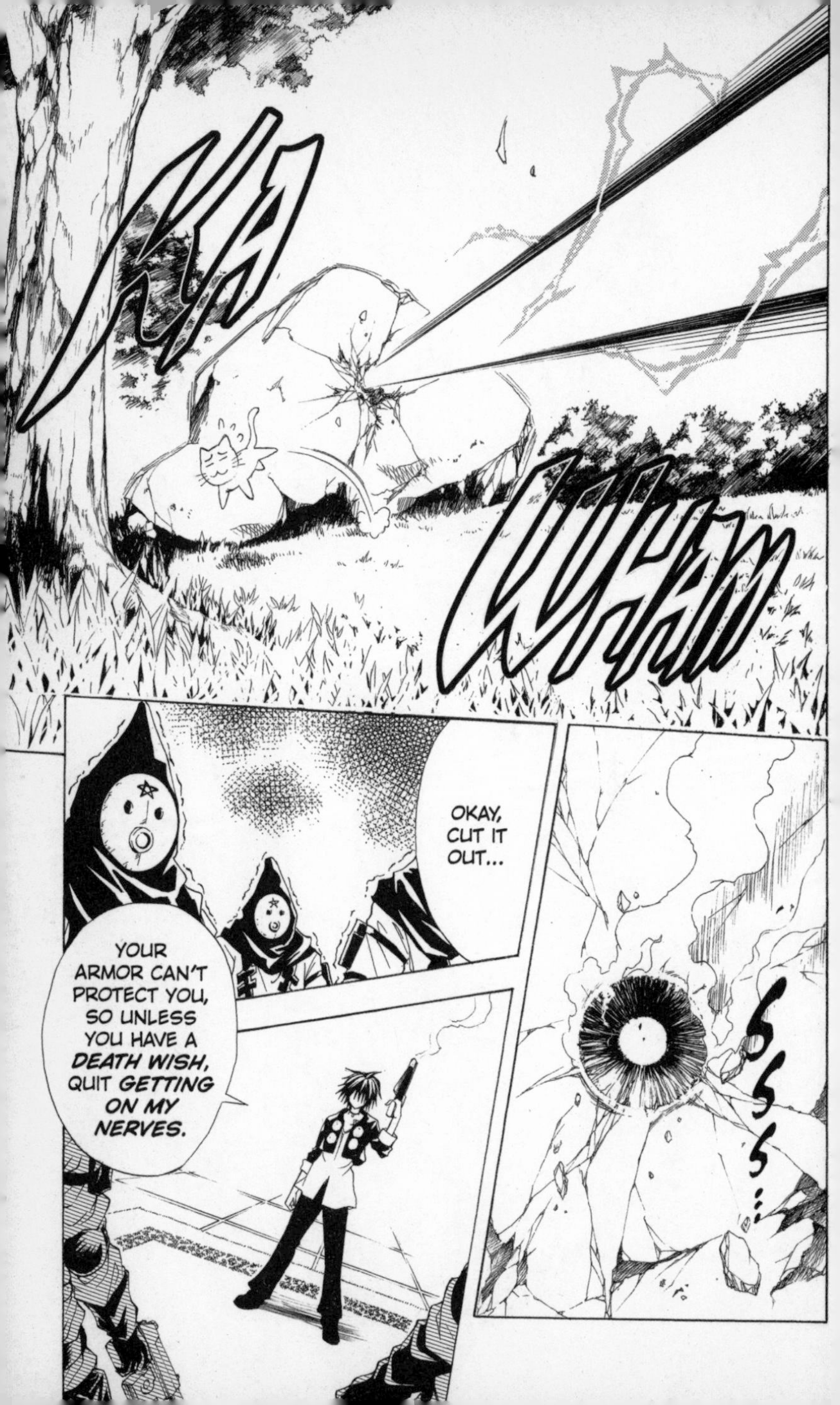
SSS...
OKAY, CUT IT OUT...
YOUR ARMOR CAN'T PROTECT YOU, SO UNLESS YOU HAVE A *DEATH WISH*, QUIT *GETTING ON MY NERVES.*

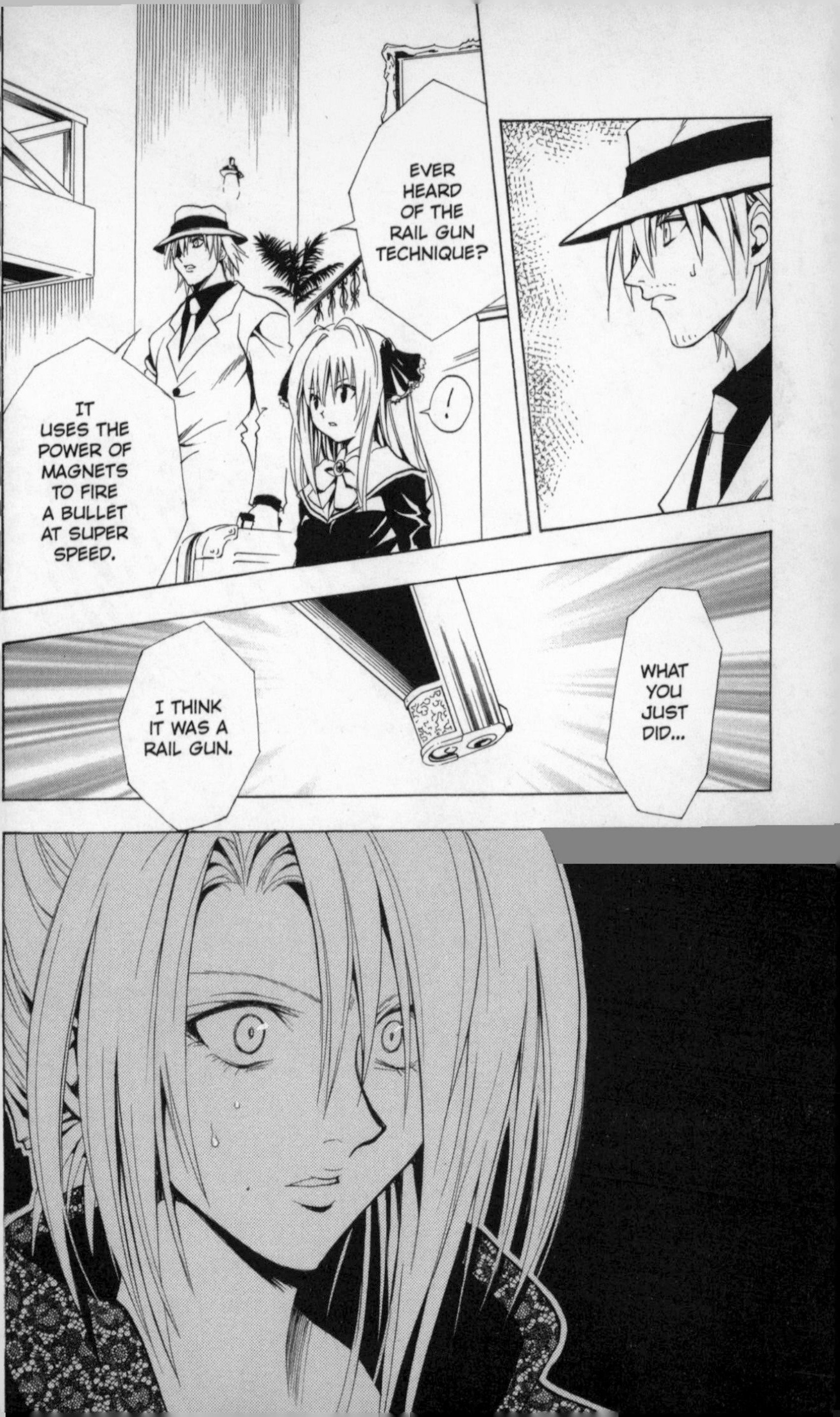
EVER HEARD OF THE RAIL GUN TECHNIQUE?
!
IT USES THE POWER OF MAGNETS TO FIRE A BULLET AT SUPER SPEED.
WHAT YOU JUST DID...
I THINK IT WAS A RAIL GUN.

RAIL GUN!

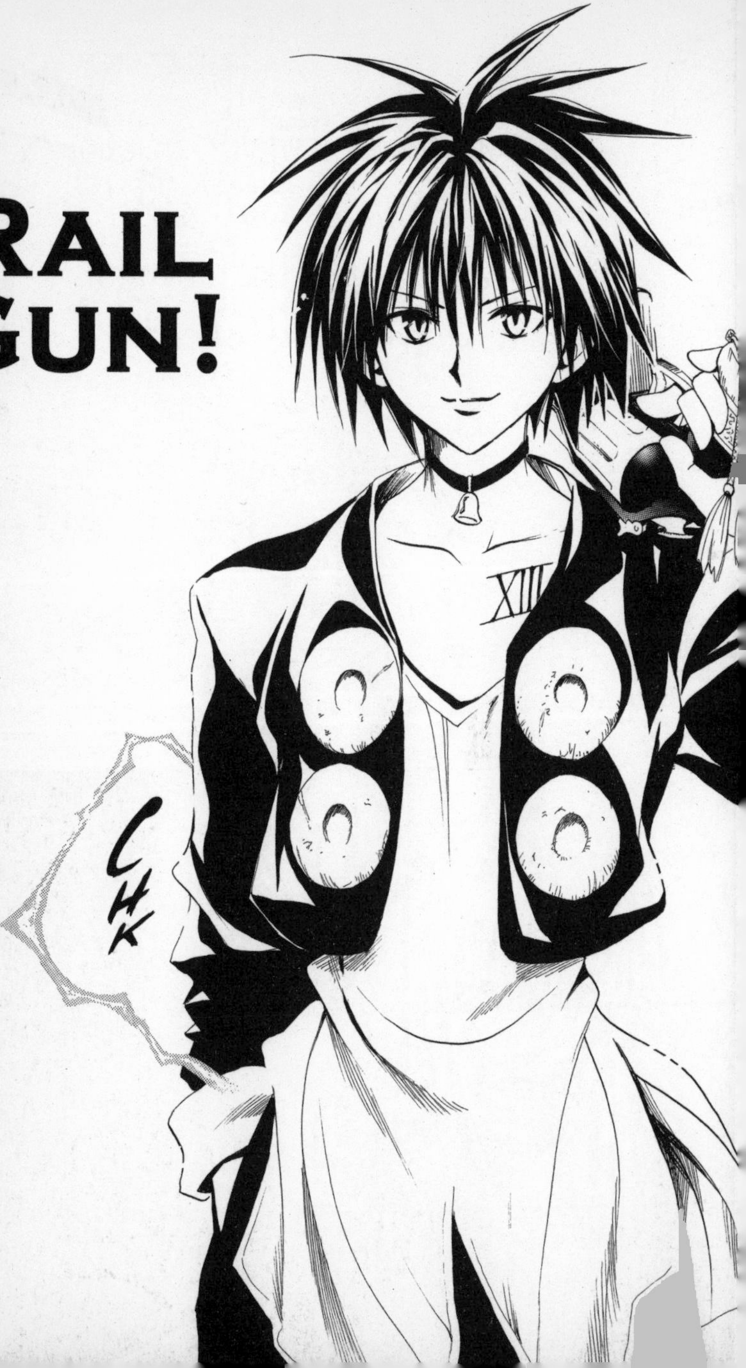
CHK

I drew several illustrations for the Black Cat novel. The novel and the manga are slightly different.

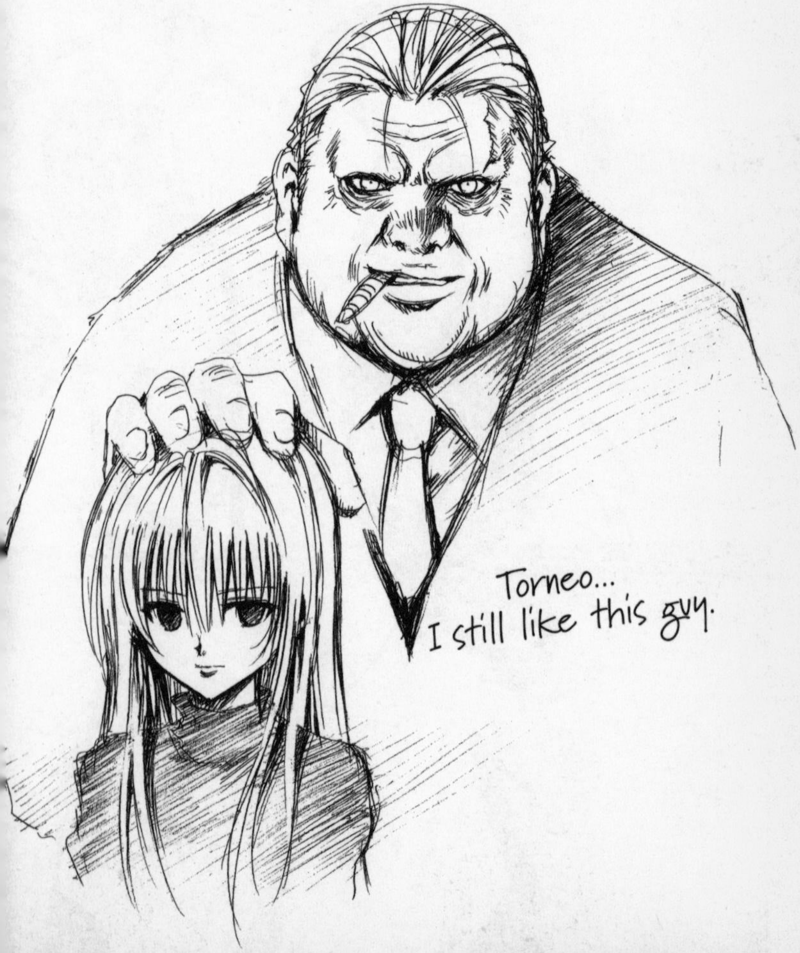
Torneo...
I still like this guy.

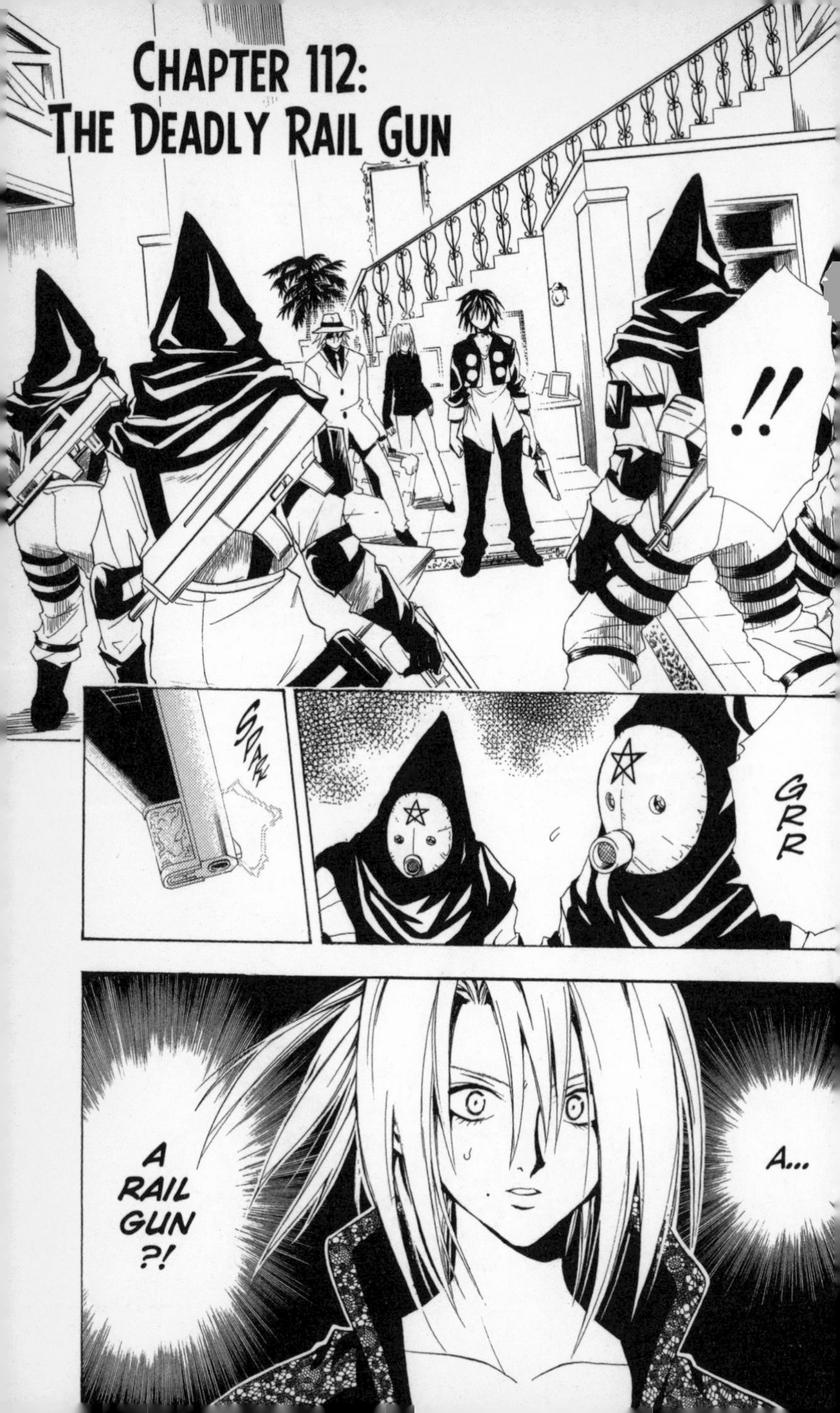
Chapter 112: The Deadly Rail Gun
!!
GRR
A...
A RAIL GUN ?!

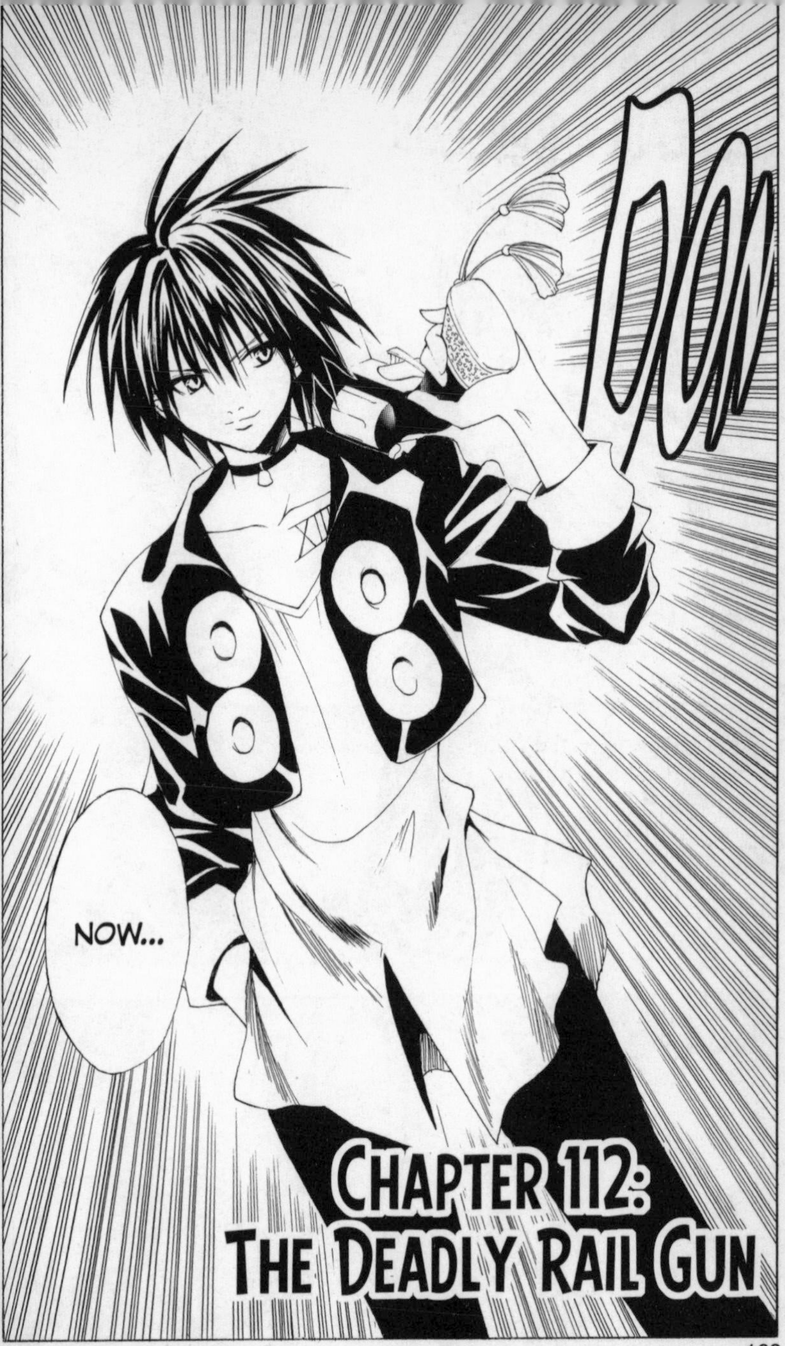
DON
NOW...
CHAPTER 112:
THE DEADLY RAIL GUN

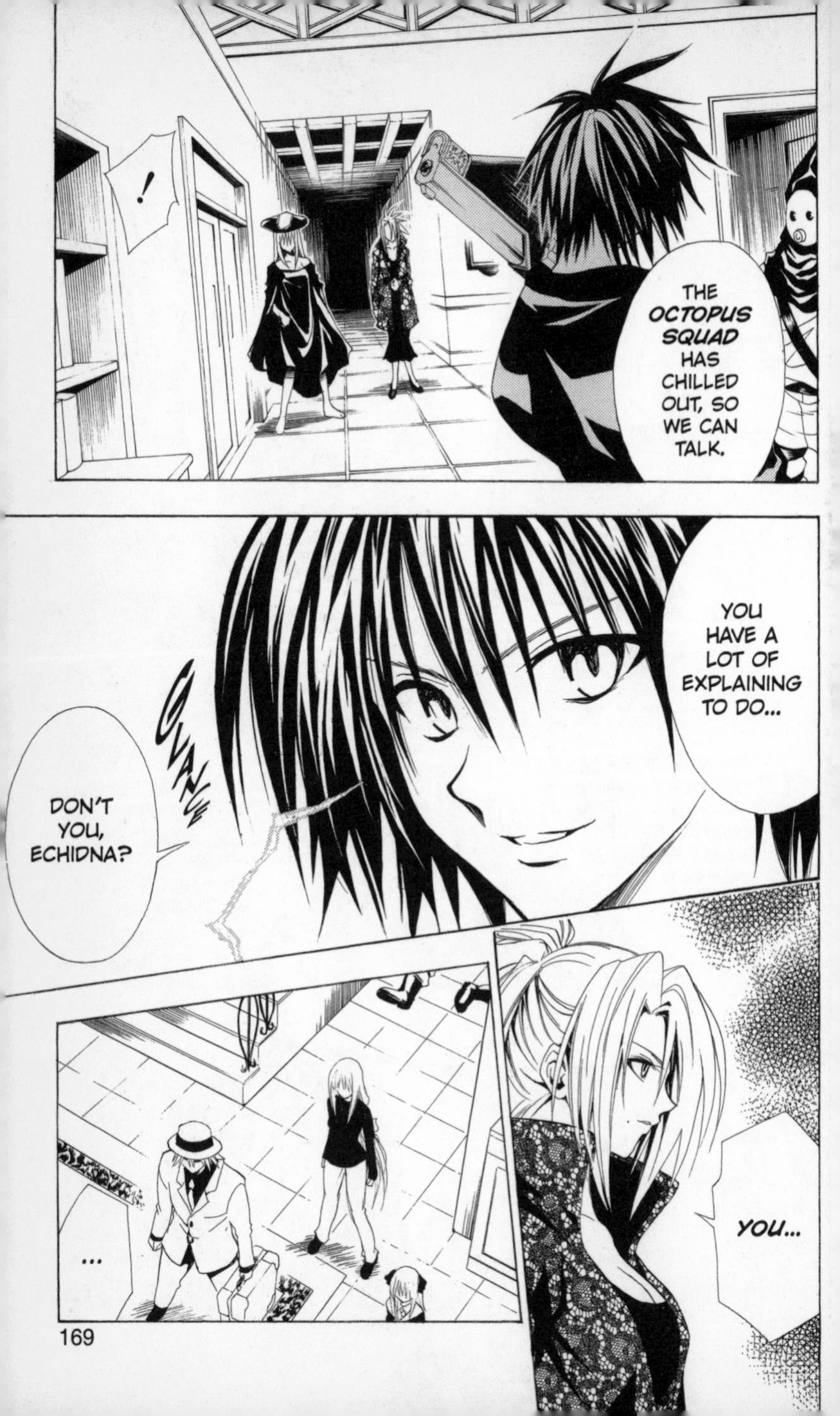
THE *OCTOPUS SQUAD* HAS CHILLED OUT, SO WE CAN TALK.
!
YOU HAVE A LOT OF EXPLAINING TO DO...
GLANCE
DON'T YOU, ECHIDNA?
YOU...
...

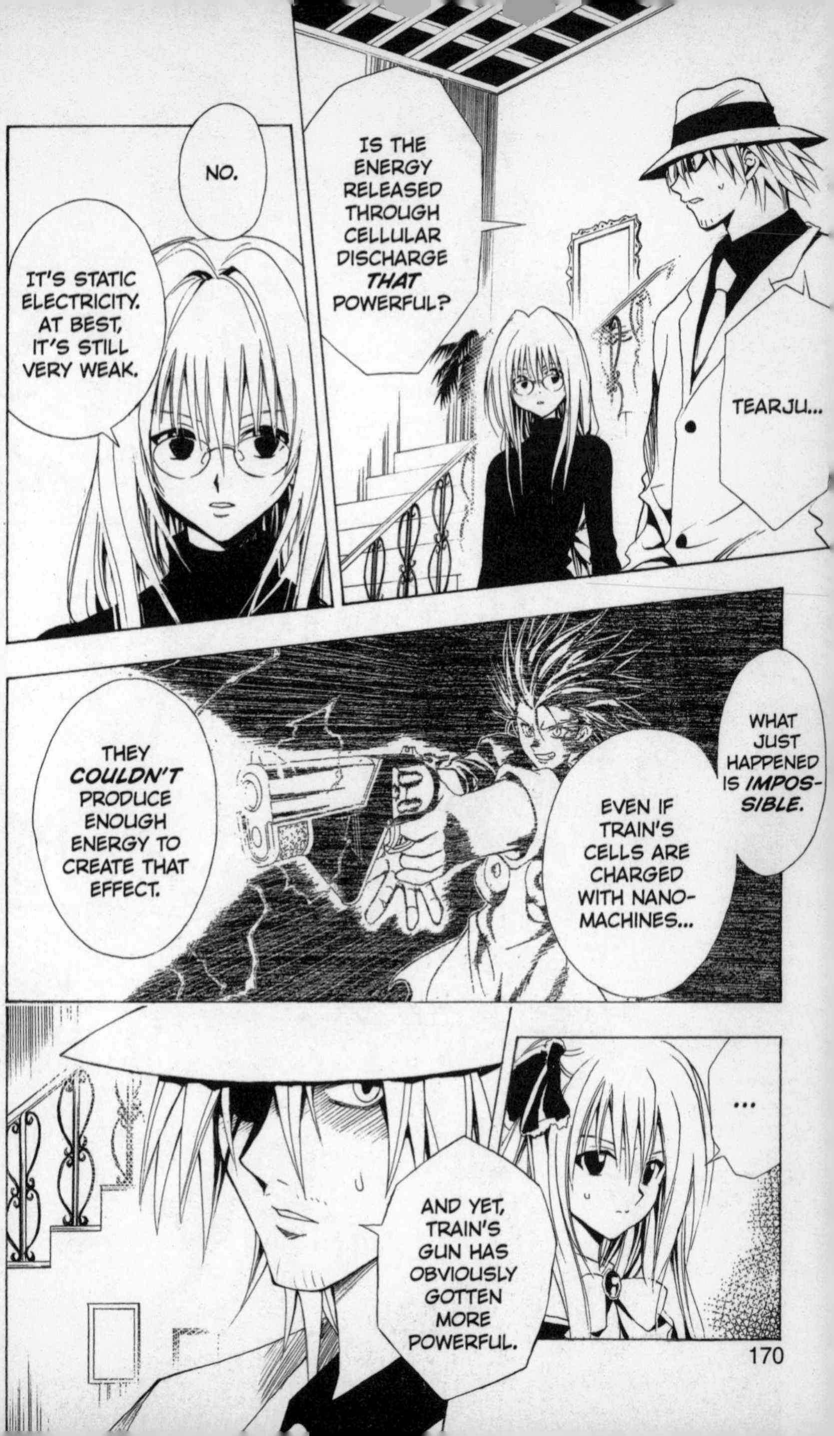

IS THE ENERGY RELEASED THROUGH CELLULAR DISCHARGE *THAT* POWERFUL?
TEARJU...
NO.
IT'S STATIC ELECTRICITY. AT BEST, IT'S STILL VERY WEAK.
WHAT JUST HAPPENED IS *IMPOSSIBLE.*
EVEN IF TRAIN'S CELLS ARE CHARGED WITH NANO-MACHINES...
THEY *COULDN'T* PRODUCE ENOUGH ENERGY TO CREATE THAT EFFECT.
...
AND YET, TRAIN'S GUN HAS OBVIOUSLY GOTTEN MORE POWERFUL.

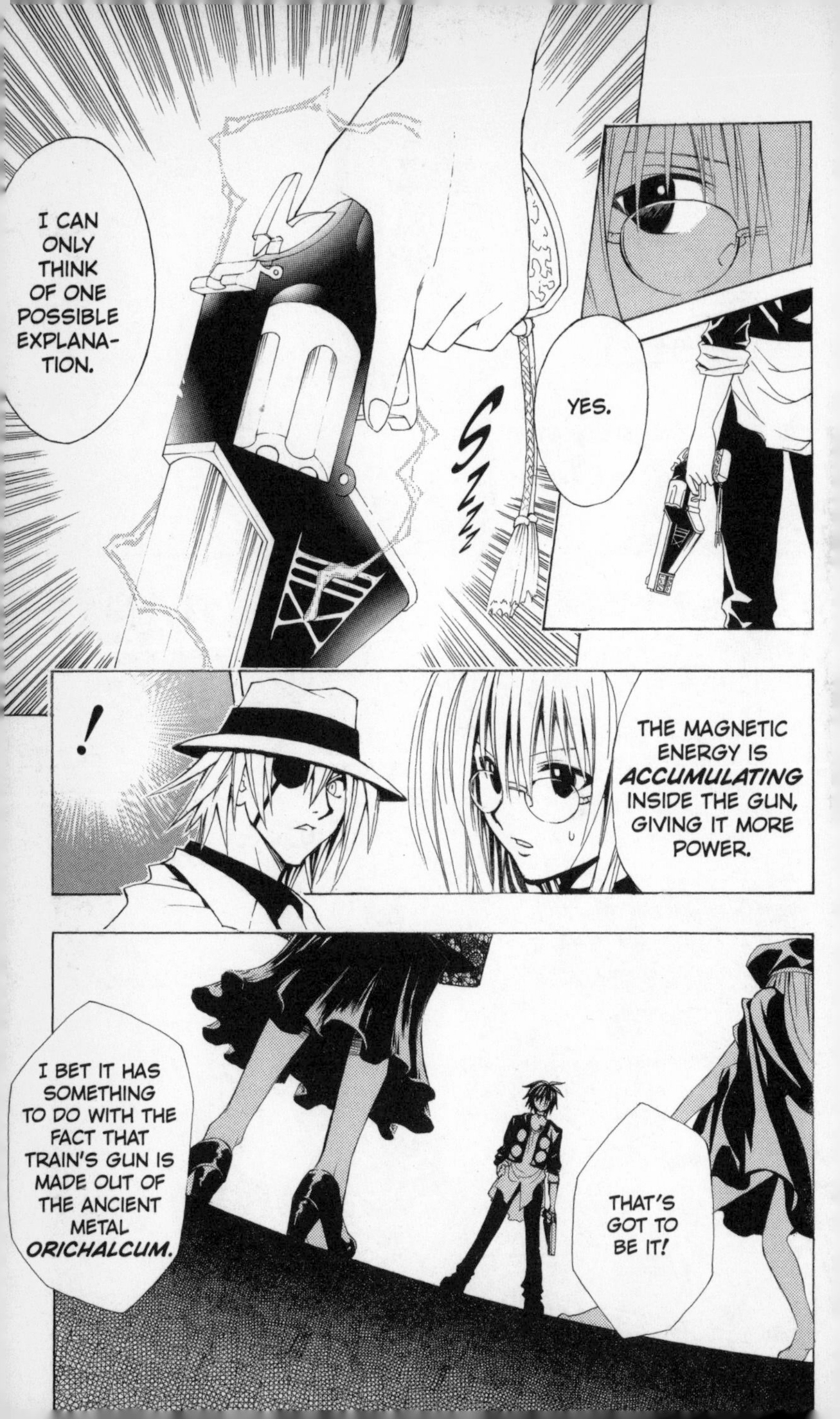
YES.
I CAN ONLY THINK OF ONE POSSIBLE EXPLANA-TION.
THE MAGNETIC ENERGY IS *ACCUMULATING* INSIDE THE GUN, GIVING IT MORE POWER.
!
THAT'S GOT TO BE IT!
I BET IT HAS SOMETHING TO DO WITH THE FACT THAT TRAIN'S GUN IS MADE OUT OF THE ANCIENT METAL *ORICHALCUM*.

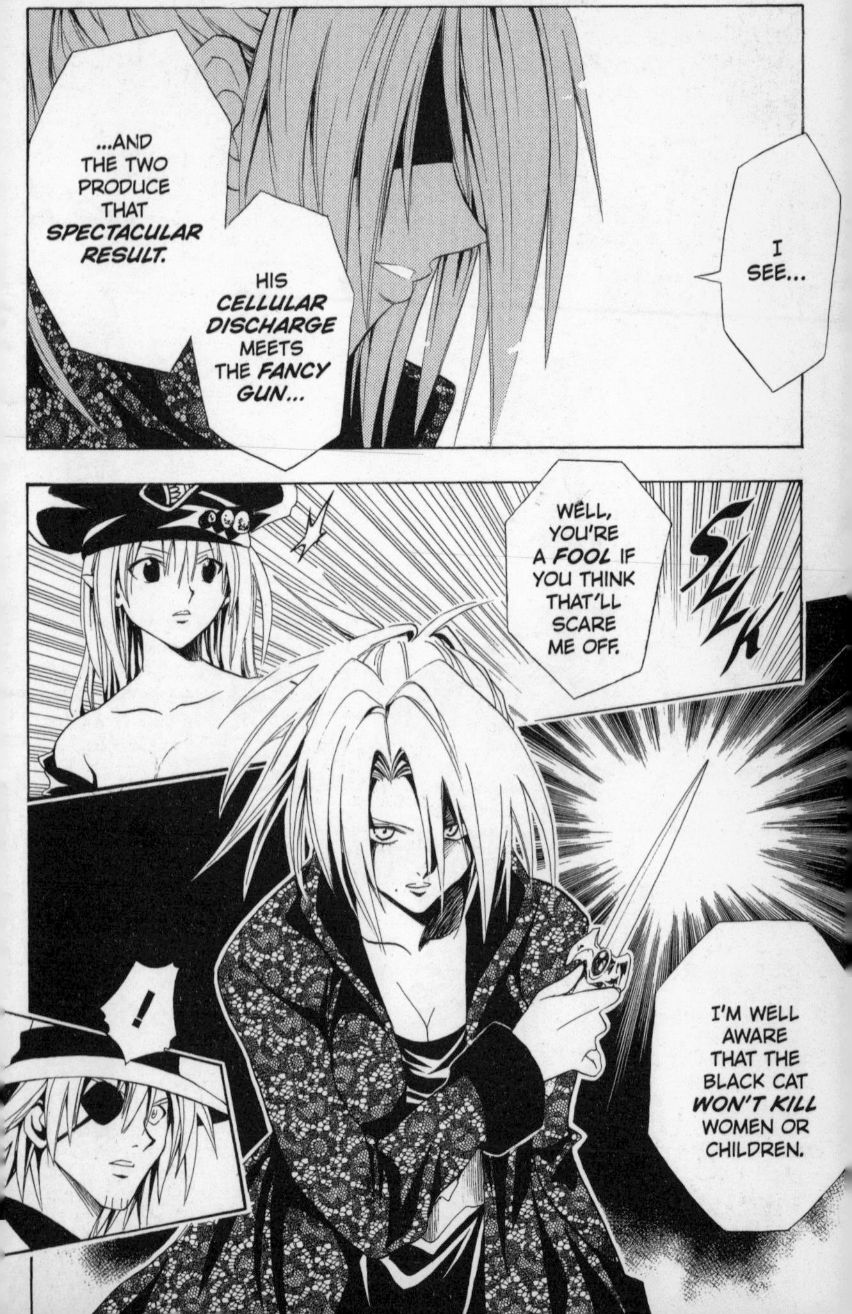
I SEE...
HIS CELLULAR DISCHARGE MEETS THE FANCY GUN...
...AND THE TWO PRODUCE THAT SPECTACULAR RESULT.
SLLK
WELL, YOU'RE A FOOL IF YOU THINK THAT'LL SCARE ME OFF.
I'M WELL AWARE THAT THE BLACK CAT WON'T KILL WOMEN OR CHILDREN.
!

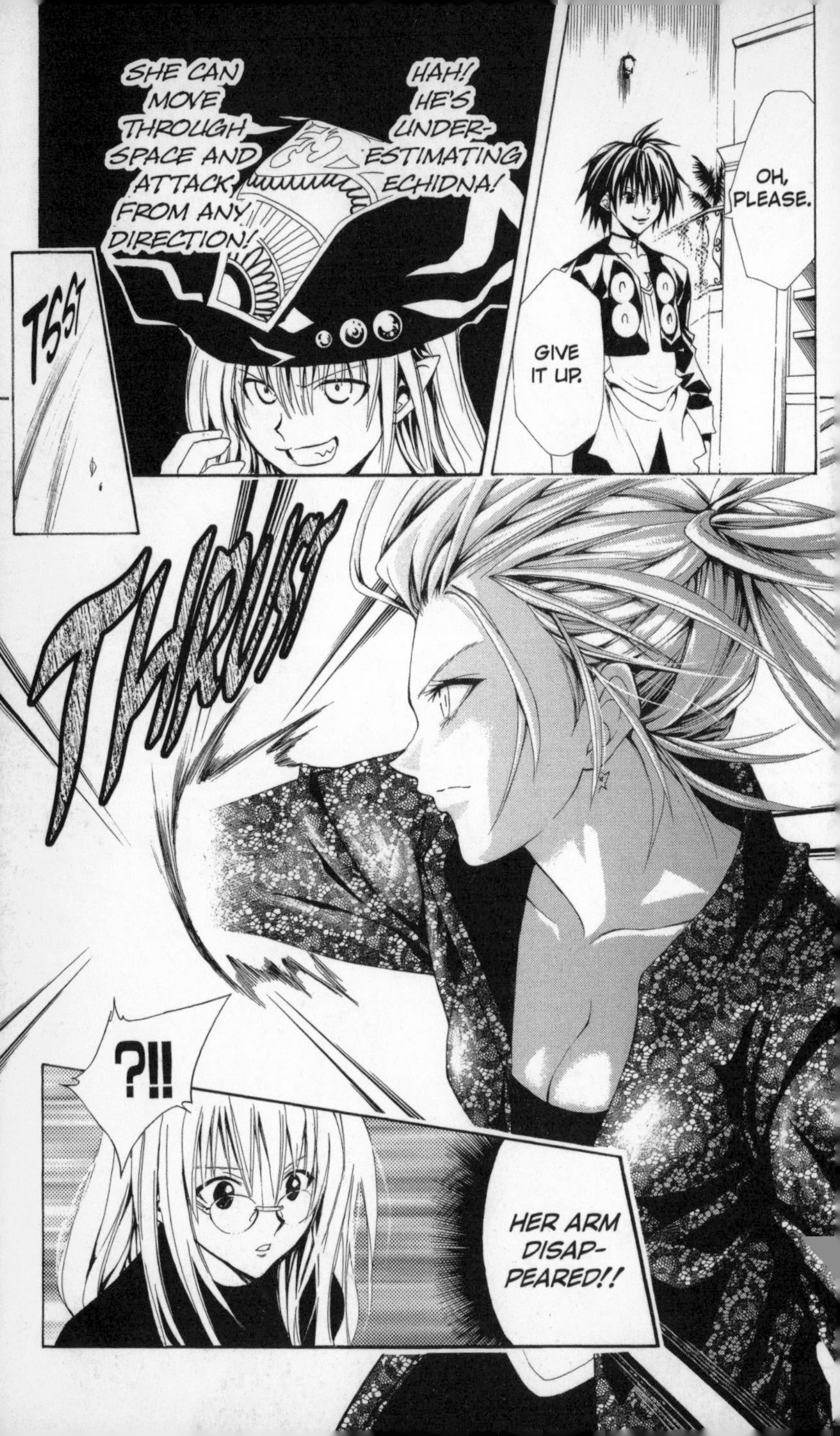
OH, PLEASE.
GIVE IT UP.
HAH! HE'S UNDER-ESTIMATING ECHIDNA!
SHE CAN MOVE THROUGH SPACE AND ATTACK FROM ANY DIRECTION!
TSST
THRUST
HER ARM DISAP-PEARED!!
?!!

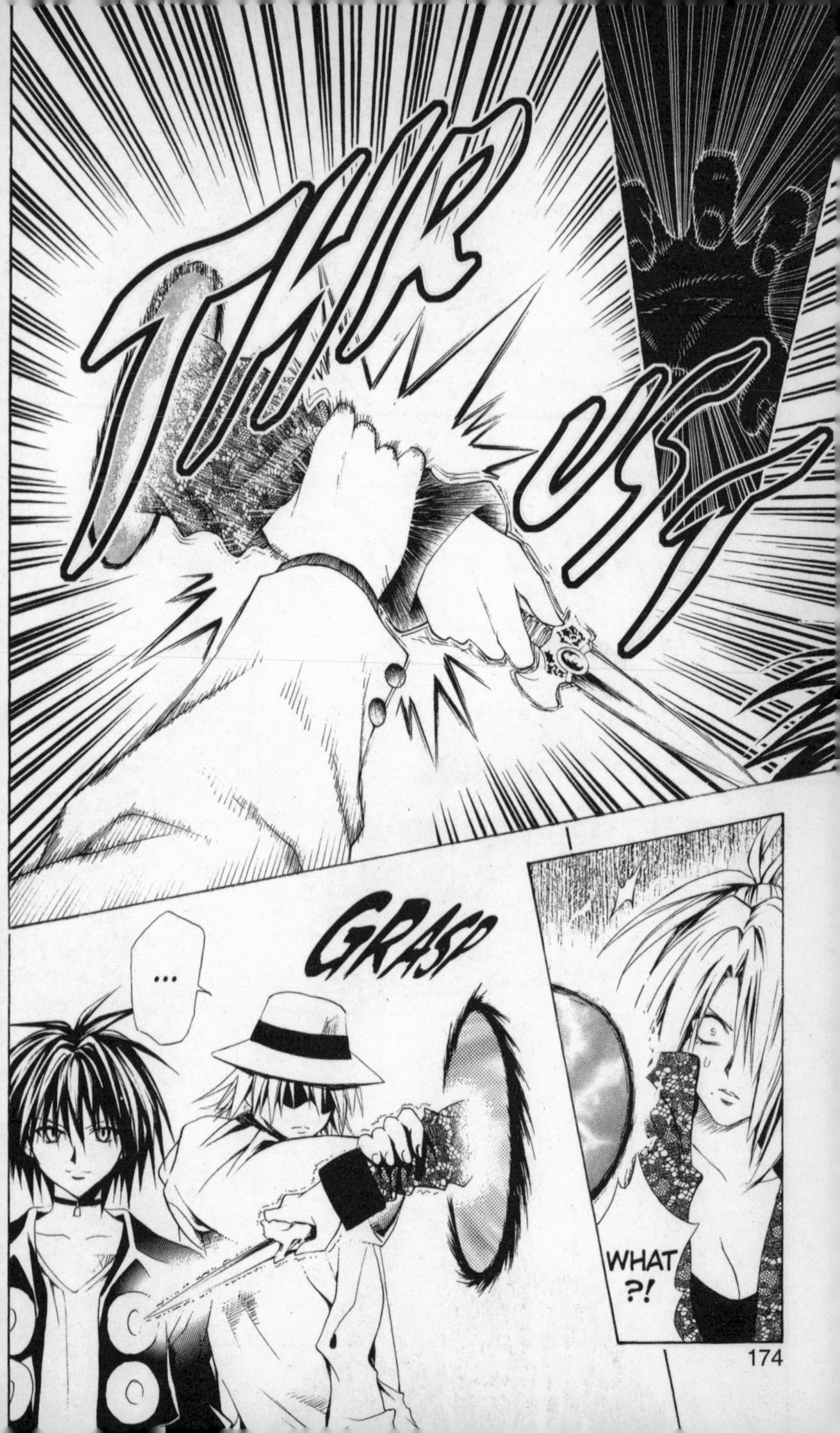
THRUST
WHAT ?!
GRASP
...

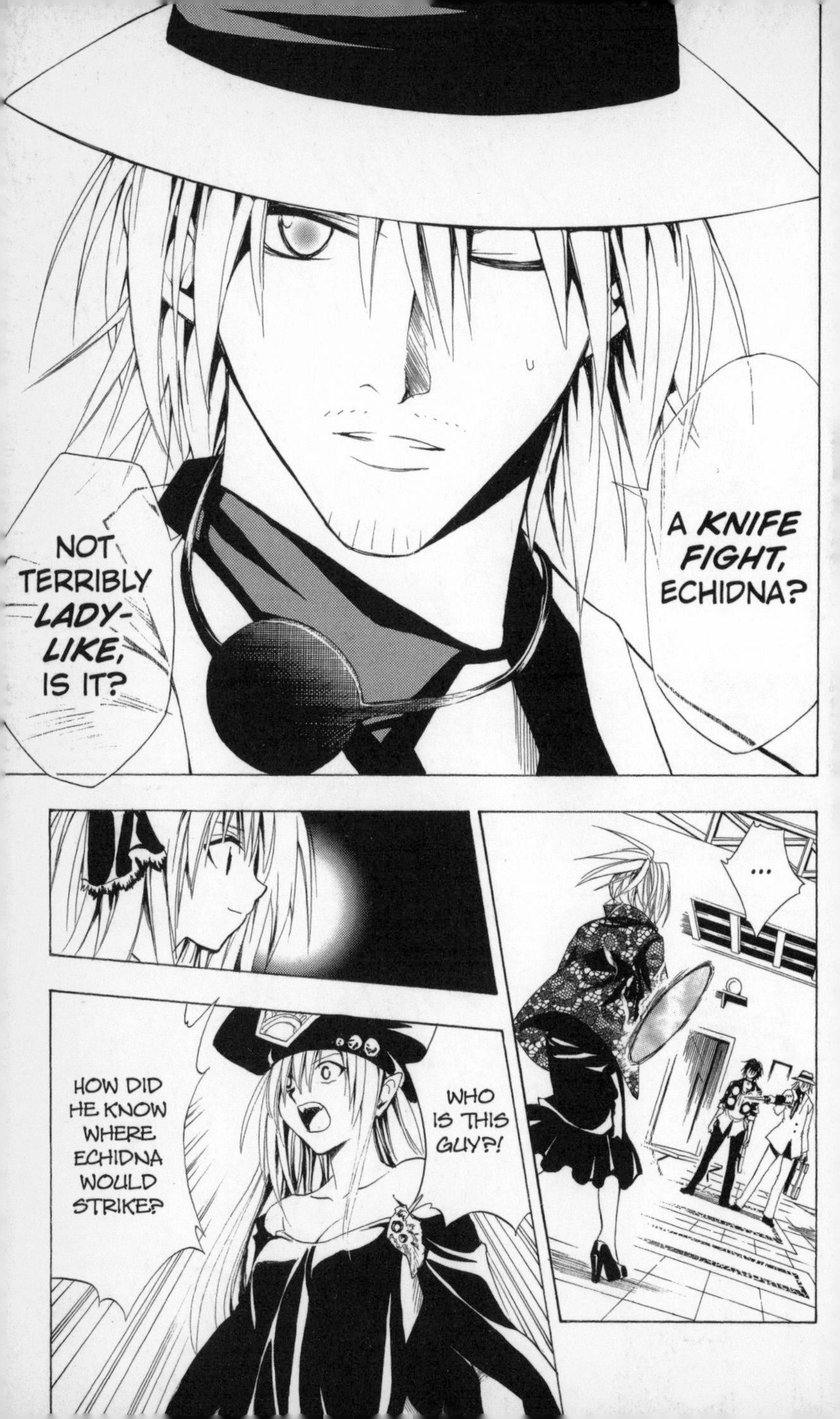
A KNIFE FIGHT, ECHIDNA?
NOT TERRIBLY LADY-LIKE, IS IT?
...
WHO IS THIS GUY?!
HOW DID HE KNOW WHERE ECHIDNA WOULD STRIKE?

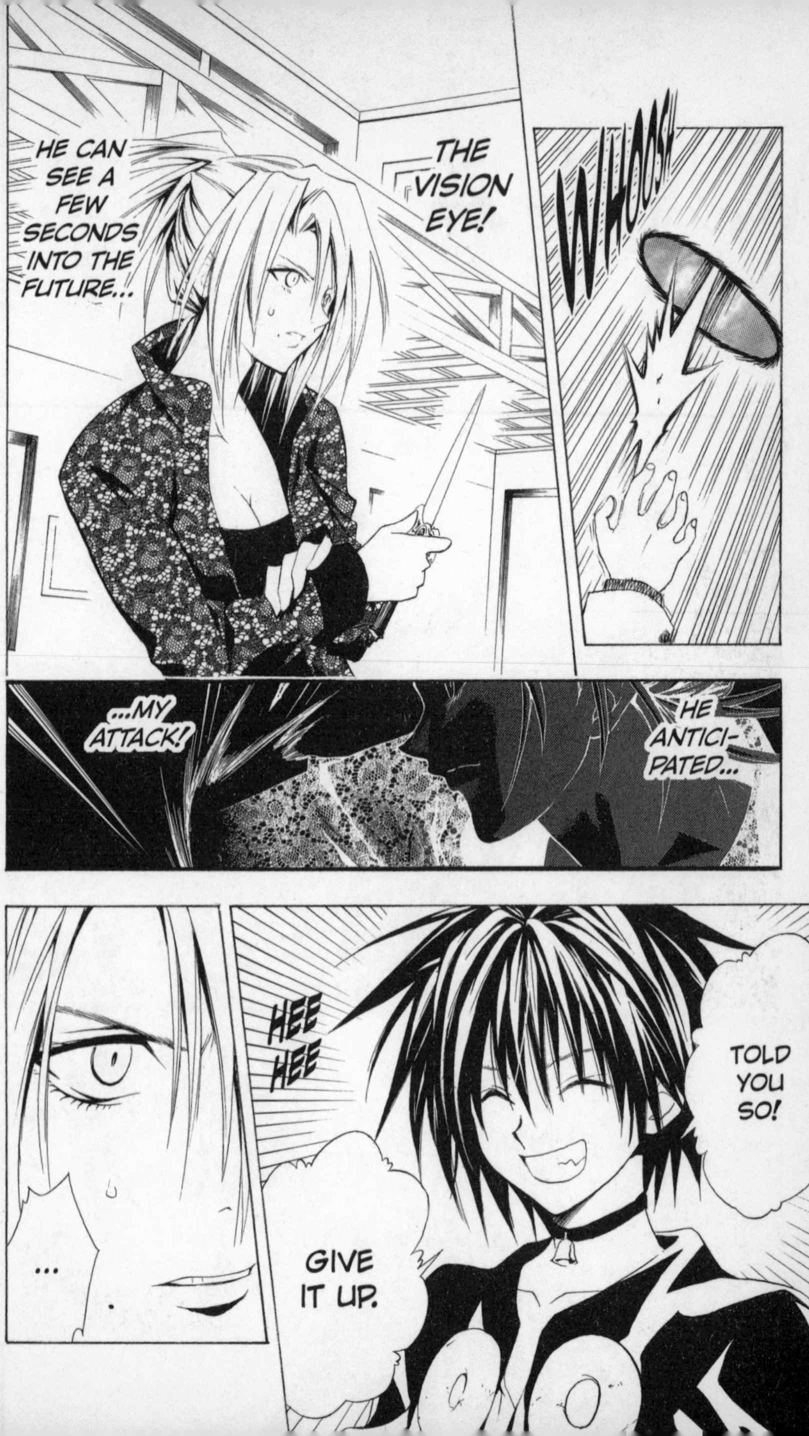
WHOOSH
THE VISION EYE!
HE CAN SEE A FEW SECONDS INTO THE FUTURE...
HE ANTICIPATED...
...MY ATTACK!
TOLD YOU SO!
HEE HEE
GIVE IT UP.
...

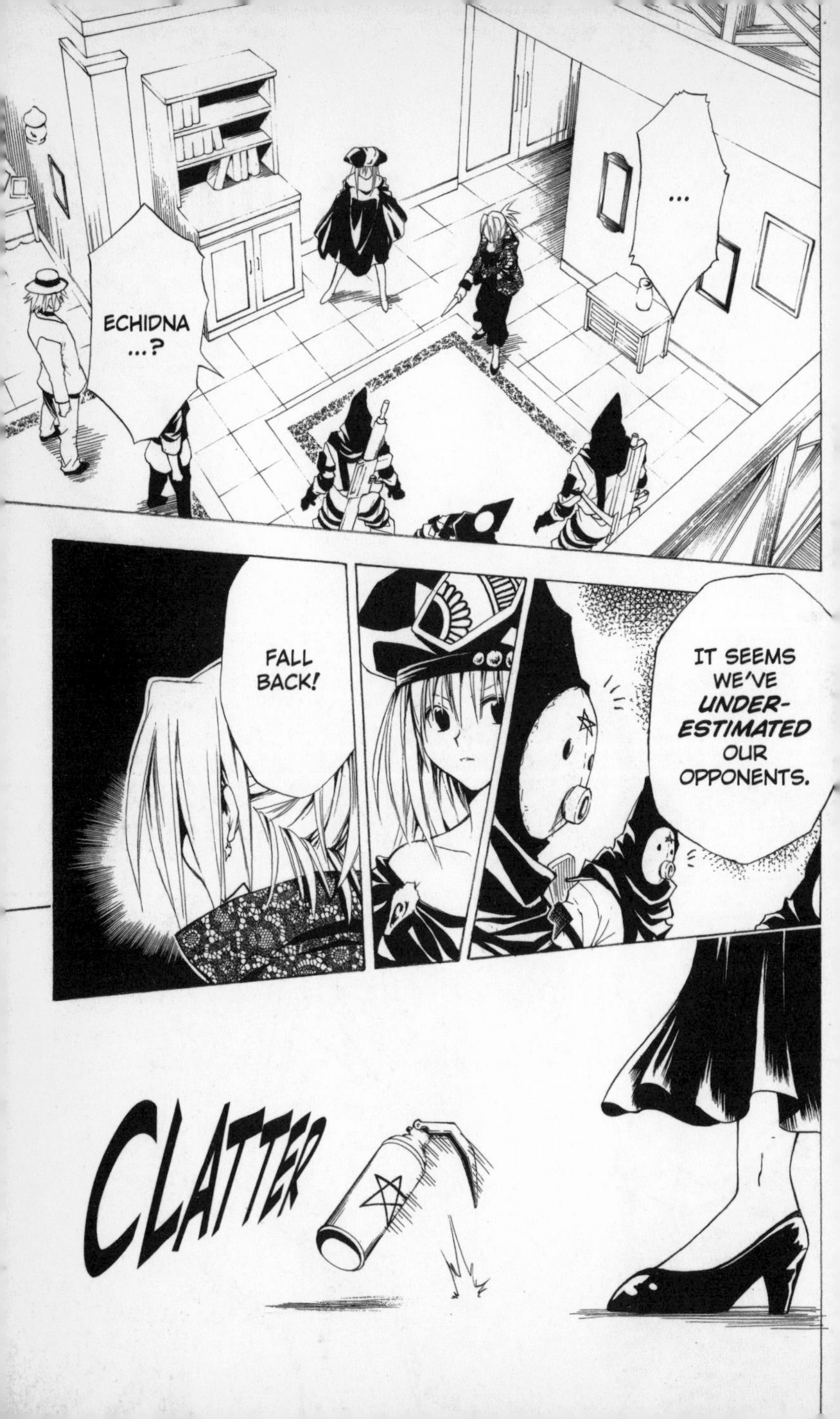
...
ECHIDNA ...?
IT SEEMS WE'VE UNDER-ESTIMATED OUR OPPONENTS.
FALL BACK!
CLATTER

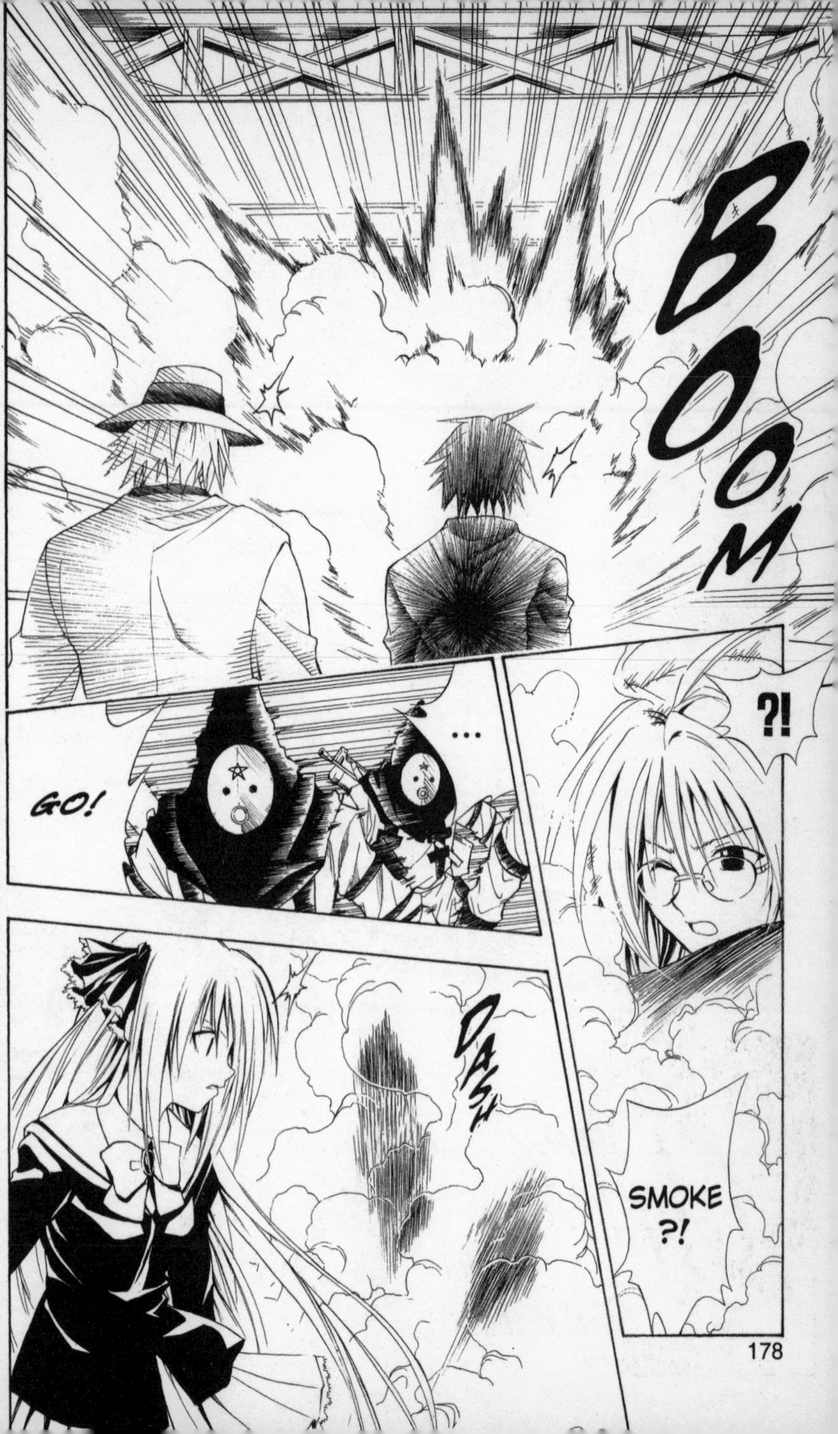
BOOM
?!
SMOKE ?!
...
GO!
DASH

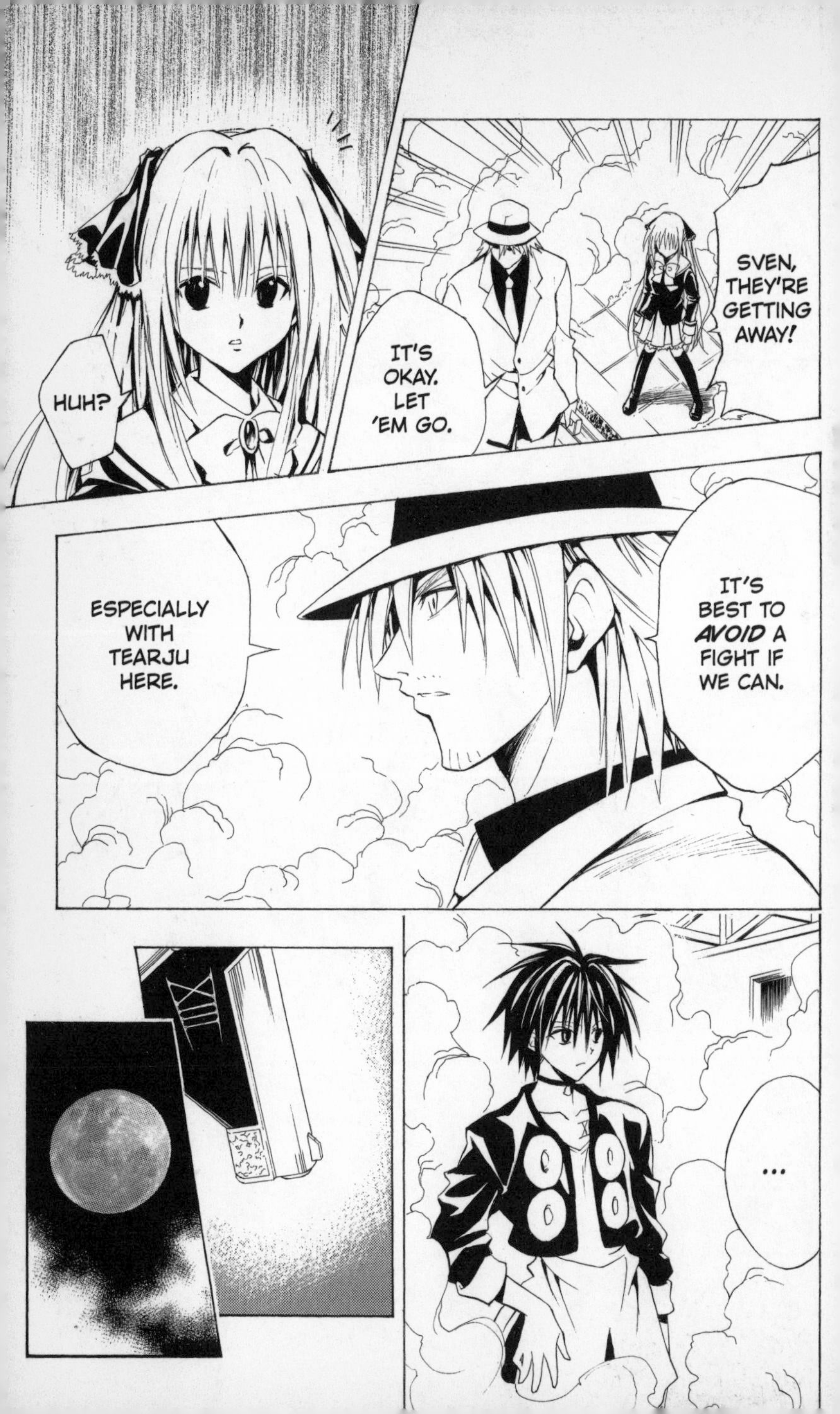
SVEN, THEY'RE GETTING AWAY!
IT'S OKAY. LET 'EM GO.
HUH?
IT'S BEST TO *AVOID* A FIGHT IF WE CAN.
ESPECIALLY WITH TEARJU HERE.
...

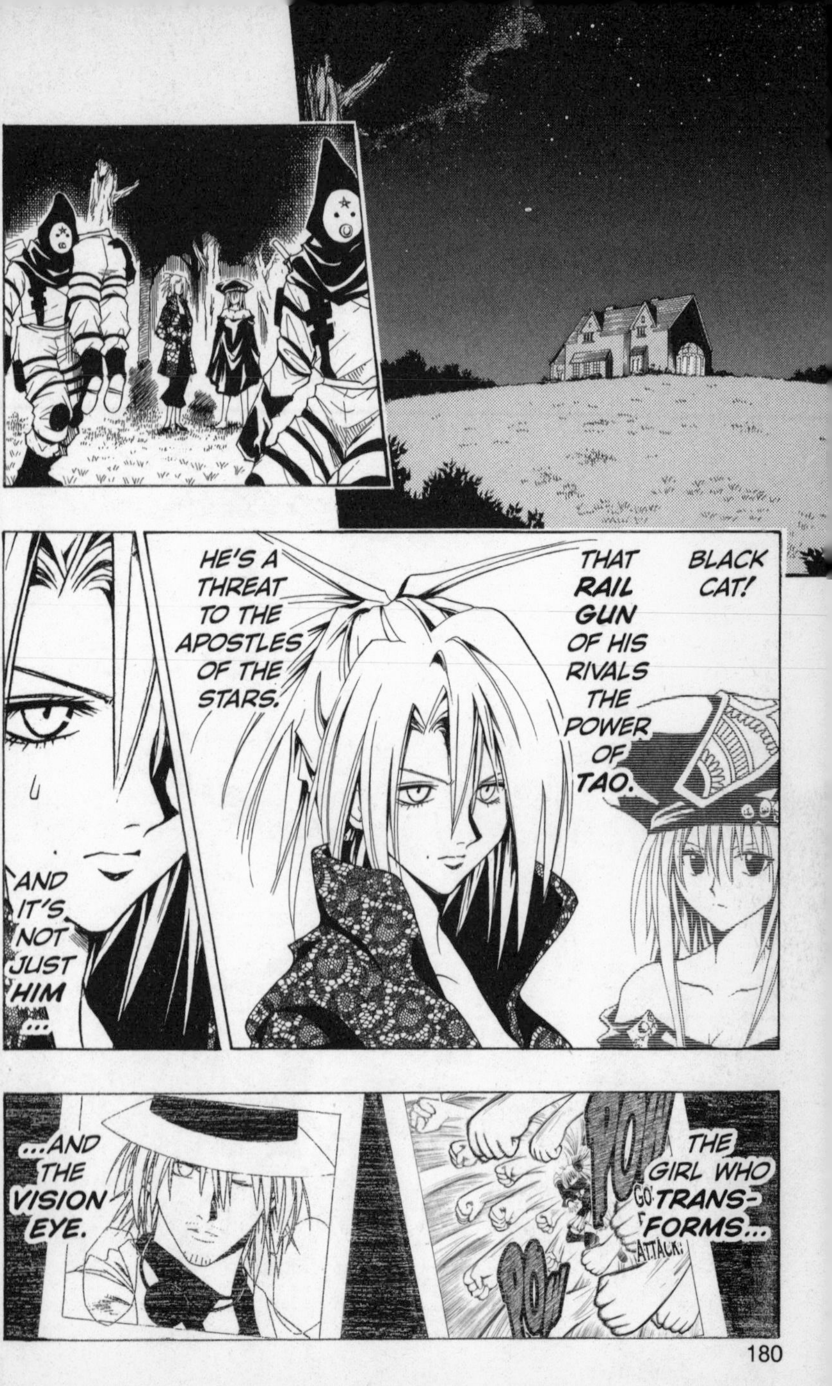
BLACK CAT!
THAT RAIL GUN OF HIS RIVALS THE POWER OF TAO.
HE'S A THREAT TO THE APOSTLES OF THE STARS.
AND IT'S NOT JUST HIM...
THE GIRL WHO TRANS-FORMS...
ATTACK!
...AND THE VISION EYE.

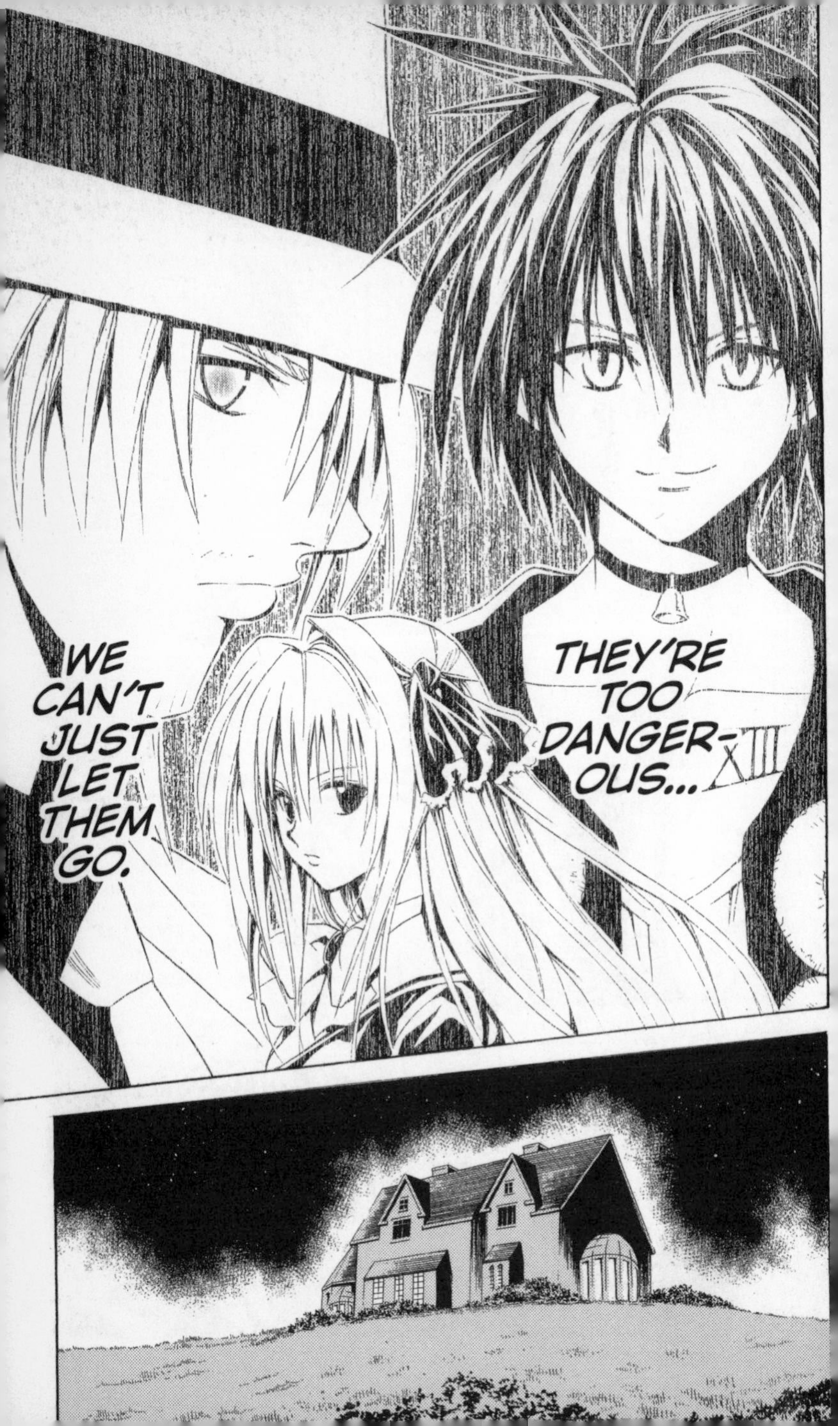
THEY'RE TOO DANGER-OUS...
WE CAN'T JUST LET THEM GO.

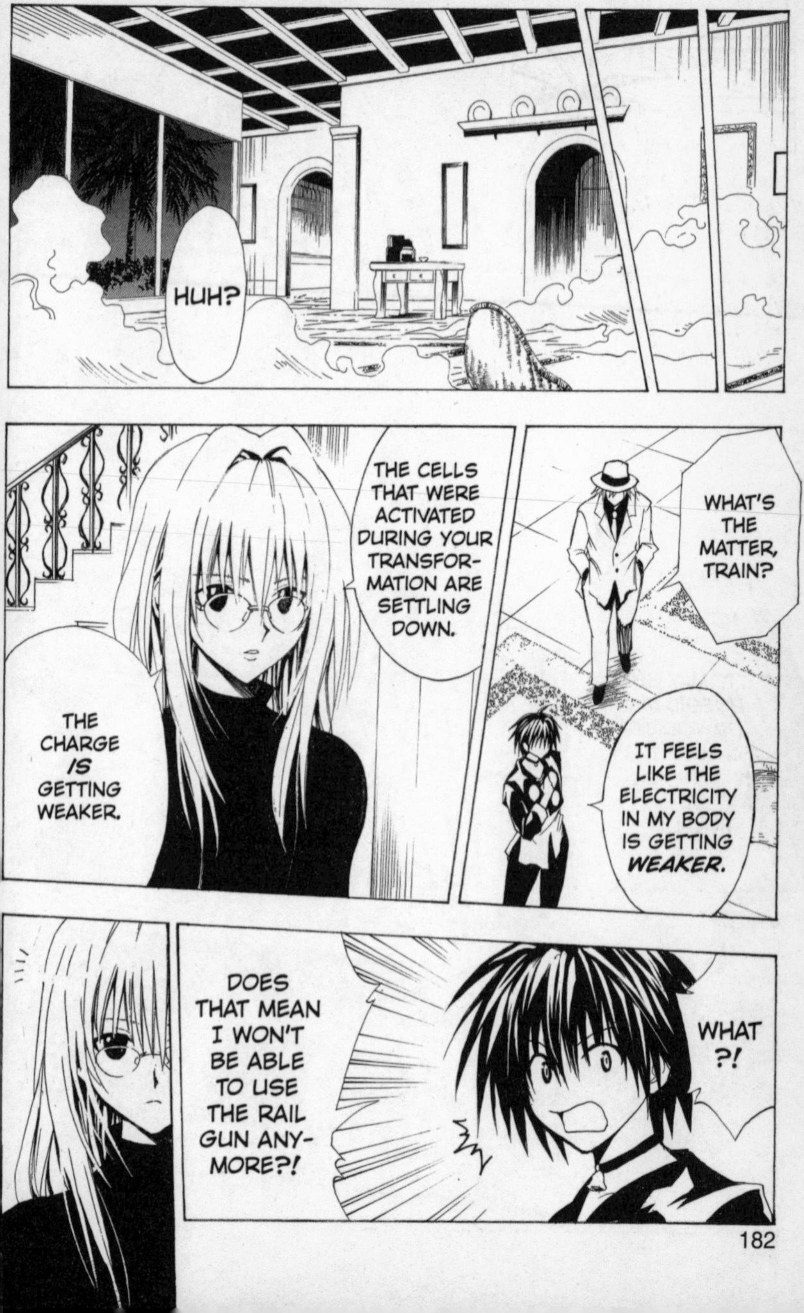
HUH?
WHAT'S THE MATTER, TRAIN?
IT FEELS LIKE THE ELECTRICITY IN MY BODY IS GETTING *WEAKER.*
THE CELLS THAT WERE ACTIVATED DURING YOUR TRANSFORMATION ARE SETTLING DOWN.
THE CHARGE *IS* GETTING WEAKER.
WHAT?!
DOES THAT MEAN I WON'T BE ABLE TO USE THE RAIL GUN ANYMORE?!

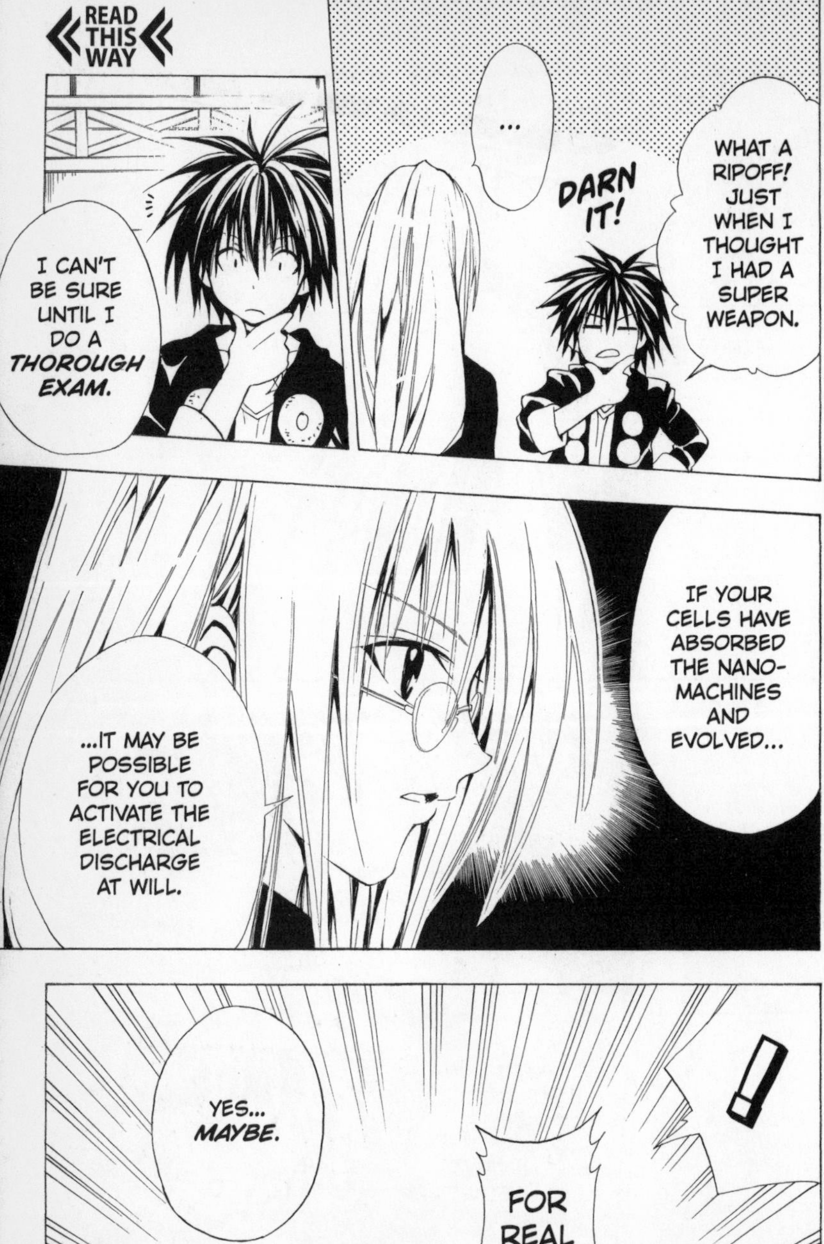
READ THIS WAY
WHAT A RIPOFF! JUST WHEN I THOUGHT I HAD A SUPER WEAPON.
DARN IT!
...
I CAN'T BE SURE UNTIL I DO A *THOROUGH EXAM.*
IF YOUR CELLS HAVE ABSORBED THE NANO-MACHINES AND EVOLVED...
...IT MAY BE POSSIBLE FOR YOU TO ACTIVATE THE ELECTRICAL DISCHARGE AT WILL.
!
FOR REAL?!
YES... *MAYBE.*

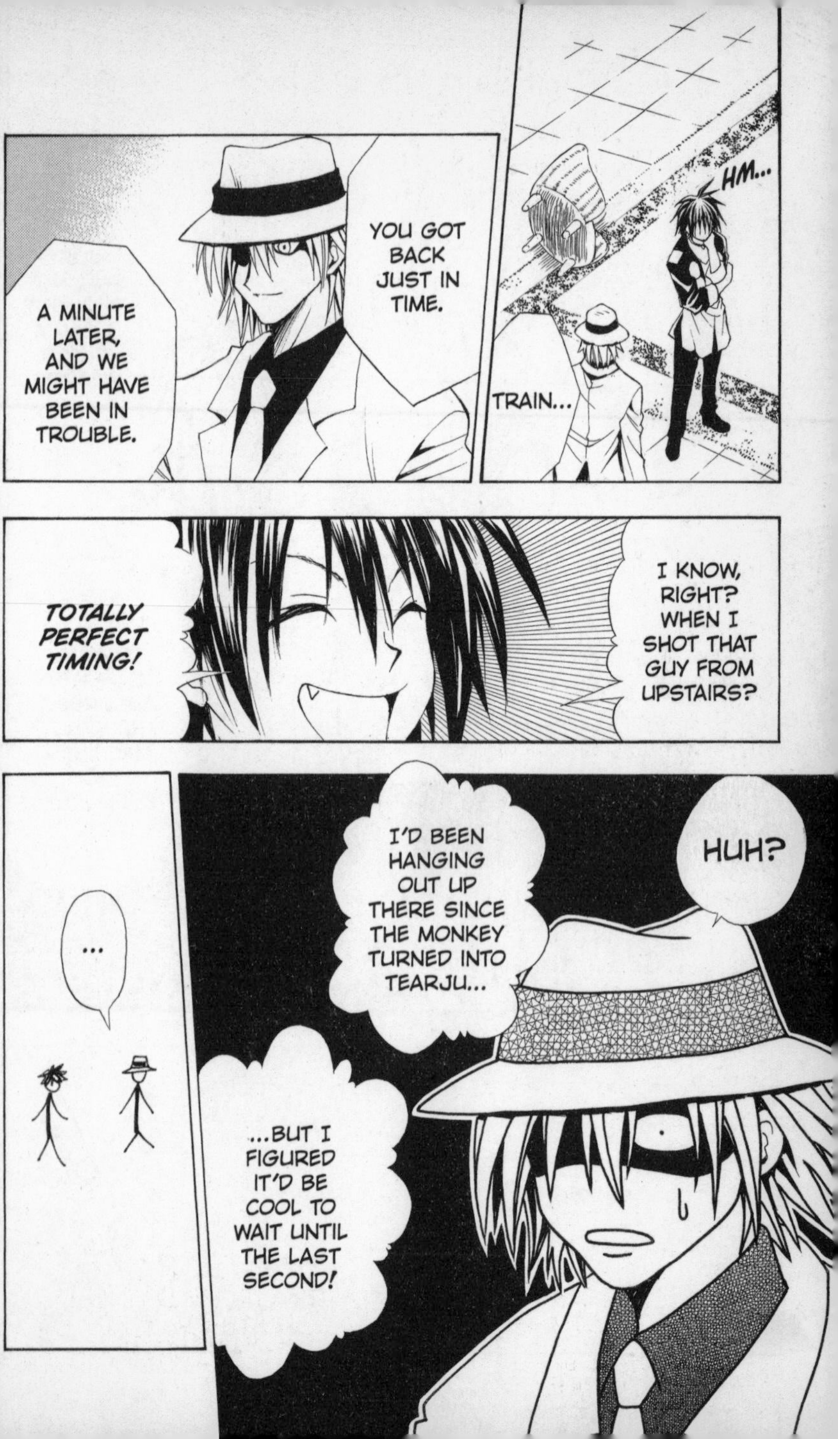
HM...
TRAIN...
YOU GOT BACK JUST IN TIME.
A MINUTE LATER, AND WE MIGHT HAVE BEEN IN TROUBLE.
I KNOW, RIGHT? WHEN I SHOT THAT GUY FROM UPSTAIRS?
TOTALLY PERFECT TIMING!
HUH?
I'D BEEN HANGING OUT UP THERE SINCE THE MONKEY TURNED INTO TEARJU...
...BUT I FIGURED IT'D BE COOL TO WAIT UNTIL THE LAST SECOND!
...

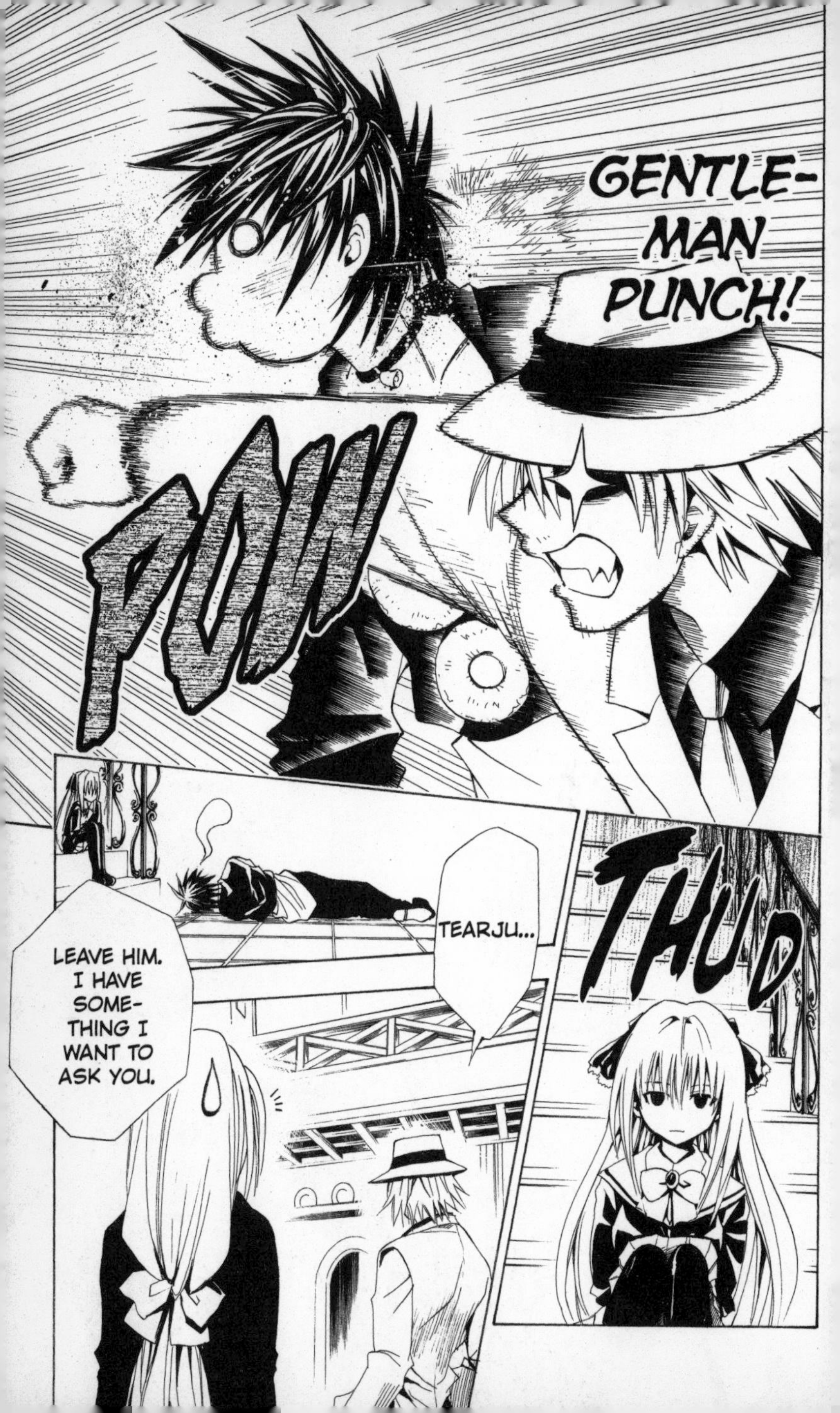
GENTLE-MAN PUNCH!
POW
THUD
TEARJU...
LEAVE HIM. I HAVE SOME-THING I WANT TO ASK YOU.

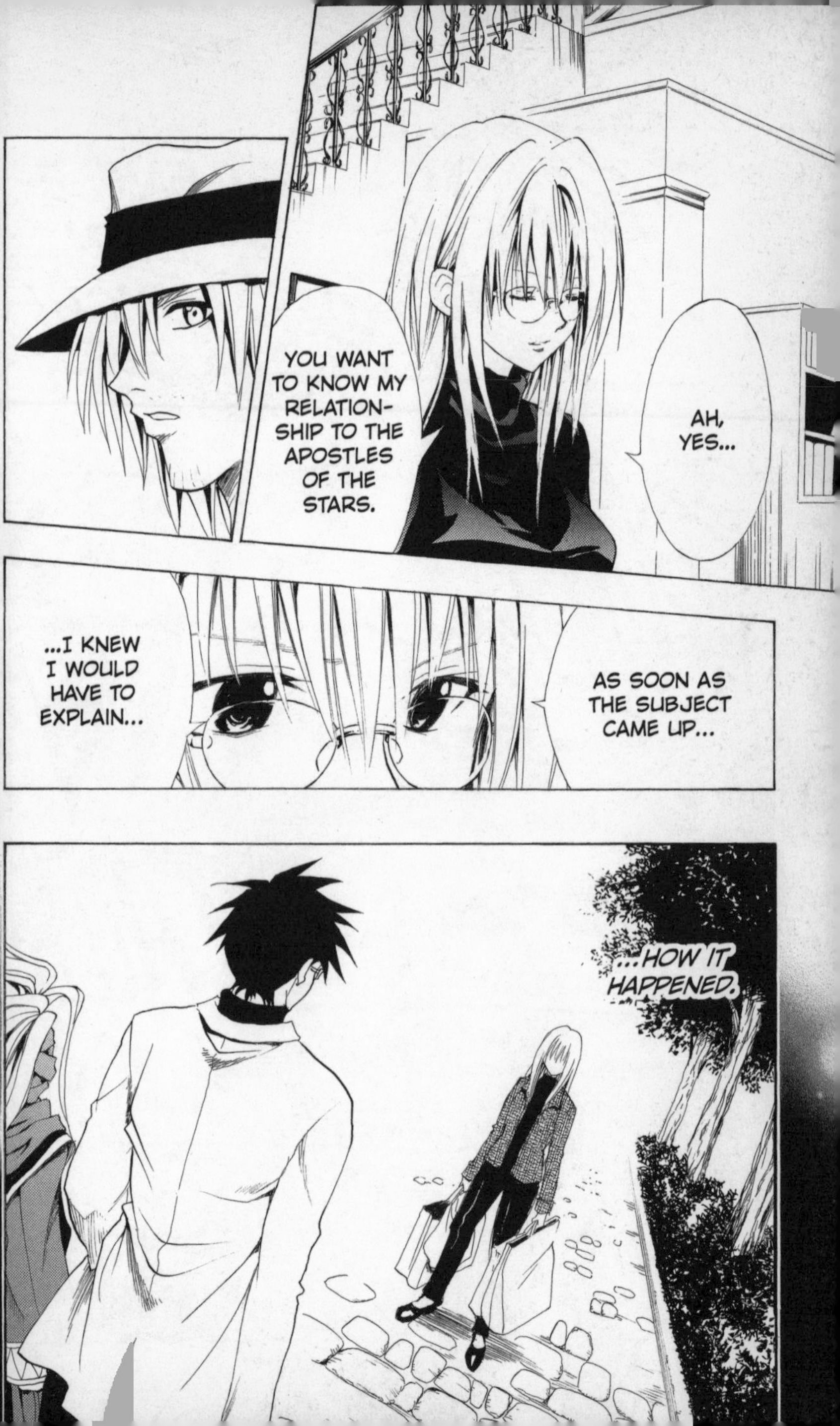
AH, YES...
YOU WANT TO KNOW MY RELATION-SHIP TO THE APOSTLES OF THE STARS.
AS SOON AS THE SUBJECT CAME UP...
...I KNEW I WOULD HAVE TO EXPLAIN...
...HOW IT HAPPENED.

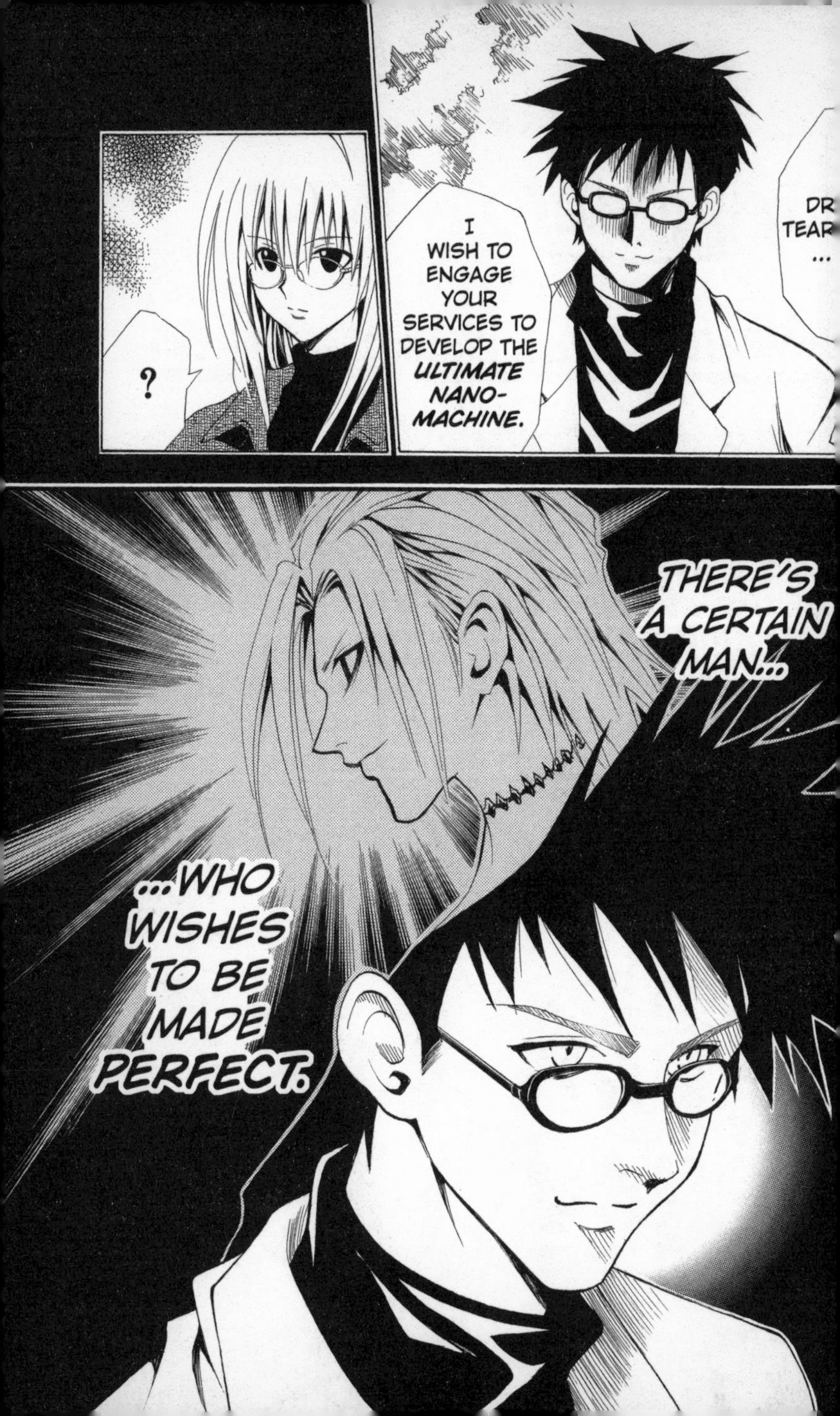
DR TEAR ...
I WISH TO ENGAGE YOUR SERVICES TO DEVELOP THE *ULTIMATE NANO-MACHINE.*
?
THERE'S A CERTAIN MAN...
...WHO WISHES TO BE MADE PERFECT.

BLACK CAT

FACTOID

MASKED WARRIORS: THE SHOOTING STAR UNIT

A NEW UNIT COMPOSED OF MEMBERS OF THE
APOSTLES OF THE STARS, FORMED TO SUPPORT
THE APOSTLES' GOAL OF REVOLUTION.
WHILE THEY ARE NOT TAOISTS, EACH IS AN
EXCEPTIONALLY SKILLED WARRIOR. THEY'VE BEEN
INVOLVED IN MOST OF CREED'S OPERATIONS SINCE
THE ASSASSINATIONS AT THE WORLD CONFERENCE,
THOUGH IT IS STILL UNCLEAR HOW MANY OF
THEM THERE ARE. TRAIN HAS FOR SOME REASON
NICKNAMED THE GROUP "THE OCTOPUS SQUAD."

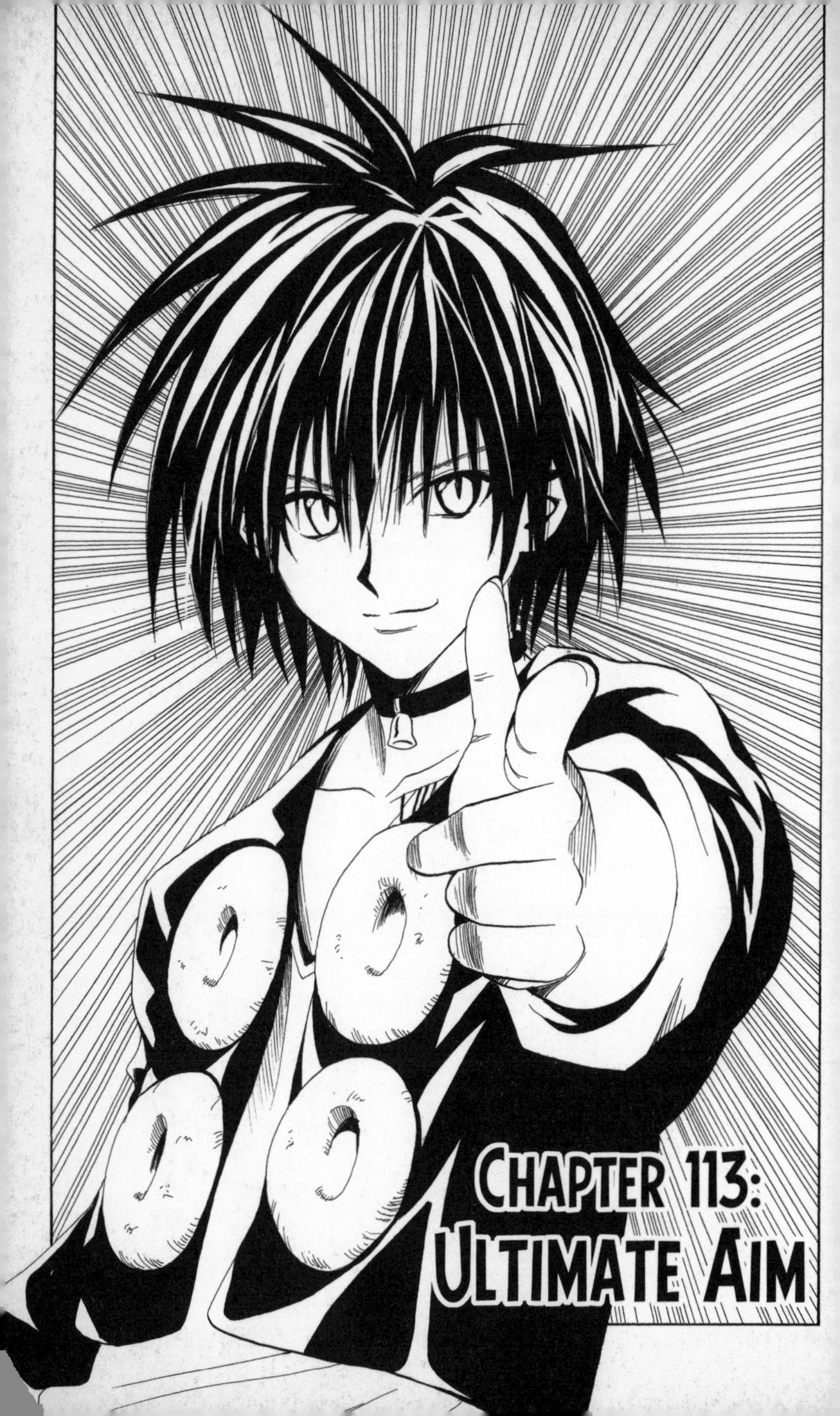
Chapter 113:
Ultimate Aim

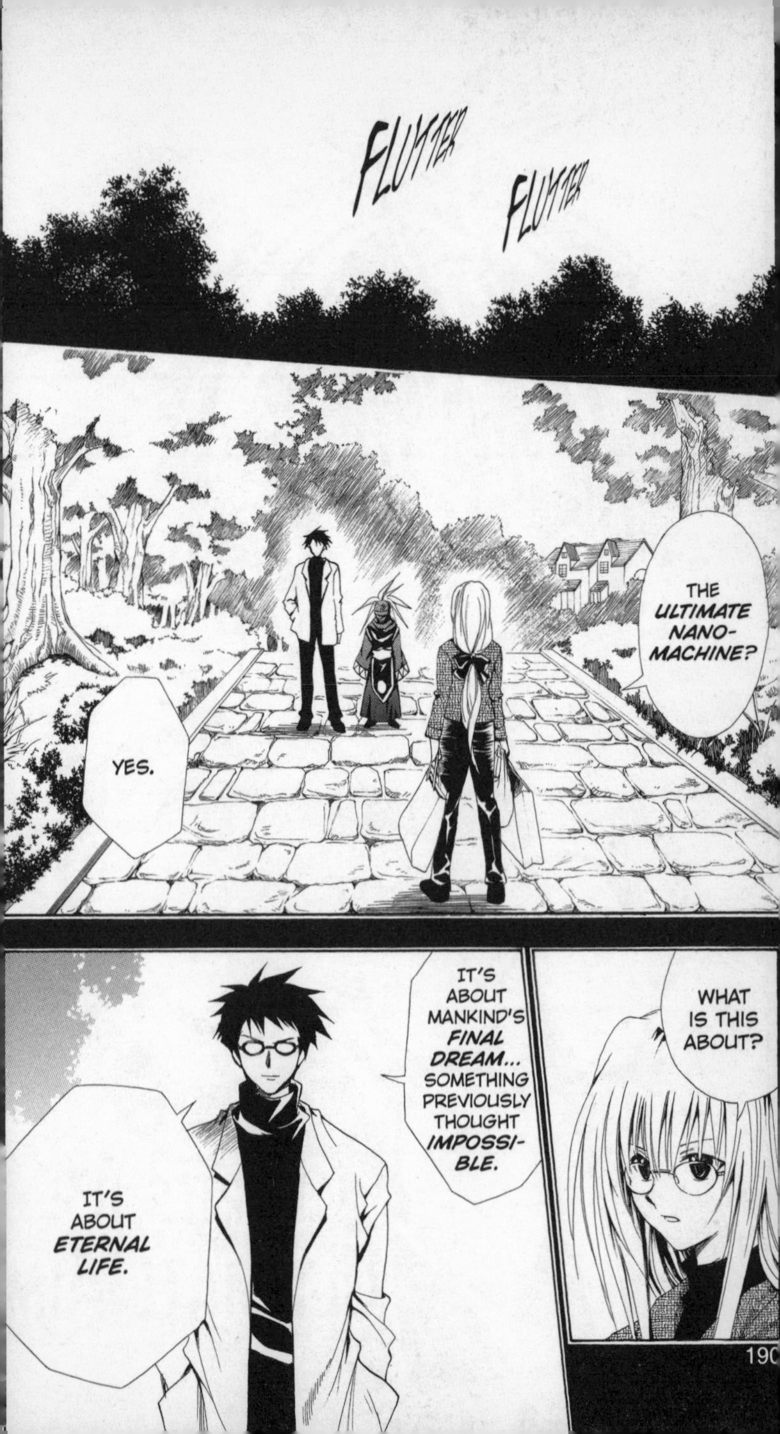
FLUTTER
FLUTTER
THE *ULTIMATE* NANO-MACHINE?
YES.
WHAT IS THIS ABOUT?
IT'S ABOUT MANKIND'S *FINAL DREAM...* SOMETHING PREVIOUSLY THOUGHT *IMPOSSI-BLE.*
IT'S ABOUT *ETERNAL LIFE.*

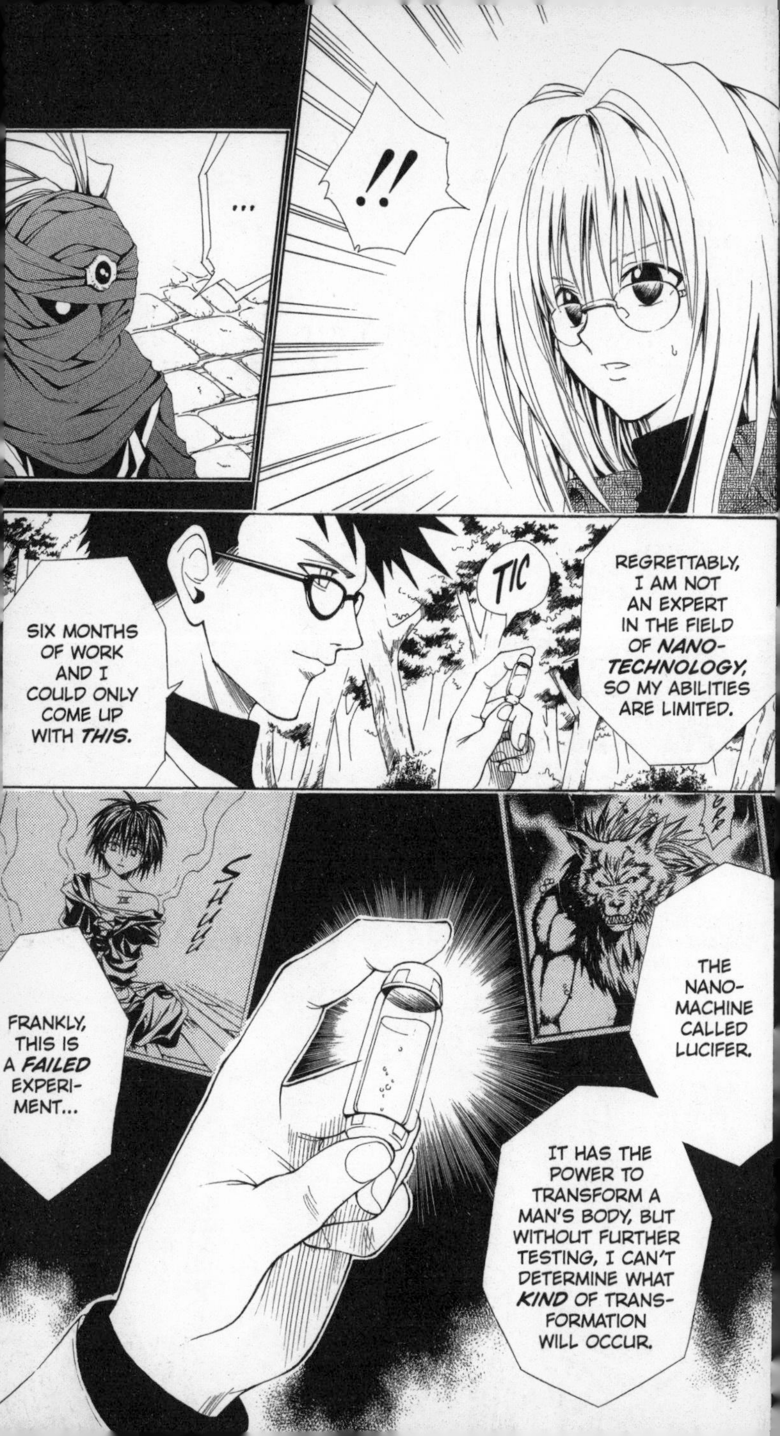

!!
...
REGRETTABLY, I AM NOT AN EXPERT IN THE FIELD OF ***NANO-TECHNOLOGY,*** SO MY ABILITIES ARE LIMITED.
TIC
SIX MONTHS OF WORK AND I COULD ONLY COME UP WITH ***THIS.***
THE NANO-MACHINE CALLED LUCIFER.
IT HAS THE POWER TO TRANSFORM A MAN'S BODY, BUT WITHOUT FURTHER TESTING, I CAN'T DETERMINE WHAT ***KIND*** OF TRANS-FORMATION WILL OCCUR.
SHUU
FRANKLY, THIS IS A ***FAILED*** EXPERI-MENT...

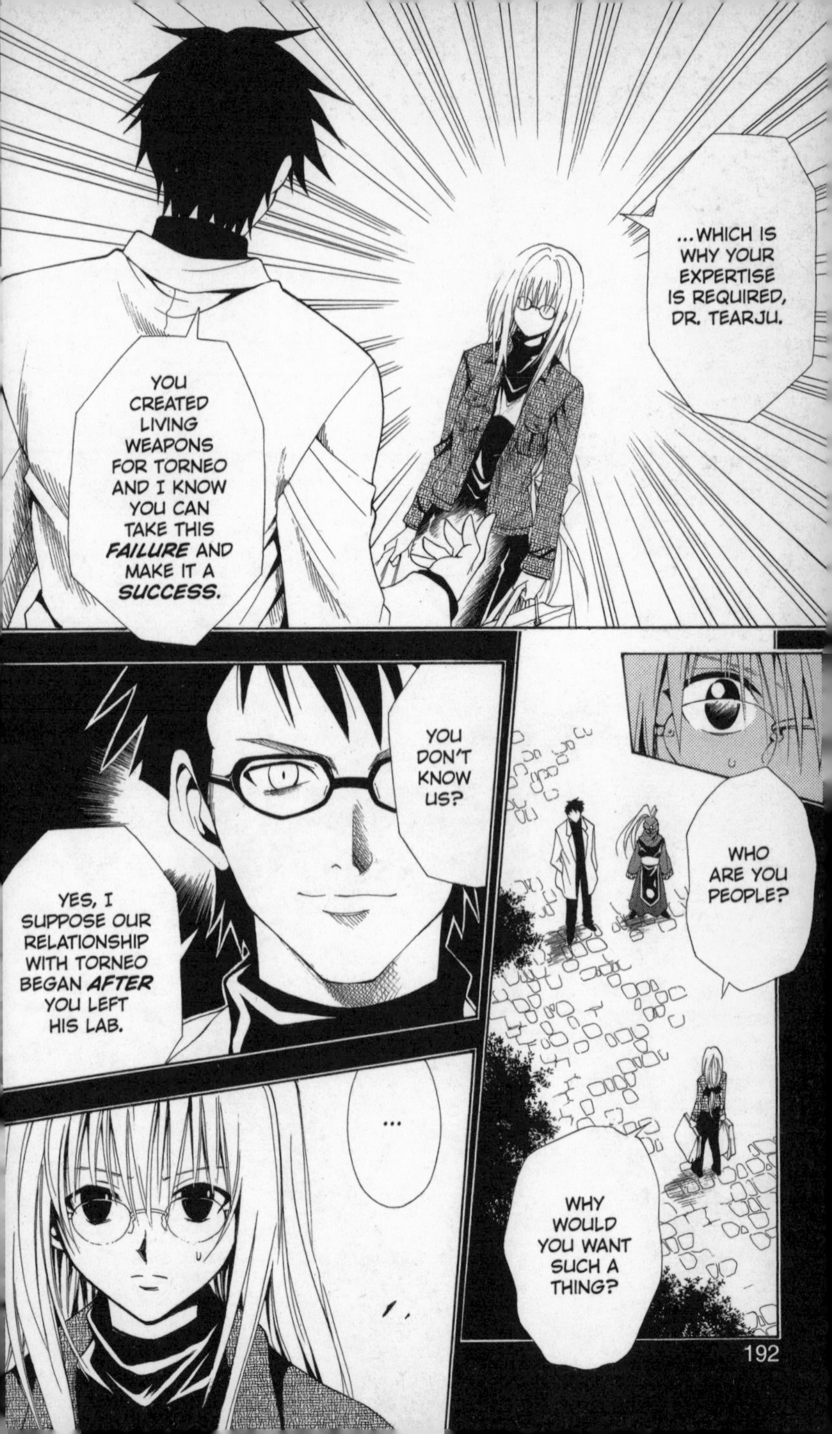
...WHICH IS WHY YOUR EXPERTISE IS REQUIRED, DR. TEARJU.
YOU CREATED LIVING WEAPONS FOR TORNEO AND I KNOW YOU CAN TAKE THIS *FAILURE* AND MAKE IT A *SUCCESS.*
WHO ARE YOU PEOPLE?
WHY WOULD YOU WANT SUCH A THING?
YOU DON'T KNOW US?
YES, I SUPPOSE OUR RELATIONSHIP WITH TORNEO BEGAN *AFTER* YOU LEFT HIS LAB.
...

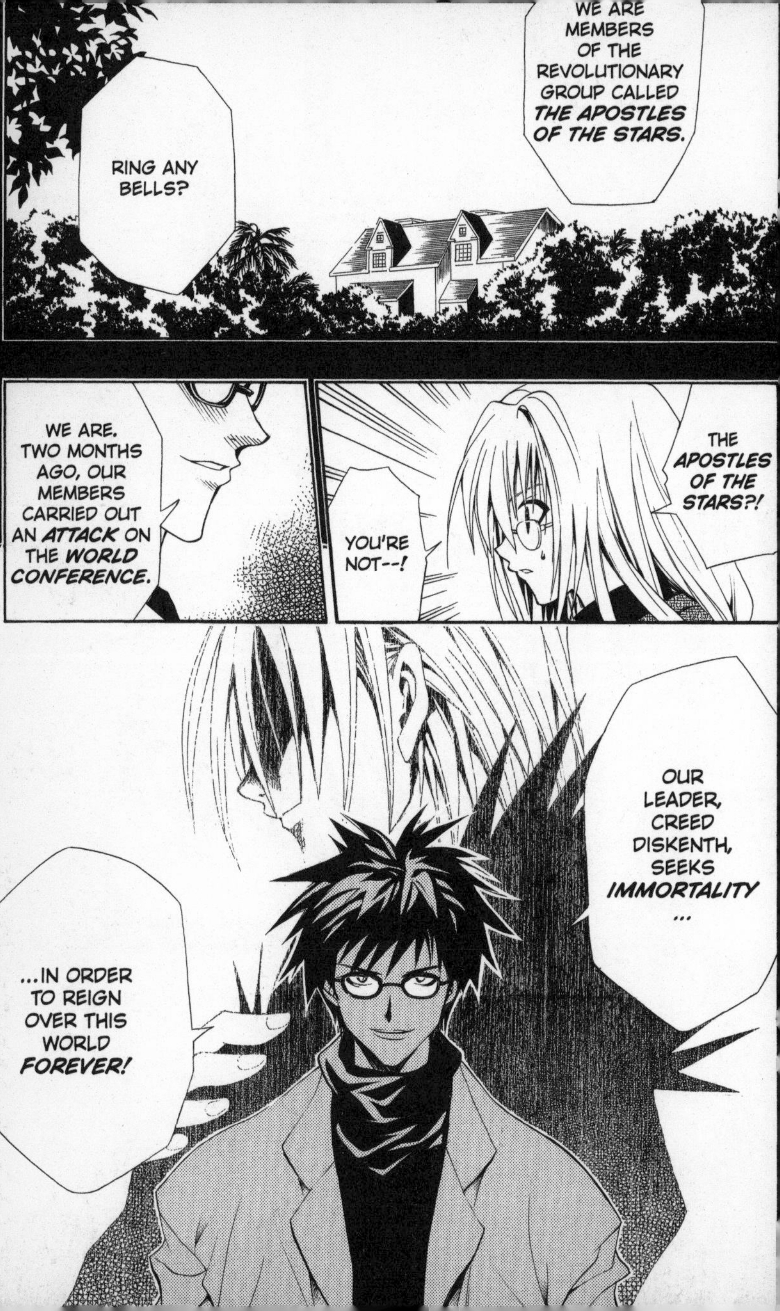
WE ARE MEMBERS OF THE REVOLUTIONARY GROUP CALLED *THE APOSTLES OF THE STARS.*
RING ANY BELLS?
THE *APOSTLES OF THE STARS?!*
YOU'RE NOT--!
WE ARE. TWO MONTHS AGO, OUR MEMBERS CARRIED OUT AN *ATTACK* ON THE *WORLD CONFERENCE.*
OUR LEADER, CREED DISKENTH, SEEKS *IMMORTALITY*...
...IN ORDER TO REIGN OVER THIS WORLD *FOREVER!*

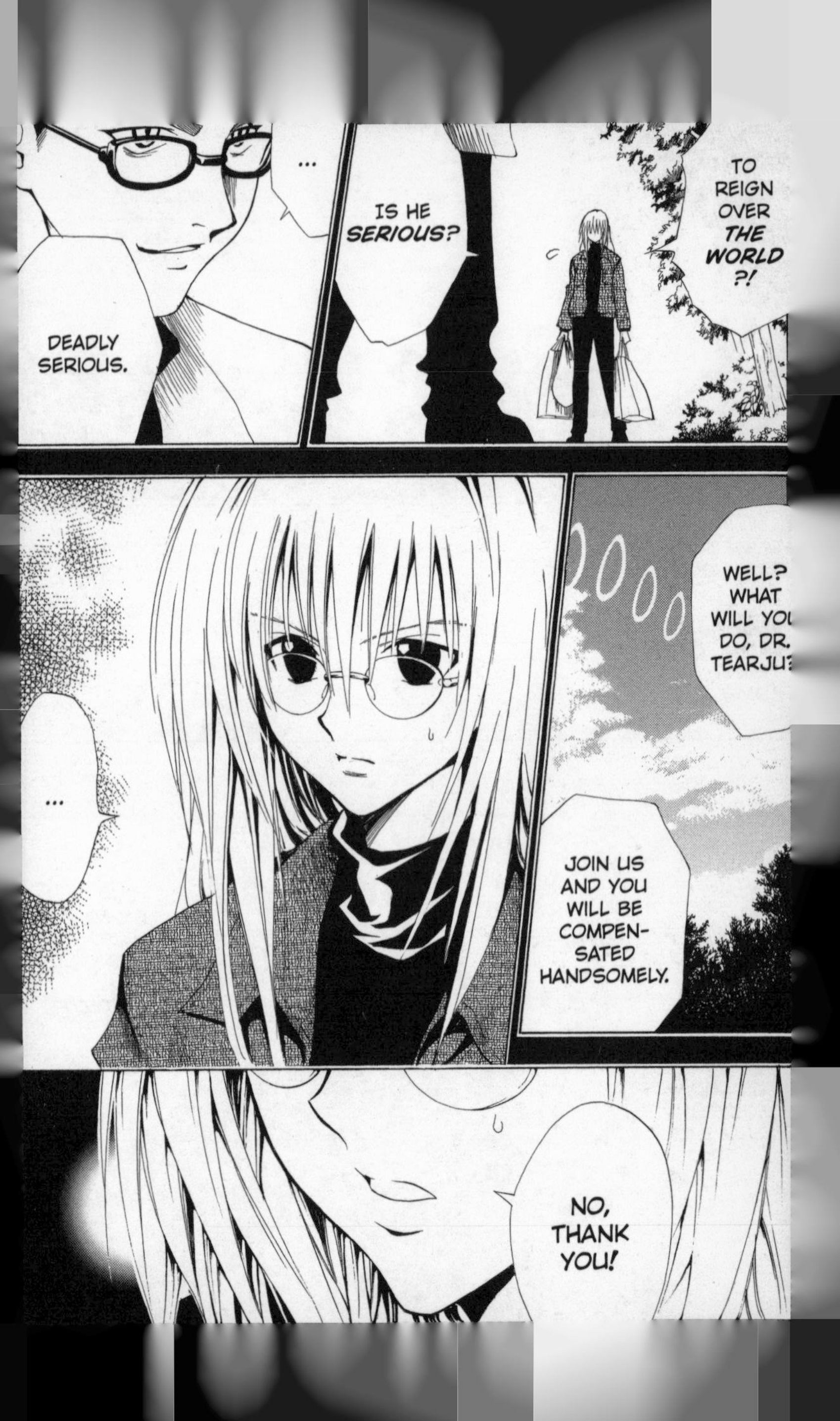
TO REIGN OVER THE WORLD ?!
IS HE SERIOUS?
...
DEADLY SERIOUS.
WELL? WHAT WILL YOU DO, DR. TEARJU?
JOIN US AND YOU WILL BE COMPEN-SATED HANDSOMELY.
...
NO, THANK YOU!

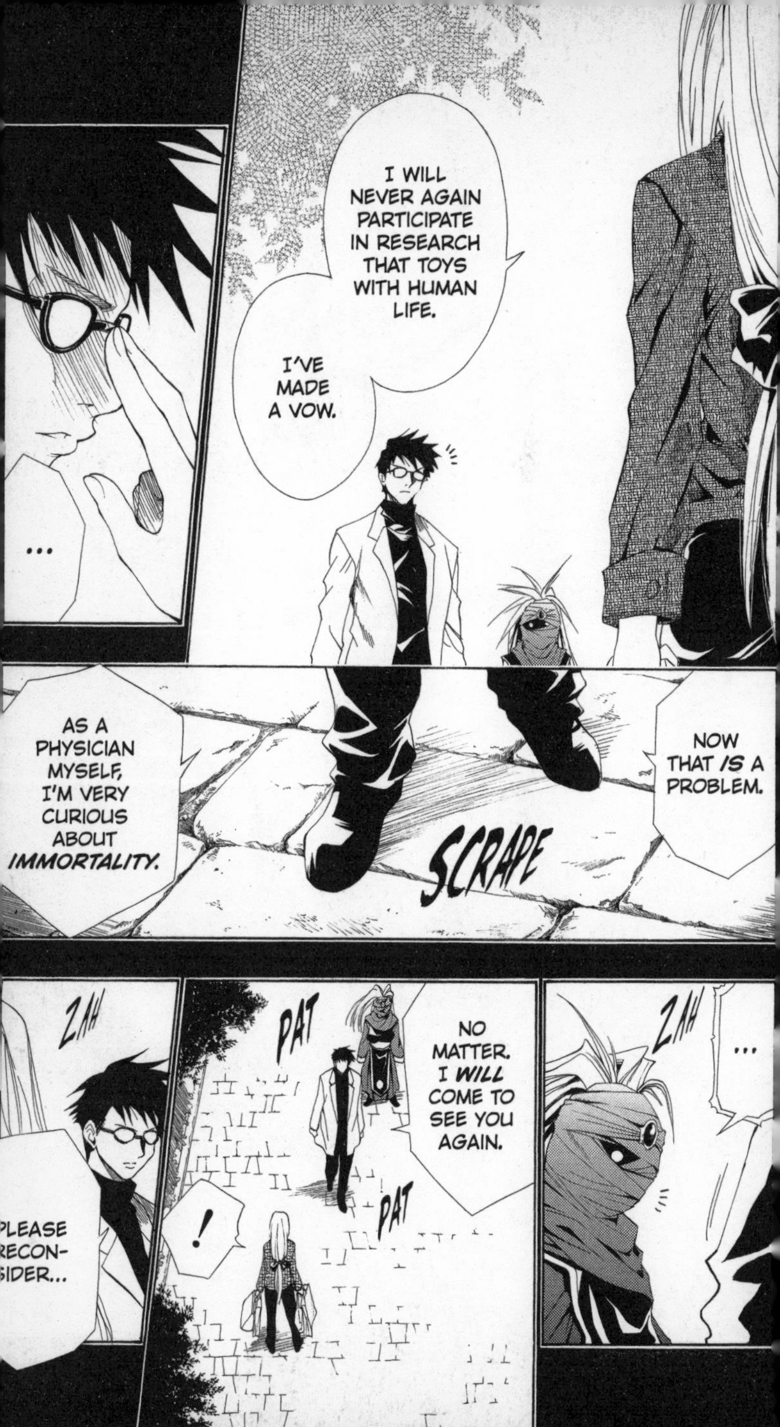
I WILL NEVER AGAIN PARTICIPATE IN RESEARCH THAT TOYS WITH HUMAN LIFE.
I'VE MADE A VOW.
...
NOW THAT *IS* A PROBLEM.
SCRAPE
AS A PHYSICIAN MYSELF, I'M VERY CURIOUS ABOUT *IMMORTALITY.*
ZAH
...
NO MATTER. I *WILL* COME TO SEE YOU AGAIN.
PAT
PAT
!
ZAH
PLEASE RECON-
SIDER...

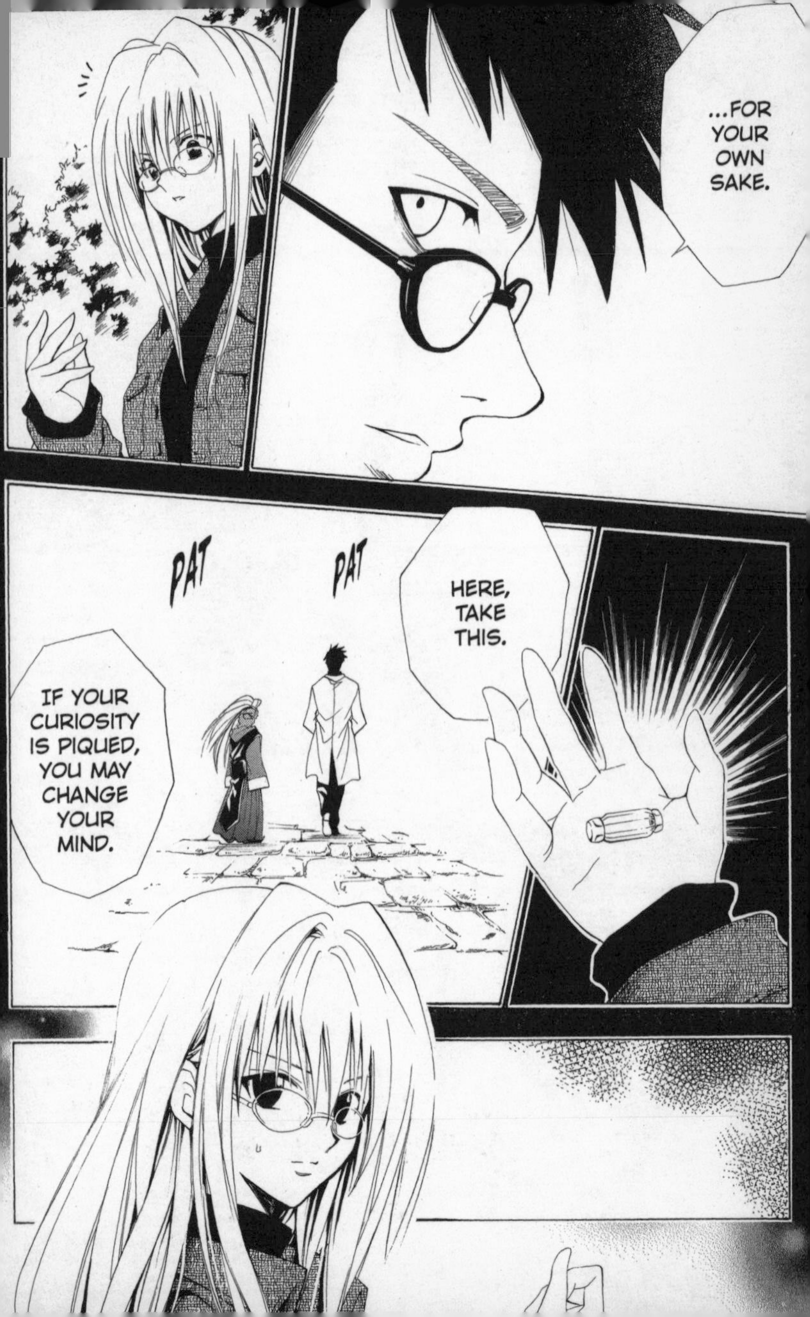
...FOR YOUR OWN SAKE.
HERE, TAKE THIS.
PAT
PAT
IF YOUR CURIOSITY IS PIQUED, YOU MAY CHANGE YOUR MIND.

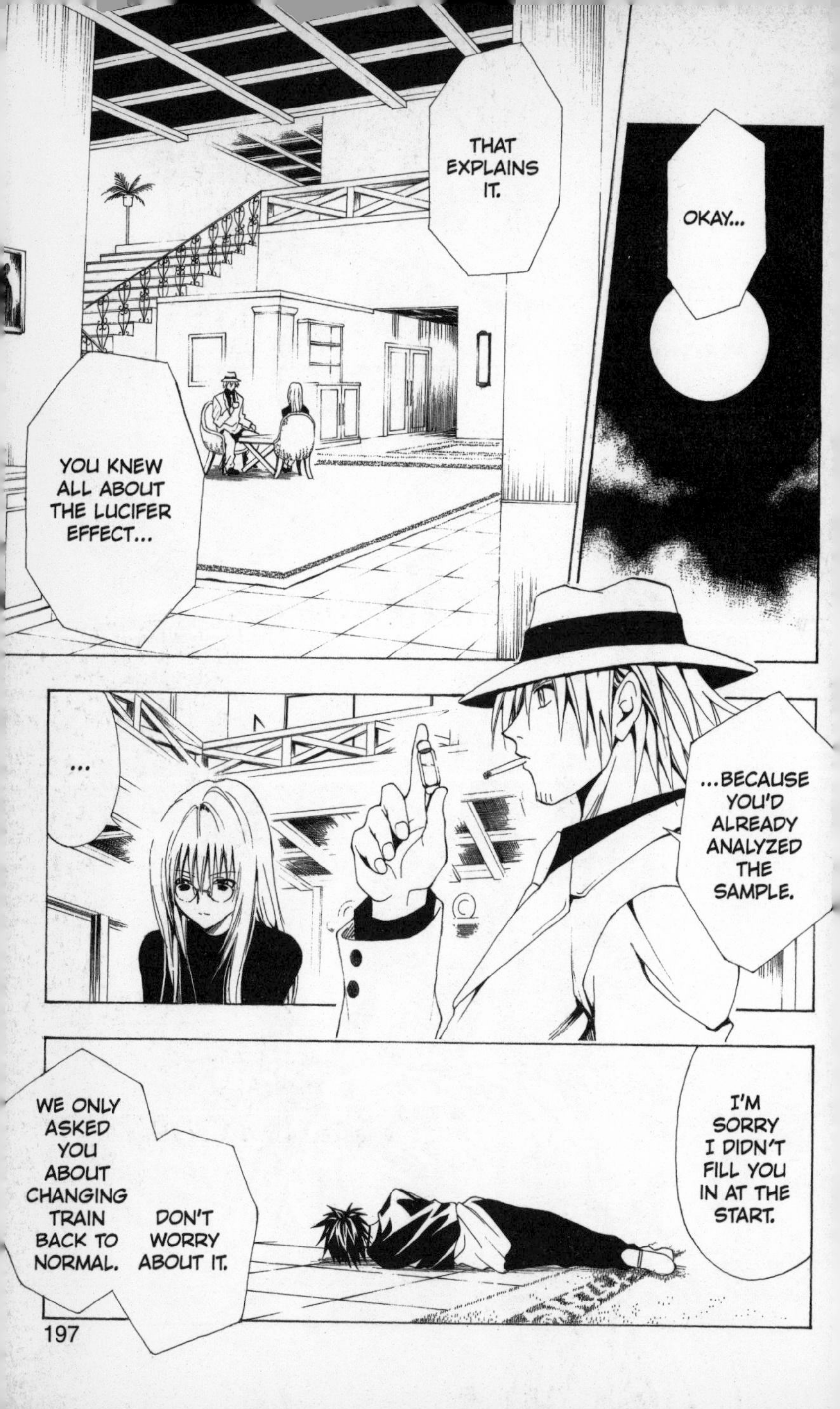
OKAY...
THAT EXPLAINS IT.
YOU KNEW ALL ABOUT THE LUCIFER EFFECT...
...BECAUSE YOU'D ALREADY ANALYZED THE SAMPLE.
...
I'M SORRY I DIDN'T FILL YOU IN AT THE START.
DON'T WORRY ABOUT IT.
WE ONLY ASKED YOU ABOUT CHANGING TRAIN BACK TO NORMAL.

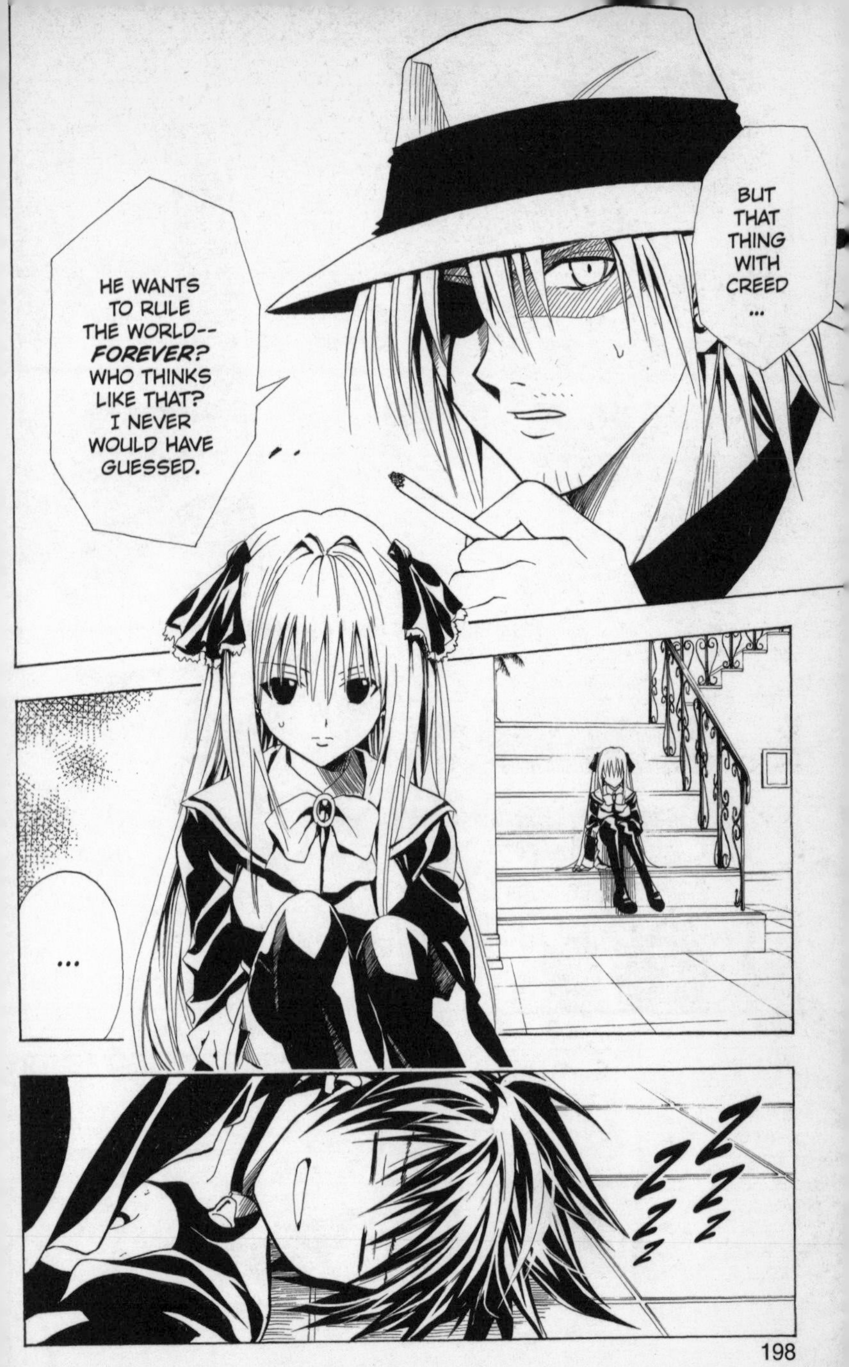
BUT THAT THING WITH CREED ...
HE WANTS TO RULE THE WORLD-- *FOREVER?* WHO THINKS LIKE THAT? I NEVER WOULD HAVE GUESSED.
...
Z Z Z Z Z Z Z Z

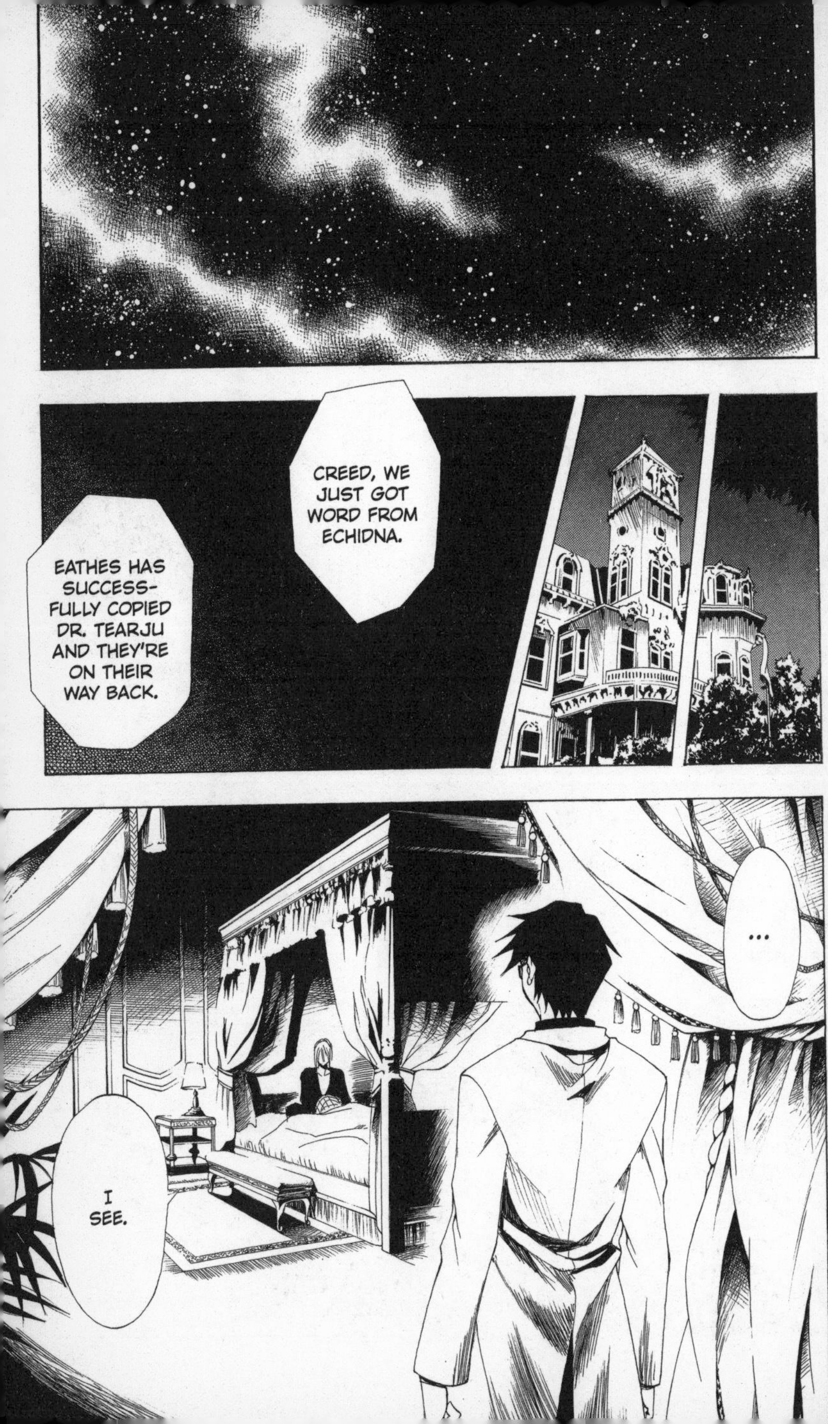
CREED, WE JUST GOT WORD FROM ECHIDNA.
EATHES HAS SUCCESS-FULLY COPIED DR. TEARJU AND THEY'RE ON THEIR WAY BACK.
...
I SEE.

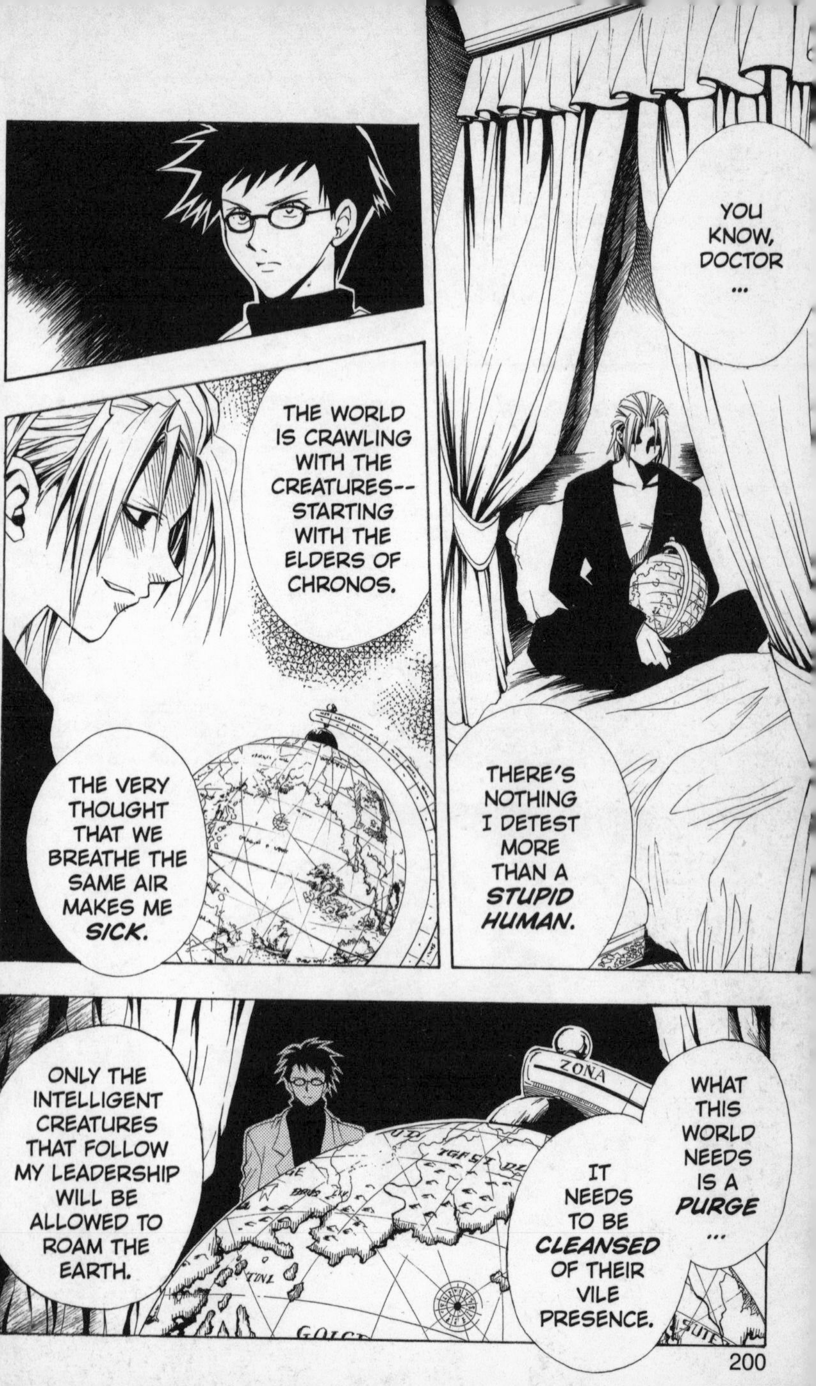
YOU KNOW, DOCTOR ...
THERE'S NOTHING I DETEST MORE THAN A ***STUPID HUMAN.***
THE WORLD IS CRAWLING WITH THE CREATURES-- STARTING WITH THE ELDERS OF CHRONOS.
THE VERY THOUGHT THAT WE BREATHE THE SAME AIR MAKES ME ***SICK.***
ZONA
WHAT THIS WORLD NEEDS IS A ***PURGE*** ...
IT NEEDS TO BE ***CLEANSED*** OF THEIR VILE PRESENCE.
ONLY THE INTELLIGENT CREATURES THAT FOLLOW MY LEADERSHIP WILL BE ALLOWED TO ROAM THE EARTH.

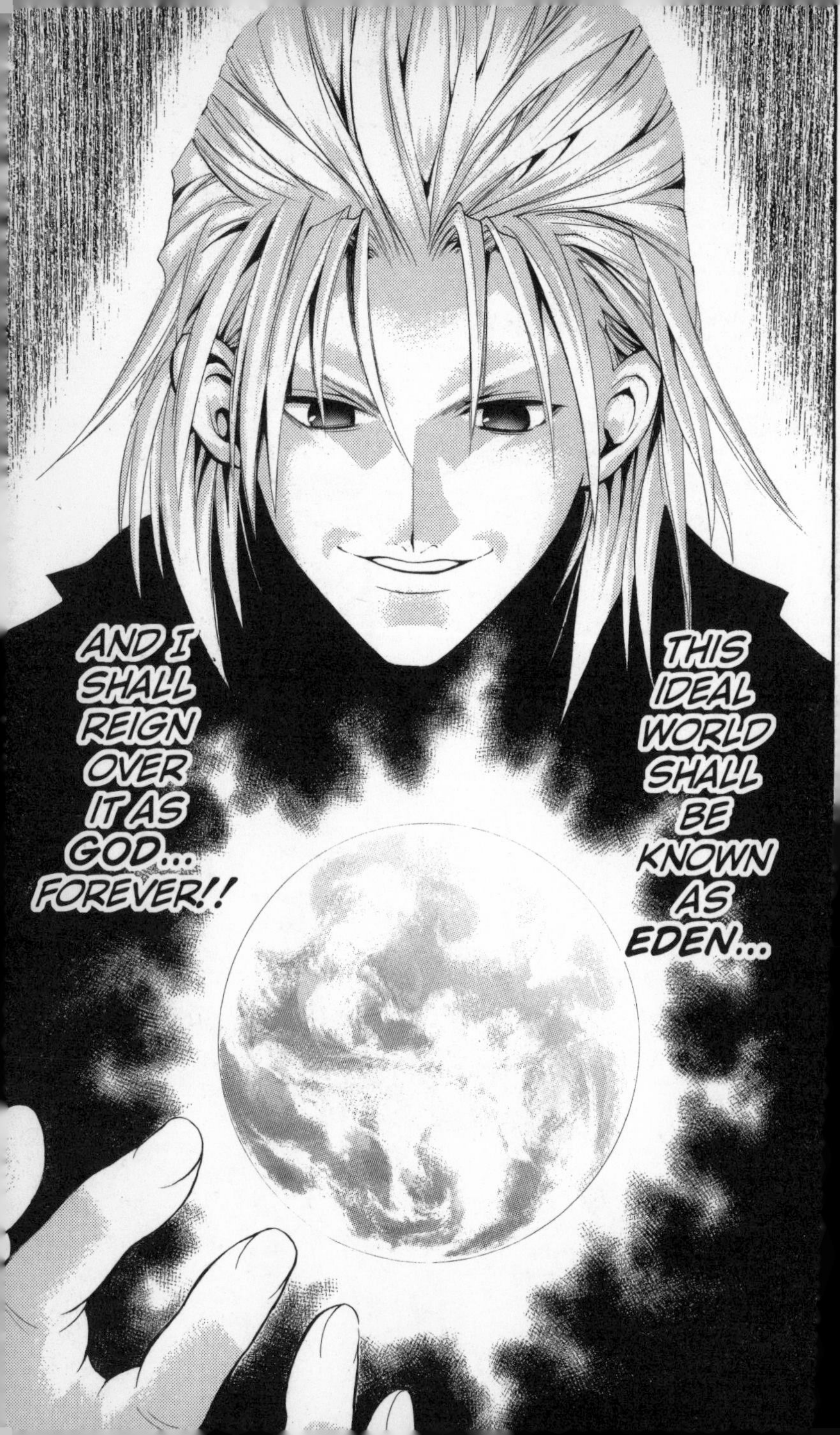
THIS IDEAL WORLD SHALL BE KNOWN AS EDEN...
AND I SHALL REIGN OVER IT AS GOD... FOREVER!!

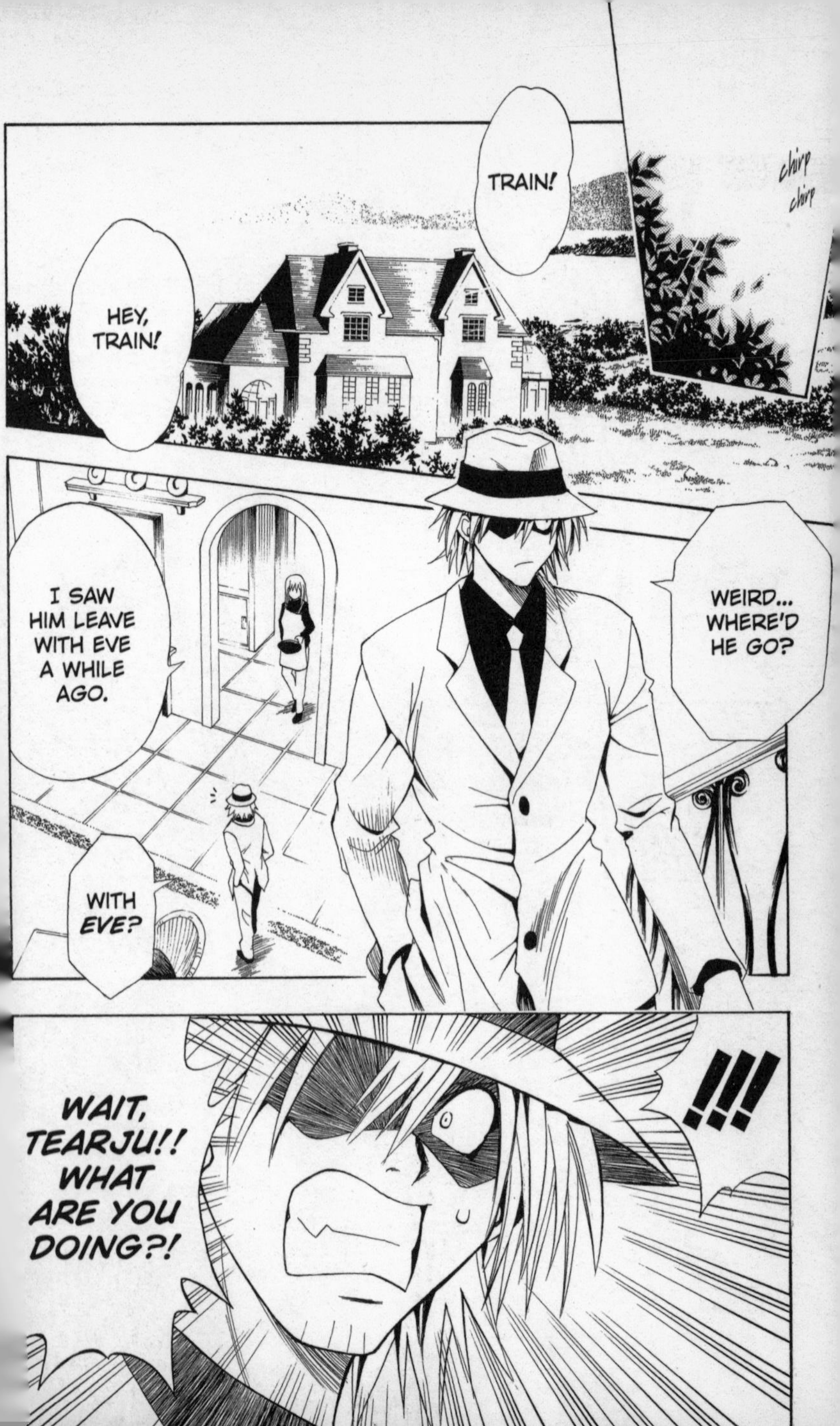
chirp chirp
TRAIN!
HEY, TRAIN!
WEIRD... WHERE'D HE GO?
I SAW HIM LEAVE WITH EVE A WHILE AGO.
WITH *EVE*?
!!!!
WAIT, TEARJU!! WHAT ARE YOU DOING?!

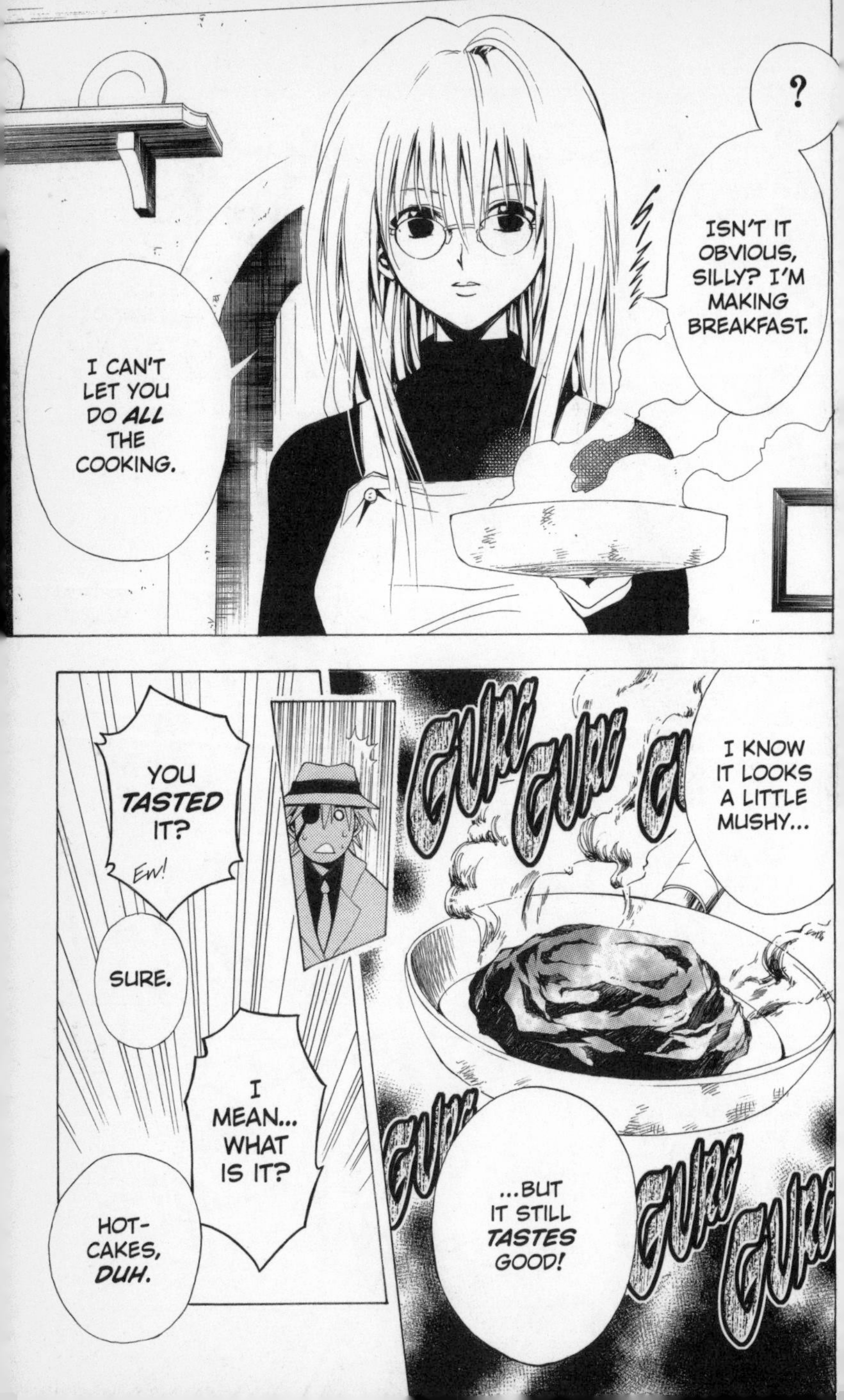
?
ISN'T IT OBVIOUS, SILLY? I'M MAKING BREAKFAST.
I CAN'T LET YOU DO *ALL* THE COOKING.
GURG GURG GURG
I KNOW IT LOOKS A LITTLE MUSHY...
...BUT IT STILL *TASTES* GOOD!
GURG GURG GURG
YOU *TASTED* IT?
Ew!
SURE.
I MEAN... WHAT IS IT?
HOT-CAKES, *DUH*.

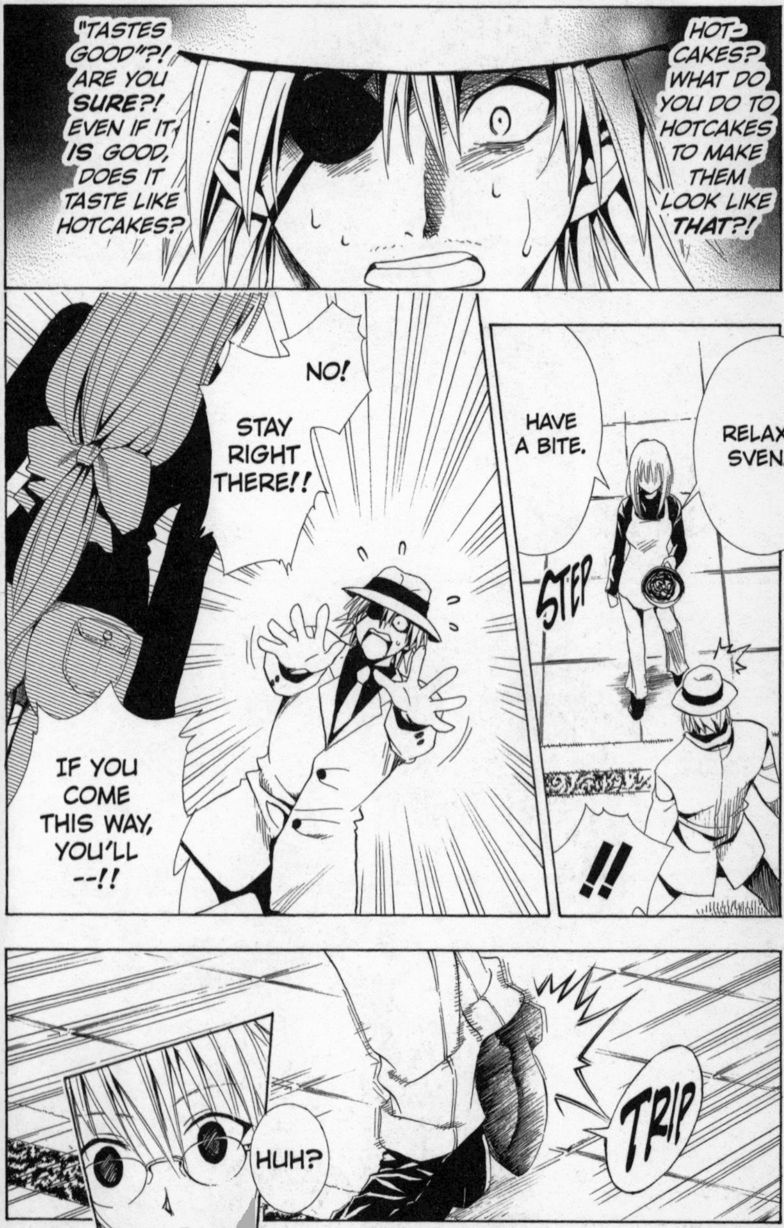
HOT-CAKES? WHAT DO YOU DO TO HOTCAKES TO MAKE THEM LOOK LIKE THAT?!
"TASTES GOOD"?! ARE YOU SURE?! EVEN IF IT IS GOOD, DOES IT TASTE LIKE HOTCAKES?
RELAX, SVEN.
HAVE A BITE.
STEP
!!
NO!
STAY RIGHT THERE!!
IF YOU COME THIS WAY, YOU'LL --!!
TRIP
HUH?

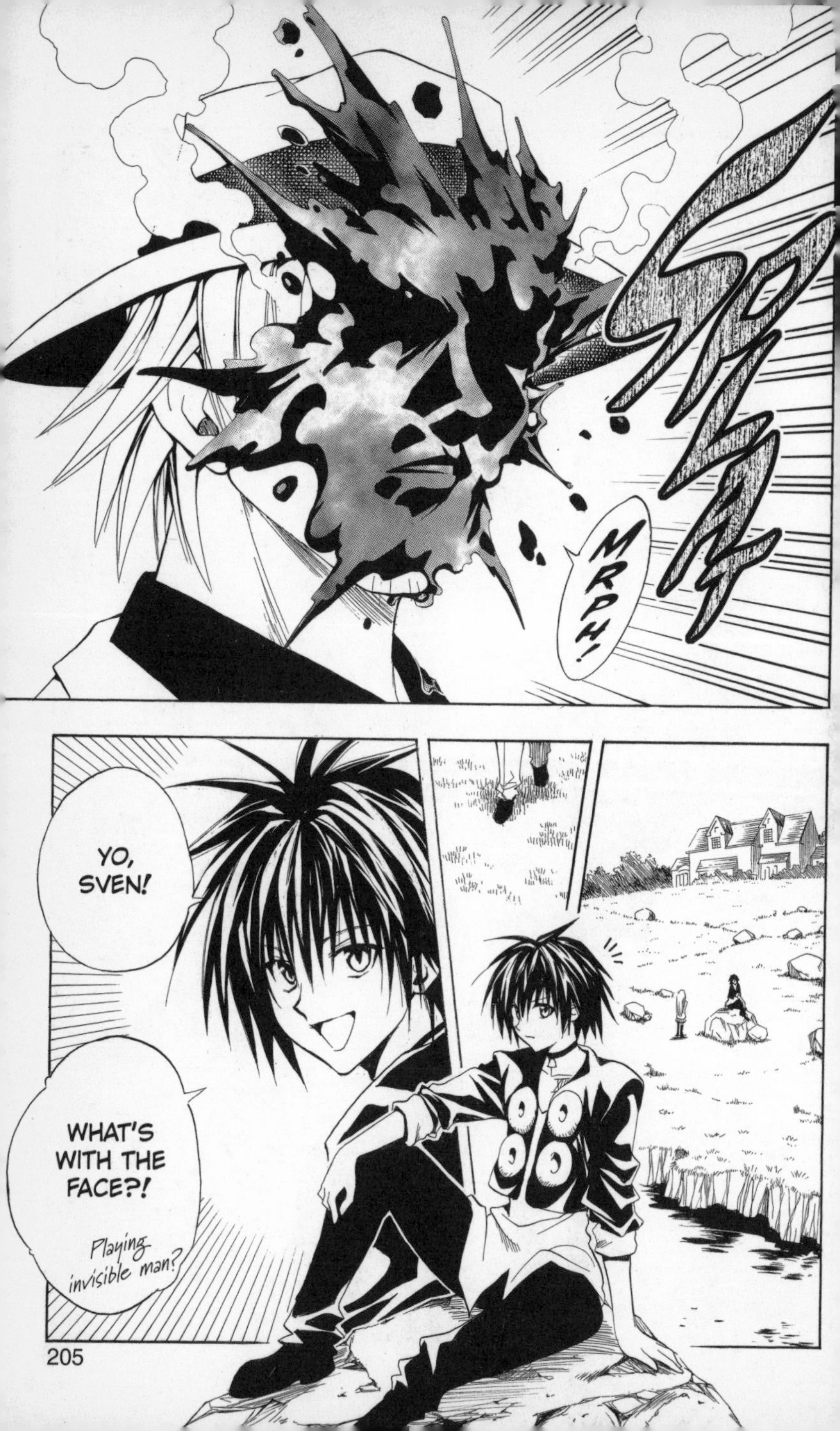
SPLAT
MRPH!
YO, SVEN!
WHAT'S WITH THE FACE?!
Playing invisible man?

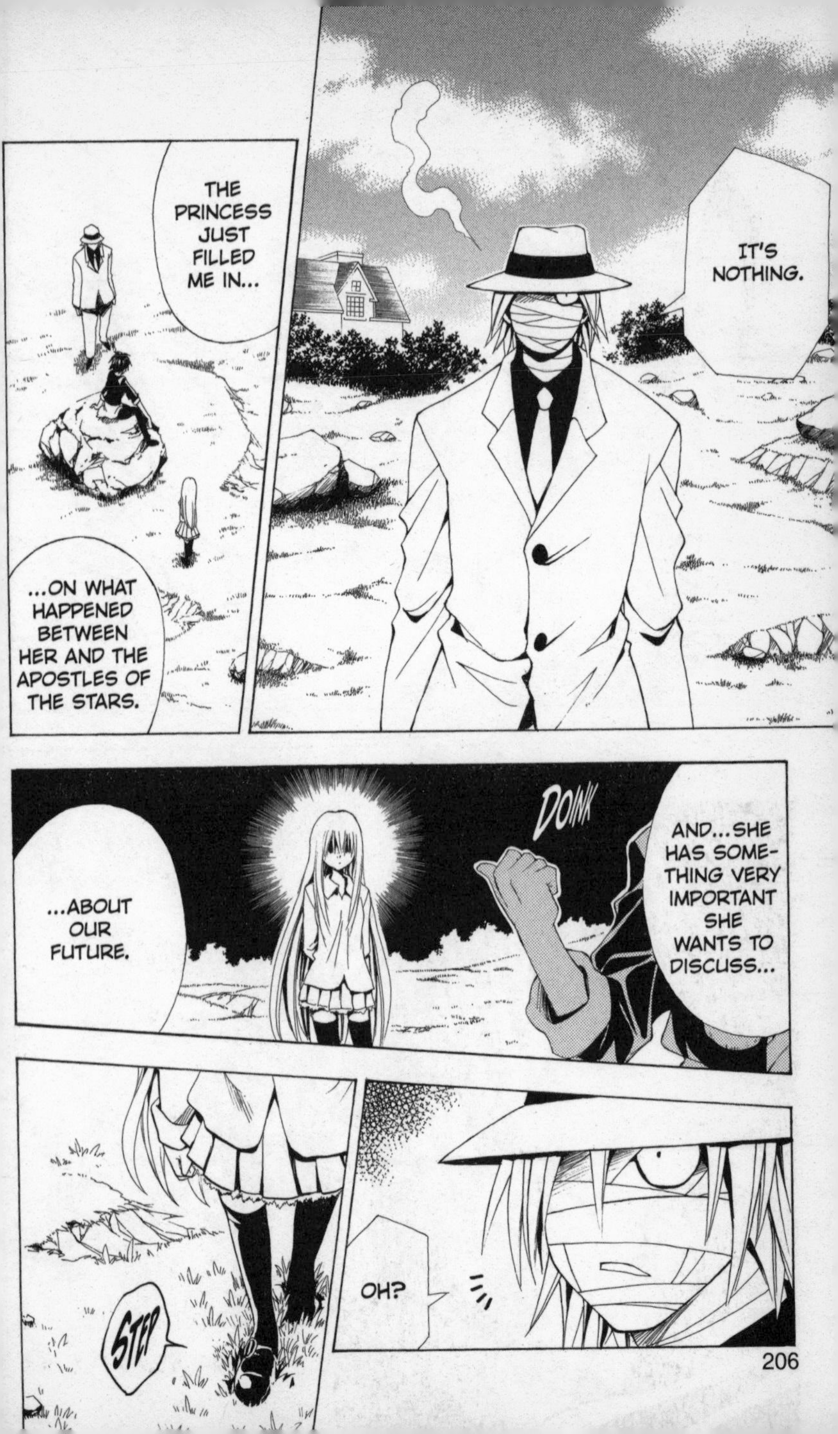
IT'S NOTHING.
THE PRINCESS JUST FILLED ME IN...
...ON WHAT HAPPENED BETWEEN HER AND THE APOSTLES OF THE STARS.
DOINK
AND...SHE HAS SOME-THING VERY IMPORTANT SHE WANTS TO DISCUSS...
...ABOUT OUR FUTURE.
OH?
STEP

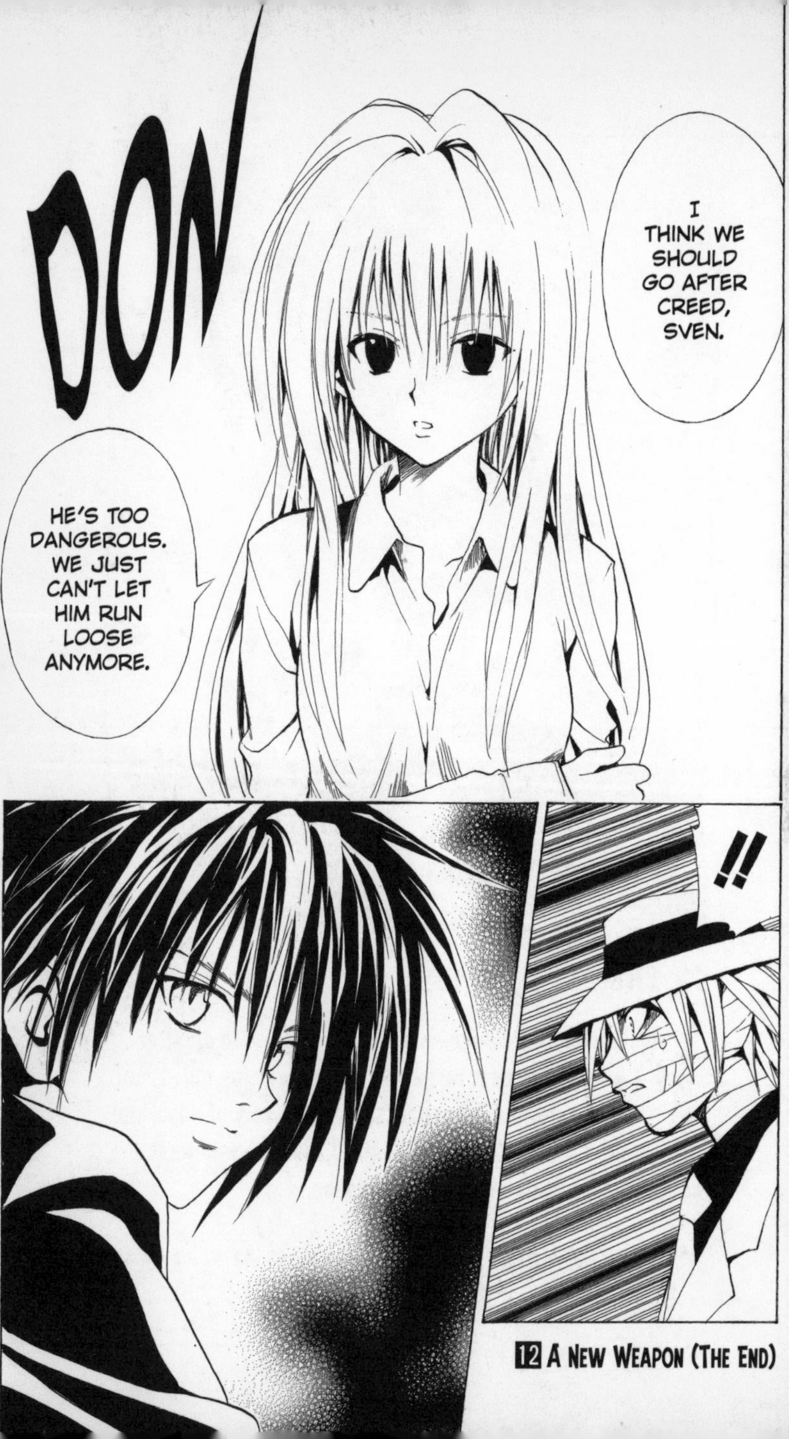
I THINK WE SHOULD GO AFTER CREED, SVEN.
DON
HE'S TOO DANGEROUS. WE JUST CAN'T LET HIM RUN LOOSE ANYMORE.
!!

12 A NEW WEAPON (THE END)

IN THE NEXT VOLUME...

Following Eve's suggestion, Train decides to go after Creed as his next target. But before setting out, Train reveals, for the first time, the tragic story of Saya and the reason for Train's hatred toward Creed, as well as the cause of Train's defection from Chronos...

AVAILABLE MARCH 2008! ◁◁◁◁◁◁◁◁

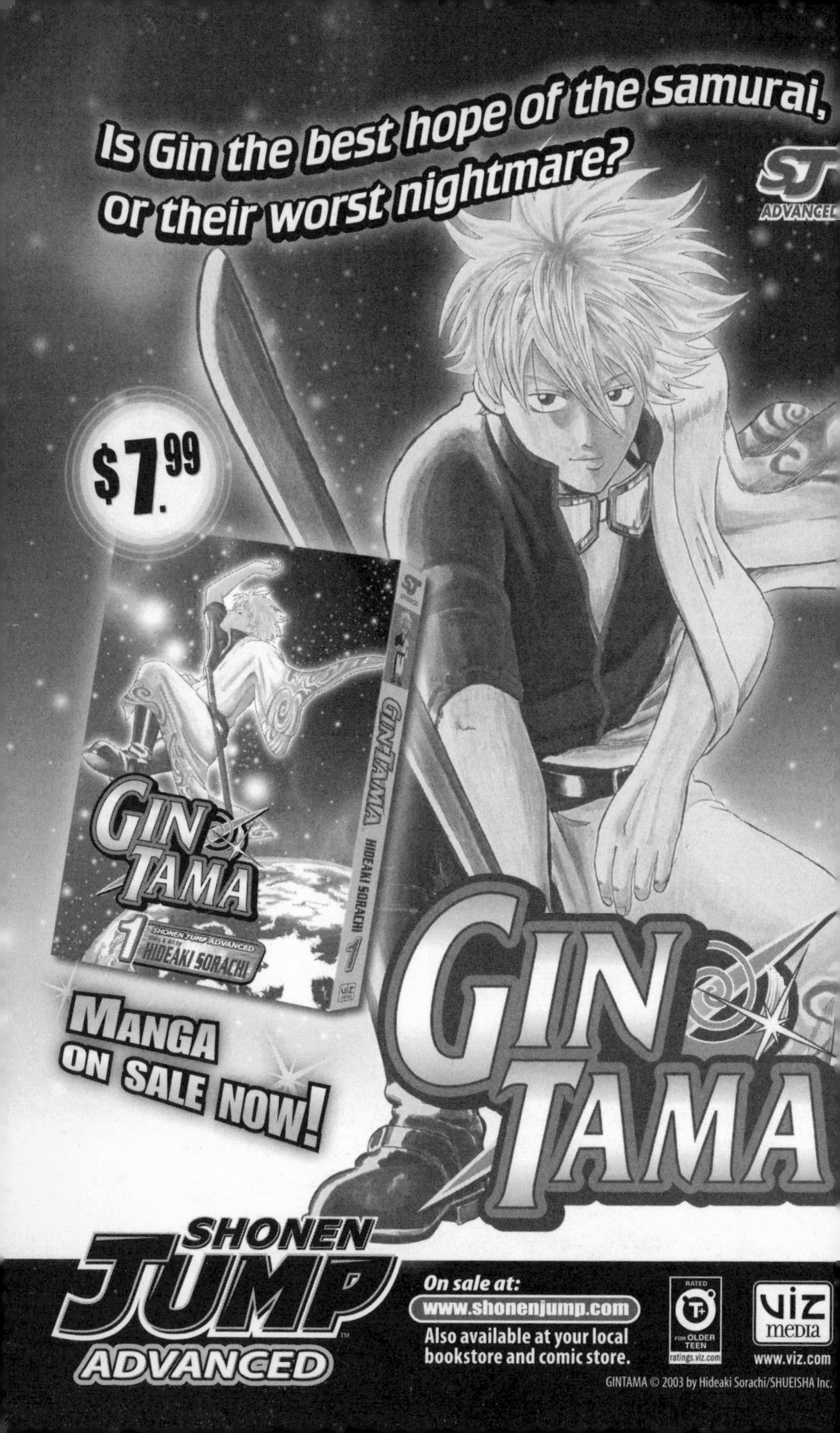
Is Gin the best hope of the samurai, or their worst nightmare?
SJ ADVANCED
$7.99
GIN TAMA
1 SHONEN JUMP ADVANCED
HIDEAKI SORACHI
MANGA ON SALE NOW!
GIN TAMA
SHONEN JUMP ADVANCED
On sale at:
www.shonenjump.com
Also available at your local bookstore and comic store.
RATED T+ FOR OLDER TEEN
ratings.viz.com
VIZ media
www.viz.com
GINTAMA © 2003 by Hideaki Sorachi/SHUEISHA Inc.

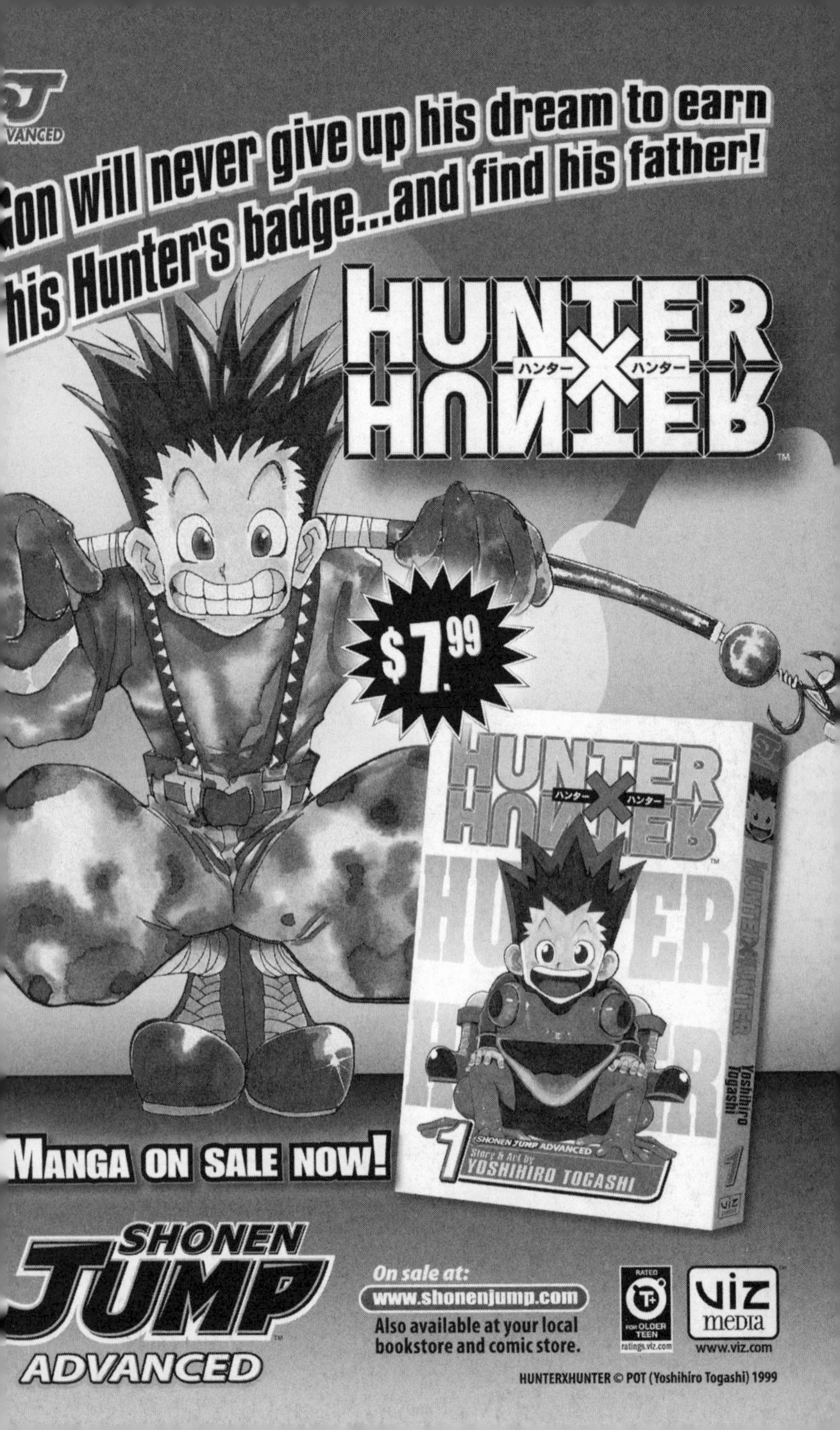
SJ ADVANCED
Gon will never give up his dream to earn his Hunter's badge...and find his father!
HUNTER × HUNTER
ハンター ハンター
$7.99
HUNTER × HUNTER
SHONEN JUMP ADVANCED
Story & Art by
YOSHIHIRO TOGASHI
Yoshihiro Togashi
MANGA ON SALE NOW!
SHONEN JUMP ADVANCED
On sale at:
www.shonenjump.com
Also available at your local bookstore and comic store.
RATED T+ FOR OLDER TEEN
ratings.viz.com
VIZ media
www.viz.com
HUNTERXHUNTER © POT (Yoshihiro Togashi) 1999

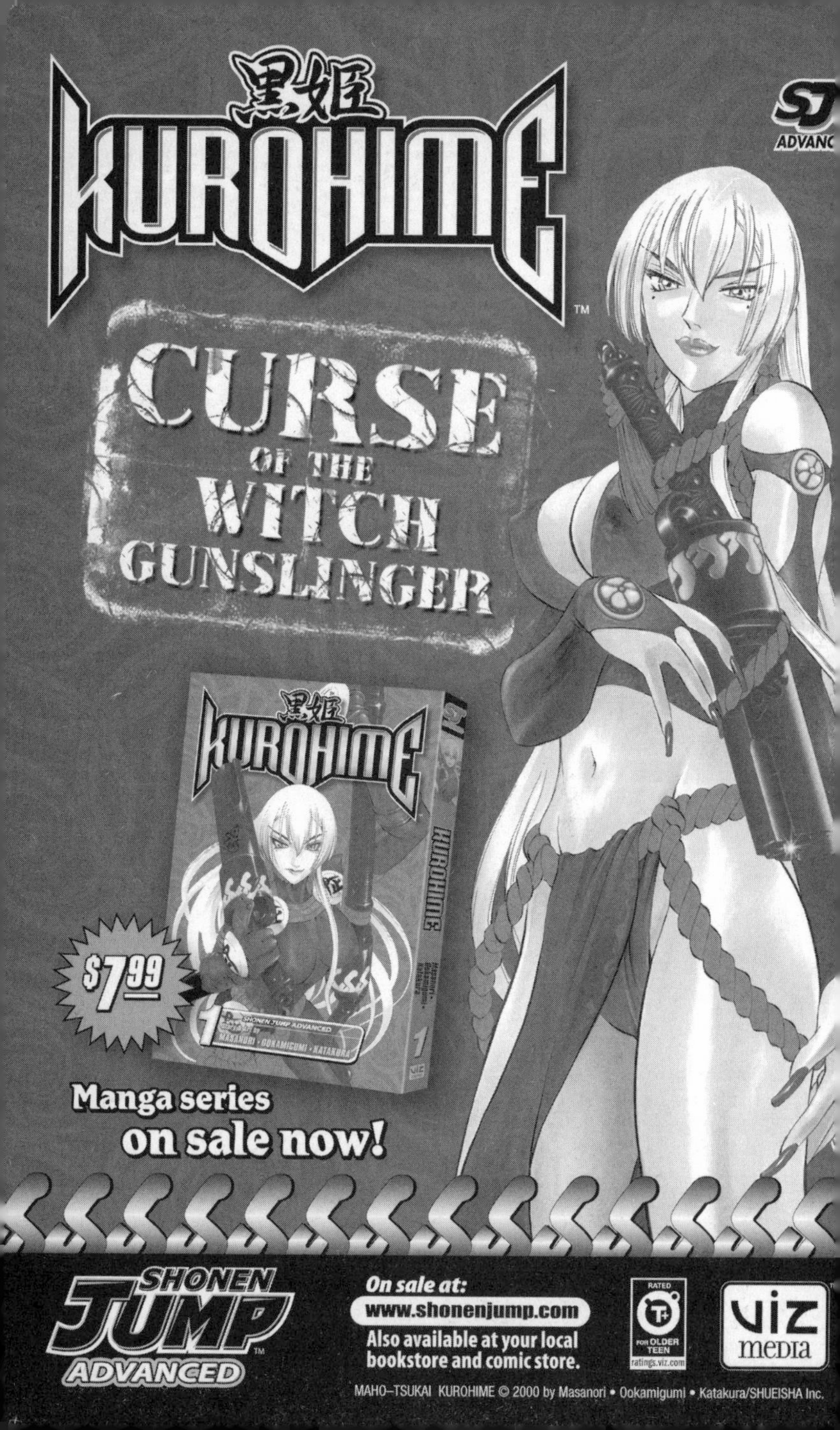
黒姫
KUROHIME™
CURSE OF THE WITCH GUNSLINGER
$7.99
Manga series on sale now!
SHONEN JUMP ADVANCED
On sale at:
www.shonenjump.com
Also available at your local bookstore and comic store.
RATED T+ FOR OLDER TEEN ratings.viz.com
viz media
MAHO-TSUKAI KUROHIME © 2000 by Masanori • Ookamigumi • Katakura/SHUEISHA Inc.

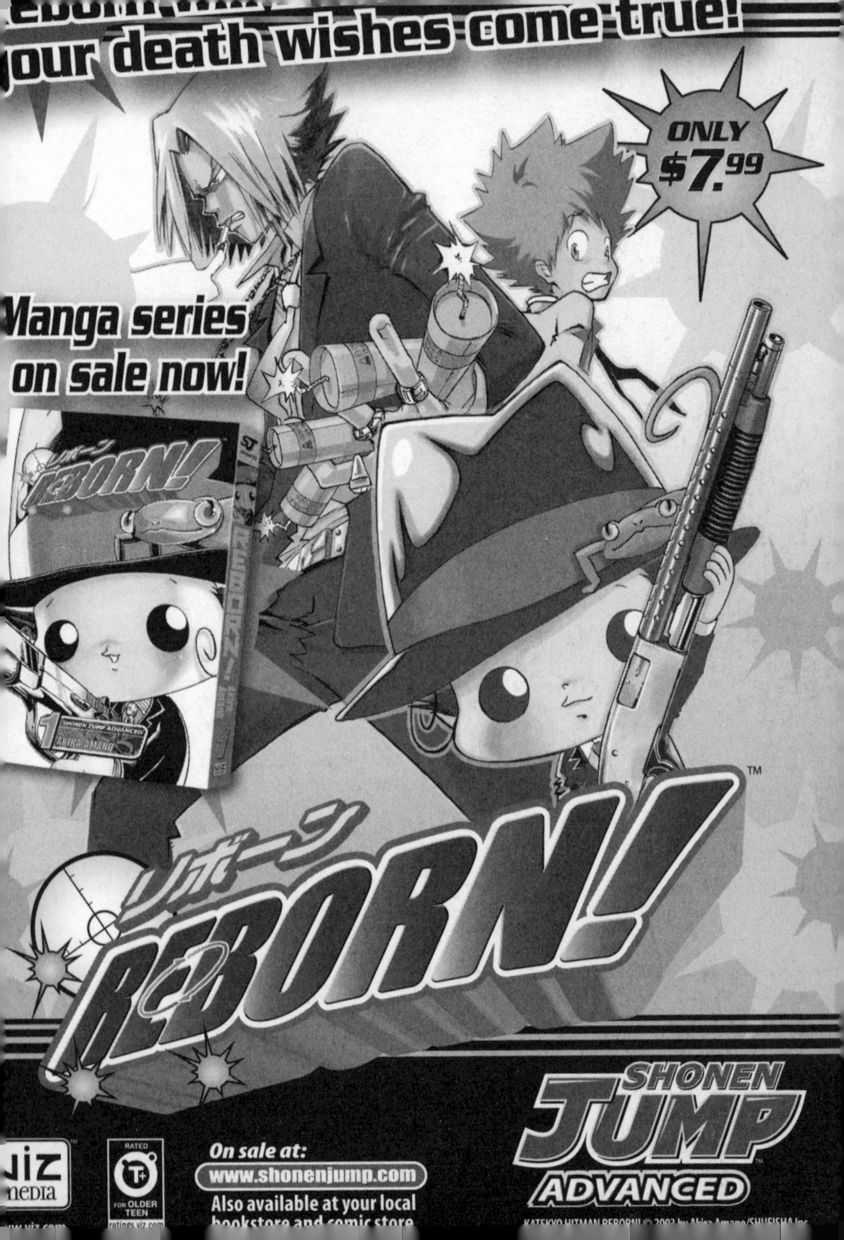

your death wishes come true!
ONLY $7.99
Manga series on sale now!
REBORN!
SHONEN JUMP ADVANCED
AKIRA AMANO
1
REBORN!
SHONEN JUMP ADVANCED
viz media
RATED T+ FOR OLDER TEEN
ratings.viz.com
On sale at:
www.shonenjump.com
Also available at your local bookstore and comic store.
KATEKYO HITMAN REBORN! © 2003 by Akira Amano/SHUEISHA Inc.

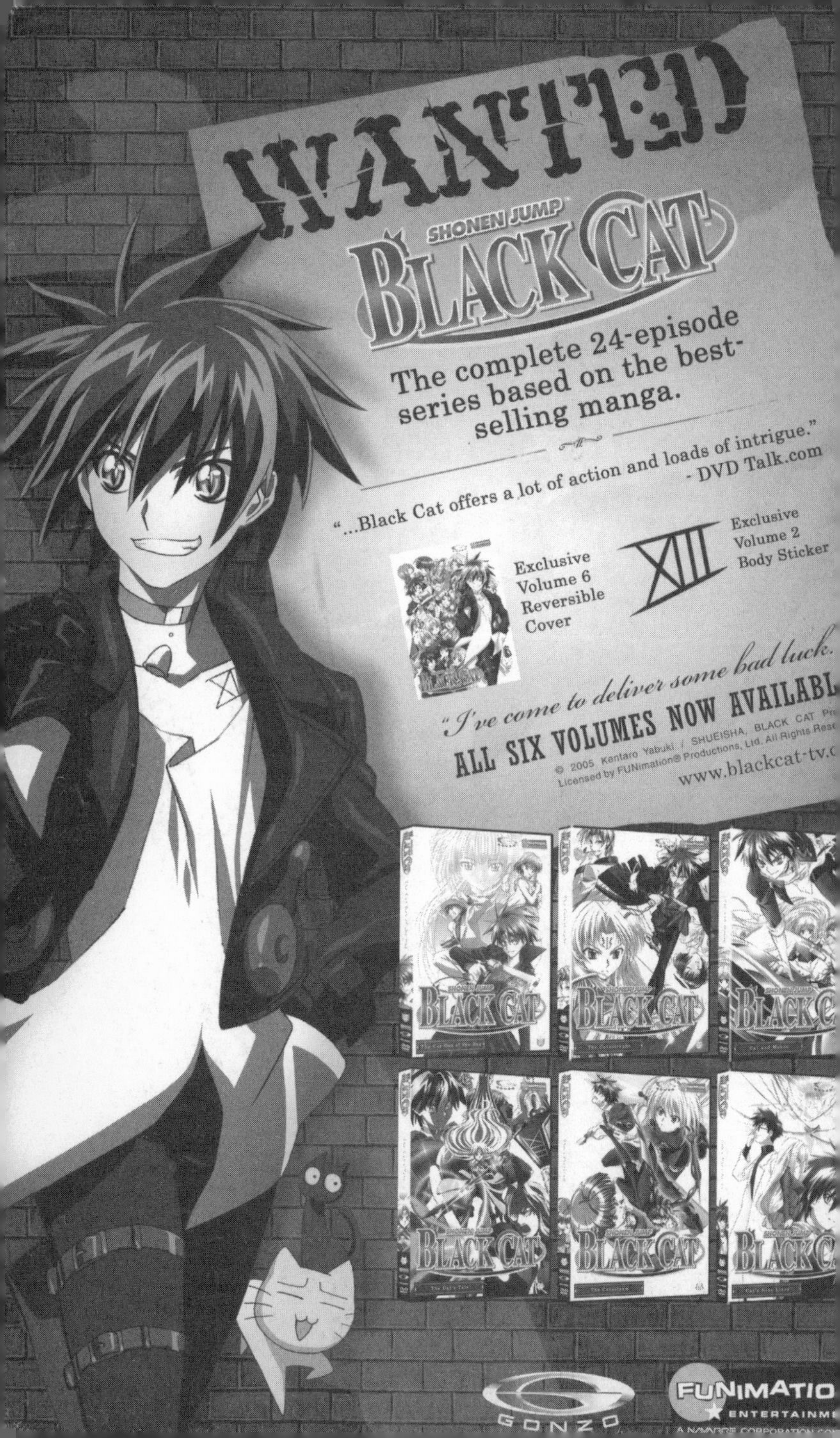
WANTED
SHONEN JUMP
BLACK CAT
The complete 24-episode series based on the best-selling manga.
"...Black Cat offers a lot of action and loads of intrigue."
- DVD Talk.com
Exclusive Volume 6 Reversible Cover
XIII
Exclusive Volume 2 Body Sticker
"I've come to deliver some bad luck.
ALL SIX VOLUMES NOW AVAILABL
© 2005 Kentaro Yabuki / SHUEISHA, BLACK CAT Pr
Licensed by FUNimation® Productions, Ltd. All Rights Rese
www.blackcat-tv.c
GONZO
FUNIMATIO
ENTERTAINM

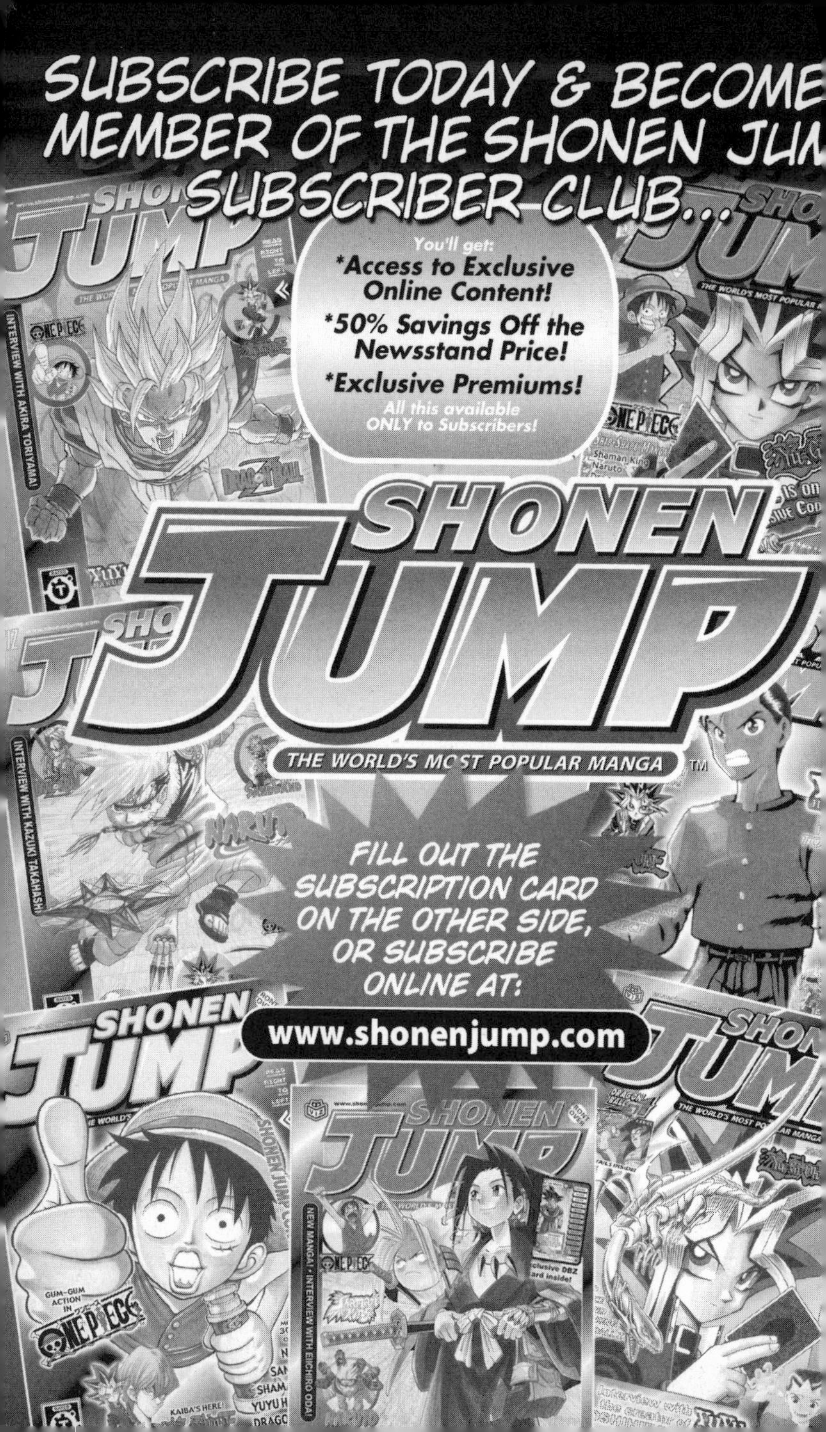
SUBSCRIBE TODAY & BECOME
MEMBER OF THE SHONEN JUM
SUBSCRIBER CLUB...
You'll get:
*Access to Exclusive Online Content!
*50% Savings Off the Newsstand Price!
*Exclusive Premiums!
All this available ONLY to Subscribers!
SHONEN JUMP
THE WORLD'S MOST POPULAR MANGA
FILL OUT THE SUBSCRIPTION CARD ON THE OTHER SIDE, OR SUBSCRIBE ONLINE AT:
www.shonenjump.com